AMERICAN
LEGAL REALISM

AMERICAN LEGAL REALISM

EDITED BY

William W. Fisher III
Morton J. Horwitz
Thomas A. Reed

New York   Oxford
OXFORD UNIVERSITY PRESS
1993

Oxford University Press

Oxford   New York   Toronto
Delhi   Bombay   Calcutta   Madras   Karachi
Kuala Lumpur   Singapore   Hong Kong   Tokyo
Nairobi   Dar es Salaam   Cape Town
Melbourne   Auckland   Madrid

and associated companies in
Berlin   Ibadan

Copyright © 1993 by Oxford University Press, Inc.

Published by Oxford University Press, Inc.

198 Madison Avenue, New York, New York 10016-4314
Oxford is a registered trademark of Oxford University Press

Library of Congress Cataloging-in-Publication Data
American legal realism / edited by William W. Fisher III, Morton J.
Horwitz, Thomas A. Reed.
p.   cm.   Includes bibliographical references.
ISBN 978-0-19-507123-8 (paper)
1. Law—Philosophy.   2. Realism.   3. Law—United States—History.
I. Fisher, William W., 1953–   II. Horwitz, Morton J., 1938–   .
III. Reed, Thomas A., 1958–   .
KF379.A43   1993   349.73—dc20   [347.3]   92–33872

6 8 9 7

Printed in the United States of America
on acid-free paper

Acknowledgments

Many people contributed to this volume. The staff of the Harvard Law Library patiently and successfully tracked down (sometimes two or three times) obscure briefs, essays, and books. Kathleen Maloney typed the bulk of the manuscript, and Marilyn L. Byrne and Lori Kelley proofread it carefully. Valerie Aubrey and Helen McInnis of Oxford University Press kept the project on track and provided many useful suggestions along the way.

In February of 1991, a preliminary plan for the book was presented to a faculty seminar at Harvard Law School. The comments of the participants were very helpful. Equally valuable were the suggestions of the five anonymous reviewers for Oxford University Press. The holders of the rights to the copyrighted books and essays included in the book have been generous in permitting us to reproduce excerpts from them. A somewhat different version of the introduction to Chapter 6 first appeared as part of an essay by William Fisher in Michael J. Lacey and Knud Haakonssen, eds., *A Culture of Rights: The Bill of Rights in Philosophy, Politics, and Law, 1791 and 1991* (New York: Cambridge University Press, 1991). We are grateful to Cambridge University Press for permission to reprint those passages.

Portions of the book were prepared while William Fisher was a Fellow at the Center for Advanced Study in the Behavioral Sciences. He is grateful for financial support provided to the Center by the Andrew W. Mellon Foundation. In addition both William Fisher and Morton Horwitz have relied heavily on the Summer Research Program of Harvard Law School.

Contents

Introduction

During the period between the two world wars, a group of American judges and scholars developed and sought to implement a novel approach to law, adjudication, and legal education—an approach now conventionally known as Legal Realism. The purpose of this volume is to make more widely available the body of writing produced by the Realists and to illuminate its central themes.

To understand Legal Realism, one must know something of the system of rules and ideas it was designed to discredit and displace. Various labels, most of them censorious, have been used to describe that system, but the most apt is "classical legal thought."[1] Formulated during the last third of the nineteenth century, classicism dominated most American legal institutions until the 1930s. Its best-known manifestation was a series of decisions by appellate courts that strengthened the positions of business corporations in their struggles with workers and consumers. For example, federal and state courts invented new legal remedies (such as the labor injunction) and new common law doctrines (such as the rule that union organizers may be held liable for interfering with employers' "contractual relations") that assisted businesses in their efforts to prevent strikes and other forms of collective action by their employees.[2] Early legislative efforts to discourage the formation or to control the behavior of monopolies were construed narrowly by most courts.[3] Last, but not least, many appellate courts around the turn of the century interpreted the "due process" clause of the Fourteenth Amendment—and similar clauses in the state constitutions—in favor of sharply restricting the ability of the state legislatures to interfere with property rights or with employers' "freedom of contract."[4]

A less well known but equally important aspect of classical legal thought was a distinctive style of judicial reasoning. Before the Civil War, an American court confronted with a difficult case typically made a conscious effort to adopt a rule and reach a decision that simultaneously advanced "public policy" (for example, by creating incentives for economic development) and secured "justice" (for example, by ensuring that no morally innocent parties suffered net economic injury or were subjected to obligations to which they had not voluntarily agreed).[5] After the war, this frankly consequentialist style of analysis fell into disfavor. Invocations of precedent—efforts to follow rules or interpretations announced in prior judicial decisions—became more common. When no prior decision seemed directly applicable, a court often would attempt to extract from the rulings made in a group of loosely related prior cases a general principle (the more abstract and encompassing the better) that could be brought to bear on the case before it. Lawyers and judges arguing in this vein did not ignore policy considerations altogether, but tended to invoke them only when selecting the "first principles" from which they could then generate particular rules to deal with particular problems.[6] By 1900, these and a host of related changes had produced a style of legal analysis dramatically different from the mode of reasoning that had been paradigmatic in 1850.[7]

Meanwhile, an influential group of law teachers was elaborating its own version of classicism. Properly organized, law was like geometry, the teachers insisted. Each doctrinal field revolved around a few fundamental axioms, derived primarily from empirical observation of how courts had in the past responded to particular sorts of problems. From those axioms, one could and should deduce—through uncontroversial, rationally compelling reasoning processes—a large number of specific rules or corollaries. The legal system of the United States, they acknowledged, did not yet fully conform to this ideal; much of the scholars' energies were devoted to identifying and urging the repudiation of rules or decisions that disturbed the conceptual order of their respective fields. But once purified of such anomalies and errors, the scholars contended, the law would be "complete" (capable of providing a single right answer to every dispute) and elegant.[8]

The causes of the development of this interrelated set of theories and doctrines are not altogether clear. Some historians attribute the theories' emergence to the conscious efforts of judges to maximize the profits and protect the property of the dominant social and economic classes in the United States—partly by inhibiting legislative initiatives that might threaten those privileges and partly by devising a style of analysis that would help to depict the extant distribution of wealth and power as legitimate.[9] Others trace the classical vision to more parochial interests of the legal profession—for example, the desire of the relatively new cadre of professional law teachers to persuade skeptical university presidents and practicing lawyers that law was a science, a technical but integrated field that could be mastered only through three years of full-time study.[10] Other historians emphasize the influence on lawyers of classical economic theory.[11] Still others attribute to lawyers in the late nineteenth century a belief that formal rationality could make the law more certain and predictable—and thereby facilitate the planning and pursuit of private ventures of all sorts.[12] Whatever its sources, by World War I the classical synthesis had come to exert a powerful influence on American law.

Not all participants in American legal culture were captivated by this vision, however. Many courts persisted in discussing and deciding cases using the mode of analysis that had been popular in the early nineteenth century.[13] Regulatory statutes were not always struck down when subjected to constitutional challenges.[14] Many lawyers in their briefs and oral arguments departed more or less consciously from the classical guidelines.[15] And a gradually growing group of scholars—some of them marching under the banner of "Sociological Jurisprudence"—criticized the work of their classical colleagues as philosophically naive and politically pernicious.[16]

In the 1920s, the volume, sophistication, and radicalism of this stream of dissident writings increased substantially. Two circumstances contributed to the surge. First, many young and energetic scholars joined the faculties of leading American law schools. Irreverent, iconoclastic, and steeped in the political tradition of Progressivism, most members of the new generation were less inclined than their elders to see virtue in the extant legal order. Second, legal scholars (and the younger teachers in particular) became more aware of developments in other academic disciplines that seemed to undermine the premises of classical legal thought. Pragmatism in philosophy, non-Euclidean geometry, Einstein's theories of physics, and new approaches in psychology and anthropology all seemed to cast doubt on the utility of systems of axioms and theorems, the value of inductive and deductive reasoning, and the power of formal rules to organize human affairs.[17]

It is the work of this enlarged and energized group of critics that legal historians typically refer to as Legal Realism, and this volume conforms to that usage. Unfortunately, the task of deciding precisely which authors and works should be accorded the label Realist is not as simple as this account might suggest. The job is complicated by three circumstances: Many of the ideas propounded by the younger scholars were derived from the work of older dissidents (whose attitudes toward the work of their successors varied substantially); the younger scholars disagreed among themselves on several issues; and there never developed a professional organization of "Legal Realists." Consequently, the scope of the Realist movement has been—and undoubtedly will continue to be—controverted.[18]

The editors' view is that the most useful definition of Legal Realism is a generous one. The heart of the movement was an effort to define and discredit classical legal theory and practice and to offer in their place

a more philosophically and politically enlightened jurisprudence. All of
the lawyers, judges, and legal scholars who contributed to that project
should, in our view, be considered Realists.

Why excavate the writings of the Realists (however the movement
is defined)? Aside from making easier the study of an important stage in
American legal and intellectual history, two considerations, we believe,
justify the venture. First, the Realists' writings contain many enduring
insights. The Realist credo is often caricatured as the proposition that
how a judge decides a case on a given day depends primarily on what he
or she had for breakfast. It is true that some of the Realists' remarks
concerning the importance to judicial decision-making of judges' personalities and prejudices are overstated and seem, in retrospect, simplis-
tic (although no Realist, in fact, took the position that a judge's diet is
critical to his or her rulings). But most of their writings on the character
of adjudication and on other issues were vastly more sophisticated and
penetrating.

Second, in several respects Legal Realism was an extraordinarily influential movement in American legal history. A large group of Realists—including Berle, Dowling, Arnold, Douglas, Frankfurter, and
Frank—served in the federal government during the New Deal, helping
to shape most of the major administrative agencies.[19] Important systems
of rules, such as the Uniform Commercial Code, were crafted by Realists and bear the marks of their jurisprudence.[20] The organization of
many of the casebooks used in modern law-school courses are directly
attributable to the Realists.[21] Even the tenor of the discussion in most
law-school classrooms—the set of understandings shared by teachers and
students of the sorts of claims that do and do not count as "legal arguments"—owes much to the Realists.

Contemporary American legal theory has also been powerfully affected by the Realist movement. The empirical orientation and the skepticism concerning the grip on social affairs of "paper rules"
characteristic of the Law and Society movement; the impatience with
doctrinal reasoning and the insistence upon judges' law-making power
that infuses most Law and Economics scholarship; the aspiration to expose "gaps, conflicts, and ambiguities" in the legal order and the fascination with the ideological functions of legal doctrine manifested in
most Critical Legal Studies writings—all are traceable to the contentions
of the Realists.

Less obviously, Legal Realism continues to exert an important influence on modern American legal scholarship through its capacity to set
the agenda—to define the questions that need answering. For reasons
that a reading of this volume will make clear, Legal Realism called into
question three related ideals cherished by most Americans: the notion
that, in the United States, the people (not unelected judges) select the
rules by which they are governed; the conviction that the institution of
judicial review reinforces rather than undermines representative democ-

racy; and the faith that ours is a government of laws, not of men. The aspiration of most of the schools of American legal theory that have proliferated since World War II has been to meet those challenges. In one way or another, the theorists have sought to demonstrate that, if courts behave responsibly, adjudication can be reasonably constrained, judicial review can be legitimate, the rule of law can be a reality, and justice can be secured. None of the successive modern schools has been wholly successful in this regard; each new group of scholars, consequently, feels obliged to confront anew the Realists' challenges.[22]

Finally, Legal Realism has had a substantial impact on American judges' understandings of their responsibilities and power. In their confirmation hearings, most candidates for judicial office still profess fidelity to the classical vision of adjudication,[23] and even in private few contemporary American judges would describe their jobs in precisely the terms the Realists used. But the majority recognize—and often worry about—the substantial amount of discretionary power they wield.[24] To a degree far greater than their counterparts in virtually any other country, American judges think of themselves as lawmakers. That self-image originates to a large degree in Legal Realism.

The content and structure of this volume reflects in several ways the understanding of Legal Realism summarized above. Our commitment to a generous definition of the movement has led us to include a number of writers not always considered Realists. Our conviction that the body of Realist writings is integrated by some central themes explains the organization of the book into eight topical chapters. And our view that Realism is best understood in view of the institutions and ideas the Realists were challenging and of the political implications of those challenges has prompted us to preface each of the chapters with an introduction sketching the relevant context.

Practical constraints have also helped shape the volume. We wished to keep the book short so that it could be sold for a price within the means of most students. At the same time, we wished to include not only the classic essays, but also some lesser known authors and works that would suggest something of the range and flavor of Legal Realism. Reconciling these goals required us to edit most of the works either modestly or severely. Some readers will undoubtedly find the resulting selections too abbreviated for their tastes or needs. For them, we have supplied a selected bibliography.

Stanford, California W.W.F.
Cambridge, Massachusetts M.J.H.
Boston, Massachusetts T.A.R.
February 1993

Note on the Texts

The spelling and punctuation in many of the Realists' works are archaic or eccentric. We have corrected only obvious errors. To save space, we have omitted the large majority of the footnotes in the Realists' essays. The few we have retained have been renumbered (consecutively within each excerpt) and placed at the end of the volume under the appropriate chapter headings.

AMERICAN
LEGAL REALISM

1

Antecedents

The Realist movement is conventionally thought to have been confined to the period between the two world wars. Realism did not, however, emerge fully formed in 1918. Many of the ideas that figured prominently in the Realists' teaching and writing were first developed—sometimes in rudimentary form, sometimes elaborately—by dissidents among the preceding generation of scholars.

By far the most important of these forerunners was Oliver Wendell Holmes, Jr. Holmes was more than simply an incipient Realist. Partly because of his brilliance, partly because of his long tenure as a justice of the United States Supreme Court, and partly because of his aphoristic, even cryptic, writing style, Holmes heavily influenced American legal theorists of many stripes. But the Realists were especially indebted to him.

Despite their avowedly patricidal inclinations, most of the Realists were eager to acknowledge this debt. They cited Holmes' works constantly. They frequently used long quotations from his books and articles as epigraphs for their own. They celebrated his judicial opinions.[1] Even Jerome Frank, who had little patience for "father worship," proclaimed Holmes "the Completely Adult Jurist."[2]

Included in this chapter are excerpts from three of Holmes' works that had especially powerful impacts on Realist thought. The first is the brief but extraordinarily rich passage from *The Common Law* (1881) that commences with the famous declaration: "The life of the law has not been logic; it has been experience."[3] Benjamin Cardozo, perhaps the premier Realist judge, said of this passage, "Here is the text to be unfolded. All that is to come will be development and commentary."[4] To be sure, the text was (and is) susceptible of many interpretations. Some

Realists saw in it a denunciation of all efforts (like those of Harvard Law School's dean, Christopher Columbus Langdell) to represent law as a "science."[5] Others read it as an assault on the classical conception of law as a coherent system of fixed axioms from which particular rules and decisions could be deduced.[6] Still others construed it as a call for a empirical, behaviorist study of legal rules.[7] Recently, the same passage has been read as the foundation of a "pragmatist" legal theory—an understanding of the nature and purpose of law shared by Holmes and an important subset of the Realists.[8] The debate will undoubtedly continue, but one thing seems clear: Most Realists found the paragraph in some way inspirational.

The second selection comes from the greatest of all of Holmes' essays, "The Path of the Law." Written originally as a speech in 1897, it represents the culmination of three decades of reflection upon the nature of law and adjudication.[9] Several of the arguments deployed in the essay recur in the writings of the Realists. The most important, undoubtedly, is the "bad-man" theory of law:

> Take the fundamental question, What constitutes the law? You will find some text writers telling you that it is something different from what is decided by the courts of Massachusetts or England, that it is a system of reason, that it is a deduction from principles of ethics or admitted axioms or what not, which may or may not coincide with the decisions. But if we take the view of our friend the bad man we shall find that he does not care two straws for the axioms or deductions, but that he does want to know what the Massachusetts or English courts are likely to do in fact. I am much of his mind. The prophecies of what the courts will do in fact, and nothing more pretentious, are what I mean by the law.[10]

The sharp distinction Holmes draws here between law and morals had a powerful impact on the thought of most Legal Realists—although it too was construed in a variety of ways.[11] Some thought it justified separating the scientific study of legal institutions from the distracting discourse of ethics. Others, like Morris Cohen, treated Holmes' argument as a useful corrective to the confused understanding of law and morality engendered by "the traditional American conception of natural rights" but denounced as "superficial" and misleading the "positivistic conception of scientific method" that their comrades were extracting from it.[12] The majority of the Realists, like Karl Llewellyn, sought in some way to straddle this divide.[13]

The utilitarian or instrumental flavor of "The Path of the Law" also found favor with the Realists. The purpose of law, Holmes insisted, was the deterrence of undesirable social consequences: "I think that the judges themselves have failed adequately to recognize their duty of weighing considerations of social advantage." Before the Civil War, this conception of adjudication as a form of social engineering had been widely shared by American judges, but in the late nineteenth century it had fallen out of favor.[14] One of the aspirations of both Holmes and the Realists was to revive it.

Finally, several of the specific doctrinal arguments made in "The Path of the Law" were recapitulated or elaborated in the more technical essays of the Realists. For example, Holmes drew upon his "bad-man" theory in developing what for the time was a radical understanding of the nature of contractual obligations. "The duty to keep a contract at common law means a prediction that you must pay damages if you do not keep it—and nothing else." Only "the confusion between legal and moral" ideas had led others to the conclusion that it was immoral to breach a contract. An approach that focuses solely on the consequences of breach, Holmes conceded, "stinks in the nostrils of those who think it advantageous to get as much ethics into the law as they can," but it is more accurate and useful, he argued, than an approach that concentrates on the moral obligations associated with promises. On a more detailed level, Holmes amplified his earlier criticisms of subjective theories of contractual duties (which grounded obligation in a "meeting of the minds" of putatively contracting parties), offering instead an objective theory (which acknowledged that judges do and should give meaning to the language employed by the parties "because of some belief as to the practice of the community or of a class, or because of some opinion as to policy"). In ways more fully set out in Chapter 3, this characterization provided an important staging ground for the Realists' assault on the classical ideal of the self-regulating market.

Holmes' remarks on torts in "The Path of the Law" were even more innovative—and indeed continue to provoke controversy among legal scholars. Distancing himself from the positions he had adopted earlier in *The Common Law*, Holmes contended that it is impossible to answer definitively the question whether a defendant who has injured someone but whose conduct was not blameworthy should be forced to pay damages to the victim. The choice between the negligence principle (defendants should be liable only if they were at fault) and the strict-liability principle (defendants should be liable even if blameless), he now insisted, "is a concealed, half conscious battle on the question of legislative policy, and if any one thinks that it can be settled deductively, or once for all, I only can say that I think he is theoretically wrong, and that I am certain that his conclusion will not be accepted in practice." Among the policy questions upon which the choice turned was the degree to which the losses associated with the myriad injuries caused by modern industries ("railroads, factories, and the like") should be borne by the public at large (through increased prices for the goods and services provided by those industries). "Loss-spreading" arguments of this sort would figure prominently in the Realists' writings on torts and indeed continue to play a large role in the discussions in today's law-school classrooms.

The last of the selections from Holmes—his 1905 dissenting opinion in *Lochner* v. *New York*—is best understood as part of a large body of criticism provoked by the emergence of the doctrine of "substantive due process." When state and federal courts began in the late nineteenth century to declare unconstitutional a significant percentage of social-welfare statutes, the sponsors and supporters of such legislation, as one might expect, were angry. Between the 1890s and the late 1930s, that anger gave rise to a series of increasingly innovative commentaries on legal and constitutional theory. A relatively conventional but nevertheless influential early venture in this genre was James Thayer's article, "The Origin and Scope of the American Doctrine of Constitutional Law." Drawing on his extensive knowledge of legal history, Thayer contended that American courts had traditionally, and properly, accorded considerable deference to legislatures' judgments that their enactments did not violate the relevant constitutions. Recent departures from that approach he attributed in part to "a pedantic and academic treatment of the texts of the constitution and the laws."

Holmes' *Lochner* dissent was more sophisticated but, as always, harder to interpret. His insistence that the courts were losing sight of "the right of the majority to embody their opinions into law" was clear enough, as was his criticism of his colleagues for trying to deduce the answer to "concrete cases" from a few "general propositions." But other portions of the opinion were more opaque. For example, Holmes did not suggest that the courts should get out of the business of judicial review altogether or even that they should limit themselves to invalidating statutes inconsistent with express provisions of the Constitution; legislation that infringes "fundamental principles as they have been understood by the traditions of our people and our law," he argued, should continue to be struck down. He gave no indication, however, what those principles were or how judges were to ascertain them. Other passages in the opinion were even more troublesome for Holmes' Progressive supporters. For example, what was one to make of his suggestion that much modern social-welfare legislation could be considered "injudicious," even "tyrannical"? Language of this sort continues to support a lively debate among legal historians concerning the extent to which Holmes may be considered a democrat.[15] At the time, however, most of the growing group of critics of the Supreme Court's constitutional jurisprudence chose to ignore these passages.

In his 1909 essay "Liberty of Contract," Roscoe Pound contributed two themes to the critics' arsenal of arguments. First, he invoked sociology—and, more broadly, a practical understanding of industrial working conditions in the United States—to criticize the conceptions of equality and individual liberty upon which much of the Supreme Court's reasoning seemed to depend. Second, instead of merely denouncing the Court's decisions and arguments as misguided, he sought to explain how the justices could have gone so far astray. A host of circumstances—ranging from the manner in which American lawyers typically are educated, to the timing of the passage of the early labor statutes, to the "mechanical" mode of reasoning that characterized the current period of American legal history—contributed, he argued, to the unfortunate line of recent decisions. During the next twenty-five years, this diagnostic and thus, inevitably, condescending style of criticism would become increasingly common, reaching its most extreme form in the work of Jerome Frank.

In "Law in Books and Law in Action," published the following year, Pound addressed a general problem of which the failings of constitutional law were, he thought, merely one symptom. American legal doctrine and theory, he argued, had lost touch in several related senses with the rest of the world. What the courts did in fact often deviated sharply from the rules ostensibly in force; jurisprudence had failed to keep up with the development of "social, economic and philosophical thinking"; and the manner in which law was made and applied in the United States was "backward." Pound contended that these failings could be traced in part to the excessive influence of a set of images and prescriptions that we would now describe as classical liberalism, the centerpiece of which was excessive celebration of the "self-reliant man." The solution: Law must be brought up to date and, specifically, must come to recognize that justice entails not merely "fair play between individuals," but "fair play between social classes."

Unfortunately, during the remainder of his career, Pound gradually retreated from the iconoclasm of these early essays. For example, his denunciation in "Law in Books" of the brutal and unequal treatment received by "the weak and friendless and lowly" at the hands of the criminal justice system contrasts sharply with his failure seventeen years later to speak out against the handling by the Massachusetts courts of the accusations against Sacco and Vanzetti.[16] His writing style also changed markedly. For the most part, his early essays were brisk, irreverent, and impassioned. Only occasionally did he lapse into ponderous generalities, such as his lumbering account in "Liberty of Contract" of the stages through which all legal systems periodically pass. Over time, however, he pontificated more and sparkled less. The sense in which Pound was a forerunner of the Realists is thus complex: His early essays they found inspirational; his later work was one of their principal targets.[17]

John Chipman Gray extended Holmes' arguments in a different direction. Building on the "bad-man" theory of law, Gray contended that an unbiased study of the actual operation of the common-law system would make it plain that judges "do make Law." By modern lights, this claim is tame. Gray's principal contentions were simply that judges' political inclinations affect their decisions and that courts occasionally jettison old rules or interpretations and announce new ones, thereby instituting "a different state of the Law." But even these modest assertions threatened to undermine the delicate set of arguments developed by James Coolidge Carter and others in their ongoing campaign against legislative "codification" of the common law.[18] And it laid the groundwork for the Realists' more radical assertions concerning the lawmaking powers of the judiciary.

The last of the forerunners featured in this chapter is Wesley Hohfeld, the *wunderkind* of the Yale Law School. Had he lived longer, Hohfeld would likely have been one of the giants of American legal theory. As it was, his two articles on judicial reasoning altered the outlook of an extraordinary number of law teachers.[19] Stylistically and substantively, they are sharply different from most of the essays in this book. The prose is turgid and abstract. Neither essay makes any mention of sociology, economics, or the law in action. Instead, they seek to derive insight from precise categorization of legal concepts. Yet, in several ways illustrated in subsequent chapters, Hohfeld's taxonomy of entitlements was of practical use to the Realists. It helped them discredit the distinction between the public and private spheres.[20] It markedly enhanced the power and precision of their critique of the classical style of legal reasoning. And it helped them explain why, in resolving most of the disputes that come before them (not merely a few anomalous "hard cases"), judges should weigh carefully the practical implications of their decisions.[21]

OLIVER WENDELL HOLMES

The Common Law

(1881)

The life of the law has not been logic: it has been experience. The felt necessities of the time, the prevalent moral and political theories, intuitions of public policy, avowed or unconscious, even the prejudices which judges share with their fellow-men, have had a good deal more to do than the syllogism in determining the rules by which men should be governed. The law embodies the story of a nation's development through many centuries, and it cannot be dealt with as if it contained only the axioms and corollaries of a book of mathematics. In order to know what it is, we must know what it has been, and what it tends to become. We must alternately consult history and existing theories of legislation. But the most difficult labor will be to understand the combination of the two into new products at every stage. The substance of the law at any given time pretty nearly corresponds, so far as it goes, with what is then understood to be convenient; but its form and machinery, and the degree to which it is able to work out desired results, depend very much upon its past....

Reprinted from *The Common Law* (Boston: Little, Brown, 1881), pp. 1–2.

JAMES B. THAYER

"The Origin and Scope of the American Doctrine of Constitutional Law"

(1893)

[The traditional understanding of the scope of judicial review was] to determine, for the mere purpose of deciding a litigated question properly submitted to the court, whether a particular disputed exercise of power was forbidden by the constitution. In doing this the court was so to discharge its office as not to deprive another department of any of its proper power, or to limit it in the proper range of its discretion. Not merely, then, do these questions, when presenting themselves in the courts for judicial action, call for a peculiarly large method in the treatment of them, but especially they require an allowance to be made by the judges for the vast and not definable range of legislative power and choice, for that wide margin of considerations which address themselves only to the practical judgment of a legislative body. Within that margin, as among all these legislative considerations, the constitutional lawmakers must be allowed a free foot. In so far as legislative choice, ranging here unfettered, may select one form of action or another, the judges must not interfere, since *their* question is a naked judicial one.

Moreover, such is the nature of this particular judicial question that the preliminary determination by the legislature is a fact of very great importance, since the constitutions expressly intrust to the legislature this determination; they cannot act without making it. Furthermore, the constitutions not merely intrust to the legislatures a preliminary determination of the question, but they contemplate that this determination may be the final one; for they secure no revision of it. It is only as litigation may spring up, and as the course of it may happen to raise the point of constitutionality, that any question for the courts can regularly emerge. It may be, then, that the mere legislative decision will accomplish results throughout the country of the profoundest importance before any judicial question can arise or be decided,—as in the case of the

Reprinted from the *Harvard Law Review*, vol. 7 (1893), pp. 135–38, 140, 143–44, 151, 155–56, by permission.

first and second charters of the United States Bank, and of the legal tender laws of thirty years ago and later. The constitutionality of a bank charter divided the cabinet of Washington, as it divided political parties for more than a generation. Yet when the first charter was given, in 1791, to last for twenty years, it ran through its whole life unchallenged in the courts, and was renewed in 1816. Only after three years from that did the question of its constitutionality come to decision in the Supreme Court of the United States. It is peculiarly important to observe that such a result is not an exceptional or unforeseen one; it is a result anticipated and clearly foreseen. Now, it is the legislature to whom this power is given,—this power, not merely of enacting laws, but of putting an interpretation on the constitution which shall deeply affect the whole country, enter into, vitally change, even revolutionize the most serious affairs, except as some individual may find it for his private interest to carry the matter into court. So of the legal tender legislation of 1863 and later....

It is plain that where a power so momentous as this primary authority to interpret is given, the actual determinations of the body to whom it is intrusted are entitled to a corresponding respect; and this not on mere grounds of courtesy or conventional respect, but on very solid and significant grounds of policy and law. The judiciary may well reflect that if they had been regarded by the people as the chief protection against legislative violation of the constitution, they would not have been allowed merely this incidental and postponed control. They would have been let in, as it was sometimes endeavored in the conventions to let them in, to a revision of the laws before they began to operate. As the opportunity of the judges to check and correct unconstitutional Acts is so limited, it may help us to understand why the extent of their control, when they do have the opportunity, should also be narrow.

It was, then, all along true, and it was foreseen, that much which is harmful and unconstitutional may take effect without any capacity in the courts to prevent it, since their whole power is a judicial one. Their interference was but one of many safeguards, and its scope was narrow.

The rigor of this limitation upon judicial action is sometimes freely recognized, yet in a perverted way which really operates to extend the judicial function beyond its just bounds. The court's duty, we are told, is the mere and simple office of construing two writings and comparing one with another, as two contracts or two statutes are construed and compared when they are said to conflict; of declaring the true meaning of each, and, if they are opposed to each other, of carrying into effect the constitution as being of superior obligation,—an ordinary and humble judicial duty, as the courts sometimes describe it. This way of putting it easily results in the wrong kind of disregard of legislative considerations; not merely in refusing to let them directly operate as grounds of judgment, but in refusing to consider them at all. Instead of taking them into account and allowing for them as furnishing possible grounds of legislative action, there takes place a pedantic and academic treatment of the texts of the constitution and the laws. And so we miss that combination of a lawyer's rigor with a statesman's breadth of view which should be found in dealing with this class of questions in constitutional law. Of this petty method we have many specimens; they are found only too easily to-day in the volumes of our current reports.

In order, however, to avoid falling into these narrow and literal methods, in order to prevent the courts from forgetting, as Marshall said, that "it is a constitution we are expounding," these literal precepts about the nature of the judicial task have been accompanied by a rule of administration which has tended, in competent hands, to give matters a very different complexion. . . .

Let us observe the course which the courts, in point of fact, have taken, in administering this interesting jurisdiction. . . .

. . . In 1811, Chief Justice Tilghman, of Pennsylvania, while asserting the power of the court to hold laws unconstitutional, but declining to exercise it in a particular case, stated this rule as follows:—

> For weighty reasons, it has been assumed as a principle in constitutional construction by the Supreme Court of the United States, by this court, and every other court of reputation in the United States, than an Act of the legislature is not to be declared void unless the violation of the constitution is so manifest as to leave no room for reasonable doubt.

When did this rule of administration begin? Very early. . . .

. . . The courts have perceived with more or less distinctness that this exercise of the judicial function does in truth go far beyond the simple business which judges sometimes describe. If their duty were in truth merely and nakedly to ascertain the meaning of the text of the constitution and of the impeached Act of the legislature, and to determine, as an academic question, whether in the court's judgment the two were in conflict, it would, to be sure, be an elevated and important office, one dealing with great matters, involving large public considerations, but yet a function far simpler than it really is. Having ascertained all this, yet there remains a question—the really momentous question—whether, after all, the court can disregard the Act. It cannot do this as a mere matter of course,—merely because it is concluded that upon a just and true construction the law is unconstitutional. That is precisely the significance of the rule of administration that the courts lay down. It can only disregard the Act when those who have the right to make laws have not merely made a mistake, but have made a very clear one,—so clear that it is not open to rational question. That is the standard of duty to which the courts bring legislative Acts; that is the test which they apply,—not merely their own judgment as to constitutionality, but their conclusion as to what judgment is permissible to another department which the constitution has charged with the duty of making it. This rule recognizes that, having regard to the great, complex, ever-unfolding exigencies of government, much which will seem unconstitutional to one man, or body of men, may reasonably not seem so to another; that the constitution often admits of different interpretations; that there is often a range of choice and judgment; that in such cases the constitution does not impose upon the legislature any one specific opinion, but leaves open this range of choice; and that whatever choice is rational is constitutional. This is the principle which the rule that I have been illustrating affirms and supports. . . .

. . . [T]here are many cases where the judges sustain an Act because they are in doubt about it; where they are not giving their own opinion that it is constitutional, but are merely leaving untouched a determination of the legislature; as in the case where a Massachusetts judge concurred in the opinion of his brethren that a legislative Act was "competent for the legislature to pass, and was not unconstitutional," "upon the single ground that the Act is not so clearly unconstitutional, its invalidity so free from reasonable doubt, as to make it the duty of the judicial department, in view of the vast interests involved in the result, to declare it void." The constant declaration of the judges that the question for them is not one of the mere and simple preponderance of reasons for or against, but of what is very plain and clear, clear beyond a reasonable doubt,—this declaration is really a steady announcement that their decisions in support of the constitutionality of legislation do not, as of course, import their own opinion of the true construction of the constitution, and that the strict meaning of their words, when they hold an Act constitutional, is merely this,—not unconstitutional beyond a reasonable doubt. It may be added that a sufficient explanation is found here of some of the decisions which have alarmed many people in recent years,—as if the courts were turning out but a broken reed. Many more such opinions are to be expected, for, while legislatures are often faithless to their trust, judges sometimes have to confess the limits of their own power. . . .

The view which has thus been presented seems to me highly important. I am not stating a new doctrine, but attempting to restate more exactly and truly an admitted one. If what I have said be sound, it is greatly to be desired that it should be more emphasized by our courts, in its full significance. It has been often remarked that private rights are more respected by the legislatures of some countries which have no written constitution, than by ours. No doubt our doctrine of constitutional law has had a tendency to drive out questions of justice and right, and to fill the mind of legislators with thoughts of mere legality, of what the constitution allows. And moreover, even in the matter of legality, they have felt little responsibility; if we are wrong, they say, the courts will correct it. If what I have been saying is true, the safe and permanent road towards reform is that of impressing upon our people a far stronger sense than they have of the great range of possible harm and evil that our system leaves open, and must leave open, to the legislatures, and of the clear limits of judicial power; so that responsibility may be brought sharply home where it belongs. The checking and cutting down of legislative power, by numerous detailed prohibitions in the constitution, cannot be accomplished without making the government petty and incompetent. This process has already been carried much too far in some of our States. Under no system can the power of courts go far to save a people from ruin; our chief protection lies elsewhere. If this be true, it is of the greatest public importance to put the matter in its true light.

OLIVER WENDELL HOLMES

"The Path of the Law"

(1897)

When we study law we are not studying a mystery but a well-known profession. We are studying what we shall want in order to appear before judges, or to advise people in such a way as to keep them out of court. The reason why it is a profession, why people will pay lawyers to argue for them or to advise them, is that in societies like ours the command of the public force is intrusted to the judges in certain cases, and the whole power of the state will be put forth, if necessary, to carry out their judgments and decrees. People want to know under what circumstances and how far they will run the risk of coming against what is so much stronger than themselves, and hence it becomes a business to find out when this danger is to be feared. The object of our study, then, is prediction, the prediction of the incidence of the public force through the instrumentality of the courts.

The means of the study are a body of reports, of treatises, and of statutes, in this country and in England, extending back for six hundred years, and now increasing annually by hundreds. In these sibylline leaves are gathered the scattered prophecies of the past upon the cases in which the axe will fall. These are what properly have been called the oracles of the law. Far the most important and pretty nearly the whole meaning of every new effort of legal thought is to make these prophecies more precise, and to generalize them into a thoroughly connected system. The process is one, from a lawyer's statement of a case, eliminating as it does all the dramatic elements with which his client's story has clothed it, and retaining only the facts of legal import, up to the final analyses and abstract universals of theoretic jurisprudence. The reason why a lawyer does not mention that his client wore a white hat when he made a contract, while Mrs. Quickly would be sure to dwell upon it along with the parcel gilt goblet and the sea-coal fire, is that he foresees that the public force will act in the same way whatever his client had upon his head. It is to make the prophecies easier to be remembered and to be understood that the teachings of the decisions of the past are put into general propositions and gathered into text–books, or

Reprinted from the *Harvard Law Review*, vol. 10 (1897), pp. 457–69, 473–74, 477–78, by permission.

that statutes are passed in a general form. The primary rights and duties with which jurisprudence busies itself again are nothing but prophecies. One of the many evil effects of the confusion between legal and moral ideas, about which I shall have something to say in a moment, is that theory is apt to get the cart before the horse, and to consider the right or the duty as something existing apart from and independent of the consequences of its breach, to which certain sanctions are added afterward. But, as I shall try to show, a legal duty so called is nothing but a prediction that if a man does or omits certain things he will be made to suffer in this or that way by judgment of the court;—and so of a legal right.

The number of our predictions when generalized and reduced to a system is not unmanageably large. They present themselves as a finite body of dogma which may be mastered within a reasonable time. It is a great mistake to be frightened by the ever increasing number of reports. The reports of a given jurisdiction in the course of a generation take up pretty much the whole body of the law, and restate it from the present point of view. We could reconstruct the corpus from them if all that went before were burned. The use of the earlier reports is mainly historical, a use about which I shall have something to say before I have finished.

I wish, if I can, to lay down some first principles for the study of this body of dogma or systematized prediction which we call the law, for men who want to use it as the instrument of their business to enable them to prophesy in their turn, and, as bearing upon the study, I wish to point out an ideal which as yet our law has not attained.

The first thing for a business-like understanding of the matter is to understand its limits, and therefore I think it desirable at once to point out and dispel a confusion between morality and law, which sometimes rises to the height of conscious theory, and more often and indeed constantly is making trouble in detail without reaching the point of consciousness. You can see very plainly that a bad man has as much reason as a good one for wishing to avoid an encounter with the public force, and therefore you can see the practical importance of the distinction between morality and law. A man who cares nothing for an ethical rule which is believed and practised by his neighbors is likely nevertheless to care a good deal to avoid being made to pay money, and will want to keep out of jail if he can.

I take it for granted that no hearer of mine will misinterpret what I have to say as the language of cynicism. The law is the witness and external deposit of our moral life. Its history is the history of the moral development of the race. The practice of it, in spite of popular jests, tends to make good citizens and good men. When I emphasize the difference between law and morals I do so with reference to a single end, that of learning and understanding the law. For that purpose you must definitely master its specific marks, and it is for that that I ask you for the moment to imagine yourselves indifferent to other and greater things.

I do not say that there is not a wider point of view from which the distinction between law and morals becomes of secondary or no importance, as all mathematical distinctions vanish in presence of the infinite. But I do say that that distinction is of the first importance for the object which we are here to consider,—a right study and mastery of the law as a business with well understood limits, a body of dogma enclosed within definite lines. I have just shown the practical reason for saying so. If you want to know the law and nothing else, you must look at it as a bad man, who cares only for the material consequences which such knowledge enables him to predict, not as a good one, who finds his reasons for conduct, whether inside the law or outside of it, in the vaguer sanctions of conscience. . . .

The confusion with which I am dealing besets confessedly legal conceptions. Take the fundamental question, What constitutes the law? You will find some text writers telling you that it is something different from what is decided by the courts of Massachusetts or England, that it is a system of reason, that it is a deduction from principles of ethics or admitted axioms or what not, which may or may not coincide with the decisions. But if we take the view of our friend the bad man we shall find that he does not care two straws for the axioms or deductions, but that he does want to know what the Massachusetts or English courts are likely to do in fact. I am much of his mind. The prophecies of what the courts will do in fact, and nothing more pretentious, are what I mean by the law. . . .

Nowhere is the confusion between legal and moral ideas more manifest than in the law of contract. Among other things, here again the so called primary rights and duties are invested with a mystic significance beyond what can be assigned and explained. The duty to keep a contract at common law means a prediction that you must pay damages if you do not keep it,—and nothing else. If you commit a tort, you are liable to pay a compensatory sum. If you commit a contract, you are liable to pay a compensatory sum unless the promised event comes to pass, and that is all the difference. But such a mode of looking at the matter stinks in the nostrils of those who think it advantageous to get as much ethics into the law as they can. . . .

I have spoken only of the common law, because there are some cases in which a logical justification can be found for speaking of civil liabilities as imposing duties in an intelligible sense. These are the relatively few in which equity will grant an injunction, and will enforce it by putting the defendant in prison or otherwise punishing him unless he complies with the order of the court. But I hardly think it advisable to shape general theory from the exception, and I think it would be bet-

ter to cease troubling ourselves about primary rights and sanctions altogether, than to describe our prophecies concerning the liabilities commonly imposed by the law in those inappropriate terms. . . .

In the law of contract the use of moral phraseology has led to equal
confusion, as I have shown in part already, but only in part. Morals deal
with the actual internal state of the individual's mind, what he actually
intends. From the time of the Romans down to now, this mode of dealing has affected the language of the law as to contract, and the language
used has reacted upon the thought. We talk about a contract as a meeting of the minds of the parties, and thence it is inferred in various cases
that there is no contract because their minds have not met; that is, because they have intended different things or because one party has not
known of the assent of the other. Yet nothing is more certain than that
parties may be bound by a contract to things which neither of them intended, and when one does not know of the other's assent. Suppose a
contract is executed in due form and in writing to deliver a lecture,
mentioning no time. One of the parties thinks that the promise will be
construed to mean at once, within a week. The other thinks that it
means when he is ready. The court says that it means within a reasonable time. The parties are bound by the contract as it is interpreted by
the court, yet neither of them meant what the court declares that they
have said. In my opinion no one will understand the true theory of contract or be able even to discuss some fundamental questions intelligently
until he has understood that all contracts are formal, that the making of
a contract depends not on the agreement of two minds in one intention,
but on the agreement of two sets of external signs,—not on the parties'
having *meant* the same thing but on their having *said* the same thing.
Furthermore, as the signs may be addressed to one sense or another,—
to sight or to hearing,—on the nature of the sign will depend the moment when the contract is made. If the sign is tangible, for instance, a
letter, the contract is made when the letter of acceptance is delivered. If
it is necessary that the minds of the parties meet, there will be no contract until the acceptance can be read,—none, for example, if the acceptance be snatched from the hand of the offerer by a third person. . . .

. . . The next thing which I wish to consider is what are the forces
which determine its content and its growth. You may assume, with
Hobbes and Bentham and Austin, that all law emanates from the sovereign, even when the first human beings to enunciate it are the judges,
or you may think that law is the voice of the Zeitgeist, or what you like.
It is all one to my present purpose. Even if every decision required the
sanction of an emperor with despotic power and a whimsical turn of
mind, we should be interested none the less, still with a view to prediction, in discovering some order, some rational explanation, and some
principle of growth for the rules which he laid down. In every system
there are such explanations and principles to be found. It is with regard

to them that a second fallacy comes in, which I think it important to expose.

The fallacy to which I refer is the notion that the only force at work in the development of the law is logic. In the broadest sense, indeed, that notion would be true. The postulate on which we think about the universe is that there is a fixed quantitative relation between every phenomenon and its antecedents and consequents. If there is such a thing as a phenomenon without these fixed quantitative relations, it is a miracle. It is outside the law of cause and effect, and as such transcends our power of thought, or at least is something to or from which we cannot reason. The condition of our thinking about the universe is that it is capable of being thought about rationally, or, in other words, that every part of it is effect and cause in the same sense in which those parts are with which we are most familiar. So in the broadest sense it is true that the law is a logical development, like everything else. The danger of which I speak is not the admission that the principles governing other phenomena also govern the law, but the notion that a given system, ours, for instance, can be worked out like mathematics from some general axioms of conduct. This is the natural error of the schools, but it is not confined to them. I once heard a very eminent judge say that he never let a decision go until he was absolutely sure that it was right. So judicial dissent often is blamed, as if it meant simply that one side or the other were not doing their sums right, and, if they would take more trouble, agreement inevitably would come.

This mode of thinking is entirely natural. The training of lawyers is a training in logic. The processes of analogy, discrimination, and deduction are those in which they are most at home. The language of judicial decision is mainly the language of logic. And the logical method and form flatter that longing for certainty and for repose which is in every human mind. But certainty generally is illusion, and repose is not the destiny of man. Behind the logical form lies a judgment as to the relative worth and importance of competing legislative grounds, often an inarticulate and unconscious judgment, it is true, and yet the very root and nerve of the whole proceeding. You can give any conclusion a logical form. You always can imply a condition in a contract. But why do you imply it? It is because of some belief as to the practice of the community or of a class, or because of some opinion as to policy, or, in short, because of some attitude of yours upon a matter not capable of exact quantitative measurement, and therefore not capable of founding exact logical conclusions. Such matters really are battle grounds where the means do not exist for determinations that shall be good for all time, and where the decision can do no more than embody the preference of a given body in a given time and place. We do not realize how large a part of our law is open to reconsideration upon a slight change in the habit of the public mind. No concrete proposition is self—evident, no matter how ready we may be to accept it, not even Mr. Herbert Spencer's Every man has a right to do what he wills, provided he interferes not with a like right on the part of his neighbors.

Why is a false and injurious statement privileged, if it is made honestly in giving information about a servant? It is because it has been thought more important that information should be given freely, than that a man should be protected from what under other circumstances would be an actionable wrong. Why is a man at liberty to set up a business which he knows will ruin his neighbor? It is because the public good is supposed to be best subserved by free competition. Obviously such judgments of relative importance may vary in different times and places. Why does a judge instruct a jury that an employer is not liable to an employee for an injury received in the course of his employment unless he is negligent, and why do the jury generally find for the plaintiff if the case is allowed to go to them? It is because the traditional policy of our law is to confine liability to cases where a prudent man might have foreseen the injury, or at least the danger, while the inclination of a very large part of the community is to make certain classes of persons insure the safety of those with whom they deal. Since the last words were written, I have seen the requirement of such insurance put forth as part of the programme of one of the best known labor organizations. There is a concealed, half conscious battle on the question of legislative policy, and if any one thinks that it can be settled deductively, or once for all, I only can say that I think he is theoretically wrong, and that I am certain that his conclusion will not be accepted in practice *semper ubique et ab omnibus*.

Indeed, I think that even now our theory upon this matter is open to reconsideration, although I am not prepared to say how I should decide if a reconsideration were proposed. Our law of torts comes from the old days of isolated, ungeneralized wrongs, assaults, slanders, and the like, where the damages might be taken to lie where they fell by legal judgment. But the torts with which our courts are kept busy to-day are mainly the incidents of certain well known businesses. They are injuries to person or property by railroads, factories, and the like. The liability for them is estimated, and sooner or later goes into the price paid by the public. The public really pays the damages, and the question of liability, if pressed far enough, is really the question how far it is desirable that the public should insure the safety of those whose work it uses. It might be said that in such cases the chance of a jury finding for the defendant is merely a chance, once in a while rather arbitrarily interrupting the regular course of recovery, most likely in the case of an unusually conscientious plaintiff, and therefore better done away with. On the other hand, the economic value even of a life to the community can be estimated, and no recovery, it may be said, ought to go beyond that amount. It is conceivable that some day in certain cases we may find ourselves imitating, on a higher plane, the tariff for life and limb which we see in the *Leges Barbarorum.*

I think that the judges themselves have failed adequately to recognize their duty of weighing considerations of social advantage. The duty is inevitable, and the result of the often proclaimed judicial aversion to deal with such considerations is simply to leave the very ground and foundation of judgments inarticulate, and often unconscious, as I have said. When socialism first began to be talked about, the comfortable classes of the community were a good deal frightened. I suspect that this fear has influenced judicial action both here and in England, yet it is certain that it is not a conscious factor in the decisions to which I refer. I think that something similar has led people who no longer hope to control the legislatures to look to the courts as expounders of the Constitutions, and that in some courts new principles have been discovered outside the bodies of those instruments, which may be generalized into acceptance of the economic doctrines which prevailed about fifty years ago, and a wholesale prohibition of what a tribunal of lawyers does not think about right. I cannot but believe that if the training of lawyers led them habitually to consider more definitely and explicitly the social advantage on which the rule they lay down must be justified, they sometimes would hesitate where now they are confident, and see that really they were taking sides upon debatable and often burning questions.

So much for the fallacy of logical form. Now let us consider the present condition of the law as a subject for study, and the ideal toward which it tends. We still are far from the point of view which I desire to see reached. No one has reached it or can reach it as yet. We are only at the beginning of a philosophical reaction, and of a reconsideration of the worth of doctrines which for the most part still are taken for granted without any deliberate, conscious, and systematic questioning of their grounds. The development of our law has gone on for nearly a thousand years, like the development of a plant, each generation taking the inevitable next step, mind, like matter, simply obeying a law of spontaneous growth. It is perfectly natural and right that it should have been so. Imitation is a necessity of human nature, as has been illustrated by a remarkable French writer, M. Tarde, in an admirable book, "Les Lois de l'Imitation." Most of the things we do, we do for no better reason than that our fathers have done them or that our neighbors do them, and the same is true of a larger part than we suspect of what we think. The reason is a good one, because our short life gives us no time for a better, but it is not the best. It does not follow, because we all are compelled to take on faith at second hand most of the rules on which we base our action and our thought, that each of us may not try to set some corner of his world in the order of reason, or that all of us collectively should not aspire to carry reason as far as it will go throughout the whole domain. In regard to the law, it is true, no doubt, that an evolutionist will hesitate to affirm universal validity for his social ideals, or for the principles which he thinks should be embodied in legislation. He is content if he can prove them best for here and now. He may be ready to admit that he knows nothing about an absolute best in the cosmos, and even that he knows next to nothing about a permanent best for men. Still it is true that a body of law is more rational and more civilized when every rule it contains is referred articulately and definitely to an end which it subserves, and when the grounds for desiring that end are stated or are ready to be stated in words.

At present, in very many cases, if we want to know why a rule of law has taken its particular shape, and more or less if we want to know why it exists at all, we go to tradition. We follow it into the Year Books, and perhaps beyond them to the customs of the Salian Franks, and somewhere in the past, in the German forests, in the needs of Norman kings, in the assumptions of a dominant class, in the absence of generalized ideas, we find out the practical motive for what now best is justified by the mere fact of its acceptance and that men are accustomed to it. The rational study of law is still to a large extent the study of history. History must be a part of the study, because without it we cannot know the precise scope of rules which it is our business to know. It is a part of the rational study, because it is the first step toward an enlightened scepticism, that is, toward a deliberate reconsideration of the worth of those rules. When you get the dragon out of his cave on to the plain and in the daylight, you can count his teeth and claws, and see just what is his strength. But to get him out is only the first step. The next is either to kill him, or to tame him and make him a useful animal. For the rational study of the law the black-letter man may be the man of the present, but the man of the future is the man of statistics and the master of economics. It is revolting to have no better reason for a rule of law than that so it was laid down in the time of Henry IV. It is still more revolting if the grounds upon which it was laid down have vanished long since, and the rule simply persists from blind imitation of the past. . . .

I trust that no one will understand me to be speaking with disrespect of the law, because I criticise it so freely. I venerate the law, and especially our system of law, as one of the vastest products of the human mind. No one knows better than I do the countless number of great intellects that have spent themselves in making some addition or improvement, the greatest of which is trifling when compared with the mighty whole. It has the final title to respect that it exists, that it is not a Hegelian dream, but a part of the lives of men. But one may criticise even what one reveres. Law is the business to which my life is devoted, and I should show less than devotion if I did not do what in me lies to improve it, and, when I perceive what seems to me the ideal of its future, if I hesitated to point it out and to press toward it with all my heart.

. . . I look forward to a time when the part played by history in the explanation of dogma shall be very small, and instead of ingenious research we shall spend our energy on a study of the ends sought to be attained and the reasons for desiring them. As a step toward that ideal it seems to me that every lawyer ought to seek an understanding of economics. The present divorce between the schools of political economy and law seems to me an evidence of how much progress in philosophical study still remains to be made. In the present state of political economy, indeed, we come again upon history on a larger scale, but there we are called on to consider and weigh the ends of legislation, the means of attaining them, and the cost. We learn that for everything we have we give up something else, and we are taught to set the advantage we gain against the other advantage we lose, and to know what we are doing when we elect. . . .

I have been speaking about the study of law, and I have said next to nothing of what commonly is talked about in that connection,—textbooks and the case system, and all the machinery with which a student comes most immediately in contact. Nor shall I say anything about them. Theory is my subject, not practical details. The modes of teaching have been improved since my time, no doubt, but ability and industry will master the raw material with any mode. Theory is the most important part of the dogma of the law, as the architect is the most important man who takes part in the building of a house. The most important improvements of the last twenty-five years are improvements in theory. It is not to be feared as unpractical, for, to the competent, it simply means going to the bottom of the subject. For the incompetent, it sometimes is true, as has been said, that an interest in general ideas means an absence of particular knowledge. I remember in army days reading of a youth who, being examined for the lowest grade and being asked a question about squadron drill, answered that he never had considered the evolutions of less than ten thousand men. But the weak and foolish must be left to their folly. The danger is that the able and practical minded should look with indifference or distrust upon ideas the connection of which with their business is remote. I heard a story, the other day, of a man who had a valet to whom he paid high wages, subject to deduction for faults. One of his deductions was, "For lack of imagination, five dollars." The lack is not confined to valets. The object of ambition, power, generally presents itself nowadays in the form of money alone. Money is the most immediate form, and is a proper object of desire. "The fortune," said Rachel, "is the measure of the intelligence." That is a good text to waken people out of a fool's paradise. But, as Hegel says, "It is in the end not the appetite, but the opinion, which has to be satisfied." To an imagination of any scope the most far-reaching form of power is not money, it is the command of ideas. If you want great examples, read Mr. Leslie Stephen's "History of English Thought in the Eighteenth Century," and see how a hundred years after his death the abstract speculations of Descartes had become a practical force controlling the conduct of men. Read the works of the great German jurists, and see how much more the world is governed to-day by Kant than by Bonaparte. We cannot all be Descartes or Kant, but we all want happiness. And happiness, I am sure from having known many successful men, cannot be won simply by being counsel for great corporations and having an income of fifty thousand dollars. An intellect great enough to win the prize needs other food besides success. The remoter and more general aspects of the law are those which give it universal interest. It is through them that you not only become a great master in your calling, but connect your subject with the universe and catch an echo of the infinite, a glimpse of its unfathomable process, a hint of the universal law.

Lochner v. *New York*

198 U.S. 45 (1905)

Section 110 of the New York "labor law" provided, among other things, that "[n]o employee shall be required or permitted to work in a biscuit, bread or cake bakery or confectionery establishment more than sixty hours in any one week, or more than ten hours in any one day, unless for the purpose of making a shorter work day on the last day of the week." The defendant was charged with permitting an employee to work more than sixty hours during one week in his Utica bakery, in contravention of the provision. He demurred on the ground that the conduct of which he was accused "did not constitute a crime." The demurrer was overruled, and the defendant was convicted and sentenced to pay a fine of $50. His conviction was affirmed by the Appellate Division of the New York Supreme Court, and then by the New York Court of Appeals. The United States Supreme Court reversed, holding that the statute impermissibly "interfere[d] with the right of contract between the employer and employes" and therefore violated the portion of the Fourteenth Amendment that forbids "any State" to "deprive any person of life, liberty, or property, without due process of law." The dissenting opinion of Justice Holmes, reprinted below, was often cited by Legal Realists as an early example of enlightened judicial reasoning.—Ed]

Mr. Justice Holmes, dissenting.

I regret sincerely that I am unable to agree with the judgment in this case, and that I think it my duty to express my dissent.

This case is decided upon an economic theory which a large part of the country does not entertain. If it were a question whether I agreed with that theory, I should desire to study it further and long before making up my mind. But I do not conceive that to be my duty, because I strongly believe that my agreement or disagreement has nothing to do with the right of a majority to embody their opinions in law. It is settled by various decisions of this court that state constitutions and state laws may regulate life in many ways which we as legislators might think as injudicious or if you like as tyrannical as this, and which equally with this interfere with the liberty to contract. Sunday laws and usury laws are ancient examples. A more modern one is the prohibition of lotteries. The liberty of the citizen to do as he likes so long as he does not interfere with the liberty of others to do the same, which has been a shibboleth for some well-known writers, is interfered with by school laws, by the Post Office, by every state or municipal institution which takes his money for purposes thought desirable, whether he likes it or not. The Fourteenth Amendment does not enact Mr. Herbert Spencer's Social Statics. The other day we sustained the Massachusetts vaccination law.... United States and state statutes and decisions cutting down the liberty to contract by way of combination are familiar to this court.... Two years ago we upheld the prohibition of sales of stock on margins or for future delivery in the Constitution of California.... The decision sustaining an eight-hour law for miners is still recent.... Some of these laws embody convictions or prejudices which judges are likely to share. Some may not. But a Constitution is not intended to embody a particular economic theory, whether of paternalism and the organic relation of the citizen to the State or of *laissez faire*.

It is made for people of fundamentally differing views, and the accident of our finding certain opinions natural and familiar, or novel, and even shocking, ought not to conclude our judgment upon the question whether statutes embodying them conflict with the Constitution of the United States.

General propositions do not decide concrete cases. The decision will depend on a judgment or intuition more subtle than any articulate major premise. But I think that the proposition just stated, if it is accepted, will carry us far toward the end. Every opinion tends to become a law. I think that the word liberty in the Fourteenth Amendment is perverted when it is held to prevent the natural outcome of a dominant opinion, unless it can be said that a rational and fair man necessarily would admit that the statute proposed would infringe fundamental principles as they have been understood by the traditions of our people and our law. It does not need research to show that no such sweeping condemnation can be passed upon the statute before us. A reasonable man might think it a proper measure on the score of health. Men whom I certainly could not pronounce unreasonable would uphold it as a first instalment of a general regulation of the hours of work. Whether in the latter aspect it would be open to the charge of inequality I think it unnecessary to discuss.

ROSCOE POUND

"Liberty of Contract"

(1909)

"The right of a person to sell his labor," says Mr. Justice Harlan, "upon such terms as he deems proper, is in its essence, the same as the right of the purchaser of labor to prescribe the conditions upon which he will accept such labor from the person offering to sell it. So the right of the employee to quit the service of the employer, for whatever reason, is the same as the right of the employer, for whatever reason, to dispense with the services of such employee. . . . In all such particulars the employer and the employee have equality of right, and any legislation that disturbs that equality is an arbitrary interference with the liberty of contract, which no government can legally justify in a free land."[1] With this positive declaration of a lawyer, the culmination of a line of decisions now nearly twenty-five years old, a statement which a recent writer on the science of jurisprudence has deemed so fundamental as to deserve quotation and exposition at an unusual length, as compared with his treatment of other points, let us compare the equally positive statement of a sociologist:

"Much of the discussion about 'equal rights' is utterly hollow. All the ado made over the system of contract is surcharged with fallacy."[2]

To everyone acquainted at first hand with actual industrial conditions the latter statement goes without saying. Why, then do courts persist in the fallacy? Why do so many of them force upon legislation an academic theory of equality in the face of practical conditions of inequality? Why do we find a great and learned court in 1908 taking the long step into the past of dealing with the relation between employer and employee in railway transportation, as if the parties were individuals—as if they were farmers haggling over the sale of a horse? Why is the legal conception of the relation of employer and employee so at variance with the common knowledge of mankind? The late President has told us that it is because individual judges project their personal, social and economic views into the law. A great German publicist holds that it is because the party bent of judges has dictated decisions. But when a doctrine is announced with equal vigor and held with equal tenacity by courts of Pennsylvania and of Arkansas, of New York and of California, of Illinois and of West Virginia,

Reprinted by permission of The Yale Law Journal Company and Fred B. Rothman & Company from *The Yale Law Journal*, vol. 18 (1909), pp. 454–58, 460–70.

of Massachusetts and of Missouri, we may not dispose of it so readily. Surely the sources of such a doctrine must lie deeper. Let us inquire then, what further and more potent causes may be discovered, how these causes have operated to bring about the present state of the law as to freedom of contract, what the present doctrine of the courts is upon that subject, and how far we may expect amelioration thereof in the near future.

It is significant that the subject, so far as the form it now takes is concerned, is a new one. The phrase "liberty of contract" is not to be found in Lieber's *Civil Liberty and Self-Government*, published in 1853. It is not to be found in Professor Burgess's *Political Science and Constitutional Law*, published in 1890. The first decision turning upon it was rendered in 1886. The first extended discussion of the right of free contract as a fundamental natural right is in Spencer's *Justice*, written in 1891. . . .

The idea that unlimited freedom of making promises was a natural right came after enforcement of promises when made, had become a matter of course. It began as a doctrine of political economy, as a phase of Adam Smith's doctrine which we commonly call *laisser faire*. It was propounded as a utilitarian principle of politics and legislation by Mill. Spencer deduced it from his formula of justice. In this way it became a chief article in the creed of those who sought to minimize the functions of the state, that the most important of its functions was to enforce by law the obligations created by contract. But we must remember that the task of the English individualists was to abolish a body of antiquated institutions that stood in the way of human progress. Freedom of contract was the best instrument at hand for the purpose. They adopted it as a means, and made it an end. While this evolution of juristic and political thought was in progress, the common law too had become thoroughly individualistic; partly from innate tendency, partly through theological influence, partly through the contests between the courts and the crown in the sixteenth and seventeenth centuries, and partly as a result of the course of thought in the eighteenth and nineteenth centuries. This bit of history may suggest the chief, although not all, of the causes of the phenomenon we are considering.

In my opinion, the causes to which we must attribute the course of American constitutional decisions upon liberty of contract are seven: (1) The currency in juristic thought of an individualist conception of justice, which exaggerates the importance of property and of contract, exaggerates private right at the expense of public right, and is hostile to legislation, taking a minimum of law-making to be the ideal; (2) what I have ventured to call on another occasion a condition of mechanical jurisprudence, a condition of juristic thought and judicial action in which deduction from conceptions has produced a cloud of rules that obscures the principles from which they were drawn, in which conceptions are developed logically at the expense of practical results and in which the artificiality characteristic of legal reasoning is exaggerated; (3) the survival of purely juristic notions of the state and of economics and politics as against the social conceptions of the present; (4) the training of judges and lawyers in eighteenth century philosophy of law and the pretended contempt for philosophy in law that keeps the legal profession in the bonds of the philosophy of the past because it is to be found in law-sheep bindings; (5) the circumstance that natural law is the theory of our bills of rights and the impossibility of applying such a theory except when all men are agreed in their moral and economic views and look to a single authority to fix them; (6) the circumstance that our earlier labor legislation came before the public was prepared for it, so that the courts largely voiced well-meant but unadvised protests of the old order against the new, at a time when the public at large was by no means committed to the new; and (7) by no means least, the sharp line between law and fact in our legal system which requires constitutionality, as a legal question, to be tried by artificial criteria of general application and prevents effective judicial investigation or consideration of the situations of fact behind or bearing upon the statutes. . . .

. . . Moreover, our constitutional models and our bills of rights were drawn in the period in which the natural law school of jurists was at its zenith, and the growing period of American law coincided with the high tide of individualistic ethics and economics. Hence his school course in political economy and his office reading of Blackstone taught the nineteenth century judge the same things as fundamentals. He became persuaded that they were the basis of the jural order, and, as often happens, the individualist conception of justice reached its complete logical development after the doctrine itself had lost its vitality. Social justice, the last conception to develop, had already begun to affect not merely legal thought but legislation and judicial decision, while the courts were working out the last extreme deductions from the older conception.

. . . As a result, and as a result of our legal history, we exaggerate the importance of property and of contract, as an incident thereof. A leader of the bar, opposing the income tax, argues that a fundamental object of our polity is "preservation of the rights of private property." Text writers tell us of the divine origin of property. The Supreme Court of Wisconsin tells us that the right to take property by will is an absolute and inherent right, not depending upon legislation. The absolute certainty which is one of our legal ideals, an ideal responsible for much that is irritatingly mechanical in our legal system, is demanded chiefly to protect property. And our courts regard the right to contract, not as a phase of liberty—a sort of freedom of mental motion and locomotion—but as a phase of property, to be protected as such. A further result is to exaggerate private right at the expense of public interest. Blackstone's proposition that "the public good is in nothing more essentially interested than in the protection of every individual's private rights," has been quoted in more than one American decision; and one of these is a case often cited in support of extreme doctrines of liberty of contract. It is but a corollary that liberty of contract cannot be restricted merely in the interest of a contracting party. His right to contract freely is to yield only to the safety, health, or moral welfare of the public. Still another result is that bench and bar distrust and object to legislation. I have discussed the history and the causes of this attitude toward legislation on another occasion. Suffice it to say here that the doctrine as to liberty of contract is bound up in the decisions of our courts with a narrow view of what constitutes special or class legislation that greatly limits effective law-making. If we can only have laws of wide generality of application, we can have only a few laws; for the wider their application the more likelihood there is of injustice in concrete cases. But from the individualist standpoint a minimum of law is desirable. The common law antipathy to legislation sympathizes with this, and in consequence we find courts saying that it is not necessary to consider the reasons that led up to the type of legislation they condemn and that the maxim that the government governs best which governs least is proper for courts to bear in mind in expounding the Constitution.

The second cause, a condition of mechanical jurisprudence, I have discussed in its relation to the legal system generally in another place. The effect of all system is apt to be petrifaction of the subject systemized. Legal science is not exempt from this tendency. Legal systems have their periods in which system decays into technicality, in which a scientific jurisprudence becomes a mechanical jurisprudence. In a period of growth through juristic speculation and judicial decision, there is little danger of this. But whenever such a period has come to an end, when its work has been done and its legal theories have come to maturity, jurisprudence tends to decay. Conceptions are fixed. The premises are no longer to be examined. Everything is reduced to simple deduction from them. Principles cease to have importance. The law becomes a body of rules. This is the condition Professor Henderson refers to when he speaks of the way of social progress as barred by barricades of dead precedents. Manifestations of mechanical jurisprudence are conspicuous in the decisions as to liberty of contract. A characteristic one is the rigorous logical deduction from predetermined conceptions in disregard of and often in the teeth of the actual facts, which was noted at the outset. Two courts, in passing on statutes abridging the power of free contract have noted the frequency of such legislation in recent times but have said that it was not necessary to consider the reasons for it. Another court has asked what right the legislature has to "*assume* that one class has the need of protection against another." Another has said that the remedy for the company store evil "is in the hands of the employee," since he is not compelled to buy from the employer, forgetting that there may be a compulsion in fact where there is none in law. Another says, that "theoretically there is among our citizens no inferior class," and of course no facts can avail against that theory. Another tells us that man and woman have the same rights, and hence a woman must be allowed to contract to work as many hours a day as a man may. We have already noted how Mr. Justice Harlan insists on a legal theory of equality of rights in the latest pronouncement of the Federal Supreme Court. Legislation designed to give laborers some measure of practical independence, which, if allowed to operate, would put them in a position of reasonable equality with their masters, is said by courts, because it infringes on a theoretical equality, to be insulting to their manhood and degrading, to put them under guardianship, to create a class of statutory laborers, and to stamp them as imbeciles. . . .

Survival of a purely juristic notion of the state and of economics and politics, in contrast with the social conception of the present, the third cause suggested, can be looked at but briefly. Formerly the juristic attitude obtained in religion, in morals, and in politics as well as in law. This fundamentally juristic conception of the world, due possibly to Roman law being the first subject of study in the universities, which gave a form of legality even to theology, has passed away elsewhere. But it lingers in the courts. Jurisprudence is the last in the march of the sciences away from the method of deduction from predetermined conceptions. The sociological movement in jurisprudence, the movement for pragmatism as a philosophy of law, the movement for the adjustment of principles and doctrines to the human conditions they are to govern rather than to assumed first principles, the movement for putting the human factor in the central place and relegating logic to its true position as an instrument, has scarcely shown itself as yet in America. Perhaps the dissenting opinion of Mr. Justice Holmes in *Lochner* v. *New York*, is the best exposition of it we have.

Another factor of no mean importance in producing the line of decisions we are considering is the training of lawyers and judges in eighteenth century theories of natural law. In a book just published by a well-known writer on legal subjects who has also been a teacher of law, the whole basis of discussion is natural law. The learned author does not indicate a suspicion that any doubt has been cast upon or may attach to his philosophical premises. In another book published last year by a well-known practitioner, it is recommended gravely that one subject of required study in preparation for the bar be "natural and civil law, and the principles, foundation, and spirit of law," and the student is expected to learn these from Grotius, Paley's *Moral and Political Philosophy*, Burlamaqui's *Natural Law*, Puffendorf, and MacIntosh's *Discourses on the Study of the Law of Nature and Nations*. Until a comparatively recent date, all legal education, whether in school or in office, began with the study of Blackstone. Probably all serious office study begins with Blackstone or some American imitator to-day. Many schools make Blackstone the first subject of instruction to-day, and in others Blackstone is a subject of examination for admission or of prescribed reading after admission, or there are courses on elementary law in which texts reproducing the theories of the introduction to and the first book of the *Commentaries* are the basis of instruction. A student who is college-trained may have had a course or courses that brought him in contact with modern thought. It is quite as likely he has not, or if he has, the natural law theories which are a matter of course in all our law books are not unlikely to persuade him that what he learned in college is immaterial in the domain of law. Constitutional law is full of natural law notions. For one thing, there is the doctrine that apart from constitutional restrictions there are individual rights resting on a natural basis, to which courts must give effect "beyond the control of the state." In the judicial discussions of liberty of contract this idea has been very prominent. The Supreme Court of Massachusetts, in passing on legislation directed against fines in cotton mills, tells us that a statute which violates "fundamental" rights "is unconstitutional and void, even though the enactment of it is not expressly forbidden." Another court reminds us that natural persons do not derive their right to contract from the law. Another court, in passing adversely upon legislation against company stores, says any classification is arbitrary and unconstitutional unless it proceeds on "the natural capacity of persons to contract." Another, in passing on a similar statute, denies that contractual capacity can be restricted, except for physical or mental disabilities. Another holds that the legislature cannot take notice of the *de facto* subjection of one class of persons to another in making contracts of employment in certain industries, but must be governed by the theoretical, jural equality. These natural law ideas are carried to an extreme by the Supreme Court of Illinois in *Ritchie* v. *People,* in which case it is announced that women have a natural equality with men and that no distinction may be drawn between them with respect to power of engaging to labor.

Closely related to the ideas just considered, and, indeed, a product of the same training, is a deep-seated conviction of the American lawyer that the doctrines of the common law are part of the universal jural order. Just as in nine cases out of ten, natural law meant for the seventeenth century and eighteenth century jurist the Roman law which he knew and had studied, for the common law lawyer it means the common law. For one thing, this feeling leads to a narrow attitude toward legislation; a tendency to hold down all statutory innovations upon the common law as far as possible. In like spirit, on this subject of liberty of contract, most of the courts which have overthrown legislation as being in derogation of liberty, have insisted that only common law incapacities can be given legal recognition; that new incapacities in fact, growing out of new conditions in business and industry, cannot be taken advantage of in legislation; that the ordinary farm-hand and the laborer in the beet fields, for example, must be treated alike. But, even more important for our purpose, this feeling operates in constitutional law to lead judges to try statutes by the measure of common law doctrines rather than by the Constitution....

Last of the causes suggested, but by no means the least efficient in bringing about the line of decisions under consideration, is the sharp line between law and fact in our legal system, due originally to the exigencies of trial by jury. The line between what is for the court to pass upon and what is for the jury, has come to be called a line between law and fact. For purposes of jury trial the line itself has to be drawn often very artificially. But, beyond that, when it is drawn the tendency is to assume that questions which analytically are pure questions of fact, when they become questions for the court to decide, must be looked at in a different way from ordinary questions of fact and must be dealt with in an academic and artificial manner because they have become questions of law. The tendency to insist upon such a line and to draw it arbitrarily, has spread from the law of trials to every part of the law. One example is to be seen in decisions as to what is a reasonable time in the law of negotiable instruments. Another may be seen in judicial pronouncements as to negligence, which are leading so many of our state legislatures to turn the whole matter over to juries in cases of personal injury. Still another may be seen in the refinements as to constructive fraud and badges of fraud which led to wide-spread legislation, making fraud a question for the jury. It is one of the chief factors in producing what I have ventured to call mechanical jurisprudence in our legal system. In constitutional law, the necessity for drawing this line and the assumption that whatever is left to the court to decide must be dealt with artificially and disposed of mechanically, operates to the disadvantage of new types of legislation. It is felt that a law cannot be constitutional now if it would have been unconstitutional one hundred years ago. *In fact* it might have been an unreasonable deprivation of liberty as things were even 50 years ago, and yet be a reasonable regulation as things are now. But the question is not one of fact. Being for the court to decide, it must be decided upon some universal proposition, valid in all places and at all times. . . . More than anything else, ignorance of the actual situations of fact for which legislation was provided and supposed lack of legal warrant for knowing them, have been responsible for the judicial overthrowing of so much social legislation.

JOHN CHIPMAN GRAY

The Nature and Sources of the Law

(1909)

Can decisions of the courts be properly considered as sources of Law? If the object of asking this question is to ascertain the fact, there can be but little doubt of the answer. Certainly the judges, in deciding cases, draw rules from precedents. They decide cases otherwise than they would have decided them had the precedents not existed, and they follow the precedents, although they may think that they ought not to have been made. Why has any question, therefore, been raised on this? It is because the judges have been unwilling to seem to be law-givers, because they have liked to say that they applied Law, but did not make it, while, if the decisions of courts were sources of Law, it could not be denied that the judges, to that extent, did make Law. . . .

[T]he classical passage is in Blackstone's Commentaries:—

As to general customs, or the common law, properly so called; this is that law, by which proceedings and determinations in the King's ordinary courts of justice are guided and directed. . . . How are these customs or maxims to be known, and by whom is their validity to be determined? The answer is, by the judges in the several courts of justice. They are the depositaries of the laws; the living oracles, who must decide in all cases of doubt, and who are bound by an oath to decide according to the law of the land. . . . Judicial decisions are the principal and the most authoritative evidence that can be given of the existence of such a custom as shall form a part of the Common Law. . . . For it is an established rule to abide by former precedents, where the same points come again in litigation; as well to keep the scale of justice even and steady, and not liable to waver with every new judge's opinion; as also because the law in that case being solemnly declared and determined, what before was uncertain, and perhaps indifferent, is now become a permanent rule, which it is not in the breast of any subsequent judge to alter or vary from, according to his private sentiments, he being sworn to determine, not according to his own private judgment, but according to the known laws and customs of the land, not delegated to pronounce a new law, but to maintain and expound the old one. Yet this rule admits of exceptions, where the former determination is most evidently contrary to reason; much more if it be clearly contrary to the Divine Law. But even in such cases the subsequent judges do not pretend to make a new law, but to vindicate the old one from misrepresentation. For if it be found that the former decision is manifestly absurd or unjust, it is declared, not that such a sentence was *bad* law, but that it was *not law;* that is, that it is not the established custom of the realm, as has been erroneously determined.

Blackstone's statement, in short, is this: The Common Law consists of general customs, but what these customs are must be known from the decisions of the courts; former precedents must be followed, a decision of a court makes what was before uncertain and indifferent a permanent rule, which subsequent judges must follow; but precedents are not absolutely binding, they can be disregarded when flatly absurd or unjust.

There seems little occasion to find fault with this statement, so far as it concerns the force and effect of precedents as a source of Law, but Blackstone's attempt to carry back further the source of Law into general custom, and make the decisions only evidence of that custom, is unfortunate.

The notion that judicial decisions are only evidence of a preëxisting law was fallen foul of by Bentham; but in Austin it found its most influential opponent. It may be questioned whether he has not devoted himself too exclusively to this part of Blackstone's remarks, and neglected the substantially accurate view of the force and effect of precedents which the commentator gives. Austin speaks of "the childish fiction, employed by our judges, that judiciary or Common Law is not made by them, but is a miraculous something made by nobody, existing, I suppose, from eternity, and merely *declared* from time to time by the judges."

Austin's views have met general acceptance. But Blackstone has not wanted defenders. One of the latest attempts to rehabilitate him is by his editor, Professor Hammond. . . .

"We do not infer that philosophers make the laws of nature, how then can we infer that judges make the law of the land?" is what Professor Hammond says. Because philosophers do not make the laws of nature, but, as Professor Hammond has just said, judges do make "historically" the laws of the land. Because the laws of nature are independent of human opinion, while the Law of the land *is* human opinion. The heavenly bodies have been governed by the same laws after the birth of Ptolemy and Copernicus and Newton that they were before, but the English people have not been governed by the same Law since Lord Mansfield's time that they were before. His decisions have made that to be Law which was not Law before, and the Law of England since his time is different from what it would have been, had he been a man of a different cast of mind.

Or, to take an instance from the Constitutional Law of the United States, suppose Chief Justice Marshall had been as ardent a Democrat (or Republican, as it was then called) as he was a Federalist. Suppose, instead of hating Thomas Jefferson and loving the United States Bank, he had hated the United States Bank and loved Thomas Jefferson, how different would be the law under which we are living to-day....

Professor Hammond truly says that...*Story*, J., in *Swift* v. *Tyson*, adopt[ed] the Blackstonian theory: "In the ordinary use of language it will hardly be contended that the decisions of Courts constitute laws." These particular consequences of Blackstone's theory are hardly such as to recommend the theory itself.

But the Supreme Court of the United States has, since this state of things was established, been compelled, by what Professor Hammond would call the aspect of historical as against that of scientific truth—that is, by the stress of the real facts of life—to abandon the theory of Blackstone in a most important class of cases, those concerning municipal bonds....

In several of the United States, bonds were issued by towns and cities, generally in aid of railroads; the Supreme Courts of the States declared that the bonds were validly issued; on the faith of these decisions the bonds were sold; and then new judges were elected and the bonds were declared invalid. Blackstone's theory was urged with great force, that the decisions of the courts did not make Law; and that the Law must be taken to have been always what the latest decisions declared it to be. But the Supreme Court ruled otherwise, and has always held firmly to the doctrine that if a contract, when made, was valid by the Law as then laid down by the courts, its obligation could not be impaired by any subsequent decision....

"The doctrine of precedent, correctly stated, forbids the assumption that a new law was created by the prior decision—or that, in Austin's words, 'the imperial decrete established a *new* principle,' in the sense of creating a new law. If it did, and the present case arose under the law so created by this precedent, we should be deciding the later case by a different law from that under which the precedent arose." And so we are. Suppose it has been generally believed that an action will lie for verbal slander, but upon the case coming before the court of final appeal, they decide, perhaps by a majority of one, that it will not. Does not any later case come before a judge under a different state of the Law? Is a judge in the same position as he was before that decision? Is there not a new element introduced? How must the Law be the same, when there is now an element, all but necessarily conclusive, which there was not before? Professor Hammond declares we must not say that the Law is changed, because such change cannot be reconciled with the simplest rule of justice; but, say what we will, the fact is that there is a new controlling element introduced into the Law. One can understand a German jurist considering such a state of things as unjust, and therefore refusing to give any weight to Judicial Precedents, but how a Common Law lawyer, who regards the system of precedent with complacency, can suppose that he can turn injustice into justice by inventing a fiction is a remarkable instance of the power of conventional expressions....

Whether it is desirable that such remarks should be made, or whether, if made, it is desirable that they should be believed, whether it is desirable that the judges' power and practice of making Law should be concealed from themselves and the public by a form of words, is a matter into which I do not care to enter. The only thing I am concerned with is the fact. Do the judges make Law? I conceive it to be clear that, under the Common Law system, they do make Law.

The opinions of another writer on the question of the law-making power of the judges, a writer whose opinions deserve to be treated with the highest respect, remain to be considered. Mr. James C. Carter published an article on "The Ideal and the Actual in the Law," in which he maintained that the judges were the discoverers and not the makers of the Law....

The main thesis of Mr. Carter's essay is the erroneousness of the theory that all Law proceeds from the commands of the sovereign. He admits fully "that all the knowledge which we really have of the Law comes from the judge," but he shrinks from saying that the judge makes Law, because he fears that this would recognize the theory that all Law comes from the command of the sovereign. If I shared the fear, I should be equally unwilling to use the expression that the judges make Law. But is this objectionable result a consequence of holding that judges make Law?

What is meant by judges making Law? It is meant that a decision *suo vigore*, without regard to its agreement or disagreement with some ideal, is a source of Law; not the only, not necessarily the controlling, source of Law, but something which has an independent and not merely evidential value. To decide cases is the necessary function of a judge; it is of the essence of judgeship; but whether a judge can establish precedents or not is not of the essence of judgeship. In England judges have the power; in Germany, generally, they have not. The sovereign might interfere to give them the power, or to deny them the power, but generally he has not interfered, and therefore, if they have the power, it does not arise from the command of the sovereign (unless we adopt the theory of Austin that whatever the sovereign permits he commands, a theory which I am at one with Mr. Carter in disapproving), but whether decisions shall establish precedents is left to the free action of the judicial mind, affected by ideas of public policy, by popular custom, and by professional opinion. These motives, operating on the minds of English and American judges, have led them to recognize decisions of the courts as sources of the Law. Judges, then, may make Law, *i.e.* establish precedents, and yet such Law may not be the product of the sovereign's command, and therefore the dilemma which Mr. Carter feels does not, it seems to me, in truth exist.

... But he says a judge rather *discovers* than makes the Law. The expression "discovered" throws light on the processes of the judicial mind. To speak of "making" the Law suggests an arbitrary will, while to speak of "discovering" it suggests the process of reason and reflection.... But while I recognize the reason which led Mr. Carter to use the word "discover," and also the fact that the word "make" may, although improperly, carry with it a suggestion of arbitrariness, I must yet regret Mr. Carter's substitution of the term "discovery" as misleading. . . .

ROSCOE POUND

"Law in Books and Law in Action"

(1910)

[I]f we look closely, distinctions between law in the books and law in action, between the rules that purport to govern the relations of man and man and those that in fact govern them, will appear, and it will be found that today also the distinction between legal theory and judicial administration is often a very real and a very deep one.

Let us take a few examples. It is a settled dogma of the books that all doubts are to be resolved in favor of the constitutionality of a statute—that the courts will not declare it in conflict with the constitution unless clearly and indubitably driven to that conclusion. But it can not be maintained that such is the actual practice, especially with respect to social legislation claimed to be in conflict with constitutional guaranties of liberty and property. The mere fact that the Court of Appeals of New York and the Supreme Court of the United States differed on such questions as the power to regulate hours of labor on municipal and public contracts, and the power to regulate the hours of labor of bakers, the former holding adversely to the one and upholding the other, while the latter court had already ruled the opposite on the first question and then reversed the ruling of the New York court on the second, speaks for itself.[1] Many more instances might be noted. But it is enough to say that any one who studies critically the course of decision upon constitutional questions in a majority of our state courts in recent years must agree with Professor Freund that the courts in practice tend to overturn all legislation which they deem unwise, and must admit the truth of Professor Dodd's statement:

> The courts have now definitely invaded the field of public policy and are quick to declare unconstitutional almost any laws of which they disapprove, particularly in the fields of social and industrial legislation. The statement still repeated by the courts that laws will not be declared unconstitutional unless their repugnance to the constitution is clear beyond a reasonable doubt, seems now to have become "a mere courteous and smoothly transmitted platitude."

Another example is to be found in those jurisdictions where the common-law doctrines as to employer's liability still obtain and in those corners of employer's liability in other jurisdictions where recent legisla-

Reprinted from the *American Law Review*, vol. 44 (1910), p. 15–17, 19–20, 22, 24–28, 30–31, 33–36.

tion has left the common law in force. It is notorious that a feeling that employers and great industrial enterprises should bear the cost of the human wear and tear incident to their operations dictates more verdicts in cases of employer's liability than the rules of law laid down in the charges of the courts. Most of the new trials directed by our highest courts of review because the verdicts returned are not sustained by the evidence are in cases of this sort. Here the law in the books is settled and defined. The law administered is very different, and only the charge of the court, rigidly examined on appeal, serves to preserve an appearance of life in the legal theory.

More striking still is the divergence between legal theory and current practice in the handling of persons suspected of crime. The "third degree" has become an every day feature of police investigation of crime. What is our law according to the books? "The prisoner," says Sir James Stephen, "is absolutely protected against all judicial questioning before or at the trial." "This," he adds, "contributes greatly to the dignity and apparent humanity of a criminal trial. It effectually avoids the appearance of harshness, not to say cruelty, which often shocks an English spectator in a French court of justice." Such is the legal rule. But prosecuting attorneys and police officers and police detectives do not hesitate to conduct the most searching, rigid and often brutal examinations of accused or suspected persons, with all the appearance of legality and of having the power of the state behind them. It is true, no rich man is ever subjected to this process to obtain proof of violation of anti-trust or rebate legislation and no powerful politician is thus dealt with in order to obtain proof of bribery and graft. The malefactor of means, the rogue who has an organization of rogues behind him to provide a lawyer and a writ of *habeas corpus* has the benefit of the law in the books. But the ordinary malefactor is bullied and even sometimes starved and tortured into confession by officers of the law. It is no doubt a sound instinct that makes us hesitate to give any such examinations the sanction of legality. We may agree with Sir James Stephen's informant that there is a deal of laziness behind it, that, to use his words, "it is far pleasanter to sit comfortably in the shade rubbing red pepper into a poor devil's eyes than to go about in the sun hunting up evidence." The fact remains, however, that the attempt of the books to compel prosecutors to use only a case-knife is failing. They will use the pickaxe in practice, and until the law has evolved some device by which they may use it in all cases the weak and friendless and lowly will be at a practical disadvantage, despite the legal theory....

Another attempt at adjusting the letter of the law to the demands of administration in concrete cases, while apparently preserving the law unaltered, is to be seen in our American ritual, for in many jurisdictions it is little else, of written opinions, discussing and deducing from the precedents with great elaboration. As one reads the reports critically the conclusion is forced upon him that this ritual covers a deal of personal government by judges, a deal of "raw equity," or, as the Germans call it, of equitable application of law, and leaves many a soft spot in what is superficially a hard and fast rule, by means of which concrete causes are decided in practice as the good sense or feelings of fair play of the tribunal may dictate. One instance of this, in constitutional law, has been spoken of. Many others might be adduced from almost any department of private law. Let one suffice. In the law as to easements it is laid down that a right may be acquired by adverse user, although the known use was not objected to, if it was in fact, adverse. But the same courts say properly that a permissive user will give no right. When, however, one turns to the cases themselves and endeavors to fit each case in the scheme, not according to what the court said was the rule, but according to the facts of that case, he soon finds that the apparent rules to a great extent are no rules, and that where to allow the right would work a hardship the courts have discussed the decisions as to permissive user, and where, in the concrete cause, it seemed fair to grant the right they have insisted on the adverse character of the claimant's conduct. And the reason is not far to seek. We have developed so minute a jurisprudence of rules, we have interposed such a cloud of minute deductions between principles and concrete cases, that our case-law has become ultra-mechanical, and is no longer an effective instrument of justice if applied with technical accuracy. In theory our judges are tied down rigidly by hard and fast rules. Discretion is reduced to a strictly defined and narrowly limited minimum. Judicial law-making has produced a wealth of rules that has exhausted the field formerly afforded for the personal sense of justice of the tribunal. Legally, the judge's heart and conscience are eliminated. He is expected to force the case into the four corners of the pigeon-hole the books have provided. In practice, flesh and blood will not bow to such a theory. The face of the law may be saved by an elaborate ritual, but men, and not rules, will administer justice....

Some of the causes of divergence between the law in the books and the law in action have been suggested already. In the first place, it is nothing new. Law has always been and no doubt will always continue to be, "in a process of becoming." It must be "as variable as man himself." "Social life," says Wundt, "like all life, is change and development. Law would be neglecting one of its most important functions if it ceased to meet the demands of this ceaseless evolution." However much the lawyer, enamored of his ideal of an absolute certainty in legal rules, may seek to evade these demands, the people will not permit it. Men will do what they are bent on doing, laws and traditions to the contrary notwithstanding. The forms may be kept, but the substance will find some fiction or some interpretation, or some court of equity or some practice of equitable application, to sanction change. Nevertheless, the divergence between law in books and law in action is more acute in some periods of legal history than in others. In all legal systems, periods of growth, periods in which the law is developing through juristic activity, alternate with periods of stability, periods in which the results of the juristic activity of the past are summed up or worked out in detail or merely corrected here and there by legislation.

Closer analysis will reveal three special causes behind the conditions in American law to which I have called attention—namely, (1) that our settled habits of juristic thought are to no small extent out of accord with current social, economic and philosophical thinking, (2) the backwardness of the art of legislation, particularly in that our legislative law-making, like our judicial law-making, is too rigid, attempts too much detail and fails to leave enough margin for judicial action in individual cases, and (3) the defects of our administrative machinery. . . .

Settled habits of juristic thought are characteristic of American legal science. Our legal scholarship is historical and analytical. In either event it begins and ends substantially in Anglo-American case law. But the fundamental conceptions of that case law are by no means those of popular thought today. . . . Today, while all other sciences, in the wake of the natural sciences, have abandoned deduction from predetermined conceptions, such is still the accepted method of jurisprudence. After philosophical, political, economic and sociological thought have given up the eighteenth-century law of nature, it is still the premise of the American lawyer. In other words, law has always been dominated by ideas of the past long after they have ceased to be vital in other departments of learning. This is an inherent difficulty in legal science, and it is closely connected with an inherent difficulty in the administration of justice according to law—namely, the inevitable difference in rate of progress between law and public opinion.

Of the defects in our American administration of justice with which fault is found today, the more serious are reducible ultimately to two general propositions: (1) over-individualism in our doctrines and rules, an over-individualist conception of justice, and (2) over-reliance upon the machinery of justice and too much of the mechanical in the administration and application of rules and doctrines. At first sight the coexistence of over-individualism in the rules of law and in the doctrines from which they proceed, with lack of individualization or too little adjustment to individual cases in the application of the rules and doctrines, is a paradox. But in truth the latter is due to exactly the same causes, and is a result of the same attitude toward law and government and of the same frame of mind as the former. The former is an assertion of the individual against his fellows individually. The latter is an assertion of the individual against his fellows collectively. The former expresses the feeling of the self-reliant man that, as a free moral agent, he is to make his own bargains and determine upon his own acts and control his own property, accepting the responsibility that goes with such power, subjecting himself to liability for the consequences of his free choice, but exempt from interference in making his choice. The latter expresses the feeling of the same self-reliant man that neither the state, nor its representative, the magistrate, is competent to judge him better than his own conscience; that he is not to be judged by the discretion of men, but by the inflexible rule of the law. Each proceeds from jealousy of oppression of the individual. The former is due to fear he may be oppressed in the interest or for the protection of others; the latter is due to fear that a magistrate, who has power to adjust rules to concrete cases and discretion in the application of legal doctrines, may misuse that power and abuse that discretion to the injury of some individual. It assumes that oppression by mechanical laws, mechanically executed, is preferable to government by other men exercising their own will and judgment, and that elimination of every personal element and procedure according to hard and fast rules necessarily constitutes justice. Each is a phase, therefore, of the extreme individualism which is one of the chief characteristics of the common law. Indeed, Berolzheimer asserts that the one distinguishing mark of common-law juristic thought is this "unlimited valuation of individual liberty and respect for individual property." ...

Eighteenth century jurists conceived that certain principles were inherent in nature, were necessary results of human nature, and that these principles were discoverable *a priori*. They held that it was the business of the jurist to discover these principles, and, when discovered, to deduce a system therefrom and test all actual rules thereby. Such is even now the orthodox method in our constitutional law. Our bills of rights are regarded as merely declaratory of fundamental natural rights. Eminent judges assert that legislation is to be judged by those rights and not by the constitutional texts in which they are declared. ...

... More than this, through the power of courts over unconstitutional legislation and the doctrine that our bills of rights are declaratory, we force it upon modern social legislation. ... For the fundamental conceptions of our traditional case law have come to be regarded as fundamental conceptions of legal science. When in a period of collectivist thinking and social legislation courts and lawyers assume that the only permissible way of thinking or of law-making is limited and defined by individualism of the old type, when, while men are seeking to promote the ends of society through social control, jurists lay it down that the only method of human discipline is "to leave each man to work out in freedom his own happiness or misery," conflict is inevitable. With jurisprudence once more in the rags of a past century, while kindred sciences have been reclothed, we may be sure that law in the books will often tend to be very different from the law in action.

Probably one may summarize this first point by saying that a gulf has grown up between social justice, which is the end men are seeking today, and legal justice; that the movement away from the puritan standpoint in our social and economic and political thought has not been followed by legal thought, and that we still adhere to the idealistic, or at least to the political interpretation of, legal science, although in kindred branches of learning the economic and social interpretation is now more and more accepted.

That the legal idea of justice is not the idea entertained in the related sciences is becoming a commonplace of the sociologists. They do not hesitate to contrast social justice and legal justice. As Professor Commons put it recently, "Justice is not merely fair play between individuals, as our legal philosophy would have it—it is fair play between social classes." And one has only to read the judicial decisions upon liberty of contract to see that his conception of legal justice is that entertained by the courts. . . .

Finally, our interpretation of jurisprudence and of legal history is either idealistic or political. Brooks Adams is the only American writer to insist upon the economic and social interpretation. But until we come to look at our legal history in this way, history on which our jurists rely chiefly is not unlikely to prove a blind guide. The history of juristic thought tells us nothing unless we know the social forces that lay behind it.

I have discussed at length the effect of stability of juristic thought and the nature of American juristic thought because those are the subjects which the lawyer must ponder. It is there that the divergence between law in books and law in action has a lesson for him. . . .

For the lawyer, the moral of the difference between law in books and law in action is not to be obsessed with the notion that the common law is the beginning of wisdom and the eternal jural order. Let us not be afraid of legislation, and let us welcome new principles, introduced by legislation, which express the spirit of the time. Let us look the facts of human conduct in the face. Let us look to economics and sociology and philosophy, and cease to assume that jurisprudence is self-sufficient. It is the work of lawyers to make the law in action conform to the law in the books, not by futile thunderings against popular lawlessness, nor eloquent exhortations to obedience of the written law, but by making the law in the books such that the law in action can conform to it, and providing a speedy, cheap and efficient legal mode of applying it. On no other terms can the two be reconciled. In a conflict between the law in books and the national will there can be but one result. Let us not become legal monks. Let us not allow our legal texts to acquire sanctity and go the way of all sacred writings. For the written word remains, but man changes. Whether laws of Manu or Zarathustra or Moses, or the fourteenth amendment, or the doctrine of the Dartmouth College Case, or Munn v. Illinois, or the latest legislative discovery in Oklahoma, all laws tell us the same tale.

WESLEY NEWCOMB HOHFELD

"Some Fundamental Legal Conceptions as Applied in Judicial Reasoning"

(1913)

Fundamental Jural Relations Contrasted With One Another.

One of the greatest hindrances to the clear understanding, the incisive statement, and the true solution of legal problems frequently arises from the express or tacit assumption that all legal relations may be reduced to "rights" and "duties" and that these latter categories are therefore adequate for the purpose of analyzing even the most complex legal interests, such as trusts, options, escrows, "future" interests, corporate interests, etc. Even if the difficulty related merely to inadequacy and ambiguity of terminology, it seriousness would nevertheless be worthy of definite recognition and persistent effort toward improvement; for in any closely reasoned problem, whether legal or non-legal, chameleon-hued words are a peril both to clear thought and to lucid expression. As a matter of fact, however, the above mentioned inadequacy and ambiguity of terms unfortunately reflect, all too often, corresponding paucity and confusion as regards actual legal conceptions. That this is so may appear in some measure from the discussion to follow.

The strictly fundamental legal relations are, after all, *sui generis;* and thus it is that attempts at formal definition are always unsatisfactory, if not altogether useless. Accordingly, the most promising line of procedure seems to consist in exhibiting all of the various relations in a scheme of "opposites" and "correlatives," and then proceeding to exemplify their individual scope and application in concrete cases. An effort will be made to pursue this method:

Jural Opposites	rights no-rights	privilege duty	power disability	immunity liability

Jural Correlatives	right duty	privilege no-right	power liability	immunity disability

Reprinted by permission of The Yale Law Journal Company and Fred B. Rothman & Company from *The Yale Law Journal*, vol. 23 (1913), pp. 28–33, 44–46, 55, 58–59.

Rights and Duties. As already intimated, the term "rights" tends to be used indiscriminately to cover what in a given case may be a privilege, a power, or an immunity, rather than a right in the strictest sense; and this looseness of usage is occasionally recognized by the authorities. . . .

Recognizing, as we must, the very broad and indiscriminate use of the term, "right," what clue do we find, in ordinary legal discourse, toward limiting the word in question to a definite and appropriate meaning? That clue lies in the correlative "duty," for it is certain that even those who use the word and the conception "right" in the broadest possible way are accustomed to thinking of "duty" as the invariable correlative. . . .

In other words, if X has a right against Y that he shall stay off the former's land, the correlative (and equivalent) is that Y is under a duty toward X to stay off the place. If, as seems desirable, we should seek a synonym for the term "right" in this limited and proper meaning, perhaps the word "claim" would prove the best. The latter has the advantage of being a monosyllable. . . .

Privileges and "No-Rights." As indicated in the above scheme of jural relations, a privilege is the opposite of a duty, and the correlative of a "no-right." In the example last put, whereas X has a *right* or *claim* that Y, the other man, should stay off the land, he himself has the *privilege* of entering on the land; or, in equivalent words, X does not have a duty to stay off. The privilege of entering is the negation of a duty to stay off. As indicated by this case, some caution is necessary at this point, for, always, when it is said that a given privilege is the mere negation of a *duty,* what is meant, of course, is a duty having a content or tenor precisely *opposite* to that of the privilege in question. Thus, if, for some special reason, X has contracted with Y to go on the former's own land, it is obvious that X has, as regards Y, both the privilege of entering and the *duty of entering.* The privilege is perfectly consistent with this sort of duty,—for the latter is of the *same* content or tenor as the privilege;—but it still holds good that, as regards Y, X's privilege of entering is the precise negation of a duty *to stay off.* Similarly, if A has not contracted with B to perform certain work for the latter, A's privilege of *not* doing so is the very negation of a duty of *doing* so. Here again the duty contrasted is of a content or tenor exactly opposite to that of the privilege.

Passing now to the question of "correlatives," it will be remembered, of course, that a duty is the invariable correlative of that legal relation which is most properly called a right or claim. That being so, if further evidence be needed as to the fundamental and important difference between a right (or claim) and a privilege, surely it is found in the fact that the correlative of the latter relation is a "no-right," there being no single term available to express the latter conception. Thus, the correlative of X's right that Y shall not enter on the land is Y's duty not to enter; but the correlative of X's privilege of entering himself is manifestly Y's "no-right" that X shall not enter.

In view of the considerations thus far emphasized, the importance of keeping the conception of a right (or claim) and the conception of a privilege quite distinct from each other seems evident; and more than that, it is equally clear that there should be a separate term to represent the latter relation. No doubt, as already indicated, it is very common to use the term "right" indiscriminately, even when the relation designated is really that of privilege; and only too often this identity of terms has involved for the particular speaker or writer a confusion or blurring of ideas. . . .

Powers and Liabilities. As indicated in the preliminary scheme of jural relations, a legal power (as distinguished, of course, from a mental or physical power) is the opposite of legal disability, and the correlative of legal liability. But what is the intrinsic nature of a legal power as such? Is it possible to analyze the conception represented by this constantly employed and very important term of legal discourse? Too close an analysis might seem metaphysical rather than useful; so that what is here presented is intended only as an approximate explanation sufficient for all practical purposes. . . .

Many examples of legal powers may readily be given. Thus, X, the owner of ordinary personal property "in a tangible object" has the power to extinguish his own legal interest (rights, powers, immunities, etc.) through that totality of operative facts known as abandonment; and—simultaneously and correlatively—to create in other persons privileges and powers relating to the abandoned object,—*e.g.,* the power to acquire title to the later by appropriating it. *Similarly,* X has the power to transfer his interest to Y,—that is, to extinguish his own interest and concomitantly create in Y a new and corresponding interest. So also X has the power to create contractual obligations of various kinds. Agency cases are likewise instructive. . . . The creation of an agency relation involves, *inter alia,* the grant of legal powers to the so-called agent, and the creation of correlative liabilities in the principal. That is to say, one party P has the power to create agency powers in another party A,—for example, the power to convey X's property, the power to impose (so-called) contractual obligations on P, the power to discharge a debt, owing to P, the power to "receive" title to property so that it shall vest in P, and so forth. . . .

Immunities and Disabilities. As already brought out, immunity is the correlative of disability ("no-power"), and the opposite, or negation, of liability. Perhaps it will also be plain, from the preliminary outline and from the discussion down to this point, that a power bears the same general contrast to an immunity that a right does to a privilege. A right is one's affirmative claim against another, and a privilege is one's freedom from the right or claim of another. Similarly, a power is one's affirmative "control" over a given legal relation as against another; whereas an immunity is one's freedom from the legal power or "control" of another as regards some legal relation. . . .

In the latter part of the preceding discussion, eight conceptions of the law have been analyzed and compared in some detail, the purpose having been to exhibit not only their intrinsic meaning and scope, but also their relations to one another and the methods by which they are applied, in judicial reasoning, to the solution of concrete problems of litigation. Before concluding this branch of the discussion a general suggestion may be ventured as to the great practical importance of a clear appreciation of the distinctions and discriminations set forth. If a homely metaphor be permitted, these eight conceptions,—rights and duties, privileges and no-rights, powers and liabilities, immunities and disabilities,—seem to be what may be called "the lowest common denominators of the law." Ten fractions (1-3, 2-5, etc.) may, *superficially,* seem so different from one another as to defy comparison. If, however, they are expressed in terms of their lowest common denominators (5–15, 6–15, etc.), comparison becomes easy, and fundamental similarity may be discovered. The same thing is of course true as regards the lowest generic conceptions to which any and all "legal quantities" may be reduced.

Reverting, for example, to the subject powers, it might be difficult at first glance to discover any essential and fundamental similarity between conditional sales of personalty, escrow transactions, option agreements, agency relations, powers of appointment, etc. But if all these relations are reduced to their lowest generic terms, the conceptions of legal power and legal liability are seen to be dominantly, though not exclusively, applicable throughout the series. By such a process it becomes possible not only to discover essential similarities and illuminating analogies in the midst of what appears superficially to be infinite and hopeless variety, but also to discern common principles of justice and policy underlying the various jural problems involved. An indirect, yet very practical, consequence is that it frequently becomes feasible, by virtue of such analysis, to use as persuasive authorities judicial precedents that might otherwise seem altogether irrelevant. If this point be valid with respect to powers, it would seem to be equally so as regards all of the other basic conceptions of the law. In short, the deeper the analysis, the greater becomes one's perception of fundamental unity and harmony in the law.

2

The Struggle over
the Meaning of Realism

A debate over the meaning of Realism was carried on in the law reviews during the 1930s. Its most famous exchange, between Roscoe Pound and Karl Llewellyn, may be the best short guide to the Realist movement, its strengths and flaws alike. That exchange is also an epitome: the older essayist, whose remarks are judicious, even highflown, is challenged by a younger debater, who is brash, colloquial, at times disorganized, but who is always on the scent and will yield on no point of logic. Their exchange bodies forth both the generational conflict that gave rise to the movement and some of the spirit of the age; by implication, it also allows a reader to evaluate many smaller matters, such as what the Realists considered fitting subjects and styles for academic writing.

The exchange began in 1930, when Karl Llewellyn, a thirty-seven-year-old professor at Columbia Law School, published "A Realistic Jurisprudence—The Next Step."[1] He had been working on parts of his essay for at least five years, and that overlavish attention shows: his argument is disproportioned, a scattershot of ideas without thematic unity. Llewellyn was already moderately well-known for his work in commercial law. His "Effect of Legal Institutions on Economics" (1925)[2] had provoked debate; so too would his contentious book of advice for law students, *The Bramble Bush* (1930). His compendious *Cases and Materials on the Law of Sales* (1930) was a casebook in the newest mode, with the editor's digests far outnumbering the cases themselves, the whole worked up with extensive annotations and reprinted statutes.[3]

Announcing "Legal Realism" as the new movement in law properly fell to one of the Young Turks; and Llewellyn, who was later acknowledged the chief Realist, was as well-situated for the task as any. To his lasting regret, Roscoe Pound made himself Llewellyn's respondent. Pound was not only Dean of Harvard Law School, he was the dean of American law, better known than most Supreme Court justices. By 1930, Pound had grown increasingly oracular and conservative. In the most shameful episode of his grand career, he was to accept an honorary degree from the University of Berlin in 1934.[4] Llewellyn and Pound had by 1930 already divided over the Sacco and Vanzetti case, Pound keeping silent, Llewellyn offering a powerful radio address condemning the Massachusetts legal process on the eve of the execution.[5]

Pound's decision to respond to Llewellyn's article may have been spurred by the feeling that a new movement in law required his imprimatur. He also may have been driven by his political differences with Llewellyn, whom he nonetheless respected. Llewellyn's coauthor, Jerome Frank, had just published *Law and the Modern Mind* (1930), a book that exasperated Pound, with its strutting assertion that lawyers and judges were typified by their "childish desire to have a fixed father-controlled universe, free of chance and error."[6] Pound found Llewellyn's less strident prose more to his liking, but must have been hurt by some of Llewellyn's contentions. At one point in his article, Llewellyn stated flatly that Pound was "a man partially caught in the traditional precept-thinking of an age that is passing."[7] And despite modulated statements of deference, Llewellyn put the matter more sharply still in a footnote: Pound's work was undone by its "constant indeterminacy." "At times the work purports clearly to travel on the level of considered and buttressed scholarly discussion; at times on the level of bed-time stories for the tired bar."[8] In "Call for a Realist Jurisprudence," his published response to Llewellyn, Pound was gracious; and in private letters, Pound mocked himself and his bar lectures and set aside the whole problem.[9] But Pound's recurrence to Llewellyn's comment about bedtime stories shows he was stung. Further, Llewellyn was not saying merely, here is the falling off of a great reputation. Instead, in pointing to Pound's avuncular relation to the bar, and to his regard for the "status quo," Llewellyn was marking Pound's failure to lead a new generation of legal reformers, for Llewellyn did not consider the bar benign; rather, it was a powerful alliance of the Haves from big firms.[10]

Unfortunately, Pound's "Call for a Realist Jurisprudence"[11] is marred by just the indeterminacy on which Llewellyn had remarked. Pound fails to mention a single name associated with Realism; and while he offers the movement a benediction of sorts, he derides or exaggerates what he takes to be prime Realist traits, such as rapt love for statistics and psychology. Llewellyn wrote Pound several times, asking him whom in particular he meant to anatomize, but Pound evaded him in his best manner, never saying quite what he had read. So Llewellyn, in his formal reply, was left both to construct a fully worked out perspective for Pound, and then to comment on it.

Two connected elements of Llewellyn's second essay, "Some Realism about Realism—Responding to Dean Pound,"[12] have drawn disproportionate attention from legal historians and contemporary critics. First, Llewellyn provided a list of twenty Realists whose work he meant to test against Pound's cloudy and debunking generalizations. Llewellyn set out those twenty as undisputed Realists, or at least ones whose inclusion Pound had not objected to, and looked at ninety pieces of their writing to see how far they conformed to Pound's presentation. A generation later, legal scholars fastened on Llewellyn's group of Realists as a definition of the movement; and quickly afterwards they criticized his omissions and errors. Plainly, though, Llewellyn used his group of Realists to permit him an essay in Realist method, a testing of Pound's hypotheses, all of which proved embarrassingly wide of the mark. That testing part of Llewellyn's essay took up ten pages, although it embodied months of law review reading, in which Jerome Frank assisted him. The second part of the essay, entitled "Real Realists," is more than three times as long. It is there that Llewellyn offers his own sense of Realism, and not merely a response to Pound. Not surprisingly, his sense of the movement is capacious, discerning, and based on wide, careful reading.[13]

In "Real Realists," Llewellyn lists in his text and notes about sixty-five people (in addition to the list of twenty) he associates with Realism. He describes Realism as a temper of mind, an attitude, a perspective, confined neither by generation nor by politics. Some of the scholars Llewellyn names remain well-known today; some became judges, others ended as teachers or government officials or working lawyers. He included the administrative lawyers Frankfurter and Landis; the early Realists Pound and Holmes; the judges Cardozo and Brandeis; the institutional economists Berle, Bonbright, Hale, Richberg, Commons, and Henderson; doctrinal writers such as Isaacs in contracts and Bohlen in torts; the social scientist Glueck and the philosopher Felix Cohen; the facile young Englishman Laski; and Thurman Arnold, a sort of psychologist of legal culture, soon to be as offensive to the old guard as Jerome Frank himself. There are other names we know less well today, or do not associate with Legal Realism, but which were for Llewellyn part of the movement broadly and properly conceived, workers such as Nelles, Angell, Freund, Haines, Greene, Weiner, and Young B. Smith.

Llewellyn meant the names he summoned to be consistent with his definition of Realism, one he maintained throughout his life: Realists, whatever their philosophy or politics, should work to depict the institution of law as it is, the law in action, and to do so vigorously and fairly. As Cardozo put the matter, "Realists," like Cardozo himself, are those who find that "considerations of analogy, of convenience, of policy, and of justice" overwhelm the old "jurisprudence of conceptions."[14] Llewellyn's was not a definition meant to foment debate; on the other hand, his fashioning of a "movement" from it made it fairer game for attack. However bland Llewellyn's "Realism," his was a critical concept—for what were judges and lawyers and academicians doing if they were not part of his "Realist jurisprudence," if they were not tough-mindedly examining what law was actually about?

The second element of Llewellyn's essay to prove controversial—this one, almost instantaneously so—was his demand for "the *temporary* divorce of Is and Ought for purposes of study."[15] We first must determine how law is working, so that when we set forth our own ideals, we can say how present law is actually fitted to them. This conception was drawn in substantial part from Holmes' "Bad-Man" theory of law, set forth in his great essay, "The Path of the Law" (1897).[16] According to a student at the time, Holmes' address was "required reading" at Llewellyn's Columbia of 1930, where it was circulated in mimeograph, treatment reserved for the incunabula of the Realist movement.[17] Llewellyn certainly did not conceal the origins of his idea. In "Realistic Jurisprudence," he proclaimed, "Holmes' mind had traveled most of the road two generations back." Indeed, one might fairly characterize substantial portions of Llewellyn's jurisprudential work as no more (and no less) than popularizations and applications of Holmes'.

Yet one great difference between Llewellyn and Holmes was in practical politics, and that difference was one that marked Realism off, even if Llewellyn preferred to define the movement otherwise. While Holmes appeared to remain aloof from or contemptuous of the great struggles of the day, Llewellyn was publicly committed to the progressive side of most questions,[18] from his defense of Sacco and Vanzetti to his founding (with Jerome Frank and others) of the National Lawyers Guild in 1937. That leftward political orientation was true not only of Llewellyn, but of most of the Realists, although it was better evident after the rise of the New Deal in 1933.

That Llewellyn failed to make an original contribution to jurisprudence, at least in his two essays on Realism, does not mean that he failed properly to define a new jurisprudential movement. That task he performed in an exemplary manner, showing the method of Realism (in his canvass of Realist authors against Pound's generalizations) just as he set forth its views. And, in part, what was fresh about Realism was, as Llewellyn perceived, a mood and a temperament, a willingness to take a set of interlocking ideas, easily traced in "recent orthodox work in law," and "*consistently, persistently, insistently to carry them through*" (Llewellyn's emphasis).[19] Even Llewellyn's style, while it is far below Holmes' in mastery, exerts its own awkward charm. It is a characteristic Karl Llewellyn touch to begin an essay, "Ferment is abroad in the law," and to repeat the term over and over, in the midst of Prohibition, while his debating partner Pound served on a commission selected by Hoover to study the Volstead Act. What are "the characteristics of these new fermenters" indeed!

KARL N. LLEWELLYN

"A Realistic Jurisprudence—The Next Step"

(1930)

I am . . . going to talk about substituting a somewhat unfamiliar, but more exciting and more useful focus, for the focus that most thinking about law in the past has had.

Two references to the course that thought has taken will help to set the perspective: one, to the tenets of the nineteenth century schools of jurisprudence; one, to the development of the concepts of rights and of interests.

For the nineteenth century schools I am content to accept one of Pound's summaries.[1] It fits with what reading in the field I have done; it is based upon vastly more reading in the field than I shall ever do. With regard to the analytical jurists, Pound stresses their interest in a body of established precepts whereby a definite legal result is supposed to be fitted to a definite set of facts; he stresses the centering of their definition upon the "aggregate of authoritative legal precepts applied by tribunals as such in a given time and place," and their presupposition of a state to make precepts and tribunals authoritative. The historical jurists, on the other hand, he finds making little distinction between law and other forms of social control; with them customary precepts, irrespective of whether they originate in the organs of politically organized societies, come in for heavy attention; central in their picture of law are the traditional techniques of decision and the traditional or customary notions of rightness. (All this, it may be added, without any too close analysis as to what is meant by "custom.") For the philosophical jurists, finally, Pound finds that "philosophical, political and ethical ideas as to the end of law and as to what legal precepts should be in view thereof" occupy the center of the stage.

I have no wish to put the tenets of these schools to the test, nor to pursue them further. Their value here is limited, but great within its limits: taken together, they hammer home the complexity of law. Each school was reaching for a single definition of all that was significant about law. Each school wound up with a definition which stressed some phases and either overlooked or greatly understressed others.... And I gather that one lesson Pound has drawn from his study of these and other schools has been to insist rather on what goes into the idea of law than on what is to be kept out of it.

Moreover, you will have noted running through his summary of their views the word "precepts." This is traditional. When men talk or think about law, they talk and think about *rules.* "Precepts" as used by Pound, for instance, I take to be roughly synonymous with rules and principles, the principles being wider in scope and proportionately vaguer in connotation, with a tendency toward idealization of some portion of the *status quo* at any given time. And I think you will find as you read Pound that the precepts are *central* to his thinking about law. Along with rules and principles—along with precepts proper, may I say?—he stresses for instance "standards" as a part of the subject matter of law. These standards seem to be those vague but useful pictures with which one approaches a wide and varied field of conduct to measure the rights of a particular situation: a conception of what a reasonable man would do in the circumstances, or of what good faith requires, and similar pictures. They differ from rules, though not from principles, partly in their vagueness; they differ from both in being not propositions in themselves, but normative approaches to working out the application of some one *term* in a major proposition. The principle, let us say, would read: a man must answer for what good faith requires. But a standard (like a concept; like any class-term, loose or sharp) functions chiefly or exclusively as *part* of a precept. Consequently, it belongs in much the same world. It, too, *centers* on precepts. But Pound mentions more as law than precepts and standards. Along with the standards he stresses also ideals as to "the end" of law. These I take to be in substance standards on a peculiarly vague and majestic scale; standards, perhaps, to be applied to rules rather than to individual transactions. Finally, he stresses—and we meet here a very different order of phenomena—"the traditional techniques of developing and applying" precepts. Only a man gifted with insight would have added to the verbal formulae and verbalized (though vague) conceptual pictures thus far catalogued, such an element *of practices,* of habits and techniques of action, of *behavior.* But only a man partially caught in the traditional precept-thinking of an age that is passing would have focussed that behavior on, have given it a major reference to, have belittled its importance by dealing with it as a phase of, those merely verbal formulae: precepts. I have no wish to argue the point. It will appeal, or it will not, and argument will be of little service. But not only this particular bit of phrasing (which might be accidental), but the use made in Pound's writings of the idea, brings out vigorously the limitations of rules, of precepts, of *words,* when made the focus, the *center of reference,* in thinking about law.[2]

Indeed, those limitations appear throughout the current analysis of law in terms of interests, rights and remedies....

Substantive rights and rules are spoken of as prevailing between people, laymen: one has, *e.g.,* a right to the performance of a contract. It is a heresy when Coke or Holmes speaks of a man having liberty under the law to perform his contract, or pay damages, at his option. It would likewise be a heresy to argue that the vital real evidence of this supposed "right" lies in an action for damages, and that the right could rather more accurately be phrased somewhat as follows: if the other party does not perform as agreed, you can sue, and *if* you have a fair lawyer, and nothing goes wrong with your witnesses or the jury, *and* you give up four or five days of time and some ten to thirty percent of the proceeds, and wait two to twenty months, you will *probably* get a judgment for a sum considerably less than what the performance would have been worth—which, if the other party is solvent and has not secreted his assets, you can in further due course collect with six percent interest for delay. To argue thus would be to confuse the remedy (which you can see) with the substantive right (which you cannot see, but which you know is there—somewhere, people tell you so). The substantive right in this body of thought has a shape and scope independent of the accidents of remedies. And herein lies the scientific advance involved in the concept. You are freed of any necessity of observing what courts do, and of limiting your discussion to that. You get back into the ultimate realities behind their doing. Obviously you can think more clearly among those ultimate realities. They are not so much obscured by inconsistency and divergence of detail. They are not answerable to fact.

Most lay thinking, it may be noted in passing, is on this level today. Typical is the current acceptance of a paper rule or statute as meaning something simply because it has paper authority—indeed, as meaning all it says, or all it is supposed to have been intended to say, simply because it has paper authority.

Far be it from me to dispute that the concepts of substantive rights and of rules of substantive law have had great value . . .

[But] a price was paid, of ambiguity—indeed of multiguity. "Rules" is a term sufficiently ambiguous. A rule may be prescriptive: "this is what *ought* to be; what the judges *ought* to do in such cases." Or it may be descriptive: "this is what *is;* what the judges *actually* do in such cases." Or it may be both at once: "this is *both* what they do *and* what they ought to do." And when theorists discuss, they will move from one of these meanings into another without notice, and with all and any gradations of connotations. In the particular case of rules "of law" a further ambiguity affects the word "rule": whether descriptive or prescriptive, there is little effort to make out *whose* action and *what* action is prescribed or described. The statement "this is the rule" typically means: "I find this formula of words in authoritative books." Does this connote:" *Courts are actually proceeding* according to this formula"; or "*Courts* always *rehearse* this formula in this connection?" Does it connote: "*People* are conducting themselves in the light of this formula"; or even "People are conducting themselves as this formula suggests that they ought to." The theorist will rarely trouble to tell you how many (if any) of these connotations are implicit in his statement: "this is the rule." But he will reason, on the next page, from some one of such implications. Which means: confusion, profuse and inevitable. . . .

. . . [T]he use of precepts, or rules, or of rights which are logical counterparts of rules—of *words*, in a word—as the *center* of reference in thinking about law, is a block to clear thinking about matters legal. I want again to make sure that I am not misunderstood. (1) I am not arguing that "rules of substantive law" are without importance. (2) I am not arguing that it is not humanly *possible* to use the interests-rights and rules-remedies analysis and still think clearly and usefully about law. (3) Least of all, am I attempting to urge the exclusion of substantive rights and rules from the field of "law." Instead of these things, I am arguing (1) that rules of substantive law are of far less importance than most legal theorizers have assumed in most of their thinking and writing, and that they are *not* the most useful center of reference for discussion of law; (2) that the presence of the term "rights and rules" in the interest set-up (a) has persistent tendency to misfocus attention on that term; (b) that the avoidance of that tendency is a great gain in clarity; and (c) that to both attempt such avoidance and retain the term is to cumber all discussion with embarrassing and quite unnecessary baggage; (3) that substantive rights and rules should be removed from their present position at the *focal point* of legal discussion, in favor [of] the *area of contact* between judicial (or official) *behavior* and the *behavior* of laymen; that the substantive rights and rules should be studied not as self-existent, nor as a major point of reference, but themselves with constant reference to that area of behavior-contacts. . . .

. . . *[T]he most significant* (I do *not* say the *only* significant) aspects of the relations of law and society lie in the field of behavior, and that words take on importance either because and insofar as they are behavior, or because and insofar as they demonstrably reflect or influence other behavior. This statement seems not worth making. Its truth is absurdly apparent. For all that, it reverses, it upsets, the whole traditional approach to law. It turns accepted theory on its head. The traditional approach is in terms of words; it centers on words; it has the utmost difficulty in getting beyond words. If nothing be said about behavior, the *tacit* assumption is that the words do reflect behavior, and if they be the words of rules of law, do influence behavior, even influence behavior effectively and precisely to conform completely to those words. . . .

"Real rules," . . . if I had my way with words, would by legal scientists be called the practices of the courts, and not "rules" at all. And statements of "rights" would be statements of likelihood that in a given situation a certain type of court action loomed in the offing. Factual terms. No more. This use of "rights," at least, has already considerable standing among the followers of Hohfeld. This concept of "real rule" has been gaining favor since it was first put into clarity by Holmes. "Paper rules" are what have been treated, traditionally, as rules of law: the accepted *doctrine* of the time and place—what the books there say "the law" is. . . .

Are "rules of law" in the accepted sense eliminated in such a course of thought? Somewhat obviously not. Whether they be pure paper rules, or are the accepted patter of the law officials, they remain present, and their presence remains an actuality—an actuality of importance—but an actuality whose *precise* importance, whose bearing and influence becomes clear. First of all they appear as what they are: rules of authoritative ought, addressed *to* officials, telling *officials* what the *officials* ought to do. To which telling the officials either pay no heed at all (the pure paper rule; the dead-letter statute; the obsolete case) or listen partly (the rule "construed" out of recognition; the rule to which lip-service only is paid, while practice runs another course) or listen with all care (the rule with which the official practice pretty accurately coincides). . . .

All this is nothing new in social science. . . . The only novel feature is the application to that most conventionalized and fiction-ridden of disciplines, the law. In essence the historical school of jurists from the one side, and Bentham and later Ihering from the other, were approaching the lines of theorizing here put forth. Holmes' mind had travelled most of the road two generations back. What has been done in the last decades that has some touch of novelty, is for theorizers to go beyond theorizing, to move, along such lines as these, into the gathering and interpretations of facts about legal behavior: Ehrlich, Nussbaum, Hedemann, Brandeis, Frankfurter, Moore, Clark, Douglas, Moley, Yntema, Klaus, Handler, Lambert—I name only enough to show that neither a single country nor a single school is involved, and to make clear that the point of view has moved beyond the stage of chatter and has proved itself in operation. . . .

. . . [T]he focus, the center of law, is not merely what the judge does, in the impact of that doing on the interested layman, but what *any* state official does, officially. . . .

. . . [T]he word "official" tacitly presupposes, connotes, reaches out to include, all those patterns of action (ordering, initiative) and obedience (including passivity) on the part of the official and of all laymen affected which *make up* the official's position and authority as such. . . .

In all the emphasis placed upon behavior I may have created the impression that a "realistic" approach would make itself unrealistic by disregarding what people *think* law is. Not so. . . .

No less important than what people think law is, is what people conceive that law should be. Any change in law is in good part a reflection of someone's desire to produce a difference. And just as attitudes and expectations must be taken into account along with overt behavior, so must purposes and the ideal pictures toward which purposes drive. . . .

. . . I have been concerned not at all with marking a periphery of law, with defining "it," with *excluding* anything at all from its field. I have argued that the trend of the most fruitful thinking about law has run steadily toward regarding law as an engine (a heterogenous multitude of

engines) having purposes, not values in itself; and that the clearer visu-
alization of the problems involved moves toward ever-decreasing emphasis
on words, and ever-increasing emphasis on observable behavior (in which
any demonstrably probable attitudes and thought-patterns should be
included)....

Included in the field of law under such an approach is everything
currently included, and a vast deal more. At the very heart, I suspect, is
the behavior of judges, peculiarly, that part of their behavior which marks
them as judges—those practices which establish the continuity of their
office with their predecessors and successors, and which make their official
contacts with other persons; but that suspicion on my part may be a relic
of the case law tradition in which we American lawyers have been raised.
Close around it on the one hand lies the behavior of other government
officials. On the other, the sets of accepted formulae which judges recite,
seek light from, try to follow. Distinguishing here the formulae with close
behavior-correspondences from others; those of frequent application from
those of infrequent. Close around these again, lie various persons' ideas
of what the law is; and especially their views of what it or some part of
it ought to accomplish. At first hand contact with officials' behavior, from
another angle, lies the social set-up where the official's acts impinge directly
on it; and behind that the social set-up which resists or furthers or reflects
the impingement of his acts. Farther from the center lies legal and social
philosophy—approaching that center more directly in proportion as the
materials with which it deals are taken directly from the center. Part of
law, in many aspects, is all of society, and all of man in society. But that
is a question of periphery and not of center, of the reach of a specific
problem in hand, not of a general discussion. As to the overlapping of
the field as thus sketched with that of other social sciences, I should be
sorry if no overlapping were observable. The social sciences are not staked
out like real estate. Even in law the sanctions for harmless trespass are not
heavy.

ROSCOE POUND

"The Call for a Realist Jurisprudence"

(1931)

A critic of nineteenth-century historical jurisprudence used to deplore that Savigny had not studied under Savigny in his youth. He had been trained in the eighteenth-century natural law and was unable to get away from certain presuppositions and modes of thought which his training had made part of his juristic make-up. Those of us who were brought up in the analytical and historical jurisprudence of the last century may well bear this in mind as we read and seek to appraise the work of the on-coming generation of American law teachers. Very likely our unconscious measure may be that of a philosophy and psychology and legal science of the past, whereas they are struggling to put things in terms of the philosophy and psychology of today, and thus to set up a legal science for the twentieth century.

Hence I approach the subject of the call for a realist jurisprudence, insistent on the part of our younger teachers of law, with some humility. But here is an important movement in the science of law, and it behooves us to understand it and be thinking about it.

First, then, what is meant by realism in this connection? As I read them, the new juristic realists hardly use realism in a technical philosophical sense. They use it rather in the sense which it bears in art. By realism they mean fidelity to nature, accurate recordings of things as they are, as contrasted with things as they are imagined to be, or wished to be, or as one feels they ought to be. They mean by realism faithful adherence to the actualities of the legal order as the basis of a science of law. But a science of law must be something more than a descriptive inventory. There must be selection and ordering of the materials so as to make them intelligible and useful. After the actualities of the legal order have been observed and recorded, it remains to do something with them. What does realism propose to do with them which we had not been doing in the past? What are the features of the program of the new realists which make it one of juristic realism?

Let us consider first the program of faithful adherence to actualities, and then the program of doing something with them when observed and recorded. The former would think of jurisprudence as an organized

Reprinted from the *Harvard Law Review*, vol. 44 (1931), pp. 697–711, by permission.

body of knowledge with respect to the phenomena of social control through politically organized society, treating of the phenomena themselves rather than preconceptions of what they must be or ought to be. But there is nothing new in the assumption of those who are striking out new paths of juristic thought that those who have gone before them have been dealing with illusions, while they alone and for the first time are dealing with realities. The rationalists put forward the same claim. They claimed to stand upon a solid and unchallengeable ground of reason in contrast to an illusion of authority and the broken down academic fiction of continuity of the empire on which the medieval conception of the binding force of the *corpus juris* had been built. When Kant's critical philosophy undermined this supposed solid foundation, the historical jurists came forward with a claim of substituting for the illusion of reason the reality of experience. Historical study of experience of adjusting human relations was to show us the course of unfolding of the idea, which alone had significance, as contrasted with the eighteenth-century illusion of a natural law discoverable by sheer reason. Next the analytical jurists made a like claim. They made no pretense of considering what had been or what would be or what ought to be. It was their boast that they treated of what was. They proceeded on the basis of "the pure fact of law." They had to do with the actual rules actually obtaining in the administration of justice in a given time and place in contrast to subjective speculations as to what rules of law should be, or deductions from what they had been. And then came the positivists. They too stood and stood alone on a solid ground of reality. To them reality was in laws of social and legal development discoverable by observation of social and legal institutions among all peoples. Our new realist rejects all these conceptions of juristic reality: Reason is an illusion. Experience is not the unfolding of an idea. No "pure fact of law" is to be found in rules since the existence of rules of law, as anything outside of the books, is an illusion. Nor have we observed the phenomena of legal institutions among all peoples with sufficient accuracy and objectivity to be in a position to formulate any laws of legal development therefrom. One may concede this and yet be skeptical as to the faith in ability to find the one unchallengeable basis free from illusion which alone the new realist takes over from the illusion-ridden jurists of the past.

If recent philosophy teaches aright, there is no absolute reality. What test of reality may a modern relativist assert in jurisprudence other than significance? But there is no absolute significance. Significance is significance for or in relation to something. Is not a valuing in terms of significance for the ends of the legal order (as the social utilitarians see it) or a valuing and defining of ends with reference to significance for civilization (as the Neo-Hegelians see it) as real as a looking at single phenomena as significant in their uniqueness or at the alogical element in judicial or legislative or juristic behavior as more significant than the logical? As in the disputes of diverse schools of jurists in the past, the difference today is one of emphasis. Received ideals, conceptions, the quest for certainty and uniformity, an authoritative technique of using authoritative legal materials, settled legal doctrines and modes of thought, and a traditional mode of legal reasoning are actual and every-day phenomena of the legal order. The question at bottom is whether a faithful representation of realities shall paint them in the foreground or instead shall put in the foreground the subjective features in the behavior of particular judges, the elements in judicial action which stand in the way of certainty and uniformity, the deficiencies of the received technique, the undefined edges and overlappings of doctrines and the deficiencies of legal reasoning. Emphasis on the fallings short of these instruments is useful in that it shows us what we have to do in making them more effective, or in making their workings more in accord with the ends of law, or in finding better instruments to take their place. The new realists have been doing good work at this point. But such critical activity, important as it is, is not the whole of jurisprudence, nor can we build a science of law which shall faithfully describe the actualities of the legal order and organize our knowledge of these actualities, merely on the basis of such criticism. There is as much actuality in the old picture as in the new. Each selects a set of aspects for emphasis. Neither portrays the whole as it is.

Let it be repeated. Faithful portrayal of what courts and law makers and jurists do is not the whole task of a science of law. One of the conspicuous actualities of the legal order is the impossibility of divorcing what they do from the question what they ought to do or what they feel they ought to do. For by and large they are trying to do what they ought to do. Their picture of what they ought to do is often decisive in determining what they do. Such pictures are actualities quite as much as the materials of legal precepts or doctrines upon which or with which they work. . . . The new realists have their own preconceptions of what is significant, and hence of what juristically must be. Most of them merely substitute a psychological must for an ethical or political or historical must.

Except as they sometimes take form and content from some one masterful leader, new movements in any field of learning do not acquire a detailed and officially orthodox creed in their formative period. Hence it is unfair to take any one item, or even set of items, from one or more of its adherents and assume that it may be fastened upon the formative school as characteristic dogma. But five items are to be found so generally in the writings of the new school, that one may be justified in pronouncing them, or most of them, the ideas of current juristic realism:

(a) One of the most common is faith in masses of figures as having significance in and of themselves. The single instance may or may not have significance, according to the purpose for which or connection in which we consider it. So with the mass or aggregate of single instances. If, for example, we are studying congestion of the criminal dockets in certain parts of the country, and its effects upon the enforcement of a particular law, and find that in those places the percentage of sentences to imprisonment runs from 4. to 6., whereas in the country at large it is 41, these figures throw much light upon the workings of "bargain days" and "cafeteria courts." ... But statistics ... are not the only objectively ascertainable data available to the jurist. In the reported decisions of the past we have a record of experience in the administration of justice, of how precepts or doctrines or institutions have worked or have failed to work, and of how and why they came to be formulated or shaped as we find them, which is as solid a basis for objectively scientific study as any mass of figures can be. I would not give over the quest for significant statistics. On the contrary, we need urgently to replace the present crude and often pointless official compilations put forth by bureaus and departments, national and state. But when we get them they will simply afford additional material. Chiefly we shall have to understand the doctrinal and institutional and legislative materials which have come down to us, both in their workings and in their possibilities, using such statistics as we find or may gather as helps toward that understanding.

(b) No less common is belief in the exclusive significance or reality of some one method or line of approach. One of these, much insisted on, is exact terminology. The analytical jurists and the Pandectists, we may remember, laid stress upon this also. But I venture to think that the utility of precise terminology and exact meanings is more in connection with differentiating problems from pseudo-problems and with formulation of results than in providing solutions. None of the fundamental problems of jurisprudence is solved by terminology, while there have been signs that rigid terminology has been used to create an appearance of solutions of questions which have been left untouched at the core. ...

Still another [mode of approach] seeks a science of law analogous to mathematical physics, and would refuse the name of science to a body of knowledge, or the epithet scientific to a method which does not conform to that type. It is conceived that observation of the phenomena of administration of justice, carried on objectively and scientifically, may give us formulas as rigidly exact and free from any personal or subjective element, either in formulation or application, as, for example, those employed by the engineer. It is argued that the only objectively valid phenomena are those discoverable by statistical investigation of the operations of judicial institutions, and the one valid method is a formulation of exact propositions on the basis thus afforded.

In the social sciences we must consider how men do act (or if one prefers, behave) in their relations and contacts with others, how they ought to act in those relations and contacts in order to maintain, further, and transmit civilization, and how to insure, as far as may be, by social, economic, political, and legal institutions or by ethical precepts, a correspondence of what takes place with what ought to be. In the narrower field of judicial application of law we must consider how judges do decide, how they ought to decide to give effect to the ends of the legal order, and how to insure as far as may be the decisions that ought to be. Undoubtedly the gathering of statistics can show us much as to how justice is administered, and how and how far legal precepts are observed and enforced. But they are expected also to show how justice must (in a psychological sense) be administered, and so to dispense with the question how it ought to be administered. This question of ought, turning ultimately on a theory of values, is the hardest one in jurisprudence. Those who long for an exact science analogous to mathematics or physics or astronomy have been inclined to seek exactness by excluding this hard problem from jurisprudence altogether. But such a jurisprudence has only an illusion of reality. For the significant question is the one excluded. . . .

. . . [T]here is a significant difference between the formulas of the engineer and the formulas of social control of which legal formulas are a specialized type. Legal formulas, or at least those to be found in the reports and the commentaries on legislative texts, are formulations of experience no less than those of the engineer. The materials of legal experience are as objective and as valid for scientific treatment as those of engineering experience. The difference is that legal formulas are put to a test to which the engineer's formulas are not subjected. Legal formulas seem to have hazy and indefinite limits, and engineering formulas sharp and definite limits, because the former operate to restrain behavior, while the latter are used to make action possible. . . . [M]en are forever pushing to the extreme limits of legal formulas, while engineers steer a conservative middle course between the limits of their formulas. In each case the formula on its face is definite enough. In the legal formula this definiteness is put to severe test by a steady current of behavior seeking to stretch the formula to the utmost. But no engineer or architect or builder would think of building to the theoretical limits of strength of materials. As a matter of course he builds well within them, and so we are able to contrast the certainty of his results with the relative uncertainty of legal results in action. This is not due to a more exact science or more strictly scientific method in the one case than in the other. In both cases experience has been formulated in rules which are valid enough at the core and indefinite or contingent enough in application at the limits. The difference lies in the nature of the tasks imposed upon the respective formulations of experience, whereby the contingent features in the application of the one are tried continually while those of the other are rarely developed. . . .

Another mode of approach to jurisprudence, often asserted to be the one path to reality, is psychological. Psychological exposure of the role of reason in human behavior, of the extent to which so-called reasons come after action as explanations instead of before action as determining factors, has made a profound impression upon the rising generation of jurists. It has led many of them to insist on the non-rational element in judicial action as reality and the rational as illusion. In contrast to the nineteenth-century emphasis on certainty and uniformity and ignoring of the continual fallings short of those ideals, they emphasize the uncertainties, the lack of uniformity, and the influence of personal and subjective factors in particular cases. This leads us to a related characteristic of the new juristic realism.

(c) Along with the assertion that the sole valid approach is by way of psychology goes usually a presupposition that some one psychological starting point is the *unum necessarium*, and that a science of law which makes use of any other type or theory of psychology is unscientific and illusory. There is nothing new in the spirit of this presupposition. It is in the right line of descent from the successive fashions in the social sciences a generation ago. The analogy of mathematical astronomy, with which the founder of sociology began, was succeeded in turn by the biological analogy—by the analogy of embryology or theories of struggle for existence—by the descriptive sociology, and by the older social psychologies. The adherents or promoters of each of these were as sure that they alone were on the one true path and that all others were groping in deep Cimmerian darkness as those who are in the van of the latest realist or scientific movements in jurisprudence today. What is common to all these fashions of juristic thought is dogmatic belief in one way of organizing knowledge about the legal ordering of society. There is little warrant in modern philosophy for this belief in the one straight and narrow path, which, indeed, is a left-over from the idealist conception of ultimate reality in a single simple idea unfolding in human experience....

It was a distinct advance when Jhering's demand for a jurisprudence of actualities led to looking at legal precepts and doctrines and institutions with reference to how they work or fail to work, and why. In keeping to this attitude the new realists are carrying on the best tradition of the last generation. Also there is a distinct advance in their frank recognition of the alogical or non-rational element in judicial action which the legal science of the nineteenth century sought to ignore. But many of these realists seek to ignore the logical and rational element and the traditional technique of application, or art of the common-law lawyer's craft, which tends to stability and uniformity of judicial action in spite of the disturbing factors. There is not and can not be the perfect uniformity and mechanical certainty of result which the last century believed in.... It is just as unreal and unjustifiably dogmatic to refuse to recognize the function of the quest for certainty as contributing to the general security. It is just as dogmatic and unreal to be blind to the extent to which the administration of justice attains certainty through rule and form and the extent to which the economic order rests thereon. It is just as unreal to refuse to see the extent to which legal technique, with all its faults, applied to authoritative legal materials, with all there defects, keeps down the alogical or unrational element or holds it to tolerable limits in practice....

(d) Another characteristic is insistence on the unique single case rather than on the approximation to a uniform course of judicial behavior....

Radical neo-realism seems to deny that there are rules or principles or conceptions or doctrines at all, because all judicial action, or at times much judicial action, can not be referred to them; because there is no definite determination whereby we may be absolutely assured that judicial action will proceed on the basis of one rather than another of two competing principles; because there is a no-man's land about most conceptions so that concrete cases have been known to fall down between them; because much takes place in the course of adjudication which does not fit precisely into the doctrinal plan. Such a view is not without its use as a protest against the assumption that law is nothing but a simple aggregate of rules. But nothing would be more unreal—in the sense of at variance with what is significant for a highly specialized form of social control through politically organized society—than to conceive of the administration of justice, or the legal adjustment of relations, or, for that matter, the working out of devices for the more efficient functioning of business in a legally ordered society, as a mere aggregate of single determinations.

(e) Finally, many of the new juristic realists conceive of law as a body of devices for the purposes of business instead of as a body of means toward general social ends. They put the whole emphasis on the exigencies of one phase of the economic order.... They give us a juristic version of what I have called the entrepreneur attitude toward law. It is instructive to contrast the Benthamist program of hands off with this program of means of enabling business organizations to function and business plans to go forward. Bentham, concerned with a science of legislation and so with the content of laws, was defining what that content should be. The new realist is concerned with what laws do and his definition would seize upon a significant economic function....

Looking at law as an aggregate of devices whereby business projects may be effected in a politically organized industrial society, there are two ways in which these devices are availed of. First, they are employed toward a better and more economical achievement of what the legal precepts in the books permit or do not forbid. Second, they are employed, or sought to be employed, to evade legal prohibitions and to enable things to be done which politically organized society has authoritatively pronounced anti-social. Thus, for example, statutes as to cooperative marketing may be used to permit mergers in contravention of the laws or policy of the laws as to restraint of trade. Eugen Ehrlich called attention to such phenomena long ago and they have been studied by the sociological jurists for their significance in the general process of social control. Certainly, here is a feature of the legal order which deserves the attention of jurists from many standpoints, and the new realists do a service in bringing it out. But if their way of looking at law is modern in its recognition of actualities ignored in the last century, it is thoroughly tied to the past in its limitations. It is a functional view. It looks at law to see how it works and what it does. It is also a narrow functional view, looking at one function, as the past looked exclusively at some one feature of the content or of the source of authority, or at some one type of form of legal precept. As in the past, one item is made to stand out at the expense of a picture of the whole. As in the past, reality is taken to be exclusively at one point or in one item. Law is more than a body of devices for business purposes, just as it is more than a body of rules for the guidance of courts. From a purely functional standpoint, the function of providing devices for business and industry is only one of the functions of the authoritative legal materials. It is a special phase of the general task of harmonizing and securing interests and upholding and furthering the social order. . . .

[L]et me essay a program of relativist-realist jurisprudence as I conceive it might be. I should formulate seven items:

1. A functional attitude, *i.e.*, study not only of what legal precepts and doctrines and institutions are, and how they have come to be, but of how they work. Thus far the sociological jurists have been going. But our new realist in jurisprudence will urge particularly study of concrete instances of rules or doctrines or institutions in action, in such number and by such methods as to be able to reach valid general conclusions.

2. Recognition of the existence of an alogical, unrational, subjective element in judicial action, and attempt by study of concrete instances of its operation to reach valid general conclusions as to the kinds of cases in which it operates most frequently, and where it operates most effectively or most unhappily for the ends of the legal order.

3. Recognition of the significance of the individual case, as contrasted with the absolute universalism of the last century, without losing sight of the significance of the generalizations and conceptions as instruments toward the ends of the legal order. At this point they have been anticipated by Stammler, but they will approach the subject in a different way through psychology.

4. Giving up of the idea of a necessary sequence from a single cause in a straight line to a single effect, and hence of the one sovereign legal remedy for every difficulty and one necessary solution of every problem. There will be recognition of a plurality of elements in all situations and of the possibility of dealing with human relations in more than one way. . . .

5. A theory of interests and of the ends of the legal order based on or consistent with modern psychology, without being tied absolutely to any particular dogmatic brand of psychology of the moment.

6. A theory of values, for the valuing of interests, consistent with modern psychology and philosophy, without being tied fast to any particular body of psychological or philosophical dogma of the moment.

7. A recognition that there are many approaches to juristic truth and that each is significant with respect to particular problems of the legal order; hence a valuing of these approaches, not absolutely or with reference to some one assumed necessary psychological or philosophical basis of jurisprudence, but with reference to how far they aid law maker, or judge, or jurist in making law and the science of law effective, the one toward the maintaining, furthering, and transmitting of civilization,

the other toward organizing the materials and laying out the course of the legal order.

Perhaps it is asking too much of any school of jurists to call upon them for so broad an outlook. But in the house of jurisprudence there are many mansions. There is more than enough room for all of us and more than enough work. If the time and energy expended on polemics were devoted to that work, jurisprudence would be more nearly abreast of its tasks.

KARL N. LLEWELLYN[1]

"Some Realism About Realism—
Responding to Dean Pound

(1931)

Ferment is abroad in the law....

Dean Pound has discussed the call and the ferment. One portion of his discussion calls in turn for our attention. He welcomed the ferment. He described it. The general terms in which he described the fermenters we seemed to recognize....

But the Dean's description... continued. On bones we knew was built a flesh we knew not of. An ugly flesh. The new realists, or "most of them," had, as the Dean read them, been guilty of a goodly number of things that careful thinkers would in the main not be proud to be caught doing. These intellectual offenses Dean Pound criticized. He criticized them tellingly. The question is one of fact: whether the offenses have been committed. For if they have, the Dean's rebukes are needed. Spare the rod and spoil the realist.

The question is one of fact. By fact it must be tried. And tried it must be. When Dean Pound speaks on jurisprudence, men listen. The profession has too long relied on him to discover, read, digest, classify and report on jurists foreign and ancient not to rely again when he speaks of would-be jurists modern and at home. We regret, therefore, peculiarly that he departed in this paper from a practice he has often followed, of indicating, in each instance when he presented a view, precisely whose view it was, and precisely where that person had set it forth. Freed of the check of the concrete, the most learned err. An error in perceiving or describing the attributes of these new fermenters would be unfortunate. For "here is an important movement in the science of law, and it behooves us to understand it and be thinking about it."

Into a series of further points in his description—points he does not approve of—we have inquired, and present the results. We speak, be it noted, for ourselves alone, and for the facts alone, not for the men whose works we have canvassed. Interpretations, judgments, and responsibility are ours. We are no spokesmen for a school....

Reprinted from the *Harvard Law Review*, vol. 44 (1931), pp. 1222, 1224–38, 1247–49, 1254–56, by permission.

[Pound] states: "five items are to be found so generally *in the writings* of the new school, *that one may be justified in pronouncing them, or most of them, the ideas of current juristic realism.*" The points of description here involved are taken with three exceptions from these five items or from their detailed development in his paper.

I

The trial of Dean Pound's indictment is not easy. It is a blanket indictment. It is blanket as to time and place and person of each offense. It specifies no one offender by his name.

We have the general indications above-mentioned: "new realists" and the like. We have the more specific indications also mentioned. Taken together, they narrow the class that may come in question. We can, therefore, check the items against a reasonable sampling of the men whom the rest of the description fits.[2] We have chosen twenty men and ninety-odd titles; representative men and pertinent titles. These we have canvassed in order to ascertain the extent to which the evidence supports the Dean's allegations. The results of our investigation are presented in summary under each point.

The Results of the Test

These statements of the Dean's points here set out are *in our language, not his.* We have done our best to reach and state his meaning. But we may misinterpret. We purport therefore to give *not what Dean Pound meant but what a reasonable reader may be expected to understand from his language.*

Point I. Much of the realists' discussion of judges' thinking sets forth what such thinkings "must" be, under some current psychological dogma, *without investigation of what recorded judicial experience reveals.*[3]
(a) Supporting: perhaps Bingham, Francis, Yntema: 3;
(b) Colorable: None;
(c) Negating: 16;
(d) No evidence noted: 1.

Point 2. One of the most common items found in the writings of the new school is *faith in masses of figures as having significance in and of themselves.*
(a) Supporting: None;
(b) Colorable: (i) Unrebutted: None; (ii) Rebutted: 1;
(c) Negating: 9;
(d) No evidence noted: 10.

Point 3. Much insisted on is the *exclusive* significance of an approach to law by way of exact terminology. Some realists believe problems are solved by terminology.

(a) Supporting: None;

(b) Colorable: (i) perhaps Unrebutted: Cook, Moore: 2; (ii) Rebutted: 1;

(c) Negating: 14;

(d) No evidence noted: 3.

Point 4. A strong group of realists expect rigidly exact and workable formulas about law to be developed in ways analogous to mathematical physics; and these formulas are expected to be workable without more as rules of what to do.

(a) Supporting: None;

(b) Colorable: (i) Unrebutted: Cook: 1; (ii) Rebutted: 1;

(c) Negating: (i) As to expecting any results *via* techniques closely analogous to mathematical physics: 5; (ii) As to awareness of great limitations on what may be expected from quantitative methods: 4 (one duplication).

(d) No evidence noted: 10.

Point 5. Many of the realists insist *that the rational element in law is an illusion.*

(a) Supporting: Conceivably Frank: 1;

(b) Colorable: (i) Unrebutted: Green: 1; (ii) Rebutted: 4;

(c) Negating: 13;

(d) No evidence noted: 1.

Point 6. Realists usually have a presupposition that some one of the competing psychologies is the *unum necessarium* for jurisprudence. (The theory of rationalization is, we believe, employed by all our subjects. It is employed by none of them as an exclusively valid attack.) We read "competing psychologies" as referring to general bodies of doctrine: *e.g.,* behaviorism or psychoanalysis in some brand. As to this:

(a) Supporting: None;

(b) Colorable: (i) Unrebutted: None; (ii) Rebutted: 2;

(c) Negating: 4;

(d) No evidence noted: 14.

Point 7. Many of the realists seek to ignore the traditional common-law technique "of application."

Examination develops that no triable issue of fact, as distinct from opinion, is joined here, since the Dean apparently conceives the traditional techniques primarily as techniques *of applying rules,* whereas the realist would include *all* the traditional techniques of deciding cases, or of the lawyer's art.

The canvass shows only that our subjects are much interested in study of the traditional techniques, so far as they can get at them, and that they weight the rule-applying aspect less heavily than does Dean Pound.

Point 8. Realists are blind to how far the administration of justice *attains certainty through rule and form.*

Again, no triable issue of fact, as opposed to opinion, is joined. The canvass shows that our subjects are much concerned with how far justice obtains certainty, and with how far it is attained—or hindered—through rule and form. But that they tend to differ with the Dean on the "how far" in both cases.

Point 9. A characteristic of the realist is conceiving of the administration of justice rather as a mere aggregate of single determinations than as an approximation to a uniform course of behavior.

Our evidence is directed to the proposition that our subjects do not conceive of judicial (and other legal) behavior as involving uniformities.

(a) Supporting: Frank: 1;

(b) Colorable: (i) Unrebutted: Green: 1; (ii) Rebutted: 4;

(c) Negating: 14;

(d) No evidence noted. None.

Point 10. Many of the realists have an exclusive interest in the business aspects of the law, and this exclusively from the standpoint of the purposes of business, rather than of society as a whole.

This could, of course, apply only to the ten commercial lawyers among our subjects:

(a) Perhaps supporting: Sturges: 1;

(b) Perhaps colorable: (i) Unrebutted (in print): Moore: 1; (ii) Rebutted: None;

(c) Negating: 7;

(d) Inadequate evidence noted (in print): 1.

Point 11. By clear implication: the work of the realists is not concerned with questions of what ought to be done by way of law.

(a) Supporting: None;

(b) Colorable: (i) Unrebutted: None; (ii) Rebutted: 3;

(c) Negating: 17;

(d) No evidence noted: None.

Point 12. By clear implication: the results, *in their attempts at description,* disregard the effects of the judges' own ideal pictures of what they ought to do.

(a) Supporting: None;

(b) Colorable: (i) Unrebutted: Moore: 1; (ii) Rebutted: None;

(c) Negating: Passages adduced from 11; but they are not particularly significant.

What counts here is the whole tone of a man's work. We should have thought the realists' concern as to the effects of the court's ideal picture of delusive certainty would be enough to negate.—Significant in this canvass is chiefly the absence of positive support.

Point 13. By clear implication: the realists are unmindful of the relativity of significance, of the way in which preconceptions necessarily condition observation, and are not on their guard against their own preconceptions, while investigating.

(a) Supporting: None;
(b) Colorable: None;
(c) Negating: 12;
(d) No evidence noted: 8.

Summary

Of eleven points on which evidence in support could be diagnosed and counted, we find such evidence as to seven—but how much? We can adduce some support for *one* point from *three of our twenty men,* for each of four further points from two of our twenty, for each of two further points from one of our twenty. *One of our twenty men* offers some support for *three of the eleven points,* three offer some support each for two of the eleven points, four offer some support each for one point. *In no instance is the support offered strong, unambiguous, or unqualified,* even on the printed record. . . .

Real Realists

. . . There is no school of realists.

. . . There is, however, a *movement* in thought and work about law. The movement, the method of attack, is wider than the number of its adherents. . . .

The common points of departure are several.[4]

(1) The conception of law in flux, of moving law, and of judicial creation of law.

(2) The conception of law as a means to social ends and not as an end in itself; so that any part needs constantly to be examined for its purpose, and for its effect, and to be judged in the light of both and of their relation to each other.

(3) The conception of society in flux, and in flux typically faster than the law, so that the probability is always given that any portion of law needs reexamination to determine how far it fits the society it purports to serve.

(4) The *temporary* divorce of Is and Ought for purposes of study. By this I mean that whereas value judgments must always be appealed to in order to set objectives for inquiry, yet during the inquiry itself into what Is, the observation, the description, and the establishment of relations between the things described are to remain *as largely as possible* uncontaminated by the desires of the observer or by what he wishes might be or thinks ought (ethically) to be. More particularly, this involves during the study of what courts are doing the effort to disregard the question what they ought to do. Such divorce of Is and Ought is, of course, not conceived as permanent. To men who begin with a suspicion that change is needed, a permanent divorce would be impossible. The argu-

ment is simply that no judgment of what Ought to be done in the future with respect to any part of law can be intelligently made without knowing objectively, as far as possible, what that part of law is now doing. . . .

(5) Distrust of traditional legal rules and concepts in so far as they purport to *describe* what either courts or people are actually doing. Hence the constant emphasis on rules as "generalized predictions of what courts will do." . . .

(6) Hand in hand with this distrust of traditional rules (on the descriptive side) goes a distrust of the theory that traditional prescriptive rule-formulations are *the* heavily operative factor in producing court decisions. This involves the tentative adoption of the theory of rationalization for the study of opinions. . . .

(7) The belief in the worthwhileness of grouping cases and legal situations into narrower categories than has been the practice in the past. . . .

(8) An insistence on evaluation of any part of law in terms of its effects, and an insistence on the worthwhileness of trying to find these effects.

(9) Insistence on *sustained and programmatic attack* on the problems of law along any of these lines. None of the ideas set forth in this list is new. Each can be matched from somewhere; each can be matched from recent orthodox work in law. New twists and combinations do appear here and there. What is as novel as it is vital is for a goodly number of men to pick up ideas which have been expressed and dropped, used for an hour and dropped, played with from time to time and dropped—to pick up such ideas and set about *consistently, persistently, insistently to carry them through*. . . .

4, 6, 7, 8 and 9 are to me the characteristic marks of the movement. Men or work fitting those specifications are to me "realistic" whatever label they may wear. . . .

Bound, as all "innovators" are, by prior thinking, these innovating "realists" brought their batteries to bear in first instance on the work of appellate courts. . . .

I. *There is first the question of what lower courts and especially trial courts are doing, and what relation their doing has to the sayings and doings of upper courts and legislatures.*

Here the question has been to begin to find out, to find some way, some ways, of getting the hitherto unavailable facts, to find some significant way or ways of classifying what business is done, how long it takes, how various parts of the procedural machinery work. (E.g., Warner, Sunderland, Millar, Clark, Yntema, Marshall, Oliphant, Douglas, Arnold, Morgan, Frankfurter, Greene, and Swazie.) Another attack begins by inquiry not into records, but into the processes of trial and their effects on the outcome of cases. (Frank, Green.) This, on the civil side, where we have (save for memoirs) been wholly in the dark. On the criminal side, beginnings lie further back. (Pound, Frankfurter, Moley and the Crime Surveys; where lawyers have drawn on the criminologists.) All that is really clear to date is that until we know more here our "rules" give us no remote suggestion of *what law means* to persons in the lower income brackets, and give us misleading suggestions as to the whole body of cases unappealed. Meantime, the techniques of the social sciences are being drawn upon and modified to make the work possible.

II. *There is the question of administrative bodies*—not merely on the side of administrative law (itself a novel concept recently enough)—but including all the action which state officials take "under the law" so far as it proves to affect people. And with this we begin departing from the orthodox. To be sure, the practicing lawyer today knows his commission as he knows his court. But the trail thus broken leads into the wilds of government, and politics, and queer events in both.

III. *There is the question of legislative regulation*—in terms of what it *means in action, and to whom,* not merely in terms of what it says. And with that, the question of what goes into producing legislative change— or blocking it—especially so far as the profession participates therein; legislative history on the official record; but as well the background of fact and interest and need. And, no less vital, there is the fact-inquiry into areas of life where maladjustment capable of legal remedy exists.

IV. Finally, and cutting now completely beyond the tradition-bounded area of law, there is the matter not of describing or predicting the action of officials—be they appellate courts, trial courts, legislators, administrators—but of describing and predicting *the effects of their action on the laymen of the community.* "Law" without effect approaches zero in its meaning. To be ignorant of its effect is to be ignorant of its meaning. To know its effect without study of the persons whom it affects is impossible. Here the antecedents of court action touch its results. To know law, then, to know *anything* of what is necessary to judge or evaluate law, we must proceed into these areas which have traditionally been conceived (save by the historical school) as not-law. Not only what courts do instead of what courts say, but also what difference it makes to anybody that they do it. And no sooner does one begin such a study than it becomes clear that there can be no broad talk of "law" nor of "the community"; but that it is a question of reaching the particular part of the community relevant to some particular part of law....

When the matter of *program in the normative aspect* is raised, the answer is: *there is none.* . . . Yet some general points of view may be hazarded.

(1) There is fairly general agreement on the importance of personnel, and of court organization, as essential to making laws have meaning. This both as to triers of fact and as to triers of law. There is some tendency, too, to urge specialization of tribunals.

(2) There is very general agreement on the need for courts to face

squarely the policy questions in their cases, and use the full freedom precedent affords in working toward conclusions that seem indicated. There is fairly general agreement that effects of rules, so far as known, should be taken account of in making or remaking the rules. There is fairly general agreement that we need improved machinery for making the facts about such effects—or about needs and conditions to be affected by a decision—available to courts.

(3) There is a strong tendency to think it wiser to narrow rather than to widen the categories in which concepts and rules *either about judging or for judging* are made.

(4) There is a strong tendency to approach most legal problems as problems in allocation of risks, and so far as possible, as problems of their reduction, and so to insist on the effects of rules on parties who not only are not in court, but are not fairly represented by the parties who are in court. To approach not only tort but business matters, in a word, as matters of *general* policy. . . .

As to whether change is called for, on any *given* point of our law, and if so, how much change, and in what direction, there is no agreement. Why should there be? A *group* philosophy or program, a *group* credo of social welfare, these realists have not. They are not a group.

3

Contracts and the Market

In 1800, the law of contracts was a relatively minor field of Anglo-American law. Most issues and relations we would now think of as contractual in character were governed by specialized bodies of law in which compulsory, status-based terms figured prominently. In the most widely circulated and influential general treatise on common-law doctrine, Blackstone's four-volume *Commentaries on the Laws of England,* only a portion of one thirty-page chapter was devoted to contracts.[1]

By 1900, contract doctrine had risen from this position of obscurity to become, in the eyes of most American lawyers, the centerpiece of the system of private law. Over the course of the intervening century, one topic after another had been swept within its ambit. Employment relations, long regulated by the law of "master and servant" (which itself had incorporated many customary norms), were now governed for the most part by the same principles used to manage sales of goods.[2] Leases had come to be thought of as contracts (albeit as special kinds of contracts) instead of as creatures of the law of property.[3] The law of agency, whose practical importance had increased enormously with the proliferation of private corporations, was deemed by most commentators and courts a subset of the law of contracts.[4] Many tort doctrines traditionally thought to be nonwaivable (such as the rule that common carriers are strictly liable for damage to cargo) could now be overridden by contracts.[5] Finally, when economic change presented the courts with new topics for classification and resolution—such as whether an employer must compensate an employee who is injured through the negligence of another employee—they usually looked for guidance to contract theories rather than, for example, tort theories.[6]

This dramatic expansion of the scope of contract law was paralleled and perhaps to some extent fostered by the emergence of two important new principles. First, during the antebellum period, American courts and treatise writers came to regard contractual obligations, not as duties imposed by the state upon private citizens, but as outgrowths or expressions of the wills of the contracting parties.[7] This "will theory" gave rise to (and was reinforced by) several doctrinal innovations: A contract could only be formed, it came to be said, through a "meeting of the minds" of the parties. Types of contracts that did not readily conform to this image, such as contracts derived from one person's detrimental reliance upon a promise made by another, were disfavored in various ways by courts and treatise writers. And traditional defenses to contractual liability, such as the doctrines of duress and undue influence, were modified so as to relieve from contractual obligations only parties whose "wills" could be said to have been "overborne" during the contracting process.[8]

Second, beginning in the middle of the nineteenth century, courts and commentators expressed growing hostility to "subjective" standards of contractual duty, offering in their place a new set of "objective" standards. For example, they argued that, if an offeree behaves in a way that a reasonable person would construe as an acceptance of an offer, a contract is formed, even if the offeree did not in fact intend to enter into the contract. Similarly, when asked to construe ambiguous language used in a contract, courts increasingly looked to the ordinary or customary meanings of the words and eschewed inquiry into the ways in which the parties intended or understood the words. These and many related doctrinal innovations were usually justified in utilitarian terms: Subjective theories, it was said, might in some cases be more precise in giving each disputant his or her due, but rendered the outcome of contractual disputes unpredictable and thus impeded commerce; objective theories occasionally did injustice but, because they increased the uniformity and consistency of decisionmaking, were better suited to a modern market economy.[9]

In the last two decades of the century, a few doctrinal developments—most of them generated by efforts to deal with the ills of unchecked industrialization and the concentration of economic power—began to threaten the integrity of this system of rules and theories. State legislatures imposed increasingly stringent regulations on railroads, insurance companies, and the sellers of food and drugs, thereby limiting the set of issues about which they could contract freely.[10] The doctrines of promissory estoppel and quantum meruit, never completely expunged from the case law, gained in importance. And some subsets of contract law evolved in ways inconsistent with the theories upon which they were ostensibly founded. For example, the elaboration of the doctrine of apparent authority in agency law had the effect

of routinely imposing on principals duties that they plainly had not in
tended to assume and that thus were difficult to reconcile with the
will theory.[11]

Few judges and commentators, however, recognized the threats
posed by these developments, and of those that did, most contrived
ways to minimize the conceptual difficulties they presented. William
Keener, for instance, was aware of the inconsistency between the courts'
enforcement of quasi-contracts and the notion that a contract derives
from a "meeting of the minds" of the parties, but sought to limit its
significance by arguing that contracts "implied in law" were both unusual and fundamentally different from "true" or "pure" contracts.[12] Before 1900, only Holmes seems to have fully appreciated the fault lines in
classical contract law—in particular, the growing tension between the
proliferation of "objective" standards, which declared irrelevant the subjective intentions of contracting parties, and the "will theory" upon
which all contractual duties were supposedly founded.[13]

The elaboration of classical contract doctrine affected in profound
ways many other fields of American law. Of these impacts, the most important was the contribution made by the common law of contracts to
the constitutional doctrine of "freedom of contract."[14] When the federal
and state courts began striking down regulatory statutes that, in their
view, interfered excessively with contractual freedom, they relied in two
ways on the private-law doctrines described above. First, the courts typically took for granted that the duties owed by one contracting party to
another are derived not from the state but from the contracting parties
themselves. On this view, when a judge orders a party to perform an
obligation he assumed in a contract (or to pay damages in lieu of performing the obligation), the judge is merely compelling that party to
fulfill a duty he himself undertook for his own ends. By contrast, a statute prescribing the terms of a contract—for example, declaring that an
employer may not insist as a condition of employment that an employee
sign a "yellow-dog contract"—imposes on contracting parties duties
they did not voluntarily select.[15] In short, much of the courts' reasoning
was founded on the assumption that, while the common law of contracts respects persons' freedom, regulatory statutes limit their freedom.
Second, the same utilitarian arguments, colored by classical economic
theory, that the courts invoked in defense of objective standards infused
their constitutional deliberations. The smooth functioning of a market
economy—which, in turn, makes for prosperity and progress—requires,
the judges believed, leaving people free to enter into whatever bargains
they choose and then providing certain, predictable remedies to enforce
such bargains. Any disruption of this system, the judges contended, unless it is necessary to overcome one of a limited set of "market failures,"
does harm, not good.[16]

Beginning around the turn of the century, a gradually growing
group of legal scholars began to challenge the classical system of con-

tract law and the conception of the relationship between law and the market it helped support. Four of the best of these critical essays are excerpted in this chapter.[17] The four writers approach the subject from different angles, but share several convictions: The classical vision is internally inconsistent. The attempt to explain all of contract doctrine on the basis of a few general principles is chimerical and destructive. Economic and social changes have rendered many specific aspects of the classical system of doctrine obsolete or pernicious. Last but not least, all legal obligations derive, not from the wills of contracting parties, but from the courts' "notions as to policy, welfare, justice, right and wrong";[18] we should make those notions explicit, modify or discard them if necessary, and then deliberately reshape accordingly the rules governing contractual relations.

As several of the critics intended, their critique of the orthodox understanding of the private law of contracts helped to destabilize the constitutional doctrine of substantive due process. More generally, it helped lay the foundation for the set of arguments considered in the next chapter: the attack on the "public/private distinction."

ARTHUR L. CORBIN

"Offer and Acceptance, and Some of the Resulting Legal Relations"

(1917)

Mutual Assent

The rule generally laid down is that the acts of offer and acceptance must be expressions of assent. This has long been the theory upon which contractual obligations have been enforced. The test question usually put is, what was the intention of the parties? It must not be supposed from this, however, that no contractual relation can exist unless the parties both foresaw and intended it. If two parties have gone through the form of offering and accepting, the law determines the legal relations that follow. Frequently these come with surprise and shock to the parties themselves. It may be said here, as in the law of torts, that the parties are presumed to intend the consequences of their acts, but this is often a violent presumption contrary to fact. To indulge such a presumption is merely to hold that the actual intention of the parties is not the determinative fact, or even that it is wholly immaterial.

Parties are bound by the reasonable meaning of what they said and not by what they thought. If A makes an offer to B which B reasonably understands to have a particular meaning, and so accepts, A is bound in accordance with B's understanding. So also, if A's offer has only one reasonable meaning, B is bound in accordance therewith, even though he accepted supposing the meaning to be otherwise. The operative act creating an obligation is the *expression* of intention and not the thought process. It may be said that the purpose of the rule is to carry out the intentions of the parties in the great majority of cases; but it seems better to say that its purpose is to secure the fulfillment of the promisee's reasonable expectations as induced by the promisor's act. In the law of contract as in the law of tort, men are expected to live up to the standard of the reasonably prudent man. If there is a misunderstanding and neither party was negligent, there is no contract. The same is true if both are equally negligent.

The legal relations consequent upon offer and acceptance are not

Reprinted by permission of The Yale Law Journal Company and Fred B. Rothman & Company from *The Yale Law Journal*, vol. 26 (1917), pp. 204–6.

wholly dependent, even upon the reasonable meaning of the words and acts of the parties. The law determines these relations in the light of subsequent circumstances, these often being totally unforeseen by the parties. In such cases it is sometimes said that the law will create that relation which the parties would have intended had they foreseen. The fact is, however, that the decision will depend upon the notions of the court as to policy, welfare, justice, right and wrong, such notions often being inarticulate and subconscious.

NATHAN ISAACS

"The Standardizing of Contracts"

(1917)

Ever since Sir Henry Maine wrote his *Ancient Law* (1861) it has been a commonplace among jurists—and some who are not jurists—that "the movement of progressive societies has hitherto been a movement from status to contract." The formula has generally been gratefully accepted as a very useful summary of many phenomena encountered in legal history. Usually, its original meaning is extended so as to embrace within the concept of "status" the immediate or the remote results of agreement. Now and then the formula has been modified or limited, or exceptions to it have been noted; then the universality of the doctrines began to be questioned; and finally its applicability to Anglo-American law has been categorically denied. In Dean Roscoe Pound's latest contribution to his forthcoming *Sociological Jurisprudence* we read:

> "But Maine's generalization as it is commonly understood shows only the course of evolution of Roman law. It has no basis in Anglo-American legal history, and the whole course of English and American law to-day is belying it unless, indeed, we are progressing backward."

The issue framed by this flat contradiction is one of fact. Viewed as an event in the history of Anglo-American juristic thought, this rejection of a fundamental concept in current jurisprudence is no mere academic quibble. The position taken by Dean Pound seems an essential part of the groundwork of his sociological jurisprudence. Thus, he remarks upon the significance of

> "the legislative development whereby duties and liabilities are imposed on the employer in the relation of employer and employee, not because he has so willed, not because he is at fault, but because the nature of the relation is deemed to call for it."

It is not only "significant"; it represents "the settled tendency of the present." For such statutes the new jurisprudence bespeaks "the sympathetic judicial development which all statutes require in order to be effective." The new school denies the soundness of the historical views of

Reprinted by permission of The Yale Law Journal Company and Fred B. Rothman & Company from *The Yale Law Journal*, vol. 27 (1917), pp. 34–40.

those courts that have been talking of freedom of contract in such matters.

Now what is the fact? Is there indeed "no basis in Anglo-American legal history" for the status-to-contract theory as generally understood? Its original application was to personal relations derived from or colored by the powers and privileges anciently residing in the family. Is it not true that the relation of master and servant was originally—and still is nominally—a domestic relation? And whether the nineteenth century was out of line with the common law or not, is it not a fact that it has made of this relation a contractual one? "Employer" and "employee" (words having reference to the contract) now seem more appropriate terms than the older "master" and "servant" (words having reference to status). What of the relation of principal and agent? Historically, the making of this relation has not depended on contract. Hence, persons incapable of making contracts are still competent to become agents. But in the living law of the last century this relation, too, has veered from status to contract. The naive statement in many text books and judicial opinions that "agency is a contract" is evidence of the tendency, if not of the law. Perhaps even the marriage relation has been made somewhat subject to contract law, at least on the property side; though, of course, here we should expect more conservatism, and marriage must still be considered a status. But when we leave the family circle and turn from the original application of the formula to its possible applications "as it is commonly understood," it becomes difficult to comprehend what is meant when we are told that the generalization has no basis in Anglo-American legal history. Holmes has shown the fact, whatever the reason, that the law of bailments was originally a law of status, and that the nineteenth century has stretched contract law so as to make a contract even of a gratuitous bailment. Perhaps here the change is in the theory of the law rather than in the law itself; but what shall we say of the law of landlord and tenant? Beginning in status as indicated by the terms still used—though "lessor" and "lessee" are displacing them—it has progressed to the point where every letting is an *agreement* of lease. A lease was formerly a conveyance of property, an instrument of status.... [T]he fact remains that most business relations have become contractual relations, and—at least until Maine's day—all business relations had shown a tendency in that direction....

Maine was, of course, no prophet. He could not foresee the twentieth century tendency of our law to go back to the *Year Books,* but as a shrewd observer of the tendencies about him, he was unsurpassed. At least, with reference to his status-to-contract generalization, whatever limitations we shall have to insert, whatever exceptions we shall be forced to engraft on the rule, we must—however reluctantly—dissent from the view that it was a mere Romanism with "no basis in Anglo-American legal history."...

Still, if Maine's observations of the past were correct, the present tendency is clearly a reaction in the opposite direction. Dean Pound enumerates, besides the instance of the workmen's compensation acts, those of public service companies, insurance, and surety companies. We may add many other cases, not only those in which the statute book says "any contract to the contrary notwithstanding," but also those in which it prescribes the terms of a relation only in the absence of a specific agreement to the contrary. In fact, because of the constitutional limitations which we inherit from the days of freedom of contract, the second class of provisions is still the more important check on the tendency that seemed to be making every contract a law unto itself. In ordinary transactions, people cannot or will not stop to make special agreements "to the contrary." Therefore, they find themselves governed by the statute with its prescribed insurance policy, its prescribed bill of lading, warehouse receipt, stock-transfer, negotiable instrument, articles of partnership, its prescribed type of sale. When the question arises whether title has passed to a buyer, they will find the answer in the mechanical rules of the code for the ascertainment of their "intention," a constructive intention. The effect is a making of contracts in wholesale lots, just as we now make corporations in wholesale lots. A practical check on the individuality of contracts, if not a theoretical limitation on the freedom of contract, and a standardization of legal relations, are the net results.

After all, the question is not so much one of status and contract as it is of a broader classification that embraces these concepts: standardized relations and individualized relations. In what Maine calls status, that is, the ancient family relations, or caste, the rights, privileges, powers and immunities (and the correlative duties, limitations, liabilities, and disabilities)[1] were thoroughly standardized. In ascertaining them, the peculiarities of the individual agreement of individual members of society were irrelevant. But so are many of the peculiarities of an agreement ignored in later stages of society where a formal contract of this or that type results in a more or less standardized relation. Here, we include not only the early Roman forms of sale and the old English conveyances of land, but marriage, the taking up of the feudal relation at other stages in the law, and the purchase of a standard insurance policy to-day. The point of likeness is that a relation results in which the details of legal rights and duties are determined not by reference to the particular intentions of the parties, but by reference to some standard set of rules made for them. In origin, these relations are, or course, contractual; in their workings, they recall the *régime* of status. Maine's original statement has reference to a classification on the basis of origins. His argument applies—and is generally applied—to a classification of relations on the basis of their workings. In this sense, the difference between status and contract is not one of kind, but one of degree; and in this sense there has clearly been a long-enduring tendency in English law from status to contract, and—in the last two generations an equally distinct veering back to status. . . .

It is, indeed, significant, not "that the nineteenth century was out of line with the common law"—for we cannot indict a century to save the reputation of a theory—but that the twentieth century is witnessing a reaction back to status. And this is not the first time that the seismograph of history has made such a record, nor the first time that it has been ignored as an exception. That medieval hardening of relations known as feudalism was also, in its beginnings, a progress from contract to status. And those whose philosophy of history is a belief in the gradual development of liberty through the principle of contract have been forced to regard feudalism as a pause in human progress, an armistice in the war between two opposite ideas, status and contract—at best, a compromise, an exceptional, disturbing element in their whole scheme. Perhaps if we were able to go back to what we accept as standard family relations, we should find their basis, too, in the hardening of individual practices into rules. Perhaps even back of caste there was a progress from the individual non-standardized conduct to the standardized. In other words, legal history has room not merely for one single line of progress in one direction or the other, but for a kind of pendulum movement back and forth between periods of standardization and periods of individualization. . . .

KARL N. LLEWELLYN

"What Price Contract?—An Essay in Perspective"

(1931)

System in Contract Law

What now of the apotheosis of technique in contract law: system? In our unsystematic legal crazy-quilt contract stands unique. It is the one field in which a grand scale orderly synthesis has been attempted, and with fair success achieved. And this has been lauded as our great legal accomplishment of the past century. To the modern Romanist the achievement must indeed appear as but partial. He sees our very object of synthesis as itself a single element in a still grander scheme: transactions. To a few American scholars, on the other hand, the reproach seems in the nature of a compliment. They doubt the wisdom of generalizations in our law on anything like the scale attempted by a single systematization of all contract. They challenge the applicability of the current generalizations to various important bodies of cases.... Their view is needed, if one is to see or to state with accuracy what courts are holding. On the other hand, the vitality of the generalizing tendency is indubitable. It may be noted not only in the scholarly work of the last seventy years, culminating in the Restatement of the Law of Contracts. It may be noted as well in the decisions....

What effect the generalizing tendency has on contract-makers, is hard to say. It facilitates the teaching of "business law," but (apart from rudimentary notions of consideration and of writing) without so far as I can discover material effect on ways of action. Rather does it promise effects on laymen chiefly by way of its effects on doctrine; not in itself and immediately, but mediately and by way of its effects on what law-men do. To be sure, a general theory of contract must almost certainly come ultimately to assert a less absolute dominion over "the entire field" than has been the case in this heyday of its hope; it will surely grow content to recognize considerable local self-government where that is demanded by particular fact-situations; it will surely come to see the demands for such self-government as no less normal than their absence. Yet as a body of

Reprinted by permission of The Yale Law Journal Company and Fred B. Rothman & Company from *The Yale Law Journal,* vol. 40 (1931), pp. 704, 748–51.

doctrine available and pressing for constant application and development *wherever no compelling reason to the contrary appears*, no man can doubt the high utility of system....

Meantime it pays to note that here, as always, doctrinal synthesis tends to distort all vision of the underlying reality. For doctrinal synthesis is and must always be in conceptual terms, in classes, in supposed uniformities, inclusive, exclusive. The battle ground of such synthesis is and must always be the marginal and even pathological case which "tests" the sweeping generalization. Thus the replacement of a will theory on the Continent, or the substantial replacement with us of "meeting of the minds" by a theory of objective manifestations apparently indicating promise, and reasonably relied on by the other party—this is indeed a great advance. It covers more cases. The more which it covers are difficult and delicate and delightful—and few. The change of theory emphasizes, too, and properly, the high importance of reasonable expectation in contract, as in life and law at large. Yet the very advance has obscured the sociological vitality of the older insight. Is it not clear that if in all but amazing cases manifestation did not roughly coincide with intent, we should have neither reasonable reliance in fact nor any law of contract to make an "objective" theory of peculiar cases necessary?

In Summa

One turns from contemplation of the work of contract as from the experience of Greek tragedy. Life struggling against form, or through form to its will—"pity and terror—." Law means so pitifully little to life. Life is so terrifyingly dependent on the law.

Marginal cases, hospital cases, most of our cases well may be. Much doctrine, however sweetly spun, serves chiefly to grow grey with dust against the rafters. Overwhelming is the certainty that any synthesis which is to match with the meaning of the law in life must expand beyond the futile limits set by present legal theory to include great blocks of what we know as property, and equity, and remedies, to cover as well the most significant parts of business associations, and who knows what besides. Overwhelming is the realization of how far a law still built in the ideology of Adam Smith has been meshed into the new order of mass-production, mass-relationships. Overwhelming in no less measure is the conviction that broad forms of words are chaos, that only in close study of the facts salvation lies.

Against these conclusions stand others. The *ad hoc* approach of case-law courts is sane, it cuts close to need, it lives, it grows. And the work of law and lawyers in the contract field, however little of the whole it constitutes, has vital meaning. It is both hinge and key of readjustment. And how, without it, shall the great gate swing open?

L. L. FULLER AND
WILLIAM R. PERDUE, JR.

"The Reliance Interest in Contract Damages"

(1936–1937)

The proposition that legal rules can be understood only with reference to the purposes they serve would today scarcely be regarded as an exciting truth. The notion that law exists as a means to an end has been commonplace for at least half a century. There is, however, no justification for assuming, because this attitude has now achieved respectability, and even triteness, that it enjoys a pervasive application in practice. Certainly there are even today few legal treatises of which it may be said that the author has throughout clearly defined the purposes which his definitions and distinctions serve. We are still all too willing to embrace the conceit that it is possible to manipulate legal concepts without the orientation which comes from the simple inquiry: toward what end is this activity directed? Nietzsche's observation, that the most common stupidity consists in forgetting what one is trying to do, retains a discomforting relevance to legal science.

In no field is this more true than in that of damages. In the assessment of damages the law tends to be conceived, not as a purposive ordering of human affairs, but as a kind of juristic mensuration. The language of the decisions sounds in terms not of command but of discovery. We *measure* the *extent* of the injury; we *determine* whether it was *caused* by the defendant's act; we *ascertain* whether the plaintiff has included the *same item* of damage twice in his complaint. One unfamiliar with the unstated premises which language of this sort conceals might almost be led to suppose that Rochester produces some ingenious instrument by which these calculations are accomplished.

It is, as a matter of fact, clear that the things which the law of damages purports to "measure" and "determine"—the "injuries," "items of damage," "causal connections," etc.—are in considerable part its own creations, and that the process of "measuring" and "determining" them

Reprinted by permission of The Yale Law Journal Company and Fred B. Rothman & Company from *The Yale Law Journal*, vol. 46 (1936–1937), pp. 52–53, 57–65, 373, 418–20.

is really a part of the process of creating them. This is obvious when courts work on the periphery of existing doctrine, but it is no less true of fundamental and established principles. For example, one frequently finds the "normal" rule of contract damages (which awards to the promisee the value of the expectancy, "the lost profit") treated as a mere corollary of a more fundamental principle, that the purpose of granting damages is to make "compensation" for injury. Yet in this case we "compensate" the plaintiff by giving him something he never had. This seems on the face of things a queer kind of "compensation." We can, to be sure, make the term "compensation" seem appropriate by saying that the defendant's breach "deprived" the plaintiff of the expectancy. But this is in essence only a metaphorical statement of the effect of the legal rule. In actuality the loss which the plaintiff suffers (deprivation of the expectancy) is not a datum of nature but the reflection of a normative order. It appears as a "loss" only by reference to an unstated *ought*. Consequently, when the law gauges damages by the value of the promised performance it is not merely measuring a quantum, but is seeking an end, however vaguely conceived this end may be.

It is for this reason that it is impossible to separate the law of contract damages from the larger body of motives and policies which constitutes the general law of contracts. It is, unfortunately for the simplicity of our subject, impossible to assume that the purposive and policy-directed element of contract law has been exhausted in the rules which define contract and breach. If this were possible the law of contract damages would indeed be simple, and we would have but one measure of recovery for all contracts. Of course this is not the case. What considerations influence the setting up of different measures of recovery for different kinds of contracts? What factors explain the rather numerous exceptions to the normal rule which measures damages by the value of the expectancy? It is clear that these questions cannot be answered without an inquiry into the reasons which underlie (or may underlie) the enforcement of promises generally.

In our own discussion we shall attempt first an analysis of the purposes which may be pursued in awarding contract damages or in "enforcing" contracts generally; then we shall attempt to inquire to what extent, and under what circumstances, these purposes have found expression in the decisions and doctrinal discussions. As the title suggests, the primary emphasis will be on what we call "the reliance interest" as a possible measure of recovery in suits for breach of contract....

Why Should the Law ever Protect the Expectation Interest?

Perhaps the most obvious answer to this question is one which we may label "psychological." This answer would run something as follows: The breach of a promise arouses in the promisee a sense of injury. This feel-

ing is not confined to cases where the promisee has relied on the promise. Whether or not he has actually changed his position because of the
promise, the promisee has formed an attitude of expectancy such that a
breach of the promise causes him to feel that he has been "deprived" of
something which was "his." Since this sentiment is a relatively uniform
one, the law has no occasion to go back of it. It accepts it as a datum
and builds its rule about it.

The difficulty with this explanation is that the law does in fact go
back of the sense of injury which the breach of a promise engenders. No
legal system attempts to invest with juristic sanction all promises. Some
rule or combination of rules effects a sifting out for enforcement of
those promises deemed important enough to society to justify the law's
concern with them. Whatever the principles which control this sifting
out process may be, they are not convertible into terms of the degree of
resentment which the breach of a particular kind of promise arouses.
Therefore, though it may be assumed that the impulse to assuage dis-
appointment is one shared by those who make and influence the law,
this impulse can hardly be regarded as the key which solves the whole
problem of the protection accorded by the law to the expectation
interest.

A second possible explanation for the rule protecting the expectancy
may be found in the much-discussed "will theory" of contract law. This
theory views the contracting parties as exercising, so to speak, a legislative power, so that the legal enforcement of a contract becomes merely
an implementing by the state of a kind of private law already established
by the parties. If A has made, in proper form, a promise to pay B one
thousand dollars, we compel A to pay this sum simply because the rule
or *lex* set up by the parties calls for this payment. *Uti lingua nuncupassit,
ita just esto.*

It is not necessary to discuss here the contribution which the will
theory is capable of making to a philosophy of contract law. Certainly
some borrowings from the theory are discernible in most attempts to ra-
tionalize the bases of contract liability. It is enough to note here that
while the will theory undoubtedly has some bearing on the problem of
contract damages, it cannot be regarded as dictating in all cases a recovery of the expectancy. If a contract represents a kind of private law, it is
a law which usually says nothing at all about what shall be done when
it is violated. A contract is in this respect like an imperfect statute which
provides no penalties, and which leaves it to the courts to find a way to
effectuate its purposes. There would, therefore, be no necessary contradiction between the will theory and a rule which limited damages to the
reliance interest. Under such a rule the penalty for violating the norm
established by the contract would simply consist in being compelled to
compensate the other party for detrimental reliance. Of course there
may be cases where the parties have so obviously anticipated that a certain form of judicial relief will be given that we can, without stretching

things, say that by implication they have "willed" that this relief should be given. This attitude finds a natural application to promises to pay a definite sum of money. But certainly as to most types of contracts it is vain to expect from the will theory a ready-made solution for the problem of damages.

A third and more promising solution of our difficulty lies in an economic or institutional approach. The essence of a credit economy lies in the fact that it tends to eliminate the distinction between present and future (promised) goods. Expectations of future values become, for purposes of trade, present values. In a society in which credit has become a significant and pervasive institution, it is inevitable that the expectancy created by an enforceable promise should be regarded as a kind of property, and breach of the promise as an injury to that property. In such a society the breach of a promise works an "actual" diminution of the promisee's assets—"actual" in the sense that it would be so appraised according to modes of thought which enter into the very fiber of our economic system. That the promisee had not "used" the property which the promise represents (had not relied on the promise) is as immaterial as the question whether the plaintiff in trespass *quare clausum fregit* was using his property at the time it was encroached upon. The analogy to ordinary forms of property goes further, for even in a suit for trespass the recovery is really for an expectancy, an expectancy of possible future uses. Where the property expectancy is limited (as where the plaintiff has only an estate for years) the recovery is reduced accordingly. Ordinary property differs from a contract right chiefly in the fact that it lies within the power of more persons to work a direct injury to the expectancy it represents. It is generally only the promisor or some one working through or upon him who is able to injure the contract expectancy in a direct enough manner to make expedient legal intervention.

The most obvious objection which can be made to the economic or institutional explanation is that it involves a *petitio principii*. A promise has present value, why? Because the law enforces it. "The expectancy," regarded as a present value, is not the cause of legal intervention but the consequence of it. This objection may be reinforced by a reference to legal history. Promises were enforced long before there was anything corresponding to a general system of "credit," and recovery was from the beginning measured by the value of the promised performance, the "agreed price." It may therefore be argued that the "credit system" when it finally emerged was itself in large part built on the foundations of a juristic development which preceded it.

The view just suggested asserts the primacy of law over economics; it sees law not as the creature but as the creator of social institutions. The shift of emphasis thus implied suggests the possibility of a fourth explanation for the law's protection of the unrelied-on expectancy, which we may call *juristic*. This explanation would seek a justification for the normal rule of recovery in some policy consciously pursued by courts and other lawmakers. It would assume that courts have protected the expectation interest because they have considered it wise to do so, not through a blind acquiescence in habitual ways of thinking and feeling, or through an equally blind deference to the individual will. Approaching the problem from this point of view, we are forced to find not a mere explanation for the rule in the form of some sentimental, volitional, or institutional datum, but articulate reasons for its existence.

What reasons can be advanced? In the first place, even if our interest were confined to protecting promisees against an out-of-pocket loss, it would still be possible to justify the rule granting the value of the expectancy, both as a cure for, and as a prophylaxis against, losses of this sort.

It is a cure for these losses in the sense that it offers the measure of recovery most likely to reimburse the plaintiff for the (often very numerous and very difficult to prove) individual acts and forbearances which make up his total reliance on the contract. If we take into account "gains prevented" by reliance, that is, losses involved in foregoing the opportunity to enter other contracts, the notion that the rule protecting the expectancy is adopted as the most effective means of compensating for detrimental reliance seems not at all far-fetched. Physicians with an extensive practice often charge their patients the full office call fee for broken appointments. Such a charge looks on the face of things like a claim to the promised fee; it seems to be based on the "expectation interest." Yet the physician making the charge will quite justifiably regard it as compensation for the loss of the opportunity to gain a similar fee from a different patient. This foregoing of other opportunities is involved to some extent in entering most contracts, and the impossibility of subjecting this type of reliance to any kind of measurement may justify a categorical rule granting the value of the expectancy as the most effective way of compensating for such losses.

The rule that the plaintiff must after the defendant's breach take steps to mitigate damages tends to corroborate the suspicion that there lies hidden behind the protection of the expectancy a concern to compensate the plaintiff for the loss of the opportunity to enter other contracts. Where after the defendant's breach the opportunity remains open to the plaintiff to sell his services or goods elsewhere, or to fill his needs from another source, he is bound to embrace that opportunity. Viewed in this way the rule of "avoidable harms" is a qualification on the protection accorded the expectancy, since it means that the plaintiff, in those cases where it is applied, is protected only to the extent that he has in reliance on the contract foregone other equally advantageous opportunities for accomplishing the same end.

But, as we have suggested, the rule measuring damages by the expectancy may also be regarded as a prophylaxis against the losses resulting from detrimental reliance. Whatever tends to discourage breach of contract tends to prevent the losses occasioned through reliance. Since the expectation interest furnishes a more easily administered measure of recovery than the reliance interest, it will in practice offer a more effective sanction against contract breach. It is therefore possible to view the rule measuring damages by the expectancy in a quasi-criminal aspect, its purpose being not so much to compensate the promisee as to penalize breach of promise by the promisor. The rule enforcing the unrelied-on promise finds the same justification, on this theory, as an ordinance which fines a man for driving through a stop-light when no other vehicle is in sight.

In seeking justification for the rule granting the value of the expectancy there is no need, however, to restrict ourselves by the assumption, hitherto made, that the rule can only be intended to cure or prevent the losses caused by reliance. A justification can be developed from a less negative point of view. It may be said that there is not only a policy in favor of preventing and undoing the harms resulting from reliance, but also a policy in favor of promoting and facilitating reliance on business agreements. As in the case of the stop-light ordinance we are interested not only in preventing collisions but in speeding traffic. Agreements can accomplish little, either for their makers or for society, unless they are made the basis for action. When business agreements are not only made but are also acted on, the division of labor is facilitated, goods find their way to the places where they are most needed, and economic activity is generally stimulated. These advantages would be threatened by any rule which limited legal protection to the reliance interest. Such a rule would in practice tend to discourage reliance. The difficulties in proving reliance and subjecting it to pecuniary measurement are such that the business man knowing, or sensing, that these obstacles stood in the way of judicial relief would hesitate to rely on a promise in any case where the legal sanction was of significance to him. To encourage reliance we must therefore dispense with its proof. For this reason it has been found wise to make recovery on a promise independent of reliance, both in the sense that in some cases the promise is enforced though not relied on (as in the bilateral business agreement) and in the sense that recovery is not limited to the detriment incurred in reliance.

The juristic explanation in its final form is then twofold. It rests the protection accorded the expectancy on (1) the need for curing and preventing the harms occasioned by reliance, and (2) on the need for facilitating reliance on business agreements. From this spelling out of a possible juristic explanation, it is clear that there is no incompatibility between it and the economic or institutional explanation. They view the same phenomenon from two different aspects. The essence of both of them lies in the word "credit." The economic explanation views credit from its institutional side; the juristic explanation views it from its rational side. The economic view sees credit as an accepted way of living;

the juristic view invites us to explore the considerations of utility which underlie this way of living, and the part which conscious human direction has played in bringing it into being.

The way in which these two points of view supplement one another becomes clearer when we examine separately the economic implications of the two aspects of the juristic explanation. If we rest the legal argument for measuring damages by the expectancy on the ground that this procedure offers the most satisfactory means of compensating the plaintiff for the loss of other opportunities to contract, it is clear that the force of the argument will depend entirely upon the existing economic environment. It would be most forceful in a hypothetical society in which all values were available on the market and where all markets were "perfect" in the economic sense. In such a society there would be no difference between the reliance interest and the expectation interest. The plaintiff's loss in foregoing to enter another contract would be identical with the expectation value of the contract he did make. The argument that granting the value of the expectancy merely compensates for that loss, loses force to the extent that actual conditions depart from those of such a hypothetical society. These observations make it clear why the development of open markets for goods tends to carry in its wake the view that a contract claim is a kind of property, a conception which—for all the importance he attached to it—MacLeod seemed to regard as the product of a kind of legal miracle. He who by entering one contract passes by the opportunity to accomplish the same end elsewhere will not be inclined to regard contract breach lightly or as a mere matter of private morality. The consciousness of what is foregone reinforces the notion that the contract creates a "right" and that the contract claim is itself a species of property.

If, on the other hand, we found the juristic explanation on the desire to promote reliance on contracts, it is not difficult again to trace a correspondence between the legal view and the actual conditions of economic life. In general our courts and our economic institutions attribute special significance to the same types of promises. The bilateral business agreement is, generally speaking, the only type of informal contract our courts are willing to enforce without proof that reliance has occurred— simply for the sake of facilitating reliance. This is, by no accident, precisely the kind of contract (the "exchange," "bargain," "trade," "deal") which furnishes the indispensable and pervasive framework for the "unmanaged" portions of our economic activity.

The inference is therefore justified that the ends of the law of contracts and those of our economic system show an essential correspondence. One may explain this either on the ground that the law (mere superstructure and ideology) reflects inertly the conditions of economic life, or on the ground that economic activity has fitted itself into the rational framework of the law. Neither explanation would be true. In fact we are dealing with a situation in which law and society have interacted.

The law measures damages by the expectancy *in part* because society views the expectancy as a present value; society views the expectancy as a present value *in part* because the law (for reasons more or less consciously articulated) gives protection to the expectancy.

The combined juristic and economic explanation which has just been developed may seem vulnerable to one serious objection. This lies in the fact that the "normal" rule, which measures damages by the expectancy, has been frequently applied to promises of a type having no conceivable relation to "the credit system," the division of labor, or the organization of economic activity. Professor Williston apparently goes so far as to assume that the "normal" rule is the only permissible rule of recovery even in the case of promises made enforceable by § 90 of the Contracts Restatement, that is, in the case of promises for which no price has been given or promised and which are enforced only because they have been seriously relied on. Most of the arguments for the rule measuring damages by the expectancy which we developed under our combined economic and juristic explanation have no application to such promises. The suggestion that the expectation interest is adopted as a kind of surrogate for the reliance interest because of the difficulty of proving reliance can scarcely be applicable to a situation where we actually insist on proof of reliance, and indeed, reliance of a "definite and substantial character." The notion that the expectancy is granted as compensation for foregoing the opportunity to enter other similar contracts is also without application in this situation, if for no other reason than because no contract is here "entered" at all. Finally the policy in favor of facilitating reliance can scarcely be extended to all promises indiscriminately. Any such policy must presuppose that reliance in the particular situation will normally have some general utility. Where we are dealing with "exchanges" or "bargains" it is easy to discern this utility since such transactions form the very mechanism by which production is organized in a capitalistic society. There seems no basis for assuming any such general utility in the promises coming under § 90, since they are restricted only by a negative definition—they are not bargains.

Is the application of the "normal" rule of damages to non-bargain promises then an unanswerable refutation of the explanation which we have attempted of the rule? We think not. In the first place, it is obviously possible that courts have, through force of habit, given a broader application to the rule than a philosophic inquiry into its possible bases would justify. In the second place, it is by no means clear, from the decisions at any rate, that the rule of recovery in the case of these "non-bargain" promises *is* necessarily that which measures damages by the expectancy. There are, as we shall show in our second installment, cases which indicate the contrary.

It is not difficult to demonstrate that the judicial treatment accorded contracts is affected by the relation between the particular contract and what we have called "the credit system." The ideal contract from the standpoint of the credit system is the (bargain) promise to pay money. Here we find a combination of legal qualities which reflects the intimate association of this type of contract with the economic institution of credit: free alienation by the creditor; free substitution of another's performance by the debtor; easy convertibility between present and future claims, the difference being measured by interest; damages measured by a mechanical standard which excludes consideration of the peculiarities of the particular situation; finally, damages measured by the expectancy, with no tendency to substitute a different measure. . . .

The Consequences of a Wider Recognition of the Reliance Interest

The cases discussed in this instalment show, we believe, that the contractual reliance interest receives a much wider (though often covert) recognition in the decisions than it does in the textbooks. There can be little question that this judicial recognition would be much enlarged if the textbooks were to abandon their present treatment of contract claims ("all or nothing") in favor of an analysis in terms of distinct contract interests such as is proposed here. This makes it necessary to consider whether a wider recognition of the reliance interest would be desirable.

Naturally, a proposal to abandon the theory that there is only one kind of contract claim is likely to engender certain fears. The first of these would be that a too cordial reception into contract law of what Gardner has called "the tort principle" would blur the lines of division separating the different branches of the law. We have already sufficiently intimated our opinion that the breaking down of these departmental barriers would represent a distinct service to legal thinking. If these ancient boundaries were erased, it would become possible to analyse the general problem of the legal sanction to be given expectancies created by words or conduct in terms of the policies involved, and it would be perceived that these policies cut across distinctions in the "nature" of the obligation. This would in turn promote a desideratum already recognized,—that the obvious (though generally unexamined) interrelations of contract, deceit, estoppel, and warranty be brought into some coherent pattern. Even, however, if one wishes to preserve intact the familiar landmarks, is there any reason why a liability to reimburse reliance on a promise should be regarded as anything but "contractual"? If one means by "contractual" a liability imposed because a promise was made and broken, then a liability to compensate losses incurred on the faith of a promise is as "contractual" as any other.

A second fear might be that the adoption of the analysis here proposed would threaten legal certainty. The assumption is very commonly made that legal certainty is necessarily promoted by limiting the alternative courses of action open to judges. Though the all-or-nothing approach may be harsh, it at least allows a man to know where he stands. This comforting supposition can be preserved only so long as one ignores the psychological realities of the judicial process. In fact, more often than not, the all-or-nothing theory introduces stresses (and with them, a fortuitous element) into the process of decision which can be eliminated only by the adoption of a more flexible scheme of legal sanctions.

Still another fear might be that a wider recognition of the reliance interest would unduly broaden the field of legal intervention. This was the danger that Kohler had in mind when he wrote, in criticism of Ihering's theory of *culpa in contrahendo,* "Not every fruitlessly paid coach or street car fare demands legal redress." That the principle of compensating losses incurred in reliance on promises cannot be given an indefinite field of application must be admitted. Inconvenience suffered when another changes his course of conduct is a constant feature of life in society, and no judicial system would be equal to the task of carrying out the literal implications of the maxim, *nemo potest mutare consilium suum in alterius iniuriam.* Nor is it an entirely adequate answer to this objection to point out that people generally have sense enough not to bring suit for fruitlessly paid street car fares. Some *serious* reliance incurred even in *reasonable* reliance on *some* promises must probably go unredressed—at least, unless the word "reasonable" be made to forfeit its ordinary meaning. Yet certainly this problem of inclusion and exclusion permits of a more rational answer (or set of answers) than to say, as Section 90 of the Restatement, for example, asks us to say: "Either your losses must have been so great as to justify us in enforcing the whole promise, or you go without remedy."

The objection just stated—viewed, as it were, from its reverse side—reveals what is the most pressing need for a wider recognition of the reliance interest, a need which extends through all the cases discussed in this instalment. The objection to the all-or-nothing attitude is not simply that it often results in the plaintiff's getting *all* when *a part* would have made him whole. The more serious objection is that in those cases where a court balks at giving him *all,* he may get *nothing* when he urgently needed and deserved *a part.* This need makes it obvious that we cannot solve the problem of reimbursing reliance simply by converting the relied-on promise into a "contract" like every other contract. The need for compensating reliance must be treated as a distinct promissory interest, deserving recognition on its own account.

4

The Critique of the
Public/Private Distinction

In the eighteenth century, most American lawyers did not assume that all political and economic actors should be classified either as private parties or as public officials. Instead, they recognized that a variety of institutions and organizations—for example, business corporations, municipal corporations, guilds, churches, and proprietors of the common fields—were most accurately described as partly private and partly public in character. The objectives of such bodies typically included both enrichment of their members and pursuit of the common weal; they enjoyed many powers (like the capacity to tax members or exercise eminent domain) typically associated with government; many of them owned substantial amounts of property and conducted their affairs partly through its management; and not all individual citizens had access to them.[1]

During the nineteenth century, a growing number of lawyers found increasingly problematic the continued exercise by these organizations of their special powers and privileges. The public and private "spheres," judges and commentators asserted with growing frequency, ought to be kept separate.[2] In turn, that shift in attitude inspired a number of important doctrinal reforms: Business corporations were stripped of some of their more "public" powers, and "general incorporation" statutes made the corporate form available to all persons.[3] Corporations "privatized" through this process were provided protections against governmental regulation comparable to the protections enjoyed by individual persons.[4] Municipal corporations, once differentiated from private corporations, were stripped of many of their proprietary functions and rendered increasingly dependent for their regulatory authority on formal delegations of power from the state legislatures.[5] The notion that government officials had property interests in their posts was repudiated.[6]

Last but not least, various private law doctrines (like the availability of punitive damages in tort suits and the authority of individuals to use self-help to abate common nuisances) that smacked of public power were eliminated or restricted.[7]

These doctrinal developments were driven or reinforced by a host of loosely related attitudes and assumptions—many of them outgrowths of the ideology of classical liberalism. In schematic form, the most important of those attitudes were as follows: Governments and their officials wield dangerous amounts of coercive power; their initiatives must therefore be scrutinized closely to ensure they do not overrun the liberties of the people. Private parties should be enabled and encouraged to enter into whatever voluntary contractual relations they please in order to advance their own conceptions of their best interests. Whereas government officials are obliged when making decisions to strive to advance the public good, private parties have no legal or moral duty to take into account the impact of their choices and actions on the common weal. The state has a responsibility to ensure that private parties are not forced into contractual relations they do not desire (thus, courts must continue to recognize fraud and duress as defenses to contractual liability), but should not seek to impose on private parties substantive conceptions of what kinds of exchanges are fair or unfair. If it respects these limits on its legitimate power, the state cannot fairly be held responsible for the distribution of wealth and power in the society—that is for the outcomes of the voluntary transactions of private parties. A polity organized along such lines would be orderly, productive, and free.[8]

The essays reprinted in this section all represent efforts by Legal Realists to discredit the foregoing composite image of how the public and private domains are and should be divided. They all seek in some way to show that coercion is ubiquitous, not rare, in the relations among private parties; that the ability of some parties (e.g., employers) to force others (e.g., unskilled laborers) to enter into and abide by certain agreements depends to a large extent on the existence and enforcement of the law of contracts and property; that the content of that body of ostensibly "private" law is largely determined by "public" policies (like fostering commerce, encouraging the transmission of property between generations in a nuclear family, or discouraging unionization); and that the state consequently is responsible to a substantial degree for the distribution of wealth and power.[9]

This line of argument had an important political point. Underlying many of the conservative judicial decisions during the classical period was an assumption that social reform statutes, because they represent governmental "intervention" into the otherwise free and voluntary interactions of private persons and institutions, are anomalous and in need of special justification. The Realists argued that that assumption was fundamentally misguided. All economic and social activity is organized by an elaborate network of legal rules. Those rules confer advantages on certain parties and disadvantages on others. Social reform statutes—such as consumer protection laws, guarantees of collective bargaining rights, or laws limiting the number of hours employees can be required to work—thus represent adjustments of the legal ground rules, designed in part to alter the relative advantages of different groups of actors, rather than intrusions by the state into a sphere in which formerly it had no role. The Realists conceded that this insight did not answer the question whether particular adjustments of the ground rules were wise. Their claim, instead, was that the courts should abandon their presumption that reform statutes were undesirable and ask: What sorts of liberties should economic actors enjoy (or, conversely, what sorts of power should some economic actors be able to exert over others), and how might the legal system be used to institute such a state of affairs?

Did the Realists' argument prevail? Did they change the way American lawyers think about the relationship between public and private activities? As has been true in most contexts, the Realists enjoyed partial but by no means complete success. Several modern legal doctrines bear the imprint of their theory. For example, the decision of the United States Supreme Court in *Shelley* v. *Kraemer* that judicial enforcement of a private, racially restrictive covenant constitutes "state action" and therefore violates the Equal Protection Clause of the Fourteenth Amendment rested in part on a recognition of the responsibility the state bears for the outcomes of ostensibly private, voluntary transactions.[10] And contemporary legal scholars of many stripes are wont to proclaim the death of the public/private distinction.[11]

In many doctrinal contexts, however, the distinction seems alive and well. Under the reigning interpretation of the First Amendment, for example, private corporations are constitutionally entitled to express their opinions on matters of public importance,[12] whereas cities enjoy no such rights and indeed must demonstrate that expenditures for expressive purposes are authorized by their charters or by state legislation.[13] Private employers remain free in most jurisdictions to discharge so-called at-will employees, whereas public employers must comply with an elaborate set of procedural rules before they can fire their workers. Popular attitudes also remain colored by the notion that there exist important, principled differences between activities undertaken in the public sphere and activities undertaken in the private sphere. For example, many sorts of gifts or promises that, when used to influence the decisionmaking of the directors of private corporations, are conventionally considered acceptable, are widely regarded as improper or illegal when used to influence the decisionmaking of government officials.[14]

In sum, here, as in many other areas, the Realist credo has partially but not fully penetrated modern American legal consciousness.

ROBERT L. HALE

"Coercion and Distribution in a Supposedly Non-Coercive State"

(1923)

> "And while the House of Peers withholds its legislative hand,
> And noble statesmen do not itch
> To interfere with matters which
> They cannot understand,
> As bright will shine Great Britain's rays
> As in King George's glorious days."
>
> —From W. S. Gilbert's *Iolanthe.*

The so-called individualist would expand this philosophy to include all statesmen, whether noble or not, and to include all economic matters as among those which they cannot understand. The practical function of economic theory is merely to prove to statesmen the wisdom of leaving such matters alone, not to aid them in the process of interfering. And in foreign as well as in domestic affairs, they should make no effort to control the natural working of economic events. This would seem to be the general view of Professor Thomas Nixon Carver, although he likewise speaks frequently as a nationalist. But a careful scrutiny will, it is thought, reveal a fallacy in this view, and will demonstrate that the systems advocated by professed upholders of *laissez-faire* are in reality permeated with coercive restrictions of individual freedom, and with restrictions, moreover, out of conformity with any formula of "equal opportunity" or of "preserving the equal rights of others." Some sort of coercive restriction of individuals, it is believed, is absolutely unavoidable, and cannot be made to conform to any Spencerian formula. Since coercive restrictions are bound to affect the distribution of income and the direction of economic activities, and are bound to affect the economic interests of persons living in foreign parts, statesmen cannot avoid interfering with economic matters, both in domestic and in foreign affairs. There is accordingly a need for the development of economic and legal theory to guide them in the process.

Reprinted from the *Political Science Quarterly*, vol. 38 (1923), pp. 470–79, by permission.

To proceed to an examination of Professor Carver's system. His "individualism" is not entirely orthodox, for he is conscious of a certain amount of restriction of liberty in the scheme he advocates. Indeed his [formulation of his thesis] is altogether too pragmatic to please the doctrinaire disciple of Spencer. In each proposed case of governmental interference, he thinks, the question is to be asked, "Are the evils to be repressed greater than those that accompany the work of repression, and are the evils to be removed by regulation greater than those that accompany the work of regulation? The method of procedure must be to consider, appraise, and compare the evils on both sides." While this test might be accepted by the so-called paternalist, as well as by the so-called individualist, Mr. Carver's final conclusions as to governmental activity do not differ materially from those of the more orthodox of the latter. The government, he thinks, should exercise sufficient constraint to prevent destruction and deception, to standardize measures, qualities and coins, to enforce contracts, to conduct certain enterprises (like lighthouses) which cannot well be carried on otherwise, to regulate monopoly prices and to control the feeble-minded and the otherwise incompetent in their own interest. It should not coerce people to work, nor should it, with rare exceptions, undertake to direct the channels into which industry should flow. It should, however, prevent any private person or group from exercising any compulsion. The government must also impose taxes; it should restrict immigration and furnish educational opportunities. Such a scheme has the appearance of exposing individuals to but little coercion at the hands of the government and to none at all at the hands of other individuals or groups. Yet it does in fact expose them to coercion at the hands of both, or at least to a kind of influence indistinguishable in its effects from coercion. This will shortly appear more clearly, it is hoped. Meanwhile, let it be kept in mind that to call an act coercive is not by any means to condemn it. It is because the word "coercion" frequently seems to carry with it the stigma of impropriety, that the coercive character of many innocent acts is so frequently denied.

What is the government doing when it "protects a property right"? Passively, it is abstaining from interference with the owner when he deals with the thing owned; actively, it is forcing the non-owner to desist from handling it, unless the owner consents. Yet Mr. Carver would have it that the government is merely preventing the non-owner from using force against the owner. This explanation is obviously at variance with the facts—for the non-owner is forbidden to handle the owner's property even where his handling of it involves no violence or force whatever. Any lawyer could have told him that the right of property is much more extensive than the mere right to protection against forcible dispossession. In protecting property the government is doing something quite apart from merely keeping the peace. It is exerting coercion wherever that is necessary to protect each owner, not merely from violence, but also from peaceful infringement of his sole right to enjoy the thing owned.

That, however, is not the most significant aspect of present-day coercion in connection with property. The owner can remove the legal duty under which the non-owner labors with respect to the owner's property. He can remove it, or keep it in force, at his discretion. To keep it in force may or may not have unpleasant consequences to the non-owner—consequences which spring from the law's creation of legal duty. To avoid these consequences, the non-owner may be willing to obey the will of the owner, provided that the obedience is not in itself more unpleasant than the consequences to be avoided. Such obedience may take the trivial form of paying five cents for legal permission to eat a particular bag of peanuts, or it may take the more significant form of working for the owner at disagreeable toil for a slight wage. In either case the conduct is motivated, not by any desire to do the act in question, but by a desire to escape a more disagreeable alternative. In the peanut case, the consequence of abstaining from a particular bag of peanuts would be, either to go without such nutriment altogether for the time being, or to conform to the terms of some other owner. Presumably at least one of these consequences would be as bad as the loss of the five cents, or the purchaser would not buy; but one of them, at least, would be no worse, or the owner would be able to compel payment of more. In the case of the labor, what would be the consequence of refusal to comply with the owner's terms? It would be either absence of wages, or obedience to the terms of some other employer. If the worker has no money of his own, the threat of any particular employer to withhold any particular amount of money would be effective in securing the worker's obedience in proportion to the difficulty with which other employers can be induced to furnish a "job." If the non-owner works for anyone, it is for the purpose of warding off the threat of at least one owner of money to withhold that money from him (with the help of the law). Suppose, now, the worker were to refuse to yield to the coercion of any employer, but were to choose instead to remain under the legal duty to abstain from the use of any of the money which anyone owns. He must eat. While there is no law against eating in the abstract, there is a law which forbids him to eat any of the food which actually exists in the community—and that law is the law of property. It can be lifted as to any specific food at the discretion of its owner, but if the owners unanimously refuse to lift the prohibition, the non-owner will starve unless he can himself produce food. And there is every likelihood that the owners will be unanimous in refusing, if he has no money. There is no law to compel them to part with their food for nothing. Unless, then, the non-owner can produce his own food, the law compels him to starve if he has no wages, and compels him to go without wages unless he obeys the behests of some employer. It is the law that coerces him into wage-work under penalty of starvation—unless he can produce food. Can he? Here again there is no law to prevent the production of food in the abstract; but in every settled country there is a law which forbids him to cultivate any particular piece of ground unless he happens to be an owner. This again is the law of property. And this again will not be likely to be lifted unless he already has money. That way of escape from the law-made dilemma of starvation or obedience is closed to him. It may seem that one way of escape has been overlooked—the acquisition of money in other ways than by wage-work. Can he not "make money" by selling goods? But here again, things cannot be produced in quantities sufficient to keep him alive, except with the use of elaborate mechanical equipment. To use any such equipment is unlawful, except on the owner's terms. Those terms usually include an implied abandonment of any claim of title to the products. In short, if he be not a property owner, the law which forbids him to produce with any of the existing equipment, and the law which forbids him to eat any of the existing food, will be lifted *only* in case he works for an employer. It is the law of property which coerces people into working for factory owners—though, as we shall see shortly, the workers can as a rule exert sufficient counter-coercion to limit materially the governing power of the owners.

Not only does the law of property secure for the owners of factories their labor; it also secures for them the revenue derived from the customers. The law compels people to desist from consuming the products of the owner's plant, except with his consent; and he will not consent unless they pay him money. They can escape, of course, by going without the product. But that does not prevent the payment being compulsory, any more than it prevents the payment of the government tax on tobacco from being compulsory. The penalty for failure to pay, in each case, may be light, but it is sufficient to compel obedience in all those cases where the consumer buys rather than go without. . . . Mr. Carver attempts to distinguish [these two situations] on the ground that in the case of the tax the government "did not produce the tobacco but only charges the manufacturer or the dealer for the privilege of manufacturing or selling." But this is equally true of the owner of the factory, if he is an absentee owner. Whether the owner has rendered a service or not bears only on the question of the justification of the income which he collects, not on whether the process of collecting it was coercive.

As already intimated, however, the owner's coercive power is weakened by the fact that both his customers and his laborers have the power to make matters more or less unpleasant for him—the customers through their law-given power to withhold access to their cash, the laborers through their *actual* power (neither created nor destroyed by the law) to withhold their services. Even without this power, it is true, he would have to give his laborers enough to sustain them, just as it is to his own interest to feed his horses enough to make them efficient. But whatever they get beyond this minimum is obtained either by reason of the employer's generosity and sense of moral obligation, or by his fear that they will exercise the threat to work elsewhere or not at all. If obtained through this fear, it is a case where he submits by so much to their wills. It is not a "voluntary" payment, but a payment as the price of escape from damaging behavior of others. Furnishing food to one's slaves is essentially different; the owner may do it reluctantly, but if there is any "coercion" it is the impersonal coercion by the facts of nature which account for the slaves' labor being less efficient without the food; he is not influenced by the will of any human being. In paying high wages to wage-earners, on the other hand, he is. But for their will to obtain the high wages, and their power of backing up that will, he has no reason for paying them. Yet he does. What else is "coercion"?

There is, however, a natural reluctance so to term it. This can be explained, I think, by the fact that some of the grosser forms of private coercion are illegal, and the undoubtedly coercive character of the pressure exerted by the property-owner is disguised. Hence the natural reaction to any recognized form of private coercion is, "forbid it." One who would not wish to take from the laboring man his power to quit the employer, or to deny him the wages that he gets for *not* quitting, is apt to resent the suggestion that those wages are in fact coercive. But were it once recognized that nearly all incomes are the result of private coercion, some with the help of the state, some without it, it would then be plain that to admit the coercive nature of the process would not be to condemn it. Yet popular thought undoubtedly does require special justification for any conduct, private or governmental, which is labeled "coercive," while it does not require such special justification for conduct to which it does not apply that term. Popular judgment of social problems, therefore, is apt to be distorted by the popular recognition or non-recognition of "coercion." Hence it may be worth while to run down into more detail the distinctions popularly made between coercion and other forms of influence over people's conduct.

"Threats" are often distinguished from "promises." If I tell a man I will do some positive act whose results will be unpleasant to him, unless he pays me money, and if as a result he pays it, I would usually be said to be collecting it by means of a "threat." If, on the other hand, I tell him I will do some positive act, whose results will be pleasant to him, *if* he pays me money, and he does, it would be said more commonly that I collected it by means of a "promise." Partly as a result of the moral connotation generally given to these terms, partly as its cause, the law more frequently interferes to prevent the doing of harmful acts than it does to compel the doing of helpful ones. Many (but not all) positive acts which are disadvantageous to others are forbidden; not so many positive acts that are advantageous to others are compelled. In other words, most torts and crimes consist of positive acts. Failure to help does not as a rule give rise to legal punishment or a right of action. Yet there are exceptions.

Certain acts not in themselves actionable at law, may give rise to legal duties to perform positive acts. If I start an automobile in motion, I have committed no legal wrong; but if subsequently I fail to perform the act of stopping it when "reasonable care" would require me to do so, the victim of my failure to act can recover damages for my non-performance. Again, and more significant, if I have promised to do certain things (with certain formalities or "consideration"), my act of promising was not a legal wrong. But if I subsequently fail to perform at the time specified, the promisee has a right of action for my failure to act. It is significant of the reluctance to admit the existence of positive legal duties, that in both cases language is used which makes my wrong conduct seem to consist of wrongful acts instead of wrongful *failure* to act. It is said, in the one case, that I "ran over" the victim, in the other that I "*committed* a breach of contract." Yet in neither was the wrong an act, but a failure to act: in the first case, my failure to make the requisite motions for stopping the car; in the second, my failure to perform the act promised.

Now suppose that instead of actually refraining from doing the acts which the law requires, I say to a man, "Pay me a thousand dollars, and when I meet you on the road walking I will use sufficient care to stop my car or to steer it so that it will not hit you; otherwise I will do nothing about it." Is that a "threat" or a "promise?" Or if I say, "Pay me a thousand dollars and I will perform the acts I have already contracted to perform"? I believe most people would call these statements threats rather than promises. Why? It may be partly due to the misleading language which speaks of the *act* of running over and the *act* of breaking a contract. But even were the fact recognized that payment were demanded as the price of *not abstaining*, I believe the demands would still be called threats. The reason, I believe, is partly because to abstain is contrary to legal duty, partly because it is adjudged to be contrary to moral duty. Popular speech in this case seems to apply the term coercion to demands made as a price of not violating a legal or moral duty, whether the duty consists of acting or of letting alone. But this criterion will not do, either.

If an act is called "coercion" when, and only when, one submits to demands in order to prevent another from violating a legal duty, then every legal system by very definition forbids the private exercise of coercion—it is not coercion unless the law does forbid it. And no action which the law forbids, and which could be used as a means of influencing another, can fail to be coercion—again by definition. Hence it would be idle to discuss whether any particular legal system forbids private coercion. And if an act is called "coercion" when, and only when, one submits to demands in order to prevent another from violating a *moral* duty, we get right back to the use of the term to express our conclusion as to the justifiability of the use of the pressure in question; with the ensuing circular reasoning of condemning an act because we have already designated it "coercive." One is likely, that is, to have a vague feeling against the use of a particular form of economic pressure, then to discover that this pressure is "coercive"—forgetting that coerciveness is not a ground for condemnation except when used in the sense of influence under pain of doing a morally unjustified act. And obviously to pronounce the pressure unjustified because it is an unjustified pressure is to reason in a circle. Hence, it seems better, in using the word "coercion," to use it in a sense which involves no moral judgment.

But popular feeling sometimes makes another distinction. If I plan to do an act or to leave something undone for no other purpose than to induce payment, that might be conceded to be a "threat." But if I plan to do a perfectly lawful act for my own good, or to abstain from working for another because I prefer to do something else with my time, then if I take payment for changing my course of conduct in either respect, it would not be called a threat. If a man pays me to keep out of a particular business, or if he pays me to work for him (when I am not legally bound by contract to do so), then it seems absurd to many to say that he paid me under threat of coercion—unless, in the first case, my sole motive in entering the business was to bring him to terms, and unless in the second I preferred working for him to any other occupation of my time, and my sole motive in abstaining was again to bring him to terms. For purposes of ordinary conversation, some other word than coercion may be preferred to describe payments made to a man who makes a sacrifice to "earn" them. But can a line be drawn? I believe the popular distinction along these lines is based on moral judgment. If a man gives up a job he likes, or if he works for another man, why shouldn't he be paid for it?—it will be asked. Perhaps he should. But unless the term "coercion" is applied only to conduct adjudged immoral, does the justifiability of the receipt of payment prevent it from being coercive?

If those distinctions are all invalid, then, which seek to remove the term "coercive" from some of the influences exerted to induce another to act against his will, it seems to follow that the income of each person in the community depends on the relative strength of his power of coercion, offensive and defensive. In fact it appears that what Mr. Carver calls the "productivity" of each factor means no more nor less than this coercive power. It is measured not by what one actually *is* producing, which could not be determined in the case of joint production, but by the extent to which production would fall off if one left and if the marginal laborer were put in his place—by the extent, that is, to which the execution of his threat of withdrawal would damage the employer. Not only does the distribution of income depend on this mutual coercion; so also does the distribution of that power to exert further compulsion which accompanies the management of an industry. Some extremely interesting suggestions of the likelihood of control by capitalists, cooperative buyers, cooperative sellers and laborers are to be found [in Mr. Carver's work.] This power is frequently highly centralized, with the result that the worker is frequently deprived, during working hours and even beyond, of all choice over his own activities.

To take this control by law from the owner of the plant and to vest it in public officials or in a guild or in a union organization elected by the workers would neither add to nor subtract from the constraint which is exercised with the aid of the government. It would merely transfer the constraining power to a different set of persons. It might result in greater or in less actual power of free initiative all round, but this sort of freedom is not to be confused with the "freedom" which means absence of governmental constraint. Mr. Carver himself points out that the governmental constraint involved in the maintenance of traffic police results in giving the average individual *greater* "freedom of movement." But "freedom of movement" does not mean freedom from governmental constraint, or even from constraint by private individuals. It means freedom from physical obstruction—in other words, greater physical *power* to move. Whether in other cases, too, physical power to exercise one's will is enhanced by a certain amount of legal restriction depends upon the peculiar facts of each case. Whether Mr. Carver's scheme of things would be more or less "free" (in the sense of giving people greater power to express their wills) than would a state of communism, depends largely on the economic results of communism respecting the character of factory work. Neither can be said to be any "freer" than the other in the sense that it involves less coercion on the part of other human beings, official or unofficial.

The distribution of income, to repeat, depends on the relative power of coercion which the different members of the community can exert against one another. Income is the price paid for not using one's coercive weapons. One of these weapons consists of the power to withhold one's labor. Another is the power to consume all that can be bought with one's lawful income instead of investing part of it. Another is the power to call on the government to lock up certain pieces of land or productive equipment. Still another is the power to decline to undertake an enterprise which may be attended with risk. By threatening to use these various weapons, one gets (with or without sacrifice) an income in the form of wages, interest, rent or profits. The resulting distribution is very far from being equal, and the inequalities are very far from corresponding to needs or to sacrifice. Most radical movements have as at least one of their aims the reduction of these inequalities, and the bringing of them into closer conformity with needs or sacrifices. Professor Carver has the same aim. He would accomplish it, however, primarily, not by altering the legal arrangements under which the various weapons are allotted, but by altering the effectiveness of the weapons. In explaining the distribution of wealth "our first problem," he says, is "to study the market value of each factor, or agent, of production in order to find out why the seller of each factor gets a large or a small share." (The study of the legal arrangements by which the seller of each comes to have control over that particular factor does not interest him.) . . .

MORRIS R. COHEN

"Property and Sovereignty"

(1927)

Property and sovereignty, as every student knows, belong to entirely different branches of the law. Sovereignty is a concept of political or public law and property belongs to civil or private law. This distinction between public and private law is a fixed feature of our law-school curriculum. It was expressed with characteristic 18th century neatness and clarity by Montesquieu, when he said that by political laws we acquire liberty and by civil law property, and that we must not apply the principles of one to the other. Montesquieu's view that political laws must in no way retrench on private property because no public good is greater than the maintenance of private property, was echoed by Blackstone and became the basis of legal thought in America. Though Austin, with his usual prolix and near-sighted sincerity, managed to throw some serious doubts on this classical distinction, it has continued to be regarded as one of the fixed divisions of the jural field. In the second volume of his *Genossenschaftsrecht* the learned Gierke treated us to some very interesting speculations as to how the Teutons became the founders of public law just as the Romans were the founders of private law. But in later years he somewhat softened this sharp distinction, and common law lawyers are inclined rather to regard the Roman system as giving more weight to public than to private law.

The distinction between property and sovereignty is generally identified with the Roman discrimination between *dominium,* the rule over things by the individual, and *imperium,* the rule over all individuals by the prince. Like other Roman distinctions, this has been regarded as absolutely fixed in the nature of things. But early Teutonic Law, the law of the Anglo-Saxons, Franks, Visigoths, Lombards and other tribes, makes no such distinction; and the state long continued to be the prince's estate so that even in the 18th century the Prince of Hesse could sell his subjects as soldiers to the King of England. The essence of feudal law— a system not confined to medieval Europe—is the inseparable connection between land tenure and personal homage involving often rather menial services on the part of the tenant and always genuine sovereignty by the landlord.

The feudal baron had, for instance, the right to determine the marriage of the ward, as well as the right to nominate the priest; and the great importance of the former as a real property right is amply attested in *Magna Carta* and in the *Statute Quia Emptores*. Likewise was the administration of justice in the baron's court an incident of land ownership; and if, unlike the French up to the Revolution, the English did not regard the office of judge as a revenue-producing incident of seigniorage to be sold in the open market (as Army Commissions were up to the time of Gladstone) the local squire did in fact continue to act as Justice of the Peace. Ownership of the land and local political sovereignty were inseparable.

Can we dismiss all this with the simple exclamation that all this is medieval and we have long outgrown it?

Well, right before our eyes the Law of Property Act of 1925 is sweeping away substantial remains of the complicated feudal Land Laws of England, by abolishing the difference between the descent of real and that of personal property, and by abolishing all legal (though not equitable) estates intermediate between leaseholds and fees simple absolute. These remains of feudalism have not been mere vestiges. They have played an important part in the national life of England. Their absurdities and indefensible abuses were pillaried with characteristic wit and learning by the peerless Maitland. The same thing had been done most judiciously by Joshua Williams, the teacher of several generations of English lawyers brought up on the seventeenth editions of his great text book on Real Property Law. Yet these and similar efforts made no impression on the actual law. What these great men did not see with sufficient clearness, was that back of the complicated law of settlement, fee-tails, copyhold estates, of the heir-at-law, of the postponement of women, and other feudal incidents, there was a great and well founded fear that by simplifying and modernizing the real property law of England the land might become more marketable. Once land becomes fully marketable it can no longer be counted on to remain in the hands of the landed aristocratic families; and this means the passing of their political power and the end of their control over the destinies of the British Empire. For if American experience has demonstrated anything, it is that the continued leadership by great families cannot be as well founded on a money as on a land economy. The same kind of talent which enables Jay Gould to acquire dominion over certain railroads enables Mr. Harriman to take it away from his sons. From the point of view of an established land economy, a money economy thus seems a state of perpetual war instead of a social order where son succeeds father. The motto that a career should be open to talent thus seems a justification of anarchy, just as the election of rulers (kings or priests) seems an anarchic procedure to those used to the regular succession of father by son.

That which was hidden from Maitland, Joshua Williams, and the other great ones, was revealed to a Welsh solicitor who in the budget of 1910 proposed to tax the land so as to force it on the market. The radically revolutionary character of this proposal was at once recognized in England. It was bitterly fought by all those who treasured what had remained of the old English aristocratic rule. When this budget finally passed, the basis of the old real property law and the effective power of the House of Lords was gone. The Legislation of 1925–26 was thus a final completion in the realm of private law of the revolution which was fought in 1910 in the forum of public law, i.e., in the field of taxation and the power of the House of Lords.

As the terms "medievalism" and "feudalism" have become with us terms of opprobrium, we are apt to think that only unenlightened selfishness has up to recently prevented English land law from cutting its medieval moorings and embarking on the sea of purely money or commercial economy. This light-hearted judgment, however, may be somewhat sobered by reflection on a second recent event—the Supreme Court decision on the Minimum Wage Law.[1] Without passing judgment at this point on the soundness of the reasoning, whereby the majority reached its decision, the result may still fairly be characterised as a high water mark of law in a purely money or commercial economy. For by that decision private monetary interests receive precedence over the sovereign duty of the state to maintain decent standards of living.

The state, which has an undisputed right to prohibit contracts against public morals or public policy, is here declared to have no right to prohibit contracts under which many receive wages less than the minimum of subsistence, so that if they are not the objects of humiliating public or private charity, they become centres of the physical and moral evils that result from systematic underfeeding and degraded standards of life. Let me repeat I do not wish here to argue the merits or demerits of the minimum wage decision. Much less am I concerned with any quixotic attempt to urge England to go back to medievalism. But the two events together show in strong relief how recent and in the main exceptional is the extreme position of the *laissez faire* doctrine, which according to the insinuation of Justice Holmes, has led the Supreme Court to read Herbert Spencer's extreme individualism into the 14th Amendment, and according to others, has enacted Cain's motto, "Am I my brother's keeper" as the supreme law of industry. Dean Pound has shown that in making a property right out of the freedom to contract, the Supreme Court has stretched the meaning of the term property to include what it has never before signified in the law or jurisprudence of any civilized country. But whether this extension is justified or not, it certainly means the passing of a certain domain of sovereignty from the state to the private employer of labor, who now has the absolute right to discharge and threaten to discharge any employee who wants to join a trade union and the absolute right to pay a wage which is injurious to a basic social interest.

It may be that economic forces will themselves correct the abuse which the Supreme Court does not allow the state to remove directly, that economic forces will eliminate parasitic industries which do not pay the minimum of subsistence, because such industries are not as economically efficient and profitable as those that pay higher wages. It was similarly argued that slavery was bound to disappear on account of its economic inefficiency. Meanwhile, however, the sovereignty of the state is limited by the manner in which the courts interpret the term "property" in the 5th and 14th amendment to the Federal Constitution and in the bills of rights in our state constitutions. This makes it imperative for us to consider the nature of private property with reference to the sovereign power of the state to look after the general welfare. A dispassionate scientific study of this requires an examination of the nature of property, its justification, and the ultimate meaning of the policies based on it.

Property as Power

Anyone who frees himself from the crudest materialism readily recognizes that as a legal term property denotes not material things but certain rights. In the world of nature apart from more or less organized society, there are things but clearly no property rights.

Further reflection shows that a property right is not to be identified with the fact of physical possession. Whatever technical definition of property we may prefer, we must recognize that a property right is a relation not between an owner and a thing, but between the owner and other individuals in reference to things. A right is always against one or more individuals. This becomes unmistakably clear if we take specifically modern forms of property such as franchises, patents, good will, etc., which constitute such a large part of the capitalized assets of our industrial and commercial enterprises.

The classical view of property as a right over things resolves it into component rights such as the *jus utendi, jus disponendi,* etc. But the essence of private property is always the right to exclude others. The law does not guarantee me the physical or social ability of actually using what it calls mine. By public regulations it may indirectly aid me by removing certain general hindrances to the enjoyment of property. But the law of property helps me directly only to exclude others from using the things which it assigns to me. If then somebody else wants to use the food, the house, the land, or the plow which the law calls mine, he has to get my consent. To the extent that these things are necessary to the life of my neighbor, the law thus confers on me a power, limited but real, to make him do what I want. If Laban has the sole disposal of his daughters and his cattle, Jacob must serve him if he desires to possess them. In a regime where land is the principal source of obtaining a livelihood, he who has the legal right over the land receives homage and service from those who wish to live on it.

The character of property as sovereign power compelling service and obedience may be obscured for us in a commercial economy by the fiction of the so-called labor contract as a free bargain and by the frequency with which service is rendered indirectly through a money payment. But not only is there actually little freedom to bargain on the part of the steel worker or miner who needs a job, but in some cases the medieval subject had as much power to bargain when he accepted the sovereignty of his lord. Today I do not directly serve my landlord if I wish to live in the city with a roof over my head, but I must work for others to pay him rent with which he obtains the personal services of others. The money needed for purchasing things must for the vast majority be acquired by hard labor and disagreeable service to those to whom the law has accorded dominion over the things necessary for subsistence.

To a philosopher this is of course not at all an argument against private property. It may well be that compulsion in the economic as well as the political realm is necessary for civilized life. But we must not overlook the actual fact that dominion over things is also *imperium* over our fellow human beings.

The extent of the power over the life of others which the legal order confers on those called owners is not fully appreciated by those who think of the law as merely protecting men in their possession. Property law does more. It determines what men shall acquire. Thus, protecting the property rights of a landlord means giving him the right to collect rent, protecting the property of a railroad or a public service corporation means giving it the right to make certain charges. Hence the ownership of land and machinery, with the rights of drawing rent, interest, etc., determines the future distribution of the goods that will come into being—determines what share of such goods various individuals shall acquire. The average life of goods that are either consumable or used for production of other goods is very short. Hence a law that merely protected men in their possession and did not also regulate the acquisition of new goods would be of little use.

From this point of view it can readily be seen that when a court rules that a gas company is entitled to a return of 6% on its investment, it is not merely protecting property already possessed, it is also determining that a portion of the future social produce shall under certain conditions go to that company. Thus not only medieval landlords but the owners of all revenue-producing property are in fact granted by the law certain powers to tax the future social product. When to this power of taxation there is added the power to command the services of large numbers who are not economically independent, we have the essence of what historically has constituted political sovereignty.

Though the sovereign power possessed by the modern large property owners assumes a somewhat different form from that formerly possessed by the lord of the land, they are not less real and no less extensive. Thus the ancient lord had a limited power to control the modes of expenditure of his subjects by direct sumptuary legislation. The modern captain of industry and of finance has no such direct power himself, though his direct or indirect influence with the legislature may in that respect be considerable. But those who have the power to standardize and advertise certain products do determine what we may buy and use. We cannot well wear clothes except within lines decreed by their manufacturers, and our food is becoming more and more restricted to the kinds that are branded and standardized.

This power of the modern owner of capital to make us feel the necessity of buying more and more of his material goods (that may be more profitable to produce than economical to use) is a phenomenon of the utmost significance to the moral philosopher. The moral philosopher must also note that the modern captain of industry or finance exercises greater influence in setting the fashion of expenditure by his personal example. Between a landed aristocracy and their tenants, the difference is sharp and fixed, so that imitation of the former's mode of life by the latter is regarded as absurd and even immoral. In a money or commercial economy differences of income and mode of life are more gradual and readily hidden so that there is great pressure to engage in lavish expenditure in order to appear in a higher class than one's income really allows. Such expenditure may even advance one's business credit. This puts pressure not merely on ever greater expenditure but more specifically on expenditure for ostentation rather than for comfort. Though a landed aristocracy may be wasteful in keeping large tracts of land for hunting purposes, the need for discipline to keep in power compels the cultivation of a certain hardihood which the modern wealthy man can ignore. An aristocracy assured of its recognized superiority need not engage in the race of lavish expenditure regardless of enjoyment.

In addition to these indirect ways in which the wealthy few determine the mode of life of the many, there is the somewhat more direct mode which bankers and financiers exercise when they determine the flow of investment, *e.g.,* when they influence building operations by the amount that they will lend on mortgages. This power becomes explicit and obvious when a needy country has to borrow foreign capital to develop its resources.

I have already mentioned that the recognition of private property as a form of sovereignty is not itself an argument against it. Some form of government we must always have. For the most part men prefer to obey and let others take the trouble to think out rules, regulations and orders. That is why we are always setting up authorities; and when we cannot find any we write to the newspaper as the final arbiter. While, however, government is a necessity, not all forms of it are of equal value. At any rate it is necessary to apply to the law of property all those considerations of social ethics and enlightened public policy which ought to be brought to the discussion of any just form of government.

LOUIS L. JAFFE

"Law Making by Private Groups"

(1937)

The historical school [of jurisprudence] attacked the concept that law was in any sense a creation of the State. Law, it maintained, was developed out of the genius of the race and merely applied by judges. We shall not rush to the defense of that thesis. It is, however, important here that custom has played an important role in determining the content of our property and commercial law. It may be answered that custom has no force until it is declared by a court to be the law. But whatever may be the preferred statement, it is the fact that the rights of the parties to the litigation are fixed by the custom as formed prior to decision. In the 16th and 17th centuries the common-law courts adopted wholesale the customs and usages of merchants, at first only in matters between merchants and later in any mercantile transaction. Holdsworth says of the law merchant: "That the usages and practice of the merchants themselves were the main source of the law is clear from the literature on the subject." The common-law courts acted chiefly on the evidence adduced before them as to the contents of the commercial custom. Nor has this process of incorporation entirely ceased. In *Goodwin* v. *Robarts,* for example, the question arose whether a certificate entitling the holder to a bond was negotiable. Benjamin argued that it was not negotiable within any existing principle of the common law or law merchant. Cockburn said of this argument that "it is founded on the view that the law merchant... is fixed and stereotyped." He then demonstrated that the courts had over a long period consistently, with the exception of the irritable Lord Holt, expanded the concept of negotiability in accordance with the prevalent view of the merchants. "Usage, adopted by the Courts, having been thus the origin of the whole of the so-called law merchant as to negotiable securities, what is there to prevent our acting upon the principle acted upon by our predecessors?"

Of considerable significance is the use made by courts in industrial negligence and compensation cases of the standards which have been worked out by the predominant opinion and practice of the industry itself. These standards are not, of course, directly binding on those who do not

Reprinted from the *Harvard Law Review,* vol. 51 (1937), pp. 212–21, by permission.

follow them but they are persuasive, often controlling evidence of what will be demanded of those who engage in the industry.

In creating custom men create the stuff of law. To be sure, the process differs in significant respects from the conscious creation and imposition of law in a moment of time. Custom evolves through a protracted period of becoming, and its quality as custom depends on its acceptance among a large number of the group concerned; essentially it is noncontroversial. It must, furthermore, be pronounced by a court to be "reasonable" and conformable to the general law. But this pushes the antithesis (admittedly this analogy is suggestive rather than persuasive) to its extreme limit. Much legislation is in large part an authoritative statement of what has been developed outside of the law and fragmentarily within the law. The industrial codes were based, in part, on practices worked out over a period of time by the trade associations. Under the Agricultural Adjustment Act there was promulgated an elaborate and complex system of marketing milk; in many respects this system represented pre-existing practice. In *Borden's Farm Products Company* v. *Ten Eyck,* a price differential in a New York statute in favor of small distributors of milk was attacked as an arbitrary and unreasonable discrimination. The Court upheld the classification relying chiefly on the fact that it had existed as trade and market custom prior to the legislation. Custom, thus, gave content to "reasonableness" and in consequence endowed the very law with that super-validity called "constitutionality."

But more important than custom is the power that men exercise over others through the protection given by the law to property and contract. Professor Morris Cohen has argued that under the influence of laissez-faire doctrine the state has relinquished to the individual the "sovereign" function of laying down the rules which govern society. It was once the exclusive province of the state to fix the prices of wages and commodities. This power was then given to the individual owner as well. And then by one of the most amazing *coups d'état* in history, the Supreme Court of the United States, under the aegis of the Fourteenth Amendment, held that this power resided exclusively in the individual. Professor Cohen says of these decisions: "Dean Pound has shown that in making a property right out of the freedom to contract, the Supreme Court has stretched the meaning of the term 'property' to include what it has never before signified in the law or jurisprudence of any civilized country. But whether this extension be justified or not, it certainly means the passing of a certain domain of Sovereignty from the state to the private employer of labour, who now has the absolute right to discharge and threaten to discharge any employee who wants to join a trade union, and the absolute right to pay a wage that is injurious to a basic social interest."

It may be thought that this suggestion is irrelevant or deliberately perverse and provocative in that it deals with economic rather than legal effects, or that it is within the law only insofar as there is consent by the parties to the application of the force of the law. In the example given above by Professor Cohen it would be said that he takes the economic substance of the agreement for its form as law, and thus confuses its quality as law with its quality in other contexts. But it is not the presumably consenting parties alone whose legal position is affected by the transaction. Consider, for example, the enormous developments of the apparently innocent doctrine of *Lumley* v. *Gye*. That doctrine makes it a tort for a third party to interfere with the performance of a contract. Thus, *pro tanto,* the contract is a rule of substance for all the world. Does that seem a trivial and unworthy reflexion in the light of our context? In itself it may be, yet the full ripe fruit of the doctrine in, let us say, the *Hitchman* case shows its significance. A coal company employs miners under a purely day to day arrangement. At the time of the hiring, the coal company states that during such employment the miner shall not be a member of a union. Upon this basis, the Supreme Court decides that *no one,* however legitimate his economic interest, can attempt to induce these employees to leave the coal company's employ or to join a union. The coal company determines the substance of these arrangements; the Court provides the sanctions.

Very recently, the New York Court of Appeals has become aware of the idea that the power of excluding by force of contract becomes equivalent to the making of law. In the last two or three years a considerable number of states have passed so-called "Fair Trade Acts." These Acts permit the producer of a commodity bearing a trade-mark to establish by contract with the initial vendee a resale price. Everyone thereafter coming into the possession of this article is forbidden "wilfully and knowingly" to sell the article at less than the resale price so fixed, though the possessor may have had no dealings with the parties to the contract. The original contract thus establishes a rule as to the chattel binding on all into whose hands it thereafter comes. Such an arrangement resembles in its effect the powers given to an original vendor of real property to impose restrictions on its use in the hands of subsequent purchasers. That doctrine, however, has been very little applied to chattels. Furthermore, the original contract for a resale price has been held to violate the federal antitrust laws and certain comparable state laws. Thus, the power to attach such restrictions to chattels did not in many jurisdictions previously exist because of reasons of policy, statutory and judicial. The legislature now confers that power, a power not substantially different in kind from others possessed by private persons. In holding the act unconstitutional, the New York Court of Appeals argues that the legislature could not fix the resale price of a book, a fortiori a private person cannot do so. This syllogism reverses an order of ideas which has prevailed since freedom of contract found sanctuary in the Fourteenth Amendment. The courts have argued again and again that it is a very law of nature that private parties have the power to make their own prices and *consequently,* the legislature has not that power. This dramatic legislative expression—and extension—of that law of nature has jarred the court of appeals into a new vision of its significance. Not so, the Supreme Court of the United States: the Supreme Courts of Illinois and California having upheld such laws, it affirmed them as in no way violating the Fourteenth Amendment. It found the rule of the legislation to be a proper analogue of the doctrine of equitable servitudes and a justified extension of the concept of legal protection of the property in a trade-mark. Referred to its own many decisions holding legislative price-fixing unconstitutional, it replied that "they constitute no authority for holding that prices in respect of 'identified goods' may not be fixed under legislative leave by contract between the parties." In the light of this demonstration, the New York Court of Appeals has reversed itself and returned to the old ways. The Fair Trade Acts and the decisions under them have this dual significance. They indicate the power over the conduct of others which the legislature is prepared to give to the owners of property; they furnish another proof of the extent to which the courts will tolerate the grant of such power where it is attached to contract and property and may be considered as growing out of the basic or "natural" property in things.

Thus property (of which contract and the right to contract, is an instance) equips the possessor with great powers of exclusion—enforced or sanctioned by the law—not in any way depending on consent, and this power to exclude is a source of regulating others' conduct, either as it prescribes complete exclusion or participation on terms. Under ordinary circumstances the fact is obscured, but monopolies in their many forms make it more palpable. Professor Robert Hale in an article on sanctions has pointed out that the exclusion of the negro in the South from inns, theatres, public places is a full-fledged regime of law with the private owners of property laying down the terms and the courts providing the sanctions, the principal one of which is the action of trespass. By this method these states have eluded the prohibition of the Fourteenth Amendment against the passage of discriminatory laws. But the line is very fine between restrictions based on the power given by the common law to exclude and an act of the legislature directly giving the power. Dissenting in the Civil Rights Cases, Mr. Justice Harlan said: "In every material sense applicable to the practical enforcement of the Fourteenth Amendment, railroad corporations, keepers of inns, and managers of places of public amusement are agents or instrumentalities of the State, because they are charged with duties to the public, and are amenable, in respect of their duties and functions, to governmental regulation. . . . that race is left (under the decision), in respect of the civil rights in question, practically at the mercy of corporations and individuals wielding power under the States."

Perhaps it is not always remembered that in days past public utilities received by franchise not only the power of operation but the power to fix rates. To be sure these rates must be "reasonable" and could be attacked in the courts. But so may the rates set by a legislature. They are neither of them no less effective rules binding on the whole public unless and until set aside on grounds of *ultra vires*. An Alabama statute authorized a street car company to make regulations concerning the use of transfers and made violations of these rules criminal. A majority of the court held it constitutional saying: "The right to make reasonable rules by street car companies . . . *exists independent of the act,* and the authority thereby given is not the delegation of authority to legislate."

Finally let us consider briefly the law of so-called voluntary associations. The law permits these associations to make their own rules with respect to admission and to rights and duties of members. The courts exercise a supervisory jurisdiction sometimes construing the rules, sometimes setting them aside. It will be said that here again we are in the realm of contract. But, if, for example, a plumbers' union has a closed shop agreement with all the builders in a certain area—and such agreements have been held valid under common law and presumably do not violate the Fourteenth Amendment—a person desiring to be a plumber has no choice but to enter the union and abide by the rules of the association and of the closed shop agreement. Indeed a man may be completely barred from a trade; it has not been uncommon in American history for powerful labor unions to bar negroes from membership and so from work. Recently a court has warned that a union will not be permitted to picket for a closed shop if it bars negroes; and the new Pennsylvania statute protecting labor in its right to organize (and realizing how greatly this protection will increase the power of unions) excludes from its definition of "labor organization" those which practice racial exclusion. A stockbroker must abide by the rules of the stock exchange. And, in England, lawyers must petition the bar for entrance and abide by its rules. It is no answer that in all these cases a person may choose not to enter the field. That is true of every branch of economic endeavor. And it has been laid down as a constitutional principle that a man has a "right" to enter any field for which he is qualified by proper law. Political parties are voluntary associations; however, so charged with public interest is the function of nomination for public office that the nominations, by large parties at least, must be in the form of public elections in manner prescribed by law. Yet in Texas where nomination by the Democratic party is equivalent to election that party has been permitted to bar negroes from membership and so, in effect, from the franchise. And the Supreme Court of the United States has held that the result does not constitute a deprivation by the state of the franchise because there has been no state action.

In sum, the great complexes of property and contract which constitute our modern industrial machine, the monopolistic associations of capital, labor, and the professions which operate it, exert under the forms and sanctions of law enormous powers of determining the substance of economic and social arrangement, in large part irrespective of the will of particular individuals. Here it is not the purpose to criticize that fact, but to show how pervasive it is. Participation in law-making by private groups under explicit statutory "delegation" does not stand then in absolute contradiction to the traditional process and conditions of law-making; it is not incompatible with the conception of law. It exposes and brings into the open, it institutionalizes a factor in law-making that we have, eagerly in fact, attempted to obscure. I do not deny that in the common law this factor operates less directly and on a more restricted scale. It tends to. approach compulsion only where by reason of economic force or special law it is linked with monopoly or can act upon persons of inferior economic power, whereas the "delegation" supplies this compulsion universally. But it does not follow that the latter is necessarily more oppressive. Tolerated, covert monopolies—power exercised indirectly—may be much more difficult to attack or to ameliorate than the edicts of majorities arrived at openly and according to the forms of law. It is a question of circumstance in each case, and without forgetting the important differences in form and in substance between the phenomena I have discussed and [more overt "delegations" of legislative power], I think that there are illuminating resemblances. . . .

M. Witmark & Sons v. Fred Fisher Music Co.

125 F.2d 949 (Court of Appeals for the Second Circuit 1942)

[The 1909 Copyright Act provided that, at the expiration of the twenty-eight year term of a copyright, "the author . . . if still living, or the widow, widower, or children of the author if the author be not living, or if such author, widow, widower, or children be not living, then the author's executors or, in the absence of a will, his next of kin shall be entitled to a renewal and extension of the copyright . . . for a further term of twenty-eight years." The issue in this case was whether an assignment by an author of his "expectancy" of the right to renew a copyright in the future is enforceable.

In 1917, George Graff, Jr., for $1,600 assigned to M. Witmark & Sons his right to renew the copyrights on 66 songs (among them "When Irish Eyes Are Smiling"). In 1939 (the twenty-eighth year of the copyrights), Witmark applied for the renewal thereof. Graff responded by applying for a renewal of the copyrights himself, and then assigned this renewal to Fred Fisher Music Company. When the latter threatened to publish one of the songs, Witmark brought suit, seeking an injunction, accounting, and damages. The District Court granted the plaintiff's motion for an injunction pendente lite.

In an opinion written by Judge Clark, the Second Circuit affirmed, holding that assignments of this sort were valid and enforceable. Excerpts from the dissenting opinion of Judge Jerome Frank follow.—Ed]

In 1917, when the contract was made, the plaintiff was a successful publisher, and the defendant Graff, an author or lyricist. It is admitted on this record that Graff was then "in desperate financial straits." By that agreement, Graff (a) released plaintiff from the obligation, existing under an earlier agreement, to pay to defendant, over a considerable future period, annual royalties, on a group of some seventy songs, which royalties "had amounted in previous years to as much as $5,000 annually"; and (b) contracted to give plaintiff his personal contingent rights to renew the copyrights on those seventy songs, if ever those rights should later ripen, i.e., if Graff should live twenty-two years longer, until 1939. The consideration was a lump payment to Graff of $1,600. The released royalties alone were almost certain, in a short period, to equal the entire consideration of $1,600; on that basis, nothing was actually received for the renewal rights. But even if we assume that nothing was paid for the released royalties and the entire $1,600 was paid for the renewal rights, then, as there were seventy songs, the amount paid for the renewal right to the particular song involved in this suit was one-seventieth of $1,600 or about $23. The right to renew a copyright twenty-two years later—a right which on no assumption could have any worth to the purchaser unless the author lived for twenty-two years more—was, of course, highly speculative. The speculation has proved immensely valuable for the plaintiff.[1]

In considering those facts, we should take judicial notice of the economic capacities and business acumen of most authors. In ascertaining that certain persons, because "often under economic compulsion," constituted a "necessitous class," our present Chief Justice in 1928, used, judicially, off-the-record knowledge which no casual inquiry would elicit—such as the contents of a report by the City Club of New York, of the Proceedings of the Association of Governmental Labor Officials, and the like.

We need not go nearly so far here. We need only take judicial notice of that which every schoolboy knows—that, usually, with a few notable exceptions (such as W. Shakespeare and G. B. Shaw), authors are hopelessly inept in business transactions and that lyricists, like the defendant Graff, often sell their songs "for a song."

Here, then, is a case where (a) the defendant was an author, one of a class of persons notoriously inexperienced in business, and the particular author was actually, at the time, in desperate financial straits, while the plaintiff was a successful and experienced publisher; (b) the property contracted for was of such a character that, when the contract was made, "neither party could know even approximately the value," so that "it was a bargain made in the dark"; and (c) the consideration was a very small sum.

That is not the kind of contract which equity will specifically enforce. Although Chancellor Kent, in a well-reasoned early case, *Seymour* v. *Delancey,* 6 Johns. Ch., N.Y., 222, concluded that inadequacy of consideration alone would bar specific performance of a contract, his views were rejected on appeal by a bare majority, 3 Cow., N.Y., 445, in what became the leading American case. More recently, however, there has been a growing tendency to adopt Chancellor Kent's view. But we need not rely on such authorities, for it is well-established that specific performance will be denied where, in addition to inadequate consideration, other factors contribute to the inequity of the bargain. Among the factors to be considered are lack of advice by one contracting party, differences in business experience or information, especially if an improvident contract is the result.

Where a small lump sum consideration is coupled with the sale by an inexperienced seller of property highly problematic in value, equity will deny relief. *Marks* v. *Gates,* 9 Cir., 154 F. 481. In *Marks* v. *Gates,* supra, the plaintiff asked for specific performance of a contract by which the defendant agreed to convey to him a twenty per cent interest in any property he should acquire in the Territory of Alaska. The consideration was $1,000 in cash, and the cancellation of a debt of $11,225. Within two years, the defendant had acquired certain mining properties, worth more than $750,000. In denying specific performance, the Circuit Court of Appeals for the Ninth Circuit said that the contract bound the defendant to convey "property of which neither party could know even approximately the value. It was a bargain made in the dark. . . . Where the consideration is so grossly inadequate as it is in the present case, and the contract is made without any knowledge at the time of its making on the part of either of the parties thereto of the nature of the property to be affected thereby, or of its value, no equitable principle is violated if specific performance is denied, and the parties are left to their legal remedies, if any they have."

For the foregoing reasons, the order for an interlocutory injunction should be reversed.[2] . . .

[Frank then argued at length that the legislative history also supported the proposition there should be "no enforcement, under the Copyright Act of 1909, of a contract for the sale of an author's renewal option if made prior to the date when the author is himself able to exercise that option."]

The chief prop of the statutory interpretation adopted by the majority opinion is that our society rests on the theory that men should have the greatest possible liberty to make such contracts as they please. I agree that that has, for long and, on the whole, desirably, been, in general, the American attitude. But while, during a part of the 19th century, the devotion to that theory was peculiarly intense, there have been in our history changes in that intensity, as this court has candidly recognized several times within recent weeks. Thus one manifestation of the most extreme enthusiasm for "liberty of contract" was the notion that courts must never depart from "the intention of the parties" to a contract. Yet our court, about a month ago, frankly confessed that that idea was a pious fiction, saying, in an opinion written by Judge Clark, that there had been much confusion in judicial statements concerning "implied" negative covenants and adding: "One may perhaps conclude that in large measure this confusion arises out of the reluctance of courts to admit that they were to a considerable extent 'remaking' a contract . . . where it seemed necessary and appropriate so to do. 'Intention of the parties' is a good formula by which to square doctrine with result. That this is true has long been an open secret." *Parev Products Co., Inc.,* v. *I.*

Rokeach & Sons, Inc., 2 Cir., 124 F.2d 147, 149. And our court has stated that, to the consensual act of the parties in entering into contracts, the courts have attached many obligations which were not in the minds of the parties, that a contract creates a status which imposes such obligations because of considerations of policy.

Consequently, it is surprising that my colleagues, uncharacteristically, in this particular case interpret the statute as if, today, laissez-faire were still in fullest bloom—as if there were still so strong a presumption against any and all restrictions on the freest possible bargaining that only the plainest language can overcome it, so that the desire of Congress to clog alienability of an author's rights, in order to protect him, must be disregarded unless that desire is set forth in wording as precise as that found in a general release.

Such was, to be sure, the attitude of the courts during the latter part of the 19th century. As Dean Pound has said, it was then "taken for gospel that law was moving and must move in the direction of abstract individual self-determination by free control.... The judges were imbued with a genuine faith in the ... doctrine of progress from status to contract. Hence it seemed to them that the constitutional requirement of due process was violated by legislative attempts to restore status and restrict the contractual powers of free men by enacting that men of full age and sound mind in particular callings should not be able to make agreements which other men might make freely.... " This attitude resulted in "an inconsistency between the doctrine of progress from status to contract, as the last generation understood it, and the principles of equity which had developed in our law, especially in the seventeenth and eighteenth centuries. The state courts held for two decades that legislative imposition of contractual incapacities in the relation of employer and employee was arbitrary and hence unconstitutional. But there were existing incapacities with which they did not think of interfering. The surviving common law incapacities could be idealized as 'natural incapacities.' Usury laws were not so easy to explain. But courts said that there had been such laws from the beginnings of American legislation, and some, ignorant of English lawmaking, that they were immemorial and universal. In other words, they were familiar historically and hence reasonable. There remained equitable restrictions on free contract, the doctrine as to penalties, the refusal to allow the holder of a penal bond to recover more than the actual damages, the doctrine of redemption of mortgaged property after the condition had become absolute, the rule against clogging the equity of redemption, the rules as to sailors' contracts and sales by reversioners. An eighteenth century chancellor had explained these by saying that necessitous persons were not free. But the courts shrank from so recognizing the facts of industrial employment in the face of the abstract freedom which they had set up as an ideal. The best they could say was that the equitable incapacities also were historical. This amounted to holding that the legislature was unable to create new contractual incapacities; that the lines had been drawn forever in the seventeenth and eighteenth centuries and that no new type of disability could be recognized. Nor did it matter that the underlying principle of these new statutory disabilities was the same as that underlying the disabilities imposed by equity."

The theory of laissez-faire was that the state, the government, was not to interfere beyond a bare minimum. That such was not the actual practice, even when laissez-faire was in its zenith, has been brilliantly shown in the writings of Robert Hale, beginning in 1923.[3] His thesis may be paraphrased thus: In outward appearance, under let-alone-ism, the extensive use of state power is rejected. In fact, however, there is a transference of much of the State's power to individuals. The contracts they make (so far as they are lawful) are enforced and protected by the State through the orders of its courts and its sheriffs. More than that, the individual has a right to refuse to sell or use his property on any terms or except on his own terms. If someone else tries to make him sell or use it except on those terms, the State, through its courts and sheriffs, will protect him from such intrusions. Liberty to contract includes liberty not to contract as one pleases. And government backs up that liberty. Laissez-faire does not mean that the State has given up most of its "interferences," but that the State is used to "interfere" in new ways at the demand of individuals. The power of government is thus exercised, indirectly, by the individual to enforce his bargains and to punish those who try to make him bargain except as he chooses.[4] The Hale thesis involves some over-statement. But its dramatic challenge of the conventional thesis helps us to attain a new and valuable perspective. It serves to high-light the public interest in individual contracts. Because of it, we can better understand why, at no time, did let-alone-ism go so far as to obliterate all direct governmental interference with contracts; why, even in the hey-day of laissez-faire, there were retained such doctrines as the rule against perpetuities and the rules as to restraints on alienation, dower rights, spendthrift trusts, the voidability of infants' contracts, etc. Laissez-faire, in other words, meant a shift of emphasis; older attitudes were not killed off but merely submerged. Hale aids us to see the legitimacy of the State's now openly acknowledged interest and direct interference in many kinds of contracts. Nothing, it has been said, exceeds like excess. Laissez-faire went too far.

It is helpful to make an historical approach to the chief interpretative device employed by my colleagues. Their opinion, I note again, relies, in effect, on a supposed spirit of our institutions, tenaciously opposed to all restraints on freedom to contract, which, it is urged, must be read into all American legislation. To make that thesis applicable here, my colleagues must assume that that spirit was operative a century ago when the 1831 Copyright Act was enacted; for the 1909 Act, it is conceded, took over from the earlier statute the provisions which we are considering in the case now before us; accordingly the relevant "time spirit" is that of 1831. In purporting to find such a spirit, then and still operative, my colleagues are, I think, misreading history. Both they and many of those who have criticized views such as they have expressed[5] have made history too smooth, have oversimplified it: Even in the so-called period of laissez-faire, of course, as in almost any so-called "historical period," there were numerous currents and cross-currents, not a single drift in one direction. The casual observer sees only the current at the surface. And so with excessive laissez-faire: It was merely—and for a relatively short time—the surface current. In the early days of the Republic, mercantilism was still visibly powerful. Alexander Hamilton was certainly not wholly in the grip of that "old Adam"—Adam Smith. Mercantilist notions—and even medieval notions⁶—persisted throughout the 19th century in America, and in many matters made themselves felt. When the 1831 Copyright Act was enacted, whole-hog laissez-faire was not yet fashionable. However, the vocabulary of full-fledged let-alone-ism became the style with the average well-to-do "educated" American after the Civil War. For a span of years, the constricting vocabulary of ultra-let-alone-ism was fashionable with much of our judiciary. As is not seldom true, the judicial fashion was out of step with a budding popular fashion in words and thoughts outside the court houses. What the courts were saying was not necessarily an index of what Congress had in mind: We lawyers are too much inclined to take our history in legal capsules; we restrict our history reading too much to what we find in the law books, neglecting the fact that "there waft into the courts only occasional gusts in the varied and perpetually changing weather of . . . transactions" occurring in the outer world. "A climate cannot be delineated from a jar of captured raindrops." Even, however, in the courthouses, there are those who, not long after the Civil War, asserted their independence of the style in words and ideas, generally prevailing in the court-rooms. Chief Justice Waite was one of them. See *Munn* v. *Illinois,* 1877, 94 U.S. 113. *Holden* v. *Hardy,* 1898, 169 U.S. 366, and *Knoxville Iron Co.* v. *Harbison,* 1901, 183 U.S., are also impressive as signs that the judicial thought-ways were not constantly running towards one point in the compass. The subsequent tussle between opposing attitudes is disclosed in a series of dissenting opinions—with Holmes as leader of the dissenters—which, latterly, have become the majority doctrine.⁷ It will not do, then, to interpret the Congressional committee reports, either of 1831 or 1909, as if they were the words of men with but a single and inflexible thought as to the folly of ever interfering with contracts.

Excessive judicial worship of let-alone-ism began, then, to melt away in the 1920s and has disappeared in the decisions, during the last decade, of the Supreme Court. "Whatever may be one's own opinion about the wisdom of trying to save the ignorant and rash from folly it is a recognized power that is used in many ways," said the Court, in 1924, in *Dillingham* v. *McLaughlin,* 264 U.S. 370, 374, construing a New York statute. We are obliged no longer to hold that the power to prevent the free disposal of rights was exhausted in such non-statutory rulings, for instance, as that contracts by public officers, executors and receivers assigning their future earnings will not, on grounds of public policy, be enforced, or in the doctrine that equity will refuse to grant specific performance of improvident contracts. Indeed, we have been warned by a successful commercial

banker and by able economists that the passion for excessive liquidity—
the eagerness to make every kind of property or idea immediately convertible into cash—was one of the causes of the Great Depression which
began in 1929, and that, unless we do something to curb that zest for
instant monetization of everything, our profit economy may collapse.

The former judicial repugnance to any legislative interference with
free bargaining involved a blindness to the effects on the public—the
community—of the conduct of individuals. Lately, we have begun to see
that any business is "affected with a public interest," if the legislature so
decides. In reaching that conclusion, the courts have, once more, realized
that what one man does with his life often affects all the rest of us. If he
is infected by a disease, many others may be victimized. If he contracts
dire poverty, crime may result and a large group may suffer. And so it is
with free bargaining. For a contract may be something more than a private
affair of the contracting parties; it may vitally affect the interests of the
public. Once that was the prevailing view; in the medieval period, and for
a long time subsequently, it was taken for granted that there was an
overriding social or public aspect of individual trafficking. Cf. *Hume* v.
Moore-McCormack Lines, 2 Cir., 121 F.2d 336, 338. That emphasis in
England on the public obligations of private persons was, however exploited in the interests of dictatorial royal dynasts and, later, to benefit an
economic oligarchy. A revolt of enterprising individuals resulted. Their
slogans were laissez-faire and the natural rights of the individual. "As is
natural in all revolts, absolute claims on one side were met with absolute
denials on the other. Hence the theory of the natural rights of the individual
took not only an absolute but a negative form: men have *in*alienable rights,
the State must never interfere with private property, etc."[8] "In the fierce
fight against... numerous irrational, tyrannical and oppressive restraints
men jump to the conclusion that the absence of all restraint is a good in
itself and indeed the one absolute good."[9]

Recognition today of the unwisdom of excessive liquidity or excessive
individualism does not at all mean a commitment to rigidity, regimentation, or undue paternalism. Here, as almost everywhere in life, there is
need for intelligent compromise. "Most of the issues of human and social
relationships are not of the black-and-white variety." We should beware
of the either-or dogmatizers. It is unnecessary to make a hard-and-fast,
all-or-nothing, antithesis between complete formal individual freedom and
complete governmental guardianship for everyone. But it is necessary to
observe that individualism, if utterly unrestrained, becomes self-
devouring.[10]

"More and more," said Lord Macmillan in 1935, "the main issue in
political science has come to be—not whether the State should intervene
at all in the regulation of our daily lives but where the frontier line ought
most wisely to be drawn between the province of state activity and that
of individual enterprise. On all hands it is now recognized that the policy
of laissez-faire, which gave us no doubt our industrial and commercial

supremacy but also gave us our slums and many other attendant evils, must give place to a new regime. . . . We have traveled far since Tom Paine—that early champion of the people's rights—proclaimed that 'The more perfect civilization is, the less occasion it has for government,. . . . Sedgwick . . . recognized that . . . social legislation is essential to the preservation of the liberty of the individual. Such measures, he saw, may promote rather than diminish freedom."

When the philosophy of 100% individualism was in vogue, the courts often soft-pedalled such considerations. They devised and interpreted legal rules and read statutes under the influence of their own notions of public policy. That process may have been largely unconscious. But, as Mr. Justice Holmes often said, there was strong policy-making in those judicial decisions.[11] The judges who decided them also uttered verbal repudiations of judicial legislation.[12] But the demolition of the purposes of Congress, through stingy statutory interpretation, is the most emphatic kind of judicial legislation. Our job is, so far as possible, to enforce the aims of Congress. We should, in the instant case, carry out what Congress meant to achieve for the protection of authors in the Copyright Act, and should not carry out, without modification, the policy of the judicial legislation found in the judicial decisions of the let-alone-ist era.

It is of considerable interest to note some of the cases cited by the majority to support their assertion that the Copyright Act must be read in the light of an alleged strong policy, said to be embedded in our legal system, unfriendly to any "restriction on free assignability": (a) There is the citation of an Illinois decision declaring unconstitutional a statute regulating assignments of wages and salaries. *Massie* v. *Cessna,* 239 Ill. 352. To cite such a case indicates sympathy, which I doubt whether my colleagues entertain, with an attitude that such legislation, because it interferes with liberty of contract, is invalid; that attitude the United States Supreme Court has, in recent decades, flatly rejected. (b) The majority also cites our recent decision, In re *Barnett,* 2 Cir., 124 F.2d 1005 where, following early New York decisions (as we were obliged to do under *Erie R. Co.* v. *Tompkins,* 304 U.S. 64), we held that an assignment of an expectancy under a will is effective, and cannot be set aside by a trustee in bankruptcy or a judgment creditor; there was in that case no statutory declaration of a contrary policy, nor was it even suggested that the consideration for the bargain was inadequate. (c) My colleagues also cite what they themselves describe as "the unusual case" of *Kelly* v. *Kelly,* 11 Cal.2d 356, in which an interest under a spendthrift trust was allowed, by indirection, to be assigned.

It is important that the "property" here involved is a creature of statute and not a common law "right of property." In *Powell* v. *Head,* L.R. 12 Ch.D.(1879), 686, 688, it was argued that the part owner of a play could grant a license for its production without the consent of the other owners because, at common law, one tenant in common of a chattel has a right to use the chattel as he pleases. Jessel, M.R., rejected this argument, saying: "I am not at all inclined to extend the antiquated and barbarous doctrines, which have been set aside partly by the Legislature and partly by the Courts of Equity, to new rights created by statute, and which are of a character wholly different from the rights of property to which these ancient doctrines apply." Cf. Holmes, J., dissenting, in *Truax* v. *Corrigan*, 257 U.S. 312, 342.

We know today that legal recognition of differences between different types of persons is not incompatible with the concept of "equality before the law," intelligently interpreted. Hughes, C.J., in *Morehead* v. *People of New York ex rel. Tipaldo*, 298 U.S. 587, 627, and in *West Coast Hotel Co.* v. *Parrish*, 300 U.S. 379, 391. Protection for those unable adequately to protect themselves must be afforded by any civilized legal system.[13] And when Congress has, as in the case of copyrights, expressed such a policy, there is no reason why the courts should frustrate it. It has been held that a person included within the provisions of a Workmen's Compensation Act cannot validly contract himself out of the statute; courts have reached that result even when the statute did not prohibit such a contractual waiver of the benefits of the legislation. *Wass* v. *Bracker Construction Co.*, 185 Minn. 70. Here, where the Committee reports show the legislative intent to arrive at a similar limitation on free bargaining by an author, it is difficult for me to see why we should pay no respect to that intention.

I agree that the courts must not rewrite statutes and import into them what they think desirable when Congress has remained silent. But there is a marked difference between the silence of Congress and a statement of its purpose not expressed with complete nicety, a middle ground between Congress saying nothing and Congress shouting. The guiding principle was formulated as follows by Mr. Justice Holmes:

"We recognize that courts have been disinclined to extend statutes modifying the common law beyond the direct operation of the words used, and that at times this disinclination has been carried very far. But it seems to us that there may be statutes that need a different treatment.... The Legislature has the power to decide what the policy of the law shall be, and if it has intimated its will, however indirectly, that will should be recognized and obeyed. The major premise of the conclusion expressed in a statute, the change of policy that induces the enactment, may not be set out in terms, but it is not an adequate discharge of duty for courts to say: We see what you are driving at, but you have not said it, and therefore we shall go on as before."

Twice recently the Supreme Court has quoted that language with approval and applied that canon of interpretation. I believe it is our duty to do likewise. My colleagues say they are willing to abide by a Congressional policy against assignability of a contingent copyright renewal. I fear that they have just missed a real opportunity to do so.

5

Law and Organizational Society

Between the Civil War and World War I, three related developments transformed the American economy. First, the scale of economic organizations increased dramatically. Many private corporations grew to sizes that during the antebellum period would have been unimaginable. By 1904, 2000 firms (approximately 1 percent of the total number of businesses in the United States) produced annually 40 percent of the nation's industrial goods. The national markets for several products (for example, oil, tobacco, and sugar) were almost completely controlled by one or by a few corporations. Agriculture was undergoing a similar transformation. Mechanized "bonanza" farms, encompassing as much as 10,000 acres of land, were multiplying. And growing numbers of farmers were joining huge economic and political associations, like the Northern and Southern alliances, that promised to defend their interests.

To some extent, the growth of these organizations was attributable to the same forces that powered the industrial revolution in the United States. Improved transportation and communications systems (especially the establishment of a national railroad and telegraph system) and the rapid growth of the cities (fueled partly by immigration) increased sharply the number of consumers a firm could reach. Urbanization also produced convenient concentrations of skilled and unskilled labor. Technological innovations (like the Bessemer process and mechanical harvesters) necessitated or placed a premium on large factories and farms. Finally, a vastly expanded pool of capital—created by a high domestic savings rate reinforced by increased foreign investment and managed by a host of new financial intermediaries—made the formation of large enterprises feasible.[1]

To some extent, the trend was also attributable to the efforts of businessmen and their lawyers through cooperation and combination to increase the scope of their operations. Some of these initiatives were designed to achieve real savings—by taking advantage of economies of scale or by integrating "vertically" the various activities that contributed to the production and marketing of a product. Many, however, had no productive purpose or effect. Instead, businessmen were seeking to curb what they saw as ruinous competition and thereby to increase or preserve their profits.[2]

The changing responses of the state and national legal systems to the spectres of oligopoly and monopoly influenced the shape of the structures the businessmen built but, in the end, did not impede (indeed, may have accelerated) their growth. Initially, most of the combinations took the form of cartels—loose trade associations of independent firms designed to stabilize the firms' shares of particular markets and to reduce price competition. When these "gentlemen's agreements" proved both difficult to enforce and unpopular, businessmen began to form trusts, organizations that held the stock of and exerted some degree of control over groups of former competitors. When these in turn proved vulnerable to attack in the state courts, corporate counsel persuaded a few states (most notably New Jersey) to amend their statutes to permit one corporation to own the stock of another. These "holding companies" proved to have disadvantages of their own, however, especially after the turn of the century when the federal government under Presidents Roosevelt and Taft began to use the hitherto dormant Sherman Antitrust Act to attack them. The businessmen's response: abandon any pretense that their firms were autonomous; merge them. The attractions of this strategy were enhanced by a series of statutes permitting a majority of the shareholders of a corporation to authorize the sale of corporate assets. The net result was that, between 1898 and 1902, thousands of formerly autonomous corporations were combined into larger and more powerful companies.[3]

The second major trend was a transformation in the way businesses were structured. Until the Civil War, almost all firms in the United States were single-unit enterprises. The large majority performed one economic function (e.g., production, marketing, finance, or communication), handled one product, and operated in a relatively small geographic area. Enterprises of this sort and scale typically were owned and managed by small groups of entrepreneurs. By World War I, things had changed radically. Almost all of the dominant businesses were multi-unit enterprises, performing and coordinating many functions and encompassing many administrative offices. Most were owned by large groups of shareholders, few of whom participated in running the businesses. That role had been assumed by an entirely new and enormously influential class of economic actors—salaried, full-time senior and middle managers. The transfer of control from owners to managers altered the objectives of most businesses; managers typically had less interest in the maximization of current profits and more interest in the long-run stability and continued growth of the enterprises to which their careers were tied. In sum, family-based and finance capitalism had been largely displaced by the modern system of managerial capitalism.[4]

The most elusive but perhaps most important of the three dimensions of change was a dramatic increase in the complexity and interconnectedness, not simply of individual firms, but of the entire economic system. The expansion of national and then international markets and the maturation of the financial system made the fates of many economic actors turn upon forces they neither controlled nor understood. The collapse of an investment banking house might set off a series of business failures, which, in turn, would throw many thousands of employees out of work. A drop in the price of wheat in Europe would destroy the fortunes of thousands of Nebraska farmers. Especially after 1900, Americans sought to reduce their vulnerability to threats of these sorts through new forms of organization. Farmers, for example, delegated much of their power over the marketing of their goods to producers' cooperatives. Workers joined unions in ever growing numbers; despite the hostility of the courts and the often violent resistance of employers, fifteen percent of the nonagricultural work force was unionized by 1914. In short, economic change and the proliferation of large organizations bred both interdependence and insecurity, breeding, in turn, yet more organizations.[5]

One of the central themes of Legal Realism was the contention that traditional legal rules and institutions were not responding adequately to these fundamental changes in the structure of the American economy. This accusation took a variety of forms, three of which are illustrated in this chapter.

The first concerned the theory and standard of liability of the law of torts. Holmes, as usual, saw the issue before anyone else. In 1896, in his great dissent in the labor picketing case of *Vegelahn* v. *Guntner,* he clearly recognized the trends discussed above. "It is plain from the slightest consideration of practical affairs, or the most superficial reading of industrial history, that free competition means combinations. It seems to me futile to set our faces against this tendency. Whether beneficial on the whole, as I think it is, or detrimental, it is inevitable." Certainly if we accept combination on the part of capital, he argued, we ought to accept it on the part of labor. More specifically, we should not declare to be torts activities undertaken by labor unions in their "struggle for life" if we privilege analogous activities by businesses.

In his magnificent essay "The Path of the Law" (excerpted in Chapter 1), Holmes derived a different set of lessons from the rise to prominence of large economic organizations. The fact that most putative torts were now committed by "railroads, factories, and the like," he argued, means that, when deciding whether to make them actionable, we should take into account the advantages or disadvantages of forcing the general public to pay for the resultant losses through increased prices for the services and commodities generated by those businesses.[6]

This idea of entrepreneurial liability became a staple of Realist analyses of torts issues. For example, in the article reprinted below, Harold Laski invoked it to justify the vicarious liability of employers for the torts of their employees. The basis of modern workmen's compensation statutes, Laski contended, "is simply that the needs of the modern state require that the burden of loss of life, or personal injury in industry, shall be charged to the expenses of production, shall be borne, that is to say, by the employer." This and similar policy recommendations were merely manifestations, in Laski's view, of a broader theme. We live "in a world where individual enterprise is so largely replaced" by the growth of large corporations that "only a social interpretation of the law" could give recognition to these changes through "the promotion of social solidarity."

The second context in which the Realists insisted upon greater attention to the transformation of the economy concerned the institutions best situated to engage in lawmaking and the modes of reasoning those institutions should employ. A fine early expression of this theme may be found in the dissenting opinion of Justice Brandeis in *International News Service* v. *Associated Press.*[7] The case raised the question of whether a wire news service could treat its news as property sufficient to entitle it to an injunction against a competitor who "stole" its dispatches. While the "injustice" of the defendant's action was "obvious," Brandeis wrote, "to give relief against it would involve more than the application of existing rules of law to new facts. It would require the making of a new rule in analogy to existing ones." That, in turn, would require of the courts informational resources and analytical powers they did not possess. Traditional analogical reasoning had "generally prove[n] adequate" in bipolar lawsuits between private parties, Brandeis argued, because such suits typically involved only "private interests." "But with the increasing complexity of society, the public interest tends to become omnipresent; and the problems presented by new demands for justice cease to be simple. Then the creation or recognition by courts of a new private right may work serious injury to the general public." Controversies of the latter sort, he insisted, could be resolved sensibly only by a legislature or administrative agency.[8]

At the end of the Realist period, James Landis made similar arguments in defense of the enormous expansion of administrative regulation during the New Deal. In *The Administrative Process,* Landis catalogued fifty years of assaults on the idea that courts were institutionally, ideologically, or technically competent to promote justice or efficiency in economic regulation. To solve the typical controversy arising out of modern economic relations, he insisted, we need not "generalizations and principles drawn from the majestic authority of textbooks and cases," but "a 'practical' judgment which is based upon all the available considerations and which has in mind the most desirable and pragmatic method of solving the particular problem."

The last of the three lines of argument developed by the Legal Realists was an effort to reorient a longstanding debate among American judges and legal scholars concerning the nature and legal status of the private corporation. In 1880, most of the disputants had subscribed to the "contractualist" or "partnership" theory, which depicted a corporation as an aggregate of its individual shareholders, created by an elaborate network of private agreements. By 1920, this view had been largely displaced by the "natural entity" theory, which depicted the corporation as something greater than the sum of its parts, an "organic whole" possessing a "will," "personality," and set of rights of its own. This shift both facilitated and was sustained by a host of doctrinal reforms (most of them favorable to the growth of corporate power): abandonment of the "ultra vires" rule; erosion of the power of states to prevent "foreign corporations" from doing business within their boundaries; strengthening of the limitations on the liability of shareholders for corporate debts; and the reduction of impediments to the merger of corporations. By no means all issues had been resolved, however; at the start of the Realist period, the law reviews were still filled with articles trying to determine the true nature of the private corporation.[9]

The Realists sought to alter the terms of this debate. It was pointless, they insisted, to argue over such things as whether a corporation could fairly be described as a "person." Such abstractions were unhelpful partly because they were indeterminate. As John Dewey argued in the essay excerpted below, each of the extant theories of the corporation "has been used to serve the same ends, and each has been used to serve opposing ends." More importantly, the Realists contended, such inquiries deflected attention from the truly important questions: How do modern corporations operate? Who controls them? If their nominal owners are no longer effectively in charge of them, what sorts of government regulations could be implemented to ensure they behave in a fashion consistent with the public's interests? The best of the books to focus on issues of these sorts was Berle and Means' *The Modern Corporation and Private Property,* the opening pages of which are reprinted below.

The first two of the three themes introduced by the Realists have been highly influential. Much of the best contemporary scholarship in the field of torts is concerned with loss spreading and more generally with the need to take into account, when crafting standards of liability, the existence and structure of large organizations. Modern administrative law likewise incorporates many of the Realists' contentions regarding the need for dispute resolution systems better suited than the traditional lawsuit to accommodate a variety of public and private interests. The fate of third of the Realists' arguments is more complex. The lines of inquiry commended by Berle and Means are still being pursued by a number of scholars. By contrast, Dewey's insistence upon the indeterminacy of theories of the corporation has largely dropped from view. Perhaps it is just as well. In retrospect, Dewey's argument appears disturbingly insensitive to the power of abstract legal theories, once invested with meaning in specific historical contexts, to shape the content of particular legal doctrines and to influence the outcome of cases.[10]

Vegelahn v. *Guntner*

167 Mass. 92 (1896)

Allen, J. The principal question in this case is whether the defendants should be enjoined against maintaining the patrol. The report shows that, following upon a strike of the plaintiff's workmen, the defendants conspired to prevent him from getting workmen, and thereby to prevent him from carrying on his business, unless and until he should adopt a certain schedule of prices. The means adopted were persuasion and social pressure, threats of personal injury or unlawful harm conveyed to persons employed or seeking employment, and a patrol of two men in front of the plaintiff's factory, maintained from half past six in the morning till half past five in the afternoon, on one of the busiest streets of Boston. The number of men was greater at times, and at times showed some little disposition to stop the plaintiff's door. The patrol proper at times went further than simple advice, not obtruded beyond the point where the other person was willing to listen; and it was found that the patrol would probably be continued, if not enjoined. There was also some evidence of persuasion to break existing contracts.

The patrol was maintained as one of the means of carrying out the defendants' plan, and it was used in combination with social pressure, threats of personal injury or unlawful harm, and persuasion to break existing contracts. It was thus one means of intimidation indirectly to the plaintiff, and directly to persons actually employed, or seeking to be employed, by the plaintiff, and of rendering such employment unpleasant or intolerable to such persons. Such an act is an unlawful interference with the rights both of employer and of employed. An employer has a right to engage all persons who are willing to work for him, at such prices as may be mutually agreed upon; and persons employed or seeking employment have a corresponding right to enter into or remain in the employment of any person or corporation willing to employ them. These rights are secured by the Constitution itself. No one can lawfully interfere by force or intimidation to prevent employers or persons employed or wishing to be employed from the exercise of these rights. . . .

The defendants contend that these acts were justifiable, because they were only seeking to secure better wages for themselves by compelling the plaintiff to accept their schedule of wages. This motive or purpose does not justify maintaining a patrol in front of the plaintiff's premises, as a means of carrying out their conspiracy. A combination among persons merely to regulate their own conduct is within allowable competition, and is lawful, although others may be indirectly affected thereby. But a combination to do injurious acts expressly directed to another, by way of intimidation or constraint, either of himself or of persons employed or seeking to be employed by him, is outside of allowable competition, and is unlawful....

A question is also presented whether the court should enjoin such interference with persons in the employment of the plaintiff who are not bound by contract to remain with him, or with persons who are not under any existing contract, but who are seeking or intending to enter into his employment. A conspiracy to interfere with the plaintiff's business by means of threats and intimidation, and by maintaining a patrol in front of his premises in order to prevent persons from entering his employment, or in order to prevent persons who are in his employment from continuing therein, is unlawful, even though such persons are not bound by contract to enter into or to continue in his employment; and the injunction should not be so limited as to relate only to persons who are bound by existing contracts.

In the opinion of a majority of the court the injunction should be in the form originally issued. *So ordered.*

Holmes, J. I agree, whatever may be the law in the case of a single defendant that when a plaintiff proves that several persons have combined and conspired to injure his business, and have done acts producing that effect, he shows temporal damage and a cause of action, unless the facts disclose, or the defendants prove, some ground of excuse or justification. And I take it to be settled, and rightly settled, that doing that damage by combined persuasion is actionable, as well as doing it by falsehood or by force.

Nevertheless, in numberless instances the law warrants the intentional infliction of temporal damage because it regards it as justified. It is on the question of what shall amount to a justification, and more especially on the nature of the considerations which really determine or ought to determine the answer to that question, that judicial reasoning seems to me often to be inadequate. The true grounds of decision are considerations of policy and of social advantage, and it is vain to suppose that solutions can be attained merely by logic and the general propositions of law which nobody disputes. Propositions as to public policy rarely are unanimously accepted, and still more rarely, if ever, are capable of unanswerable proof. They require a special training to enable any one even to form an intelligent opinion about them. In the early stages of law, at least, they generally are acted on rather as inarticulate instincts than as definite ideas for which a rational defence is ready.

To illustrate what I have said in the last paragraph, it has been the law for centuries that a man may set up a business in a country town too small to support more than one, although he expects and intends thereby to ruin some one already there, and succeeds in his intent. In such a case he is not held to act "unlawfully and without justifiable cause."...The reason, of course, is that the doctrine generally has been accepted that free competition is worth more to society than it costs, and that on this ground the infliction of the damage is privileged. Yet even this proposition nowadays is disputed by a considerable body of persons, including many whose intelligence is not to be denied, little as we may agree with them.

I have chosen this illustration partly with reference to what I have to say next. It shows without the need of further authority that the policy of allowing free competition justifies the intentional inflicting of temporal damage, including the damage of interference with a man's business, by some means, when the damage is done not for its own sake, but as an instrumentality in reaching the end of victory in the battle of trade. In such a case it cannot matter whether the plaintiff is the only rival of the defendant, and so is aimed at specifically, or is one of a class all of whom are hit. The only debatable ground is the nature of the means by which such damage may be inflicted. We all agree that it cannot be done by force or threats of force. We all agree, I presume, that it may be done by persuasion to leave a rival's shop and come to the defendant's. It may be done by the refusal or withdrawal of various pecuniary advantages which, apart from this consequence, are within the defendant's lawful control. It may be done by the withdrawal, or threat to withdraw, such advantages from third persons who have a right to deal or not to deal with the plaintiff, as a means of inducing them not to deal with him either as customers or servants.

I pause here to remark that the word "threats" often is used as if, when it appeared that threats had been made, it appeared that unlawful conduct had begun. But it depends on what you threaten. As a general rule, even if subject to some exceptions, what you may do in a certain event you may threaten to do, that is, give warning of your intention to do in that event, and thus allow the other person the chance of avoiding the consequences. So as to "compulsion," it depends on how you "compel." So as to "annoyance" or "intimidation."...

I have seen the suggestion made that the conflict between employers and employed is not competition. But I venture to assume that none of my brethren would rely on that suggestion. If the policy on which our law is founded is too narrowly expressed in the term free competition, we may substitute free struggle for life. Certainly the policy is not limited to struggles between persons of the same class competing for the same end. It applies to all conflicts of temporal interests.

So far, I suppose, we are agreed. But there is a notion which latterly has been insisted on a good deal, that a combination of persons to do what any one of them lawfully might do by himself will make the otherwise lawful conduct unlawful. It would be rash to say that some as yet unformulated truth may not be hidden under this proposition. But in the general form in which it has been presented and accepted by many courts, I think it plainly untrue, both on authority and on principle. [Citations omitted.] But it is not necessary to cite cases; it is plain from the slightest consideration of practical affairs, or the most superficial reading of industrial history, that free competition means combination, and that the organization of the world, now going on so fast, means an ever increasing might and scope of combination. It seems to me futile to set our faces against this tendency. Whether beneficial on the whole, as I think it, or detrimental, it is inevitable, unless the fundamental axioms of society, and even the fundamental conditions of life, are to be changed.

One of the eternal conflicts out of which life is made up is that between the effort of every man to get the most he can for his services, and that of society, disguised under the name of capital, to get his services for the least possible return. Combination on the one side is patent and powerful. Combination on the other is the necessary and desirable counterpart, if the battle is to be carried on in a fair and equal way....

If it be true that working men may combine with a view, among other things, to getting as much as they can for their labor, just as capital may combine with a view to getting the greatest possible return, it must be true that when combined they have the same liberty that combined capital has to support their interest by argument, persuasion, and the bestowal or refusal of those advantages which they otherwise lawfully control. I can remember when many people thought that, apart from violence or breach of contract, strikes were wicked, as organized refusals to work. I suppose that intelligent economists and legislators have given up that notion today. I feel pretty confident that they equally will abandon the idea that an organized refusal by workmen of social intercourse with a man who shall enter their antagonist's employ is wrong, if it is dissociated from any threat of violence, and is made for the sole object of prevailing if possible in a contest with their employer about the rate of wages. The fact, that the immediate object of the act by which the benefit to themselves is to be gained is to injure their antagonist, does not necessarily make it unlawful, any more than when a great house lowers the price of certain goods for the purpose, and with the effect, of driving a smaller antagonist from the business. Indeed, the question seems to me to have been decided as long ago as 1842 by the good sense of Chief Justice Shaw, in *Commonwealth* v. *Hunt,* 4 Met. 111....

HAROLD J. LASKI

"The Basis of Vicarious Liability"

(1917)

I

If a master choose to give orders to his servant, no one can fail to understand why he should be held liable for the consequences of their commission. Nor is the case in substance different when he ratifies his servant's act. To stamp what is done for him with the seal of his approval is tacitly, but obviously, to accept the act as his own; and that is true no less where the ratification is implicit, than where it is expressly made manifest. No one, moreover, deems it necessary to take objection to liability which is consequent upon a general negligence. I may knowingly employ a clearly incompetent person. I may consciously fail to provide proper means for the performance of the allotted work. I may fail to give my servant information which I know to be essential to the right completion of his task. I may fail to take adequate precautions against the commission of a tort in my presence. In cases such as these, where the master is directly involved, it is essential to any scheme of law that he should be held liable for such damage as his servant may cause. . . .

. . . The age has passed when each man might bear untroubled the burden of his own life; to-day, the complexities of social organization seem, too often, to have cast us, like some Old Man of the Sea, upon the shoulders of our fellows. Where, above all, the men of Mediaeval England gloried in their own labor, we, or, at least, many of us, take pleasure in dividends that have been vicariously earned. It is an age of abundant service. Vast numbers are working for other men and obeying their commands. Service implies action. A tells B to perform some work. When B's work entails loss to C, what is the relation of A to the transaction? We have maxims and to spare upon this question. *Respondeat superior* is an argument which, like David, has slain its tens of thousands. Its seeming simplicity conceals in fact a veritable hornet's nest of stinging difficulties. It is the merest dogma, and in no sense explanation.

Reprinted by permission of The Yale Law Journal Company and Fred B. Rothman & Company from *The Yale Law Journal,* vol. 26 (1917), pp. 105–9, 111–15, 121–24, 134–35.

For while everyone can see that the master ought to answer for acts he has authorized, why should he be liable either where no authorization can be shown, or where express prohibition of an act exists? ... Where another does no more than fulfill your command, you may with accuracy be said to act. That is as legally clear as it is morally unimpeachable. But what of cases where your servant performs acts incidental to your business without express authority for their performance? What of acts done in positive disobedience to command? Can we be said actually to have performed acts which at first acquaintance we are anxious to repudiate? ...

II

... Our skepticism is the consequence of a too great reliance upon the historic method. We have laid insistence rather upon the origins of law than upon the ends it is to serve. When the history of the modern extension of vicarious liability is examined, no one can question the high degree of its mysteriousness. ... Yet, by 1800, the novelties have forced their way to acceptance. ... It becomes possible to assert that, special authority apart, the duties assigned to a servant give him the power to bind his master in such contracts as come within the scope of his employment. But the law goes further, and makes the master generally liable for his servant's torts so long as they are fairly and reasonably to be traced to his service; though no burden is thrown upon the employer where no such connection can be shown. ...

Almost within a century the doctrines of hallowed antiquity are reversed. No attention, as it seems, is paid to historic antecedent. The whole change is, so one may urge, outstanding proof of the oft-controverted fact that judges can and do make law. Clearly, good reason is essential for so striking a revolution of opinion. ...

III

... The law of a business world is not made for amusement. Some solid reality there must have been in the reasons for its acceptance; and its very persistence in the face of bitter criticism is itself suggestive. We make men pay for faults they have not committed. ... But the rules of law have usually some purpose behind them. Men like Holt and Blackburn are something more than whimsical innovators. The basis of our principles is to be found in the economic conditions of the time. Business has ceased to be mere matter of private concern. A man who embarks upon commercial enterprise is something more—even in the eyes of the law—than a gay adventurer in search of a fortune. The results of his speculation are bound to affect the public; and the state, as the guardian of its interests, is compelled to lay down conditions upon which he may pursue his profession. ... The basis of the rule, in fact, is public policy. One knows, of course, that "public policy" is a doctrine for which the judges have cher-

ished no special affection. "I, for one," said Burrough, J., "protest...
against arguing too strongly upon public policy; it is a very unruly horse,
and when you get astride it, you never know where it will carry you. It
may lead you from the sound law. It is never argued upon at all but when
other points fail." But such an attitude is, in truth, but the prophetic
anticipation of the Victorian distrust of governmental interference. It is
becoming more and more clear that we may not be content with an
individualistic commercial law. Just as that individualism was the natural
reaction from the too strict and local paternalism of mediaeval policy—
perhaps aided by the inherent self-centredness of Puritan thought—so we
are compelled to turn away from every conception of the business relation
which does not see the public as an effective, if silent, partner in every
enterprise. That is the real meaning of Factory and Employers' Liability
Acts as of compulsory education, and the establishment of a minimum
wage. It is simply a legal attempt to see the individual in his social context.
That, at which we industrially aim, is the maximum public good as we
see it. In that respect, the employer is himself no more than a public
servant, to whom, for special purposes, a certain additional freedom of
action, and therefore a greater measure of responsibility has been vouch-
safed. If that employer is compelled to bear the burden of his servant's
torts even when he is himself personally without fault, it is because in a
social distribution of profit and loss, the balance of least disturbance seems
thereby best to be obtained.

What, then, we have to ask of ourselves is whether the positive benefits
to be derived from the present rule do not in fact outweigh the hardships
it may on occasion inflict. We cannot run a human world on the principles
of formal logic. The test of our rule's worth must, in fact, be purely
empirical in character. We have to study the social consequences of its
application, and deduce therefrom its logic. We have to search for the
mechanism of our law in life as it actually is, rather than fit the life we
live to *a priori* rules of rigid legal system. The way in which the modern
conception has grown is, in fact, very comparable to the method by which
special liabilities are attached to innkeepers, to those who have wild ani-
mals, to those who start a fire, to those who engage as public carriers.
The meaning of the legal sword of Damocles forged for their penalization
is rightly to be found, not in the particular relation they bear to their
charge, but in the general relation to society into which their occupation
brings them. In such an aspect as this it may be urged that Holt found
good reason for the incisive certitude of his dicta in an age which saw so
enormous a growth of corporate enterprise. It was, says Dean Wigmore,
"a conscious effort to adjust the rule of law to the expediency of mercantile
affairs." Something of this, it may be urged, was perceived by Bentham
in a passage which has not perhaps received its due meed of attention.
"The obligation imposed upon the master," he says, "acts as a punishment,
and diminishes the chances of similar misfortunes. He is interested in
knowing the character, and watching over the conduct of them for whom

he is answerable. The law makes him an inspector of police, a domestic magistrate, by rendering him liable for their imprudence." Even when we allow for the curiosities of the author's characteristic phraseology, it is yet clear that he has seized upon an important truth. If we allow the master to be careless of his servant's torts we lose hold upon the most valuable check in the conduct of social life.

The real problem in vicarious liability, in fact, is not so much the rectitude of its basal principles, as the degree in which they are to be applied. Nor can we anticipate the manner in which that problem is to be solved. What must strike the observer in the study of the cases is that each is in itself a separate issue; the employer of a railway conductor whose habit it is to kiss the female passengers of pleasing appearance must be dealt with differently from a bank of which the cashier fraudulently induces a customer to accept certain bills. "Each case," says Professor Frankfurter, "must be determined by the facts relevant to it.... we are dealing, in truth, not with a question of law but with the application of an undisputed formula to a constantly changing and growing variety of economic and social facts. Each case, therefore, calls for a new and distinct consideration, not only of the general facts of industry, but of the specific facts in regard to the employment in question." The issue in vicarious liability is not different from that in regard to labor legislation. Just as our conception of the constitutionality of statutes will depend upon the contemporary interpretation of liberty, so the content of the liability enforced at any given moment upon a master for his servant's torts, must be shifted to fit the new facts it will continually encounter. It is not a very serious objection, in this age when incorporation has become but a formal informality, to urge that the growth of the doctrine is a dangerous blow aimed at the stability of property. The doctrine will grow or contract according as the facts to which it is applied seem to warrant growth or contraction. It will have in view, not the history that is to be justified, but the end that is to be attained. It will let the future take care of itself by protecting it against the invasion of dogmas which grow painfully antique. It will strive, in fact, to make elastic that bed of Procrustes in which the client of law too often takes his rest. If, as Best, C.J., remarked, our law is to be "bottomed on plain, broad principles," it is well to see that they do not also, even though unconsciously, include its superstructure. For each age has to begin anew its legal thinking.

IV

The problem of scope of employment has become largely confused by the efforts of the courts to provide, somehow or other, a test of negligence on the part of the master. Thus, masters are to be held liable for their servant's torts when the latter are acting "for the master's benefit" when, as seems to be assumed, he is less careful than we may demand—or in such wise that a probable authority would from the nature of the case have been given—a fiction of implied command being, so far as one can see, relied upon. It seems far easier to attempt a humanist application of public policy to the problems presented by the cases. The fiction of implied authority is so constantly breaking down, it so obviously results in patent anomalies as to be as dangerous as it is unsatisfactory. . . .

What is here suggested is the simple thesis that only a social interpretation of the law will give us a satisfactory clue to the bewildering labyrinth that confronts us. If the judges continue to apply general principles founded on a dangerous and unsatisfying fiction, only confusion of a lamentable kind can result. It is hardly possible, as the case now stands, to avoid a perplexing variety of opinion as to whether any given issue comes within the scope of "implied authority" or not. But it is possible to have sufficient confidence in the good sense of the courts to ask for a frankly communal application of the law. The promotion of social solidarity is an end it is peculiarly incumbent upon the law to promote, since its own strength, and even life, depends upon the growth of that sentiment. The fiction of implied authority is no more than a barbarous relic of individualistic interpretation. It savors too dangerously of the time when the courts held that they were to do no more than apply a given remedy to a given set of facts concerning John Doe and Richard Roe—with a lofty unconcern for the world at large. We are passing beyond that stage. The meaning to be given to the scope of employment is bound more and more to affect vitally the whole future of industry. It is according as lawyers realize this, that they will be equipped to deal adequately with the facts of life. It is, it is true, an interpretation they may not find in the books. But law is perhaps in need of the stimulus of a freer atmosphere.

V

Such an attitude is the more important when the depersonalization of industry is borne in mind. Machinery and corporate enterprise have effected a revolution, the very beginnings of which we are able only dimly to conceive. The old, intimate relation between master and servant can hardly now return. The apprentice no longer marries his master's daughter, for the simple reason that his master no longer has a daughter, or, if he does, that daughter is a corporation who is not given in marriage. The modern business man is either a director or a manager and he sees nothing, often enough knows nothing, of his servants. That is, of course, the natural consequence of the scale of modern commercial enterprise, but it is a consequence of which the results need careful emphasis. And alongside this industrial impersonalism has gone the incredible development of machinery so that, as Mr. Birrell has grimly noted, it is with arms and legs that the courts are largely concerned. Now these corporations, are, in the eyes even of the law, juristic persons, and since they act as an ordinary individual would act in a similar situation, that is to say by agents and servants, it is clearly reasonable, that they should, equally with individuals, be held vicariously liable for such acts as those agents and servants may perform. But it has not proved easy to establish this doctrine in anything like its necessary completeness.

The hesitations that have been characteristic of our policy lie at the door of our conception of the corporation. So long as we think of it as a fiction created only for certain ends which are legal, the doctrine of implied authority logically prevents us from admitting, that it can be guilty of authorizing illegal acts. Having made it mindless, we are unwilling to admit it guilty of acts which seem to carry with them the stamp of conscious immorality. But immediately we surrender so inadequate a theory, the ground for the extension of vicarious liability to the corporate person is very clear. It acts and is acted for; it must then pay the penalty for its habits. In a world where individual enterprise is so largely replaced, the security of business relationships would be enormously impaired unless we had the means of preventing a company from repudiating its servants' torts. The reason is not that companies are well able to pay; for it is not the business of law to see that a debtor is solvent, but to provide a remedy for admitted wrong.

The enforcement of such vicarious liability is more urgent for another reason. The dissolution of individual business enterprise into the corporation system has tended to harden the conditions of commercial life. The impersonality of a company employing say five thousand men is perhaps inevitable; but in its methods of operation, it tends to be less careful of human life, more socially wasteful than the individual has been. But its consequences to society are equally momentous, and we dare not judge it differently. It is necessary, for instance, to see to it that we have pure food and unadulterated milk, and it can make no difference to us whether the offender against our requirements be individual or corporate. It is only by enforcing vicarious liability that we can hope to make effective those labor laws intended to promote the welfare of the workers; for it is too frequently the corporation that evades the statute or attempts to discredit it. It is useless to argue that the responsibility rests upon the agent; for it is unfortunately too clear that men may act very differently in their institutional relations than in their ordinary mode of life....

VIII

What has been here attempted is, in fact, a part of the sociological analysis of law. We do not sufficiently realize how greatly our legal ideas have been affected by their peculiar relation to the history of landed property. Primitive jurisprudence concerns itself, for the most part, with the protection of individual rights. Certain men are blameworthy; they have invaded the property of other men. It is then necessary to obtain protection against them. That ancient but tenacious individualism is in truth the coronation of anarchy; and the time comes when a spirit of community supersedes it. But either because that notion is prematurely born, or else because it is inadequately translated into terms of actual life, it results in the cramping of single-handed effort. It passes away; and the consequence is the beatification of *laissez-faire*. But it becomes increasingly evident that society cannot be governed on the principles of commercial nihilism. To assume that freedom and equality consist in unlimited competition is simply to travesty the facts. We come once more to an age of collective endeavor. We begin the re-interpretation of law in the terms of our collective needs.

Novelty for our principles, we may not in some sort deny; though, in truth, if it is by history that we are to be judged a plethora of anti-quarianism might not be wanting. But it is on different ground that we take our stand. It is our business to set law to the rhythm of modern life. It is the harmonization of warring interests with which we are concerned. How to evolve from a seeming conflict the social gain it is the endeavor of law to promote—this is the problem by which we are confronted. We would base our legal decisions not on the facts of yesterday, but on the possibilities of to-morrow. We would seek the welfare of society in the principles we enunciate. We have been told on the highest authority that no other matter is entitled to be weighed.

International News Service v. *Associated Press*

248 U.S. 215 (1918)

Mr. Justice Pitney delivered the opinion of the Court.

The parties are competitors in the gathering and distribution of news and its publication for profit in newspapers throughout the United States. The Associated Press, which was complainant in the District Court, is a coöperative organization, incorporated under the Membership Corporations law of the State of New York, its members being individuals who are either proprietors or representatives of about 950 daily newspapers published in all parts of the United States....

Defendant is a corporation organized under the laws of the State of New Jersey, whose business is the gathering and selling of news to its customers and clients, consisting of newspapers published throughout the United States, under contracts by which they pay certain amounts at stated times for defendant's service. It has wide-spread news-gathering agencies; the cost of its operations amounts, it is said, to more than $2,000,000 per annum; and it serves about 400 newspapers located in the various cities of the United States and abroad, a few of which are represented, also, in the membership of the Associated Press.

The parties are in the keenest competition between themselves in the distribution of news throughout the United States; and so, as a rule, are the newspapers that they serve, in their several districts....

The bill was filed to restrain the pirating of complainant's news by defendant in three ways: First, by bribing employees of newspapers published by complainant's members to furnish Associated Press news to defendant before publication, for transmission by telegraph and telephone to defendant's clients for publication by them; Second, by inducing Associated Press members to violate its by-laws and permit defendant to obtain news before publication; and, Third, by copying news from bulletin boards and from early editions of complainant's newspapers and selling this, either bodily or after rewriting it, to defendant's customers.

The District Court, upon consideration of the bill and answer, with voluminous affidavits on both sides, granted a preliminary injunction under the first and second heads, but refused at that stage to restrain the systematic practice admittedly pursued by defendant, of taking news bodily from the bulletin boards and early editions of complainant's newspapers and selling it as its own. . . .

We need spend no time, however, upon the general question of property in news matter at common law, or the application of the copyright act, since it seems to us the case must turn upon the question of unfair competition in business. And, in our opinion, this does not depend upon any general right of property analogous to the common-law right of the proprietor of an unpublished work to prevent its publication without his consent; nor is it foreclosed by showing that the benefits of the copyright act have been waived. We are dealing here not with restrictions upon publication but with the very facilities and processes of publication. The peculiar value of news is in the spreading of it while it is fresh; and it is evident that a valuable property interest in the news, as news, cannot be maintained by keeping it secret. Besides, except for matters improperly disclosed, or published in breach of trust or confidence, or in violation of law, none of which is involved in this branch of the case, the news of current events may be regarded as common property. What we are concerned with is the business of making it known to the world, in which both parties to the present suit are engaged. . . . The parties are competitors in this field; and, on fundamental principles, applicable here as elsewhere, when the rights or privileges of the one are liable to conflict with those of the other, each party is under a duty so to conduct its own business as not unnecessarily or unfairly to injure that of the other. . . .

. . . The question here is not so much the rights of either party as against the public but their rights as between themselves. . . . And although we may and do assume that neither party has any remaining property interest as against the public in uncopyrighted news matter after the moment of its first publication, it by no means follows that there is no remaining property interest in it as between themselves. For, to both of them alike, news matter, however little susceptible of ownership or dominion in the absolute sense, is stock in trade, to be gathered at the cost of enterprise, organization, skill, labor, and money, and to be distributed and sold to those who will pay money for it, as for any other merchandise. Regarding the news, therefore, as but the material out of which both parties are seeking to make profits at the same time and in the same field, we hardly can fail to recognize that for this purpose, and as between them, it must be regarded as *quasi* property, irrespective of the rights of either as against the public. . . .

The decree of the Circuit Court of Appeals will be *Affirmed*.

Mr. Justice Clarke took no part in the consideration or decision of this case.

Mr. Justice Holmes:

When an uncopyrighted combination of words is published there is no general right to forbid other people repeating them—in other words there is no property in the combination or in the thoughts or facts that the words express. Property, a creation of law, does not arise from value, although exchangeable—a matter of fact. Many exchangeable values may be destroyed intentionally without compensation. Property depends upon exclusion by law from interference, and a person is not excluded from using any combination of words merely because some one has used it before, even if it took labor and genius to make it. If a given person is to be prohibited from making the use of words that his neighbors are free to make some other ground must be found. One such ground is vaguely expressed in the phrase unfair trade. This means that the words are repeated by a competitor in business in such a way as to convey a misrepresentation that materially injures the person who first used them, by appropriating credit of some kind which the first user has earned. The ordinary case is a representation by device, appearance, or other indirection that the defendant's goods come from the plaintiff. But the only reason why it is actionable to make such a representation is that it tends to give the defendant an advantage in his competition with the plaintiff and that it is thought undesirable that an advantage should be gained in that way. Apart from that the defendant may use such unpatented devices and uncopyrighted combinations of words as he likes. The ordinary case, I say, is palming off the defendant's product as the plaintiff's but the same evil may follow from the opposite falsehood—from saying, whether in words or by implication, that the plaintiff's product is the defendant's, and that, it seems to me, is what has happened here.

Fresh news is got only by enterprise and expense. To produce such news as it is produced by the defendant represents by implication that it has been acquired by the defendant's enterprise and at its expense. When it comes from one of the great news collecting agencies like the Associated Press, the source generally is indicated, plainly importing that credit; and that such a representation is implied may be inferred with some confidence from the unwillingness of the defendant to give the credit and tell the truth. If the plaintiff produces the news at the same time that the defendant does, the defendant's presentation impliedly denies to the plaintiff the credit of collecting the facts and assumes that credit to the defendant. If the plaintiff is later in Western cities it naturally will be supposed to have obtained its information from the defendant. The falsehood is a little more subtle, the injury a little more indirect, than in ordinary cases of unfair trade, but I think that the principle that condemns the one condemns the other. It is a question of how strong an infusion of fraud is necessary to turn a flavor into a poison. The dose seems to me strong enough here to need a remedy from the law. But as, in my view, the only ground of complaint that can be recognized without legislation is the implied misstatement, it can be corrected by stating the truth; and a suitable acknowledgement of the source is all that the plaintiff can require. I think that within the limits recognized by the decision of the Court the defendant should be enjoined from publishing news obtained from the Associated

Press for   hours after publication by the plaintiff unless it gives express credit to the Associated Press; the number of hours and the form of acknowledgement to be settled by the District Court.

Mr. Justice McKenna concurs in this opinion.

Mr. Justice Brandeis dissenting.

No question of statutory copyright is involved. The sole question for our consideration is this: Was the International News Service properly enjoined from using, or causing to be used gainfully, news of which it acquired knowledge by lawful means (namely, by reading publicly posted bulletins or papers purchased by it in the open market) merely because the news had been originally gathered by the Associated Press and continued to be of value to some of its members, or because it did not reveal the source from which it was acquired?

The "ticker" cases, the cases concerning literary and artistic compositions, and cases of unfair competition were relied upon in support of the injunction. But it is admitted that none of those cases affords a complete analogy with that before us. The question presented for decision is new; and it is important.

News is a report of recent occurrences. The business of the news agency is to gather systematically knowledge of such occurrences of interest and to distribute reports thereof. The Associated Press contended that knowledge so acquired is property, because it costs money and labor to produce and because it has value for which those who have it not are ready to pay; that it remains property and is entitled to protection as long as it has commercial value as news; and that to protect it effectively the defendant must be enjoined from making, or causing to be made, any gainful use of it while it retains such value. An essential element of individual property is the legal right to exclude others from enjoying it. If the property is private, the right of exclusion may be absolute; if the property is affected with a public interest, the right of exclusion is qualified. But the fact that a product of the mind has cost its producer money and labor, and has a value for which others are willing to pay, is not sufficient to ensure to it this legal attribute of property. The general rule of law is, that the noblest of human productions—knowledge, truths ascertained, conceptions, and ideas—become, after voluntary communication to others, free as the air to common use. Upon these incorporeal productions the attribute of property is continued after such communication only in certain classes of cases where public policy has seemed to demand it. These exceptions are confined to productions which, in some degree, involve creation, invention, or discovery. But by no means all such are endowed with this attribute of property. The creations which are recognized as property by the common law are literary, dramatic, musical, and other artistic creations; and these have also protection under the copyright statutes. The inventions and discoveries upon which this attribute of property is conferred only by statute, are the few comprised within patent law. There are also many other cases in which courts interfere to prevent curtailment of plaintiff's enjoyment of incorporeal productions; and in which the right to relief is often called a property right, but is such only in a special sense. In those cases, the plaintiff has no absolute right to the protection of his production; he has merely the qualified right to be protected as against the defendant's acts, because of the special relation in which the latter stands or the wrongful method or means employed in acquiring the knowledge or the manner in which it is used. Protection of this character is afforded where the suit is based upon breach of contract or of trust or upon unfair competition.

The knowledge for which protection is sought in the case at bar is not of a kind upon which the law has heretofore conferred the attributes of property; nor is the manner of its acquisition or use nor the purpose to which it is applied, such as has heretofore been recognized as entitling a plaintiff to relief. . . .

Plaintiff further contended that defendant's practice constitutes unfair competition, because there is "appropriation without cost to itself of values created by" the plaintiff; and it is upon this ground that the decision of this court appears to be based. To appropriate and use for profit, knowledge and ideas produced by other men, without making compensation or even acknowledgement, may be inconsistent with a finer sense of propriety; but, with the exceptions indicated above, the law has heretofore sanctioned the practice. Thus it was held that one may ordinarily make and sell anything in any form, may copy with exactness that which another has produced, or may otherwise use his ideas without his consent and without the payment of compensation, and yet not inflict a legal injury; and that ordinarily one is at perfect liberty to find out, if he can by lawful means, trade secrets of another, however valuable, and then use the knowledge so acquired gainfully, although it cost the original owner much in effort and in money to collect or produce.

Such taking and gainful use of a product of another which, for reasons of public policy, the law has refused to endow with the attributes of property, does not become unlawful because the product happens to have been taken from a rival and is used in competition with him. The unfairness in competition which hitherto has been recognized by the law as a basis for relief, lay in the manner or means of conducting the business; and the manner or means held legally unfair, involves either fraud or force or the doing of acts otherwise prohibited by law. . . .

The great development of agencies now furnishing country-wide distribution of news, the vastness of our territory, and improvements in the means or transmitting intelligence, have made it possible for a news agency or newspapers to obtain, without paying compensation, the fruit of another's efforts and to use news so obtained gainfully in competition with the original collector. The injustice of such action is obvious. But to give relief against it would involve more than the application of existing rules of law to new facts. It would require the making of a new rule in analogy to existing ones. The unwritten law possesses capacity for growth; and has often satisfied new demands for justice by invoking analogies or by expanding a rule or principle. This process has been in the main wisely applied and should not be discontinued. Where the problem is relatively simple, as it is apt to be when private interests only are involved, it generally proves adequate. But with the increasing complexity of society, the public interest tends to become omnipresent; and the problems presented by new demands for justice cease to be simple. Then the creation or recognition by courts of a new private right may work serious injury to the general public, unless boundaries of the right are definitely established and wisely guarded. In order to reconcile the new private right with the public interest, it may be necessary to prescribe limitations and rules for its enjoyment; and also to provide administrative machinery for enforcing the rules. It is largely for this reason that, in the effort to meet the many new demands for justice incident to a rapidly changing civilization, resort to legislation has latterly been had with increasing frequency.

The rule for which the plaintiff contends would effect an important extension of property rights and a corresponding curtailment of the free use of knowledge and of ideas; and the facts of this case admonish us of the danger involved in recognizing such a property right in news, without imposing upon news-gatherers corresponding obligations. . . .

Courts are ill-equipped to make the investigations which should precede a determination of the limitations which should be set upon any property right in news or of the circumstances under which news gathered by a private agency should be deemed affected with a public interest. Courts would be powerless to prescribe the detailed regulations essential to full enjoyment of the rights conferred or to introduce the machinery required for enforcement of such regulations. Considerations such as these should lead us to decline to establish a new rule of law in the effort to redress a newly-disclosed wrong, although the propriety of some remedy appears to be clear.

JOHN DEWEY

"The Historic Background of Corporate Legal Personality"

(1926)

The purpose of the article is . . . to point out some of the non-legal factors which have found their way into the discussion of the personality of so-called natural and artificial persons, and to indicate the original conditions which gave these extraneous factors their efficacy. The postulate, which has been a controlling principle although usually made unconsciously, leading to the merging of popular and philosophical notions of the person with the legal notion, is the conception that before anything can be a jural person it must intrinsically possess certain properties, the existence of which is necessary to constitute anything a person. If the conception as to the nature of these inherent and essential attributes had remained constant perhaps no harm would have resulted from shoving such a notion under the legal idea; the legal doctrine would at least have remained as constant as that of the nature of the seat of personality. But the history of western culture shows a chameleon-like change in the latter notion; this change has never, moreover, effected complete replacement of an earlier by a later idea. Almost all concepts have persisted side by side in a confused intermixture. Hence their influence upon legal doctrine has necessarily been to generate confusion and conflict. . . .

The fact of the case is that there is no clear-cut line, logical or practical, through the different theories which have been advanced and which are still advanced in behalf of the "real" personality of either "natural" or associated persons. Each theory has been used to serve the same ends, and each has been used to serve opposing ends. The doctrine of the personality of the state has been advanced to place the state above legal responsibility on the ground that such a person has no superior person—save God—to whom to answer; and in behalf of a doctrine of the responsibility of the state and its officers to law, since to be a person is to have legal powers and duties. The personality of the state has been opposed to both the personality of "natural" singular persons and to the personality of groups. In the latter connection it has been employed both to make the state the

Reprinted by permission of The Yale Law Journal Company and Fred B. Rothman & Company from *The Yale Law Journal*, vol. 35 (1926), pp. 655, 658, 669–70.

supreme and culminating personality in a hierarchy, to make it but *primus inter pares,* and to reduce it to merely one among many, sometimes more important than others and sometimes less so. These are political rather than legal considerations, but they have affected law. In legal doctrines proper, both theories have been upheld for the same purpose, and each for opposed ends. Corporate groups less than the state have had real personality ascribed to them, both in order to make them more amenable to liability, as in the case of trade-unions, and to exalt their dignity and vital power, as against external control. Their personality has been denied for like reasons; they have been pulverized into mere aggregates of separate persons in order to protect other laborers from them, to make more difficult their unified action in trade disputes, as in collective bargaining, and to enable union property to escape liability, the associated individuals in their severalty having property to levy upon. The group personality theory has been asserted both as a check upon what was regarded as anarchic and dissolving individualism, to set up something more abiding and worthful than a single human being, and to increase the power and dignity of the single being as over against the state. Even the doctrine that true personality resides only in the "natural" person has been worked in opposed directions. It was first used to give church or state a short and direct road of approach which would lessen the power of the singular being over against the collective being, while lately, through being affected by "natural" in the sense of natural rights, it has been employed to exalt private, at the expense of public, interests.

ADOLF A. BERLE AND GARDINER C. MEANS

The Modern Corporation and Private Property

(1932)

Corporations have ceased to be merely legal devices through which the private business transactions of individuals may be carried on. Though still much used for this purpose, the corporate form has acquired a larger significance. The corporation has, in fact, become both a method of property tenure and a means of organizing economic life. Grown to tremendous proportions, there may be said to have evolved a "corporate system"—as there was once a feudal system—which has attracted to itself a combination of attributes and powers, and has attained a degree of prominence entitling it to be dealt with as a major social institution.

We are examining this institution probably before it has attained its zenith. Spectacular as its rise has been, every indication seems to be that the system will move forward to proportions which would stagger imagination today; just as the corporate system of today was beyond the imagination of most statesmen and business men at the opening of the present century. Only by remembering that men still living can recall a time when the present situation was hardly dreamed of, can we enforce the conclusion that the new order may easily become completely dominant during the lifetime of our children. For that reason, if for no other, it is desirable to examine this system, bearing in mind that its impact on the life of the country and of every individual is certain to be great; it may even determine a large part of the behaviour of most men living under it.

Organization of property has played a constant part in the balance of powers which go to make up the life of any era. We need not resolve the controversy as to whether property interests are invariably controlling. The cynical view of many historians insists that property interests have at all times, visible or invisible, been dominant. Following this grim analysis, one commentator on the rise of corporations observed that they had become the "master instruments of civilization." Another expressed his depression at the fact that the system had at length reached a point definitely committing civilization to the rule of a plutocracy. Still others have seen in the system a transition phase towards ultimate socialism or communism. Acceptance of any of these beliefs may be delayed; but the underlying thought expressed in them all is that the corporate system has become the principal factor in economic organization through its mobilization of property interests.

In its new aspect the corporation is a means whereby the wealth of innumerable individuals has been concentrated into huge aggregates and whereby control over this wealth has been surrendered to a unified direction. The power attendant upon such concentration has brought forth princes of industry, whose position in the community is yet to be defined. The surrender of control over their wealth by investors has effectively broken the old property relations and has raised the problem of defining these relationships anew. The direction of industry by persons other than those who have ventured their wealth has raised the question of the motive force back of such direction and the effective distribution of the returns from business enterprise.

These corporations have arisen in field after field as the myriad independent and competing units of private business have given way to the few large groupings of the modern quasi-public corporation. The typical business unit of the 19th century was owned by individuals or small groups; was managed by them or their appointees; and was, in the main, limited in size by the personal wealth of the individuals in control. These units have been supplanted in ever greater measure by great aggregations in which tens and even hundreds of thousands of workers and property worth hundreds of millions of dollars, belonging to tens or even hundreds of thousands of individuals, are combined through the corporate mechanism into a single producing organization under unified control and management. . . .

Such an organization of economic activity rests upon two developments, each of which has made possible an extension of the area under unified control. The factory system, the basis of the industrial revolution, brought an increasingly large number of workers directly under a single management. Then, the modern corporation, equally revolutionary in its effect, placed the wealth of innumerable individuals under the same central control. By each of these changes the power of those in control was immensely enlarged and the status of those involved, worker or property owner, was radically changed. The independent worker who entered the factory became a wage laborer surrendering the direction of his labor to his industrial master. The property owner who invests in a modern corporation so far surrenders his wealth to those in control of the corporation that he has exchanged the position of independent owner for one in which he may become merely recipient of the wages of capital.

In and of itself, the corporate device does not necessarily bring about this change. It has long been possible for an individual to incorporate his business even though it still represents his own investment, his own activities, and his own business transactions; he has in fact merely created a legal *alter ego* by setting up a corporation as the nominal vehicle. If the corporate form had done nothing more than this, we should have only an interesting custom according to which business would be carried on by individuals adopting for that purpose certain legal clothing. It would involve no radial shift in property tenure or in the organization of economic activity; it would inaugurate no "system" comparable to the institutions of feudalism.

The corporate system appears only when this type of private or "close" corporation has given way to an essentially different form, the quasi-public corporation: a corporation in which a large measure of separation of ownership and control has taken place through the multiplication of owners.

Such separation may exist in varying degrees. Where the men ultimately responsible for running a corporation own a majority of the voting stock while the remainder is widely diffused, control and part ownership are in their hands. Only for the remaining owners is there separation from control. Frequently, however, ownership is so widely scattered that working control can be maintained with but a minority interest. The Rockefeller family, for example, is reported to have retained direct or indirect minority interests in many of the Standard Oil Companies; and in the case of the Standard Oil Company of Indiana, this interest, amounting to only 14.5 per cent combined with the strategic position of its holders, has proved sufficient for the control of the corporation. In such a case the greater bulk of ownership is virtually without control. Separation of ownership and control becomes almost complete when not even a substantial minority interest exists, as in the American Telephone and Telegraph Company whose largest holder is reported to own less than one per cent of the company's stock. Under such conditions control may be held by the directors or titular managers who can employ the proxy machinery to become a self-perpetuating body, even though as a group they own but a small fraction of the stock outstanding. In each of these types, majority control, minority control, and management control, the separation of ownership from control has become effective—a large body of security holders has been created who exercise virtually no control over the wealth which they or their predecessors in interest have contributed to the enterprise. In the case of management control, the ownership interest held by the controlling group amounts to but a very small fraction of the total ownership. Corporations where this separation has become an important factor may be classed as quasi-public in character in contradistinction to the private, or closely held corporation in which no important separation of ownership and control has taken place.

Growing out of this separation are two characteristics, almost as typical of the quasi-public corporation as the separation itself—mere size and the public market for its securities. It is precisely this separation of control from ownership which makes possible tremendous aggregations of property. The Fords and the Mellons, whose personal wealth is sufficient to finance great enterprises, are so few, that they only emphasize the dependence of the large enterprise on the wealth of more than the individual or group of individuals who may be in control. The quasi-public corporation commands its supply of capital from a group of investors frequently described as the "investing public." It draws these savings to itself either directly, as individuals purchase stocks or bonds, or indirectly, as insurance companies, banks, and investment trusts receive these savings and invest them in corporate securities. To secure these funds it must commonly avail itself of an open market in its securities—usually by listing shares on a stock exchange, or, less importantly, by maintaining a private or "unlisted" market. So essential, in fact, is the open market to the quasi-public corporation that it may be considered almost as characteristic of that type of corporation as the separation of ownership from control and the great aggregation of wealth. . . .

Though the American law makes no distinction between the private corporation and the quasi-public, the economics of the two are essentially different. The separation of ownership from control produces a condition where the interests of owner and of ultimate manager may, and often do, diverge, and where many of the checks which formerly operated to limit the use of power disappear. Size alone tends to give these giant corporations a social significance not attached to the smaller units of private enterprise. By the use of the open market for securities, each of these corporations assumes obligations towards the investing public which transform it from a legal method clothing the rule of a few individuals into an institution at least nominally serving investors who have embarked their funds in its enterprise. New responsibilities towards the owners, the workers, the consumers, and the State thus rest upon the shoulders of those in control. In creating these new relationships, the quasi-public corporation may fairly be said to work a revolution. It has destroyed the unity that we commonly call property—has divided ownership into nominal ownership and the power formerly joined to it. Thereby the corporation has changed the nature of profit-seeking enterprise. . . .

JAMES M. LANDIS

The Administrative Process

(1938)

When we come to the more significant agencies it will be seen that they have as the central theme of their activity either the orderly supervision of a specific industry or, as in the case of the Federal Trade Commission, an extension of a particular branch of the police work of the general government. Their tasks are regulatory, it is true, but, with certain exceptions, regulatory in a broad sense, for to them is committed the initial shaping and enforcement of industrial policies.

The advantages of specialization in the field of regulatory activity seem obvious enough. But our governmental organization of the nineteenth century proceeded upon a different theory. Indeed, theorists have lifted the inexpertness that characterized our nineteenth-century governmental mechanisms to the level of a political principle. Such a practical politician as Andrew Jackson took occasion to urge the Congress to take measures against permitting the civil servants of the government a "long continuance" in office. But expertness cannot derive otherwise. It springs only from that continuity of interest, that ability and desire to devote fifty-two weeks a year, year after year, to a particular problem. With the rise of regulation, the need for expertness became dominant; for the art of regulating an industry requires knowledge of the details of its operation, ability to shift requirements as the condition of the industry may dictate, the pursuit of energetic measures upon the appearance of an emergency, and the power through enforcement to realize conclusions as to policy.

If the administrative process is to fill the need for expertness, obviously, as regulation increases, the number of our administrative authorities must increase. The most superficial criticism which can be directed toward the development of the administrative process is that which bases its objections merely upon numerical growth. A consequence of an expanding interest of government in various phases of the industrial scene must be the creation of more administrative agencies if the demand for expertness is to be met. Increasing their number of itself need not disturb us, provided that the relationships between them, and in turn their relationship to the other departments of government, are properly solved. Efficiency in the processes of governmental regulation is best served by the creation of more rather than less agencies. And it is efficiency that is the desperate need. . . .

A marked tendency of modern legislation is to deal with regulatory problems by setting forth less frequently in the legislation itself the particular rules that shall control. More commonly the administrative is given power to prescribe governing regulations in certain spheres of activity. Delegation is thus on the increase. If we contrast, for example, the form of the Interstate Commerce Act with that of the Securities Exchange Act, the difference is immense. Detailed regulative provisions encumber the Interstate Commerce Act. Indeed, that Act has ceased to have the appearance of a constituent document and resembles rather a regulative code. Students of it will recall sympathetically the outcry by Frederick J. Stimson against its cumbrous form, and wish that he had had the opportunity to make good on his boast that the Act could be redrawn "with two days' honest work" to say and effect the same things in four pages. The result of using such a technique is to call over and over again for Congressional amendments. Hardly a Congressional session concludes which has not passed some amendment of a minor or major nature to the Interstate Commerce Act. The Securities Exchange Act presents a very different situation. There, with broad, rule-making powers vested in the Commission, amendment becomes necessary only when the administrative is faced with primary problems affecting its powers.

Such delegation of powers means, of course, that the operative rules will be found outside the statute book. But it does not follow from this that these rules lack that publicity which, clearly, should attend the imposition of regulatory requirements. Since the establishment of the Federal Register the regulations of administrative agencies are as accessible, if not more so, than the enactments of the Congress. The chief virtue of this modern tendency toward delegation is that it is conducive to flexibility—a prime quality of good administration. The administrative is always in session. Its processes operate with comparative rapidity. By centralization in the drafting of its rules it can preserve the outlines of formal order in its requirements. The agency's compactness gives some assurance against the entry of impertinent considerations into the deliberations relating to a projected solution. I have seen as little as twenty minutes elapse between the drafting and promulgation of a permissive rule where the exigencies of the situation called for quick action. On the other hand, I have watched and participated with the experts for over two years in a vain attempt to find a solution to a problem which continues to defy even a tentative, experimental answer.

Despite the outcry from time to time by individual members of the Congress against the grant of powers to the administrative to formulate regulatory provisions, on the whole that process today has the respect of the members of the legislative branch of the federal government. Those with experience in legislative matters or with an insight into the difficulties attendant upon bridging the chasm between the phrase "Be it enacted" and law in the sense of controlling human affairs, recognize that it is easier to plot a way through a labyrinth of detail when it is done in the comparative quiet of a conference room than when it is attempted amid the turmoil of a legislative chamber or committee room....

Standards, if adequately drafted, afford great protection to administration. By limiting the area of the exercise of discretion they tend to routinize administration and to that degree relieve it from the play of political and economic pressures which otherwise might be harmful. The pressing problem today, however, is to get the administrative to assume the responsibilities that it properly should assume. Political and official life to too great an extent tends to favor routinization. The assumption of responsibility by an agency is always a gamble that may well make more enemies than friends. The easiest course is frequently that of inaction. A legalistic approach that reads a governing statue with the hope of finding limitations upon authority rather than grants of power with which to act decisively is thus common. One of the ablest administrators that it was my good fortune to know, I believe, never read, at least more than casually, the statues that he translated into reality. He assumed that they gave him power to deal with the broad problems of an industry and, upon that understanding, he sought his own solutions. Limitations upon his powers that counsel brought to his attention, naturally, he respected; but there is an enormous difference between the legalistic form of approach that from the negative vantage of statutory limitations looks to see what it must do, and the approach that considers a problem from the standpoint of finding out what it can do....

No one can fail to recognize that there are dangers implicit in this combination of functions in an administrative agency. The curious fact remains, however, that the tendency toward this combination has been notably upon the increase. The reasons that underlie the passage of a particular statute may on occasion be dismissed as capricious or as poorly founded. But to dismiss lightly a long continuing and definite legislative development is, perhaps, to miss deep-seated causes that underlie a succession of practical legislative judgments.

Inquiry as to the nature of these causes will reveal that they center about inadequacies attending the judicial process in the settling of those claims that have been committed to the administrative for protection. It would, for example, have been possible in 1914 to have made the Federal Trade Commission simply another specialized arm of the Attorney General's office, for the actual remedial device given to that agency was similar to an injunction issued by a court of equity. But in the field of industrial regulation deep and enduring disappointments had already resulted from the judicial attitude toward railroad legislation and toward the Sherman Act. Judicial interpretation of the statutory standards laid down by the Congress plainly gave the judges power to mold the statute to their own conceptions; and that molding had too frequently set at naught the public and political effort which had so hopefully expended itself in the passage of the statute. Judicial interpretation suffered not only from inexpertness but more from the slowness of that process to attune itself to the demands of the day. There was thus hesitation by the Congress to wait for the viewpoint of the judiciary to tally with the growing conceptions that an administrative agency might evolve as a consequence of its continuing concern with the well-being of industry. Of this lag in the judicial process, Dicey, in his *Lectures on the Relation of Law and Public Opinion in England during the Nineteenth Century,* had occasion to make these remarks. He says, speaking of the strict construction given by the judges to the Common Law Procedure Act of 1854:

> However this may be, we may, at any rate as regards the nineteenth century, lay it down as a rule that judge-made law has, owing to the training and age of our judges, tended at any given moment to represent the convictions of an earlier era than the ideas represented by parliamentary legislation. If a statute, as already stated, is apt to reproduce the public opinion not so much of today as of yesterday, judge-made law occasionally represents the opinion of the day before yesterday.

To lodge a great, interpretative power in the judiciary involved the risk that a policy, which initially was given to the administrative to formulate, might be thwarted at its most significant fulcrum by judgments antagonistic to its own.

These reasons, which were responsible for placing adjudication in the hands of the administrative in the case of the Federal Trade Commission, were more patently present when the administrative had large powers of rule-making. They were also active in fields, such as labor, which revealed continuing judicial sterilization of legislative attempts to equip workmen with the ability to use their bargaining power. The Clayton Act, which was heralded as labor's Magna Charta because it was thought to be a shield against the application of the Sherman Act to labor combinations, was literally destroyed by judicial interpretation. It is true that the language of that Act did not compel a different judicial attitude, but no trace of the will that prompted the legislative to suggest some different treatment of labor combinations can be found seeping through to the decisions. Administrative adjudication thus was resorted to in the field of labor in the hope that it would buttress the legislative will to turn the existing current of judicial decision.

Intelligent coordination between policy-making and enforcement is, of course, essential in the business of regulating industrial enterprise. If such qualities as flexibility and expertness are demanded in the field of rule-making, the intensity of that demand is no less in the area of adjudication. To place adjudication outside the administrative process would tend to threaten the carrying through of those policies whose formulation was so deliberately given to the administrative. But the fact that there is this fusion of prosecution and adjudication in a single administrative agency does not imply the absence of all checks. It implies simply the absence of the traditional check. And so it becomes worth while to examine those checks that actually inhere in the administrative process to safeguard it against the rise of arbitrariness in the imposition of administrative penalties.

An examination of the administrative process shows the presence of several checks. The first is the fact that that process, as distinguished from the judicial process, moves in a narrow field. Even in that field its discretion, as we have seen, is bounded by limitations that hem in the delegation to it of the power to act. The human claims that come before it for consideration are thus limited. The administrative is not open to the broad range of human sympathies to which the judicial process is subject. Again, as an agency of government confined to a fairly narrow field, its singleness of concern quickly develops a professionalism of spirit—an attitude that perhaps more than rules affords assurance of informed and balanced judgments. Precedents and habits as to the disposition of claims quickly tend to make its discretion, such as it is, the "equitable discretion" of a Court of Chancery. Thirdly, a statutory condition of its power to act by way of order is normally the requirement of findings of fact necessary to support an order—findings of fact that must be both detailed and informative. A fourth check, too often ignored, springs from the relationship of adjudication to policy. I have referred to the fact that the necessity for their conformance brought adjudication under the wing of the administrative. But the necessity for this conformance also affords a check upon adjudication. The policies initiated by the administrative must be "right" from an industrial standpoint. They must promote the economic soundness of the industry subject to the charge of the administrative. The same considerations, however, lead to "rightness" in the disposition of claims. For arbitrariness and unfairness in adjudication will as easily wreck the regulatory controls of the administrative as those same qualities on the rule-making side. . . .

6

Legal Reasoning

Many of the Realists' writings were devoted to the questions of how lawyers and judges should think about and seek to resolve cases. In retrospect, their reflections on those matters seem to fall into two categories: criticisms of what the Realists took to be the then-dominant style of reasoning, and suggestions as to how disputes could be resolved more intelligently.

The foundation of the critical aspect of the Realist credo was a positivist theory of the nature of law. They denounced the various metaphysical definitions of law that figured prominently in classical jurisprudence, offering in their place the empirical definition developed by Oliver Wendell Holmes: "The prophecies of what the courts will do in fact, and nothing more pretentious, are what I mean by law."[1] More specifically, the Realists argued that an accurate statement of the law governing a given case consists of an assessment of the probability that a judge or jury would grant relief to the plaintiff. In Karl Llewellyn's words: "a right... exists to the extent that a likelihood exists that A can induce a court to squeeze, out of B, A's damages."[2]

In making such prophecies, the Realists claimed, "traditional legal rules and concepts" have limited value. A few Realists sometimes argued that doctrine plays no role whatsoever in courts' decisionmaking and thus is useless in predicting outcomes.[3] Most took a more moderate position, arguing that judges sometimes to some degree pay attention to the "paper rules," but that they are also influenced powerfully by other considerations.[4]

The Realists explained on two grounds the limited role of doctrine in determining how cases are decided. First, invoking recent developments in philosophy, they argued that deductive logic and analogical reasoning are more flexible and open-ended analytical tools than the classical judges and scholars assumed; it is therefore naive to believe it possible either to derive particular legal rules from general concepts and particular outcomes from the application of rules to facts or to derive the answer to one case from a prior decision in a related case.[5] Second, the Realists insisted that much legal doctrine is internally inconsistent. "Legal Principles—and rules as well—are in the habit of hunting in pairs"; to any given dispute, at least two are likely to be equally relevant, and to point in opposite directions. Common law precedents and canons of statutory construction, they contended, are arranged in similar patterns.[6] Thus, even if equipped with effective logical implements, judges could not derive determinate answers from the "traditional rules."[7]

If doctrine does not wholly determine the outcomes of cases, what other forces are influential? On this question the Realists differed. A few contended that the typical judge resolves controversies largely on the basis of "hunches." "The vital motivating impulse for decision is an intuitive sense of what is right or wrong in the particular case."[8] Those who saw doctrine as more significant usually pointed to the "personality" of the judge as an important supplementary factor. A judge's "biases," they argued, affect his response to a given dispute in two ways: they influence his assessment of the credibility of the parties and witnesses and thus mold his perception of the facts of the case, and they help shape his sense of how the law ought to respond to those facts.[9] Some Realists—most notably, Jerome Frank—argued that those biases are derived, in turn, from life experiences peculiar to the judge. The majority, however, emphasized the more systemic and social determinants of judges' "prejudices" (such as the outlook and interests of the social class from which most judges are drawn), a position that helped them explain why most judges presented with a given case would reach the same result.[10]

Why, then, do judges pretend, when they write opinions explaining their decisions, that they are will-less, that they are doing no more than applying settled law? Drawing on recent developments in psychology and sociology, the Realists answered that judicial opinions serve the functions of rationalization and legitimation. By making each decision seem inevitable, opinions deflect popular criticism of the courts' rulings and conceal from the judges themselves the true bases of their rulings.[11]

Those, then, are the principal features of the Realists' assault on what they regarded as orthodox legal theory. The Realists' proposals for reshaping American law—and, specifically, their suggestions regarding how judges should decide cases—were less systematic and insightful. Indeed, the weakness of their affirmative program contributed significantly to the deterioration of the movement in the early 1940s. Among their desultory reflections on "ought-questions," however, were a few crucial insights and recommendations that were to figure prominently in legal scholarship after World War II.

The Realists' detractors accused them of being nominalists—of believing that universals and abstractions are nothing more than convenient devices for the communication of ideas and that the only respect in which the various referents of a general term are truly alike is that they happen to be called by the same name.[12] As applied to some members of the movement, the charge is accurate.[13] The majority, however, took a more moderate position: They believed that it is possible to identify or develop generalizations—specifically, legal concepts and rules—that capture or correspond to natural categories of human behavior and ways of controlling it. But they insisted that, to be meaningful and useful, such generalizations must be empirically based (derived from verifiable data) and narrow (incorporating only a small collection of manifestly similar situations or propositions).[14]

The philosophic stance just described undergirded three related proposals for transforming the substance and practice of law, which may be described collectively as particularism. First, the Realists argued that scholars and judges should jettison most of the accepted "black letter" rules and develop "working rules" that would more accurately describe the actual behavior of courts. Such empirically grounded rules would undoubtedly be much more specific than the propositions that currently dominate treatises and judicial opinions, because in practice most judges adjust their decisions to accommodate the peculiarities of the controversies they confront. The principal virtue of detailed "real rules" of this sort is that they would enable lawyers to advise their clients more intelligently.[15]

Second, the Realists argued that most extant legal concepts must be disaggregated if they are to be of any use in describing the behavior of courts or facilitating legal reform. Concepts like title, property right, and due process are hopelessly general. Relying heavily on the work of Wesley Hohfeld, the Realists insisted that all legal relationships, properly understood, consist of combinations of elemental entitlements that come in eight (and only eight) varieties—rights, privileges, powers, immunities, duties, no-rights, liabilities, and disabilities.[16] The existence of any one of these entitlements necessarily implies the existence of one other (its "correlative") and the nonexistence of a third (its "opposite"). Beyond that, however, there exists no inexorable or natural pattern of these relationships; it in no sense "follows" from the fact that X enjoys a particular legal privilege that X should also enjoy corresponding legal rights or powers. So, for example, the answer to the question whether picketing a place of business violates any right of the owner of the business can be derived neither from the abstract concept of ownership nor from the fact that the owner has the legal privilege of hiring whom he or she pleases, but rather can be obtained only through a conscious policy decision.[17] Disaggregation of a legal concept thus requires assessment of the social desirability of each of the myriad entitlements it hitherto encompassed and concealed.[18]

Third, the Realists argued that such policy decisions must be "particular" in an additional sense: they must refer to specific sets of socio-economic circumstances. It makes no sense to develop a rule governing all contracts or even all mortgages. The contexts in which contracts and mortgages are entered into and enforced vary dramatically; a set of entitlements appropriate in one might be entirely inappropriate in another.[19]

Different groups of Realists extended this last argument in two different directions. The first set argued that social reality is so variegated that even narrow rules are unhelpful; each dispute should be decided on its own facts. The responsible adjudicator, they claimed, should employ a variety of procedural devices to develop a rich understanding of the social setting and idiosyncratic circumstances of each individual case that comes before him and then, keeping in view and attempting to neutralize "his own prejudices, biases, antipathies, and the like," determine the best resolution of the controversy.[20] The second group believed that social reality, though complex, could be managed sensibly with narrow rules. On the basis of a thorough study of a particular industry or social practice, including examination of how its participants respond to different legal regimes, they claimed, a judge could, in the course of a particular decision, announce a specific legal norm, which would then guide and aid courts confronted in the future with similar problems.[21]

The second major component of the Realists' affirmative program is captured by the phrase *purposive adjudication*. For guidance in decision-making, many Realists argued, courts should depend primarily on consciously articulated social policies. Those Realists who saw any value in rules thought they ought to function not as powerful constraints on adjudication but as tentative expressions of how particular sets of policies impinge on particular social problems. Realists who saw rules as altogether unhelpful believed that the deliberate pursuit of social policies through the resolution of individual controversies is the only stabilizing force in adjudication.[22]

In the Realists' view, direct reference to the purposes of rules is both the key to *wise* construction of them and the only way in which they can be applied to facts with any degree of consistency and determinacy. Even the best rules cannot be applied deductively by judges in deciding concrete cases; the most such rules can do is "focus" and guide analysis of "problems of policy" and "suggest *lines* of wise *direction* of solution, for consideration." In sum, to think that a judge could decide a case by reading the rule and ignoring its "reason" is senseless.[23]

Because one's awareness of the purposes of legal rules is so important to interpreting them, the Realists argued, "only the rule which shows its reason on its face has ground to claim maximum chance of *continuing* effectiveness."[24] That insight, in turn, had important implications for the design of both statutory and common law norms. Legislators who wish to provide citizens and judges meaningful guidance should make their objectives clear when drafting and adopting statutes.[25] Judges who wish the norms they announce to be of any use in the future likewise should make explicit the policies on which they rest. In Llewellyn's characteristically eccentric prose, the "rightest and most beautiful type of legal rule, is the singing rule with purpose and with reason clear."[26]

But even "singing" common law rules, the Realists contended, are ephemeral in one crucial respect. The articulation of the objectives of a rule make it *possible* for courts in subsequent cases to follow it (more or less). But if those courts disagree with the policies, they should modify the rule.[27] It was this last attitude—that judges engaged in common law adjudication have the right and duty constantly to reconsider and revise the policies announced by their predecessors and the rules in which those policies were expressed—that doomed the project, first sketched by Holmes, of rebuilding legal doctrine from the ground up. Holmes had substantially anticipated the Realists in his contention that responsible decisionmaking requires the conscious application of policies to the facts of individual cases.[28] Holmes, however, had believed that the accretion of answers to such particular questions would gradually give rise to a detailed, consistent, and relatively stable body of doctrine that would inform private parties what they could and could not do and enable them to adjust their conduct accordingly.[29] The Realists' conviction that even highly specific common law rules should be continually reexamined compelled them to renounce Holmes' ambition.[30]

If the content of each of the myriad particular rules that constitute legal doctrine ought to be determined by a conscious policy decision, and if the interpretation and application of any rule requires reference to its purposes, lawmakers (legislators and judges) must have a clear and coherent vision of which policies are important and which are not. Unfortunately, it is on this crucial point that the Realists' writings were least satisfactory. Few members of the movement devoted significant attention to the content of the principles or policies that lawmakers should strive to implement, and the reflections of those who did take up such topics suffered from two general defects: eclecticism and excessive dependence on customary practices and standards.[31]

Virtually every time a Realist discussed the concerns that ought to guide reformulation of the legal rules governing a particular subfield or problem, he stressed the variety of conflicting policies that bore on the issue. For example, in an article written near the close of the Realist period, Llewellyn advised judges when reforming a particular aspect of the common law to strive simultaneously to foster social cooperation or "team play"; create incentives for productive activity and the development of leadership skills; make the "legal machinery" as efficient as possible; render the law accessible to the public; equalize "men's ... access to desired things—positions, powers, enjoyments, opportunities—things of which there are too few to meet all desires"; and provide "a right portion of favor, of unearned aid or indulgence to those who need it, provided the favor be so handled as not to turn its beneficiaries into laggards, spongers, sluggards."[32] To similar effect is Felix Cohen's insistence that our "standards of legal criticism" be inclusive. "Modern ethics has made it clear that no realm of values can be set apart from the fulsomeness of life. Justice, like beauty, or health, can be defined only in terms of the full set of human values, the things that men approve or enjoy for their own sake."[33]

One aspect of the Realists' outlook that may have contributed to such eclecticism was their ambivalence concerning the origins and status of moral propositions. A few members of the movement forthrightly adopted the stance of ethical relativism, insisting that "human experience discloses no ultimates ... [;] ultimates are phantoms drifting on a stream of day-dreams."[34] Most, however, equivocated on this issue. For example, in a book seeking to provide lawyers a system of values, Felix Cohen acknowledged that, as far as his own "vision ... extends," two "theories of ethics ... appear equally valid as explanations of the world of value": relativistic naturalism, which holds that "intrinsic goodness is relative, definable, and identical with a relation to an approving individual"; and "the theory that intrinsic goodness is absolute, indefinable, and equivalent in application to positive pleasantness." But although he concedes that "between these incompatible alternatives, we have discovered no rational basis of choice," he "fl[ies] forth on the pinions of faith" and does his best to persuade the reader of the merits of the second theory.[35] This ambivalence colors most Realist writings; the authors seem torn between a conviction that values are subjective and arbitrary and a residual belief (perhaps traceable to the ideology of Progressivism) that there do exist objective standards of justice and the public good, which the law should strive to advance.[36] In view of their tenuous hold on the notion that justice means more than personal taste, it is not surprising that most Realists were remarkably catholic in their definitions of the social good.

Most Realists sensed that, by arguing that a wide variety of policies will bear on any given problem, they were putting judges—and themselves, as critics of particular doctrines—in an uncomfortable position. How is a judge or scholar to weigh or choose between competing purposes? One member of the movement, Felix Cohen, confronted and tried to resolve this problem. After insisting on the breadth of the set of values that shapers of the law should take into account, Cohen set out to integrate those values into a coherent standard. The proper "starting point," he argued, is "the nonverbal agreement of men as to the content of the good life, whether determined broadly for a civilization or narrowly for a particular class or community." That vision should then be subjected to "continued refinement" through "critical analysis of possible ethical systems." Specifically, reflection upon "the nature of goodness" pointed toward "the hedonistic hypothesis" (by which he meant a version of utilitarianism) as the most plausible and attractive general ethical criterion. That insight, in turn, provided the makings of a standard for criticism and decision making: "The political task of hedonism is plain,—in thought, the translation of the books of the law into the universal language of human joys and sufferings,—in practice, the struggle for the attainment of the ideals thus discovered."[37]

Few Realists, however, took the path marked by Cohen. The large majority attempted in one of two ways not to solve but to evade the dilemma created by their ethical pluralism. The first tactic was simply to delay the project of considering "oughts."[38] A significant number of Realists purported to concentrate their energies on "identify[ing] ... the social consequences of particular legal measures and devices," disclaiming any ambition to "evaluate" those effects. They justified thus limiting their analyses on the ground that tracing the impacts of alternative legal regimes was an important and difficult job, demanding considerable time and attention. "When that task is well under way, there will be other seasons and other specialists more appropriate for doing the tasks of evaluation."[39]

The second tactic also involved a self-conscious turn from reflection upon ideals to examination of social reality, but for the purpose not of postponing the task of evaluation but rather of deriving substantive values from customary practices and beliefs. There were many variants of this maneuver; what they shared was the assumption that it is possible to determine what the law ought to be by studying how people in fact behave and what they in fact value.[40]

The most common defense of the foregoing assumption rested on a traditional Marxist conception of the nature and function of law: Although "changes in material culture ... precede and control changes in ... nonmaterial culture," including legal institutions, the latter all too often "lag behind" the former.[41] If legal analysts wish to shorten that lag, they must first acquire a thorough understanding of the evolving ways in which different institutions and industries operate. And the ambition of bringing the law more into conformity with underlying material conditions provided Realists who took this route a normative criterion for legal criticism and decisionmaking.[42]

This functionalist argument seems to have been supplemented in the minds of a few Realists by a conviction that the customary mores of a particular community should guide the resolution of controversies among its members. Llewellyn, in particular, believed that "indwelling" in "every fact-pattern of common life"—inherent in the circumstances themselves and the ways in which people perceive and respond to them—is an "immanent law," which a lawmaker can and should strive to "uncover and implement."[43] No other Realist was as explicit as Llewellyn on this score, but many seem to have shared his orientation.

To summarize, three attitudes both stimulated and hampered the Realists' efforts to rebuild American legal doctrine: (1) particularism, encompassing the related propositions that only narrow, empirically grounded "working rules" are helpful in predicting courts' decisions; that both analytical precision and wise policy making require the disaggregation of extant legal concepts; and that detailed knowledge of particular socioeconomic contexts is a precondition to sensible lawmaking;

(2) purposive adjudication—the conviction that legal rules can be intelligently applied only by keeping constantly in view the shifting mix of social policies they serve; and (3) ethical pluralism—the belief, partly rooted in ambivalence regarding the existence of objective standards of justice and the public good, that myriad, often conflicting social values are implicated by every legal issue—conjoined with hope that deference to customary values and practices would provide a way of reconciling competing concerns.

BENJAMIN N. CARDOZO

The Nature of the Judicial Process

(1921)

[In Law and the Modern Mind, *Jerome Frank described Benjamin Cardozo as follows: "One of the greatest American judges, he is in the forefront of those who realistically face the unavoidable uncertainties in law, the actualities of judicial law-making."[1] Cardozo's response was equivocal. In a letter to Frank, he seemed to agree with the characterization and to take pleasure in the compliment. However, in a subsequent speech before the New York Bar Association, he sought to distance himself from Frank and his comrades.[2] The speech may explain why Cardozo is often not included in studies of Legal Realism. It is undeniable, nevertheless, that Cardozo's early writings on the responsibilities of a judge anticipated in many ways the arguments of Llewellyn, Frank, and Cohen.—Ed]*

Few rules in our time are so well established that they may not be called upon any day to justify their existence as means adapted to an end. If they do not function, they are diseased. If they are diseased, they must not propagate their kind. Sometimes they are cut out and extirpated altogether. Sometimes they are left with the shadow of continued life, but sterilized, truncated, impotent for harm.

We get a striking illustration of the force of logical consistency, then of its gradual breaking down before the demands of practical convenience in isolated or exceptional instances, and finally of the generative force of the exceptions as a new stock, in the cases that deal with the right of a beneficiary to recover on a contract. England has been logically consistent and has refused the right of action altogether. New York and most states yielded to the demands of convenience and enforced the right of action, but at first only exceptionally and subject to many restrictions. Gradually the exceptions broadened till today they have left little of the rule. It survives chiefly in those cases where intention would be frustrated or convenience impaired by the extension of the right of action to others than the contracting parties. Rules derived by a process of logical deduction from pre-established conceptions of contract and obligation have broken down before the slow and steady and erosive action of utility and justice.

We see the same process at work in other fields. We no longer interpret contracts with meticulous adherence to the letter when in conflict with the spirit. We read covenants into them by implication when we find them "instinct with an obligation" imperfectly expressed. "The law has outgrown its primitive stage of formalism when the precise word was the sovereign talisman, and every slip was fatal." Perhaps it is in the field of procedure that we have witnessed the chief changes; though greater ones must yet be wrought. Indictments and civil pleadings are viewed with indulgent eyes. Rulings upon questions of evidence are held with increasing frequency to come within the discretion of the judge presiding at the trial. Errors are no longer ground for the upsetting of judgments with the ensuing horror of new trials, unless the appellate court is satisfied that they have affected the result. Legislation has sometimes been necessary to free us from the old fetters. Sometimes the conservatism of judges has threatened for an interval to rob the legislation of its efficacy. This danger was disclosed in the attitude of the courts toward the reforms embodied in codes of practice, in the days when they were first enacted. Precedents established in those times exert an unhappy influence even now. None the less, the tendency today is in the direction of a growing liberalism. The new spirit has made its way gradually; and its progress, unnoticed step by step, is visible in retrospect as we look back upon the distance traversed. The old forms remain, but they are filled with a new content. We are getting away from what Ehrlich calls "die spielerische und die mathematische Entscheidung," the conception of a lawsuit either as a mathematical problem or as a sportsman's game. Our own Wigmore has done much to make that conception out of date. We are thinking of the end which the law serves, and fitting its rules to the task of service.

This conception of the end of the law as determining the direction of its growth, which was Jhering's great contribution to the theory of jurisprudence, finds its organon, its instrument, in the method of sociology. Not the origin, but the goal, is the main thing. There can be no wisdom in the choice of a path unless we know where it will lead. The teleological conception of his function must be ever in the judge's mind. This means, of course, that the juristic philosophy of the common law is at bottom the philosophy of pragmatism. Its truth is relative, not absolute. The rule that functions well produces a title deed to recognition. Only in determining how it functions we must not view it too narrowly. We must not sacrifice the general to the particular. We must not throw to the winds the advantages of consistency and uniformity to do justice in the instance. We must keep within those interstitial limits which precedent and custom and the long and silent and almost indefinable practice of other judges through the centuries of the common law have set to judge-made innovations. But within the limits thus set, within the range over which choice moves, the final principle of selection for judges, as for legislators, is one of fitness to an end. "Le but est la vie interne, l'âme cachée, mais génératrice, de tous les droits." We do not pick our rules of law full-blossomed from the trees. Every judge consulting his own experience must be conscious of times when a free exercise of will, directed of set purpose to the furtherance of the common good, determined the form and tendency of a rule which at that moment took its origin in one creative act. Savigny's conception of law as something realized without struggle or aim or purpose, a process of silent growth, the fruition in life and manners of a people's history and genius, gives a picture incomplete and partial. It is true if we understand it to mean that the judge in shaping the rules of law must heed the *mores* of his day. It is one-sided and therefore false in so far as it implies that the *mores* of the day automatically shape rules which, full grown and ready made, are handed to the judge. Legal norms are confused with legal principles—*Entscheidungsnormen* with *Rechtssätze*. Law is, indeed, an historical growth, for it is an expression of customary morality which develops silently and unconsciously from one age to another. That is the great truth in Savigny's theory of its origin. But law is also a conscious or purposed growth, for the expression of customary morality will be false unless the mind of the judge is directed to the attainment of the moral end and its embodiment in legal forms. Nothing less than conscious effort will be adequate if the end in view is to prevail. The standards or patterns of utility and morals will be found by the judge in the life of the community. They will be found in the same way by the legislator. That does not mean, however, that the work of the one any more than that of the other is a replica of nature's forms.

There has been much debate among foreign jurists whether the norms of right and useful conduct, the patterns of social welfare, are to be found by the judge in conformity with an objective or a subjective standard. Opposing schools of thought have battled for each view. At times, the controversy has seemed to turn upon the use of words and little more. So far as the distinction has practical significance, the traditions of our jurisprudence commit us to the objective standard. I do not mean, of course, that this ideal of objective vision is ever perfectly attained. We cannot transcend the limitations of the *ego* and see anything as it really is. None the less, the ideal is one to be striven for within the limits of our capacity. This truth, when clearly perceived, tends to unify the judge's function. His duty to declare the law in accordance with reason and justice is seen to be a phase of his duty to declare it in accordance with custom. It is the customary morality of right-minded men and women which he is to enforce by his decree. A jurisprudence that is not constantly brought into relation to objective or external standards incurs the risk of degenerating into what the Germans call "Die Gefühlsjurisprudenz," a jurisprudence of mere sentiment or feeling. A judicial judgment, says Stammler, "should be a judgment of objective right, and no subjective and free opinion; a verdict and not a mere personal fiat. Evil stands the case when it is to be said of a judicial decree as the saying goes in the play of the 'Two Gentlemen of Verona' (Act I, sc. ii):

'I have no other but a woman's reason;
I think him so, because I think him so.' "

Scholars of distinction have argued for a more subjective standard. "We all agree," says Professor Gray, "that many cases should be decided by the courts on notions of right and wrong, and, of course, everyone will agree that a judge is likely to share the notions of right and wrong prevalent in the community in which he lives; but suppose in a case where there is nothing to guide him but notions of right and wrong, that his notions of right and wrong differ from those of the community—which ought he to follow—his own notions, or the notions of the community? Mr. Carter's theory ["Origin and Sources of Law," J. C. Carter] requires him to say that the judge must follow the notions of the community. I believe that he should follow his own notions." The hypothesis that Professor Gray offers us is not likely to be realized in practice. Rare indeed must be the case when, with conflicting notions of right conduct, there will be nothing else to sway the balance. If, however, the case supposed were here, a judge, I think, would err if he were to impose upon the community as a rule of life his own idiosyncrasies of conduct or belief. Let us suppose, for illustration, a judge who looked upon theatre-going as a sin. Would he be doing right if, in a field where the rule of law was still unsettled, he permitted this conviction, though known to be in conflict with the dominant standard of right conduct, to govern his decision? My own notion is that he would be under a duty to conform to the accepted standards of the community, the *mores* of the times. This does not mean, however, that a judge is powerless to raise the level of prevailing conduct. In one field or another of activity, practices in opposition to the sentiments and standards of the age may grow up and threaten to intrench themselves if not dislodged. Despite their temporary hold, they do not stand comparison with accepted norms of morals. Indolence or passivity has tolerated what the considerate judgment of the community condemns. In such cases, one of the highest functions of the judge is to establish the true relation between conduct and profession. There are even times, to speak somewhat paradoxically, when nothing less than a subjective measure will satisfy objective standards. Some relations in life impose a duty to act in accordance with the customary morality and nothing more. In those the customary morality must be the standard for the judge. *Caveat emptor* is a maxim that will often have to be followed when the morality which it expresses is not that of sensitive souls. Other relations in life, as, e.g., those of trustee and beneficiary, or principal and surety, impose a duty to act in accordance with the highest standards which a man of the most delicate conscience and the nicest sense of honor might impose upon himself. In such cases, to enforce adherence to those standards becomes the duty of the judge. Whether novel situations are to be brought within one class of relations or within the other must be determined, as they arise, by considerations of analogy, of convenience, of fitness, and of justice.

The truth, indeed, is, as I have said, that the distinction between the subjective or individual and the objective or general conscience, in the field where the judge is not limited by established rules, is shadowy and evanescent, and tends to become one of words and little more. For the casuist and the philosopher, it has its speculative interest. In the practical administration of justice, it will seldom be decisive for the judge. This is admitted by Brütt, one of the staunchest upholders of the theory of objective right. The perception of objective right takes the color of the subjective mind. The conclusions of the subjective mind take the color of customary practices and objectified beliefs. There is constant and subtle interaction between what is without and what is within. We may hold, on the one side, with Tarde and his school, that all social innovations come "from individual inventions spread by imitation," or on the other side, with Durkheim and his school, that all such innovations come "through the action of the social mind." In either view, whether the impulse spreads from the individual or from society, from within or from without, neither the components nor the mass can work in independence of each other. The personal and the general mind and will are inseparably united. The difference, as one theory of judicial duty or the other prevails, involves at most a little change of emphasis, of the method of approach, of the point of view, the angle, from which problems are envisaged. Only dimly and by force of an influence subconscious, or nearly so, will the difference be reflected in the decisions of the courts.

My analysis of the judicial process comes then to this, and little more: logic, and history, and custom, and utility, and the accepted standards of right conduct, are the forces which singly or in combination shape the progress of the law. Which of these forces shall dominate in any case must depend largely upon the comparative importance or value of the social interests that will be thereby promoted or impaired. One of the most fundamental social interests is that law shall be uniform and impartial. There must be nothing in its action that savors of prejudice or favor or even arbitrary whim or fitfulness. Therefore in the main there shall be adherence to precedent. There shall be symmetrical development, consistently with history or custom when history or custom has been the motive force, or the chief one, in giving shape to existing rules, and with logic or philosophy when the motive power has been theirs. But symmetrical development may be bought at too high a price. Uniformity ceases to be a good when it becomes uniformity of oppression. The social interest served by symmetry or certainty must then be balanced against the social interest served by equity and fairness or other elements of social welfare. These may enjoin upon the judge the duty of drawing the line at another angle, of staking the path along new courses, of marking a new point of departure from which others who come after him will set out upon their journey.

If you ask how he is to know when one interest outweighs another, I can only answer that he must get his knowledge just as the legislator gets it, from experience and study and reflection; in brief, from life itself. Here, indeed, is the point of contact between the legislator's work and his. The choice of methods, the appraisement of values, must in the end be guided by like considerations for the one as for the other. Each indeed is legislating within the limits of his competence. No doubt the limits for the judge are narrower. He legislates only between gaps. He fills the open spaces in the law. How far he may go without traveling beyond the walls of the interstices cannot be staked out for him upon a chart. He must learn it for himself as he gains the sense of fitness and proportion that comes with years of habitude in the practice of an art. Even within the gaps, restrictions not easy to define, but felt, however impalpable they may be, by every judge and lawyer, hedge and circumscribe his action. They are established by the traditions of the centuries, by the example of other judges, his predecessors and his colleagues, by the collective judgment of the profession, and by the duty of adherence to the pervading spirit of the law. . . . None the less, within the confines of these open spaces and those of precedent and tradition, choice moves with a freedom which stamps its action as creative. The law which is the resulting product is not found, but made. The process, being legislative, demands the legislator's wisdom.

Pennsylvania Coal Company v. *Mahon*

260 U.S. 393 (1922)

Mr. Justice Holmes delivered the opinion of the Court.

This is a bill in equity brought by the defendants in error to prevent the Pennsylvania Coal Company from mining under their property in such way as to remove the supports and cause a subsidence of the surface and of their house. The bill sets out a deed executed by the Coal Company in 1878, under which the plaintiffs claim. The deed conveys the surface, but in express terms reserves the right to remove all the coal under the same, and the grantee takes the premises with the risk, and waives all claim for damages that may arise from mining out the coal. But the plaintiffs say that whatever may have been the Coal Company's rights, they were taken away by an Act of Pennsylvania, approved May 27, 1921, commonly known there as the Kohler Act. The Court of Common Pleas found that if not restrained the defendant would cause the damage to prevent which the bill was brought, but denied an injunction, holding that the statute if applied to this case would be unconstitutional. On appeal the Supreme Court of the State agreed that the defendant had contract and property rights protected by the Constitution of the United States, but held that the statute was a legitimate exercise of the police power and directed a decree for the plaintiffs. A writ of error was granted bringing the case to this Court.

The statute forbids the mining of anthracite coal in such way as to cause the subsidence of, among other things, any structure used as a human habitation, with certain exceptions, including among them land where the surface is owned by the owner of the underlying coal and is distant more than one hundred and fifty feet from any improved property belonging to any other person. As applied to this case the statute is admitted to destroy previously existing rights of property and contract. The question is whether the police power can be stretched so far.

Government hardly could go on if to some extent values incident to property could not be diminished without paying for every such change in the general law. As long recognized, some values are enjoyed under an implied limitation and must yield to the police power. But obviously the implied limitation must have its limits, or the contract and due process clauses are gone. One fact for consideration in determining such limits is the extent of the diminution. When it reaches a certain magnitude, in most if not in all cases there must be an exercise of eminent domain and compensation to sustain the act. So the question depends upon the particular facts. The greatest weight is given to the judgment of the legislature, but it always is open to interested parties to contend that the legislature has gone beyond its constitutional power.

This is the case of a single private house. No doubt there is a public interest even in this, as there is in every purchase and sale and in all that happens within the commonwealth. Some existing rights may be modified even in such a case. But usually in ordinary private affairs the public interest does not warrant much of this kind of interference. A source of damage to such a house is not a public nuisance even if similar damage is inflicted on others in different places. The damage is not common or public. The extent of the public interest is shown by the statute to be limited, since the statute ordinarily does not apply to land when the surface is owned by the owner of the coal. Furthermore, it is not justified as a protection of personal safety. That could be provided for by notice. Indeed the very foundation of this bill is that the defendant gave timely notice of its intent to mine under the house. On the other hand the extent of the taking is great. It purports to abolish what is recognized in Pennsylvania as an estate in land—a very valuable estate—and what is declared by the Court below to be a contract hitherto binding the plaintiffs. If we were called upon to deal with the plaintiffs' position alone, we should think it clear that the statute does not disclose a public interest sufficient to warrant so extensive a destruction of the defendant's constitutionally protected rights.

But the case has been treated as one in which the general validity of the act should be discussed. The Attorney General of the State, the City of Scranton, and the representatives of other extensive interests were allowed to take part in the argument below and have submitted their contentions here. It seems, therefore, to be our duty to go farther in the statement of our opinion, in order that it may be known at once, and that further suits should not be brought in vain.

·It is our opinion that the act cannot be sustained as an exercise of the police power, so far as it affects the mining of coal under streets or cities in places where the right to mine such coal has been reserved. As said in a Pennsylvania case, "For practical purposes, the right to coal consists in the right to mine it." What makes the right to mine coal valuable is that it can be exercised with profit. To make it commercially impracticable to mine certain coal has very nearly the same effect for constitutional purposes as appropriating or destroying it. This we think that we are warranted in assuming that the statute does.

It is true that in *Plymouth Coal Co.* v. *Pennsylvania*, 232 U.S. 531 [1914], it was held competent for the legislature to require a pillar of coal to be left along the line of adjoining property, that, with the pillar on the other side of the line, would be a barrier sufficient for the safety of the employees of either mine in case the other should be abandoned and allowed to fill with water. But that was a requirement for the safety of employees invited into the mine, and secured an average reciprocity of advantage that has been recognized as a justification of various laws.

The rights of the public in a street purchased or laid out by eminent domain are those that it has paid for. If in any case its representatives have been so short sighted as to acquire only surface rights without the right of support, we see no more authority for supplying the latter without compensation than there was for taking the right of way in the first place and refusing to pay for it because the public wanted it very much. The protection of private property in the Fifth Amendment presupposes that it is wanted for public use, but provides that it shall not be taken for such use without compensation. A similar assumption is made in the decisions upon the Fourteenth Amendment. When this seemingly absolute protection is found to be qualified by the police power, the natural tendency of human nature is to extend the qualification more and more until at last private property disappears. But that cannot be accomplished in this way under the Constitution of the United States.

The general rule at least is, that while property may be regulated to a certain extent, if regulation goes too far it will be recognized as a taking. It may be doubted how far exceptional cases, like the blowing up of a house to stop a conflagration, go—and if they go beyond the general rule, whether they do not stand as much upon tradition as upon principle.[1] In general it is not plain that a man's misfortunes or necessities will justify his shifting the damages to his neighbor's shoulders. We are in danger of forgetting that a strong public desire to improve the public condition is not enough to warrant achieving the desire by a shorter cut than the constitutional way of paying for the change. As we already have said, this is a question of degree—and therefore cannot be disposed of by general propositions. But we regard this as going beyond any of the cases decided by this Court. The late decisions upon laws dealing with the congestion of Washington and New York, caused by the war, dealt with laws intended to meet a temporary emergency and providing for compensation determined to be reasonable by an impartial board.[2] They went to the verge of the law but fell far short of the present act.

We assume, of course, that the statute was passed upon the conviction that an exigency existed that would warrant it, and we assume that an exigency exists that would warrant the exercise of eminent domain. But the question at bottom is upon whom the loss of the changes desired should fall. So far as private persons or communities have seen fit to take the risk of acquiring only surface rights, we cannot see that the fact that their risk has become a danger warrants the giving to them greater rights than they bought.

Decree reversed.

Mr. Justice Brandeis, dissenting.

The Kohler Act prohibits, under certain conditions, the mining of anthracite coal within the limits of a city in such a manner or to such an extent "as to cause the . . . subsidence of any dwelling or other structure used as a human habitation, or any factory, store, or other industrial or mercantile establishment in which human labor is employed." Coal in place is land; and the right of the owner to use his land is not absolute. He may not so use it as to create a public nuisance; and uses, once harmless, may, owing to changed conditions, seriously threaten the public welfare. Whenever they do, the legislature has power to prohibit such uses without paying compensation; and the power to prohibit extends alike to the manner, the character and the purpose of the use. Are we justified in declaring that the Legislature of Pennsylvania has, in restricting the right to mine anthracite, exercised this power so arbitrarily as to violate the Fourteenth Amendment?

Every restriction upon the use of property imposed in the exercise of the police power deprives the owner of some right theretofore enjoyed, and is, in that sense, an abridgment by the State of rights in property without making compensation. But restriction imposed to protect the public health, safety or morals from dangers threatened is not a taking. The restriction here in question is merely the prohibition of a noxious use. The property so restricted remains in the possession of its owner. The State does not appropriate it or make any use of it. The State merely prevents the owner from making a use which interferes with paramount rights of the public. Whenever the use prohibited ceases to be noxious,— as it may because of further change in local or social conditions,—the restriction will have to be removed and the owner will again be free to enjoy his property as heretofore.

The restriction upon the use of this property can not, of course, be lawfully imposed, unless its purpose is to protect the public. But the purpose of a restriction does not cease to be public, because incidentally some private persons may thereby receive gratuitously valuable special benefits. Thus, owners of low buildings may obtain, through statutory restrictions upon the height of neighboring structures, benefits equivalent to an easement of light and air. Furthermore, a restriction, though imposed for a public purpose, will not be lawful, unless the restriction is an appropriate means to the public end. But to keep coal in place is surely an appropriate means of preventing subsidence of the surface; and ordinarily it is the only available means. Restriction upon use does not become inappropriate as a means, merely because it deprives the owner of the only use to which the property can then be profitably put. The liquor and the oleomargarine cases settled that.[3] Nor is a restriction imposed through exercise of the police power inappropriate as a means, merely because the same end might be effected through exercise of the power of eminent domain, or otherwise at public expense. Every restriction upon the height of buildings might be secured through acquiring by eminent domain the right of each owner to build above the limiting height; but it is settled that the State need not resort to that power. If by mining anthracite coal the owner would necessarily unloose poisonous gasses, I suppose no one would doubt the power of the State to prevent the mining, without buying his coal fields. And why may not the State, likewise, without paying compensation, prohibit one from digging so deep or excavating so near the surface, as to expose the community to like dangers? In the latter case, as in the former, carrying on the business would be a public nuisance.

It is said that one fact for consideration in determining whether the limits of the police power have been exceeded is the extent of the resulting diminution in value; and that here the restriction destroys existing rights of property and contract. But values are relative. If we are to consider the value of the coal kept in place by the restriction, we should compare it with the value of all other parts of the land. That is, with the value not of the coal alone, but with the value of the whole property. The rights of an owner as against the public are not increased by dividing the interests in his property into surface and subsoil. The sum of the rights in the parts can not be greater than the rights in the whole. The estate of an owner in land is grandiloquently described as extending *ab orco usque ad coelum.*[4] But I suppose no one would contend that by selling his interest above one hundred feet from the surface he could prevent the State from limiting, by the police power, the height of structures in a city. And why should a sale of underground rights bar the State's power? For aught that appears the value of the coal kept in place by the restriction may be negligible as compared with the value of the whole property, or even as compared with that part of it which is represented by the coal remaining in place and which may be extracted despite the statute. Ordinarily a police regulation, general in operation, will not be held void as to a particular property, although proof is offered that owing to conditions peculiar to it the restriction could not reasonably be applied. But even if the particular facts are to govern, the statue should, in my opinion, be upheld in this case. For the defendant has failed to adduce any evidence from which it appears that to restrict its mining operations was an unreasonable exercise of the police power. Where the surface and the coal belong to the same person, self-interest would ordinarily prevent mining to such an extent as to cause a subsidence. It was, doubtless, for this reason that the legislature, estimating the degrees of danger, deemed statutory restriction unnecessary for the public safety under such conditions.

It is said that this is a case of a single dwelling house; that the restriction upon mining abolishes a valuable estate hitherto secured by a contract with the plaintiffs; and that the restriction upon mining cannot be justified as a protection of personal safety, since that could be provided for by notice. The propriety of deferring a good deal to tribunals on the spot has been repeatedly recognized. May we say that notice would afford adequate protection of the public safety where the legislature and the highest court of the State, with greater knowledge of local conditions, have declared, in effect, that it would not? If public safety is imperiled, surely neither grant, nor contract, can prevail against the exercise of the police power. The rule that the State's power to take appropriate measures to guard the safety of all who may be within its jurisdiction may not be bargained away was applied to compel carriers to establish grade crossings at their own expense, despite contracts to the contrary; and, likewise, to supersede, by an employers' liability act, the provision of a charter exempting a railroad from liability for death of employees, since the civil liability was deemed a matter of public concern, and not a mere private right. Nor can existing contracts between private individuals preclude exercise of the police power. "One whose rights, such as they are, are subject to state restriction, cannot remove them from the power of the State by making a contract about them." The fact that this suit is brought by a private person is, of course, immaterial to protect the community through invoking the aid, as litigant, of interested private citizens is not a novelty in our law. That it may be done in Pennsylvania was decided by its Supreme Court in this case. And it is for a State to say how its public policy shall be enforced.

This case involves only mining which causes subsidence of a dwelling house. But the Kohler Act contains provisions in addition to that quoted above; and as to these, also, an opinion is expressed. These provisions deal with mining under cities to such an extent as to cause subsidence of—

(a) Any public building or any structure customarily used by the public as a place of resort, assemblage, or amusement, including, but not being limited to, churches, schools, hospitals, theatres, hotels, and railroad stations.

(b) Any street, road, bridge, or other public passageway, dedicated to public use or habitually used by the public.

(c) Any track, roadbed, right of way, pipe, conduit, wire, or other facility, used in the service of the public by any municipal corporation or public service company as defined by the Public Service Company Law.

A prohibition of mining which causes subsidence of such structures and facilities is obviously enacted for a public purpose; and it seems, likewise, clear that mere notice of intention to mine would not in this connection secure the public safety. Yet it is said that these provisions of the act cannot be sustained as an exercise of the police power where the right to mine such coal has been reserved. The conclusion seems to rest upon the assumption that in order to justify such exercise of the police power there must be "an average reciprocity of advantage" as between the owner of the property restricted and the rest of the community; and that here such reciprocity is absent. Reciprocity of advantage is an important consideration, and may even be an essential, where the State's power is exercised for the purpose of conferring benefits upon the property of a neighborhood, as in drainage projects, or upon adjoining owners, as by party wall provisions. But where the police power is exercised, not to confer benefits upon property owners, but to protect the public from detriment and danger, there is, in my opinion, no room for considering reciprocity of advantage. There was no reciprocal advantage to the [owners of property adversely affected by several of the state statutes this Court has upheld—] unless it be the advantage of living and doing business in a civilized community. That reciprocal advantage is given by the act to the coal operators.

JOHN DEWEY

"Logical Method and Law"

(1924)

Human conduct, broadly viewed, falls into two sorts: Particular cases overlap, but the difference is discernible on any large scale consideration of conduct. Sometimes human beings act with a minimum of foresight, without examination of what they are doing and of probable consequences. They act not upon deliberation but from routine, instinct, the direct pressure of appetite, or a blind 'hunch.' It would be a mistake to suppose that such behavior is always inefficient or unsuccessful. When we do not like it, we condemn it as capricious, arbitrary, careless, negligent. But in other cases, we praise the marvellous rectitude of instinct or intuition; we are inclined to accept the offhand appraisal of an expert in preference to elaborately calculated conclusions of a man who is ill-informed. There is the old story of the layman who was appointed to a position in India where he would have to pass in his official capacity on various matters in controversy between natives. Upon consulting a legal friend, he was told to use his common-sense and announce his decisions firmly; in the majority of cases his natural decision as to what was fair and reasonable would suffice. But, his friend added: "Never try to give reasons, for they will usually be wrong."

In the other sort of case, action follows upon a decision, and the decision is the outcome of inquiry, comparison of alternatives, weighing of facts; deliberation or thinking has intervened. Considerations which have weight in reaching the conclusion as to what is to be done, or which are employed to justify it when it is questioned, are called 'reasons.' If they are stated in sufficiently general terms they are 'principles.' When the operation is formulated in a compact way, the decision is called a conclusion, and the considerations which led up to it are called the premises. Decisions of the first type may be reasonable: that is, they may be adapted to good results; those of the second type are reasoned or rational, increasingly so, in the degree of care and thoroughness with which inquiry has been conducted and the order in which connections have been established between the considerations dealt with.

Now I define logical theory as an account of the procedures followed in reaching decisions of the second type, in those cases in which subsequent experience shows that they were the best which could have been used under the conditions. This definition would be questioned by many authorities, and it is only fair to say that it does not represent the orthodox or the prevailing view. But it is stated at the outset so that the reader may be aware of the conception of logic which underlies the following discussion. If we take an objection which will be brought against this conception by adherents of the traditional notion, it will serve to clarify its meaning. It will be said that the definition restricts thinking to the processes antecedent to making a decision or a deliberate choice; and, thereby, in confining logical procedure to practical matters, fails to take even a glance at those cases in which true logical method is best exemplified: namely, scientific, especially mathematical, subjects.

A partial answer to this objection is that the especial topic of our present discussion is logical method in legal reasoning and judicial decision, and that such cases at least are similar in general type to decisions made by engineers, merchants, physicians, bankers, etc., in the pursuit of their callings. In law we are certainly concerned with the necessity of settling upon a course of action to be pursued, giving judgment of one sort or another in favor of adoption of one mode of conduct and against another. But the scope of the position taken will appear more clearly if we do not content ourselves with this *ad hoc* reply.

If we consider the procedure of the mathematician or of any man of science, as it concretely occurs, instead of considering simply the relations of consistent implication which subsist between the propositions in which his finally approved conclusions are set forth, we find that he, as well as an intelligent farmer or business man or physician, is constantly engaged in making decisions; and that in order to make them wisely he summons before his mental gaze various considerations, and accepts and rejects them with a view to making his decision as rational as possible. The concrete subject with which he deals, the material he investigates, accepts, rejects, employs in reaching and justifying his decision, is different from that of farmer, lawyer, or merchant, but the course of the operation, the form of the procedure, is similar. The scientific man has the advantage of working under much more narrowly and exactly controlled conditions, with the aid of symbols artfully devised to protect his procedure. For that reason it is natural and proper that we should, in our formal treatises, take operations of this type as standards and models, and should treat ordinary 'practical' reasonings leading up to decisions as to what is to be done as only approximations. But every thinker, as an investigator, mathematician, or physicist as well as 'practical man,' thinks in order to determine *his* decisions and conduct—his conduct as a specialized agent working in a carefully delimited field.

It may be replied, of course, that this is an arbitrary notion of logic, and that in reality logic is an affair of the relations and orders of relations which subsist between propositions which constitute the accepted subject-matter of a science; that relations are independent of operations of inquiry and of reaching conclusions or decisions. I shall not stop to try to controvert this position, but shall use it to point [out] the essential difference between it and the position taken in this article. According to the latter, logical systematization with a view to the utmost generality and consistency of propositions is indispensable but is not ultimate. It is an instrumentality, not an end. It is a means of improving, facilitating, clarifying the inquiry that leads up to concrete decisions; primarily that particular inquiry which has just been engaged in, but secondarily, and of greater ultimate importance, other inquiries directed at making other decisions in similar fields. And here at least I may fall back for confirmation upon the special theme of law. It is most important that rules of law should form as coherent generalized logical systems as possible. But these logical systematizations of law in any field, whether of crime, contracts or torts, with their reduction of a multitude of decisions to a few general principles that are logically consistent with one another while it may be an end in itself for a particular student, is clearly in last resort subservient to the economical and effective reaching of decisions in particular cases.

It follows that logic is ultimately an empirical and concrete discipline. Men first employ certain ways of investigating, and of collecting, recording and using data in reaching conclusions, in making decisions; they draw inferences and make their checks and tests in various ways. These different ways constitute the empirical raw material of logical theory. The latter thus comes into existence without any conscious thought of logic, just as forms of speech take place without conscious reference to rules of syntax or of rhetorical propriety. But it is gradually learned that some methods which are used work better than others. Some yield conclusions that do not stand the test of further situations; they produce conflicts and confusion; decisions dependent upon them have to be retracted or revised. Other methods are found to yield conclusions which are available in subsequent inquiries as well as confirmed by them. There first occurs a kind of natural selection of the methods which afford the better type of conclusion, better for subsequent usage, just as happens in the development of rules for conducting any art. Afterwards the methods are themselves studied critically. Successful ones are not only selected and collated, but the causes of their effective operation are discovered. Thus logical theory becomes scientific.

The bearing of the conception of logic which is here advanced upon legal thinking and decisions may be brought out by examining the apparent disparity which exists between actual legal development and the strict requirements of logical theory. Justice Holmes has generalized the situation by saying that "the whole outline of the law is the resultant of a conflict at every point between logic and good sense—the one striving to work fiction out to consistent results, the other restraining and at last

overcoming that effort when the results become too manifestly unjust."
This statement he substantiates by a thorough examination of the development of certain legal notions. Upon its surface, such a statement implies a different view of the nature of logic than that stated. It implies that logic is not the method *of* good sense, that it has as it were a substance and life of its own which conflicts with the requirements of good decisions with respect to concrete subject-matters. The difference, however, is largely verbal. What Justice Holmes terms logic is formal consistency, consistency of concepts with one another irrespective of the consequences of their application to concrete matters-of-fact. We might state the fact by saying that concepts once developed have a kind of intrinsic inertia on their own account; once developed the law of habit applies to them. It is practically economical to use a concept ready at hand rather than to take time and trouble and effort to change it or to devise a new one. The use of prior ready-made and familiar concepts also gives rise to a sense of stability, of guarantee against sudden and arbitrary changes of the rules which determine the consequences which legally attend acts. It is the nature of any concept, as it is of any habit to change more slowly than do the concrete circumstances with reference to which it is employed. Experience shows that the relative fixity of concepts affords men with a specious sense of protection, of assurance against the troublesome flux of events. Thus Justice Holmes says, "The language of judicial decision is mainly the language of logic. And the logical method and form flatter that longing for certainty and for repose which is in every human mind. But certainty generally is an illusion." From the view of logical method here set forth, however, the undoubted facts which Justice Holmes has in mind do not concern logic but rather certain tendencies of the human creatures who use logic; tendencies which a sound logic will guard against. For they spring from the momentum of habit once forced, and express the effect of habit upon our feelings of ease and stability—feelings which have little to do with the actual facts of the case.

However this is only part of the story. The rest of the story is brought to light in some other passages of Justice Holmes. "The actual life of the law has not been logic: it has been experience. The felt necessities of the times, the prevalent moral and political theories, intuitions of public policy, avowed or unconscious, even the prejudices which judges share with their fellow-men, have had a good deal more to do than the syllogism in determining the rules by which men should be governed." In other words, Justice Holmes is thinking of logic as equivalent with the syllogism, as he is quite entitled to do in accord with the orthodox tradition. From the standpoint of the syllogism as the logical model which was made current by scholasticism there *is* an antithesis between experience and logic, between logic and good sense. For the philosophy embodied in the formal theory of the syllogism asserted that thought or reason has fixed forms of its own, anterior to and independent of concrete subject-matters, and to which the latter have to be adapted whether or no. This defines the negative aspect of this discussion; and it shows by contrast the need of another kind of logic which shall reduce the influence of habit, and shall facilitate the use of good sense regarding matters of social consequence.

In other words, there are different logics in use. One of these, the one which has had greatest historic currency and exercised greatest influence on legal decisions, is that of the syllogism. To this logic the strictures of Justice Holmes apply in full force. For it purports to be a logic of rigid demonstration, not of search and discovery. It claims to be a logic of fixed forms, rather than of methods of reaching intelligent decisions in concrete situations, or of methods employed in adjusting disputed issues in behalf of the public and enduring interest. Those ignorant of formal logic, the logic of the abstract relations of ready-made conceptions to one another, have at least heard of the standard syllogism: All men are mortal; Socrates is a man; therefore, he is mortal. This is offered as the model of all proof or demonstration. It implies that what we need and must procure is first a fixed general *principle*, the so-called major premise, such as 'all men are mortal;' then in the second place, a fact which belongs intrinsically and obviously to a class of things to which the general principle applies: Socrates is a man. Then the conclusion automatically follows: Socrates is mortal. According to this model every demonstrative or strictly logical conclusion 'subsumes' a particular under an appropriate universal. It implies the prior and given existence of particulars and universals.

It thus implies that for every possible case which may arise, there is a fixed antecedent rule already at hand; that the case in question is either simple and unambiguous, or is resolvable by direct inspection into a collection of simple and indubitable facts, such as, 'Socrates is a man.' It thus tends, when it is accepted, to produce and confirm what Professor Pound has called mechanical jurisprudence; it flatters that longing for certainty of which Justice Holmes speaks; it reinforces those inert factors in human nature which make men hug as long as possible any idea which has once gained lodgment in the mind.

In a certain sense it is foolish to criticise the model supplied by the syllogism. The statements made about men and Socrates are obviously true, and the connection between them is undoubted. The trouble is that while the syllogism sets forth the *results* of thinking, it has nothing to do with the *operation* of thinking. Take the case of Socrates being tried before the Athenian citizens, and the thinking which had to be done to reach a decision. Certainly the issue was not whether Socrates was mortal; the point was whether this mortality would or should occur at a specified date and in a specified way. Now that is just what does not and cannot follow from a general principle or a major premise. Again to quote Justice Holmes, "General propositions do not decide concrete cases." No concrete proposition, that is to say one with material dated in time and placed in space, follows from any general statements or from any connection between them.

If we trust to an experimental logic, we find that general principles emerge as statements of generic ways in which it has been found helpful to treat concrete cases. The real force of the proposition that all men are mortal is found in the expectancy tables of insurance companies, which with their accompanying rates show how it is prudent and socially useful to deal with human mortality. The 'universal' stated in the major premise is not outside of and antecedent to particular cases; neither is it a selection of something found in a variety of cases. It is an indication of a single way of treating cases for certain purposes or consequences in spite of their diversity. Hence its meaning and worth are subject to inquiry and revision in view of what happens, what the consequences are, when it is used as a method of treatment.

As a matter of fact, men do not begin thinking with premises. They begin with some complicated and confused case, apparently admitting of alternative modes of treatment and solution. Premises only gradually emerge from analysis of the total situation. The problem is not to draw a conclusion from given premises; that can best be done by a piece of inanimate machinery by fingering a keyboard. The problem is to *find* statements of general principle and of particular fact, which are worthy to serve as premises. As a matter of actual fact, we generally begin with some vague anticipation of a conclusion (or at least of alternative conclusions), and then we look around for principles and data which will substantiate it or which will enable us to choose intelligently between rival conclusions. No lawyer ever thought out the case of a client in terms of the syllogism. He begins with a conclusion which he intends to reach, favorable to his client of course, and then analyzes the facts of the situation to find material out of which to construct a favorable statement of facts, to *form* a minor premise. At the same time he goes over recorded cases to find rules of law employed in cases which can be presented as similar, rules which will substantiate a certain way of looking at and interpreting the facts. And as his acquaintance with rules of law judged applicable widens, he probably alters perspective and emphasis in selection of the facts which are to form his evidential data. And as he learns more of the facts of the case he may modify his selection of rules of law upon which he bases his case.

I do not for a moment set up this procedure as a model of scientific method; it is too precommitted to the establishment of a particular and partisan conclusion to serve as such a model. But it does illustrate, in spite of this deficiency, the particular point which is being made here: namely, that thinking actually sets out from a more or less confused situation, which is vague and ambiguous with respect to the conclusion it indicates, and that the formation of both major premise and minor proceed tentatively and correlatively in the course of analysis of this situation and of prior rules. As soon as acceptable premises are given and of course the judge and jury have eventually to do with their becoming accepted—and the conclusion is also given. In strict logic, the conclusion does not follow from premises; conclusions and premises are two ways of stating the same thing. Thinking may be defined either as a development of premises or development of a conclusion; as far as it is one operation it is the other.

Courts not only reach decisions; they expound them, and the exposition must state justifying reasons. The mental operations therein involved are somewhat different from those involved in arriving at a conclusion. The logic of exposition is different from that of search and inquiry. In the latter, the situation as it exists is more or less doubtful, indeterminate, and problematic with respect to what it signifies. It unfolds itself gradually and is susceptible of dramatic surprise; at all events it has, for the time being, two sides. Exposition implies that a definitive solution is reached, that the situation is now determinate with respect to its legal implication. Its purpose is to set forth grounds for the decision reached so that it will not appear as an arbitrary dictum, and so that it will indicate a rule for dealing with similar cases in the future. It is highly probable that the need of justifying to others conclusions reached and decisions made has been the chief cause of the origin and development of logical operations in the precise sense; of abstraction, generalization, regard for consistency of implications. It is quite conceivable that if no one had ever had to account to others for his decisions, logical operations would never have developed, but men would use exclusively methods of inarticulate intuition and impression, feeling; so that only after considerable experience in accounting for their decisions to others who demanded a reason, or exculpation, and were not satisfied till they got it, did men begin to give an account to themselves of the process of reaching a conclusion in a justified way. However this may be, it is certain that in judicial decisions the only alternative to arbitrary dicta, accepted by the parties to a controversy only because of the authority or prestige of the judge, is a rational statement which formulates grounds and exposes connecting or logical links.

It is at this point that the chief stimulus and temptation to mechanical logic and abstract use of formal concepts come in. Just because the personal element cannot be wholly excluded, while at the same time the decision must assume as nearly as possible an impersonal, objective, rational form, the temptation is to surrender the vital logic which has actually yielded the conclusion and to substitute for it forms of speech which are rigorous in appearance and which give an illusion of certitude.

Another moving force is the undoubted need for the maximum possible of stability and regularity of expectation in determining courses of conduct. Men need to know the legal consequences which society through the courts will attach to their specific transactions, the liabilities they are assuming, the fruits they may count upon in entering upon a given course of action.

This is a legitimate requirement from the standpoint of the interests of the community and of particular individuals. Enormous confusion has resulted, however, from confusion of *theoretical* certainty and practical certainty. There is a wide gap separating the reasonable proposition that judicial decisions should possess the maximum possible regularity in order to enable persons in planning their conduct to foresee the legal import of their acts, and the absurd because impossible proposition that every decision should flow with formal logical necessity from antecedently known premises. To attain the former result there are required general principles of interpreting cases—rules of law—and procedures of pleading and trying cases which do not alter arbitrarily. But principles of interpretation do not signify rules so rigid that they can be stated once for all and then be literally and mechanically adhered to. For the situations to which they are to be applied do not literally repeat one another in all details, and questions of degree of this factor or that have the chief weight in determining which general rule will be employed to judge the situation in question. A large part of what has been asserted concerning the necessity of absolutely uniform and immutable antecedent rules of law is in effect an attempt to evade the really important issue of finding and employing rules of law, substantive and procedural, which will actually secure to the members of the community a reasonable measure of practical certainty of expectation in framing their courses of conduct. The mechanical ease of the court in disposing of cases and not the actual security of agents is the real cause, for example, of making rules of pleading hard and fast. The result introduces an unnecessary element of gamble into the behavior of those seeking settlement of disputes, while it affords to the judges only that factitious ease and simplicity which is supplied by any routine habit of action. It substitutes a mechanical procedure for the need of analytic thought.

There is of course every reason why rules of law should be as regular and as definite as possible. But the amount and kind of antecedent assurance which is actually attainable is a matter of fact, not of form. It is large wherever social conditions are pretty uniform, and when industry, commerce, transportation, etc., move in the channels of old customs. It is much less wherever invention is active and when new devices in business and communication bring about new forms of human relationship. Thus the use of power machinery radically modifies the old terms of association of master and servant and fellow servants; rapid transportation brings into general use commercial bills of lading; mass production engenders organization of laborers and collective bargaining; industrial conditions favor concentration of capital. In part legislation endeavors to reshape old rules of law to make them applicable to new conditions. But statutes have never kept up with the variety and subtlety of social change. They cannot at the very best avoid some ambiguity, which is due not only to carelessness but also to the intrinsic impossibility of foreseeing all possible circumstances, since without such foresight definitions must be vague and classifications indeterminate. Hence to claim that old forms are ready at hand that cover every case and that may be applied by formal syllogizing is to pretend to a certainty and regularity which cannot exist in fact. The effect of the pretension is to increase practical uncertainty and social instability. Just because circumstances are really novel and not covered by old rules, it is a gamble which old rule will be declared regulative of a particular case, so that shrewd and enterprising men are encouraged to sail close to the wind and trust to ingenious lawyers to find some rule under which they can get off scot free.

The facts involved in this discussion are commonplace and they are not offered as presenting anything original or novel. What we are concerned with is their bearing upon the logic of judicial decisions. For the implications are more revolutionary than they might at first seem to be. They indicate either that logic must be abandoned or that it must be a logic *relative to consequences rather than to antecedents,* a logic of prediction of probabilities rather than one of deduction of certainties. For the purposes of a logic of inquiry into probable consequences, general principles can only be tools justified by the work they do. They are means of intellectual survey, analysis, and insight into the factors of the situation to be dealt with. Like other tools they must be modified when they are applied to new conditions and new results have to be achieved. Here is where the great practical evil of the doctrine of immutable and necessary antecedent rules comes in. It sanctifies the old; adherence to it in practise constantly widens the gap between current social conditions and the principles used by the courts. The effect is to breed irritation, disrespect for law, together with virtual alliance between the judiciary and entrenched interests that correspond most nearly to the conditions under which the rules of law were previously laid down.

Failure to recognize that general legal rules and principles are working hypotheses, needing to be constantly tested by the way in which they work out in application to concrete situations, explains the otherwise paradoxical fact that the slogans of the liberalism of one period often become the bulwarks of reaction in a subsequent era. There was a time in the eighteenth century when the great social need was emancipation of industry and trade from a multitude of restrictions which held over from the feudal estate of Europe. Adapted well enough to the localized and fixed conditions of that earlier age, they became hindrances and annoyances as the effects of methods, use of coal and steam, showed themselves. The movement of emancipation expressed itself in principles of liberty in use of property, and freedom of contract, which were embodied in a mass of legal decisions. But the absolutistic logic of rigid syllogistic forms infected these ideas. It was soon forgotten that they were relative to analysis of existing situations in order to secure orderly methods in behalf of economic social welfare. Thus these principles became in turn so rigid as to be almost as socially obstructive as "immutable" feudal laws had been in their day.

That the remarks which have been made, commonplace as they are in themselves, have a profound practical import may also be seen in the present reaction against the individualistic formulae of an older liberalism. The last thirty years has seen an intermittent tendency in the direction of legislation, and to a less extent of judicial decision, towards what is vaguely known as "social justice," toward formulae of a collectivistic character. Now it is quite possible that the newer rules may be needed and useful at a certain juncture, and yet that they may also become harmful and socially obstructive if they are hardened into absolute and fixed antecedent premises. But if they are conceived as tools to be adapted to the conditions in which they are employed rather than as absolute and intrinsic "principles," attention will go to the facts of social life, and the rules will not be allowed to engross attention and become absolute truths to be maintained intact at all costs. Otherwise we shall in the end merely have substituted one set of formally absolute and immutable syllogistic premises for another set.

If we recur then to our introductory conception that logic is really a theory about empirical phenomena, subject to growth and improvement like any other empirical discipline, we recur to it with an added conviction: namely, that the issue is not a purely speculative one, but implies consequences vastly significant for practise. I should indeed not hesitate to assert that the sanctification of ready-made antecedent universal principles as methods of thinking is the chief obstacle to the kind of thinking which is the indispensable prerequisite of steady, secure and intelligent social reforms in general and social advance by means of law in particular. If this be so infiltration into law of a more experimental and flexible logic is a social as well as an intellectual need.

MAX RADIN

"The Theory of Judicial Decision: Or How Judges Think"

(1925)

[This article was originally delivered as an address at a luncheon meeting of the San Francisco Bar Association. It was later reprinted in The San Francisco Recorder *(a local legal newspaper) and finally in the* American Bar Association Journal.]

A southern gentleman seated on a fence in the Kentucky landscape, handed his friend a brown jug which jug the aforesaid friend lifted to his lips and partook, it seems, of a considerable part of the contents thereof. The friend was arrested. Drinking is not a crime according to the Volstead law but being in possession of liquor or container is. Now was the friend in possession? Ah, that is a difficult matter, gentlemen. The great Savigny wrote a classical treatise on Possession, many times translated. So did the still greater von Ihering. There is the well-known book of Pollock and Wright. Saleilles in France had a definite theory on the general subject, as also did Huber, who wrote so large a part of the excellent Swiss Code. Is possession protected as an outwork of ownership or as a social good valuable for itself? There are hard problems into the solution of which the men I have mentioned have wrought philosophy, economics, history in different proportions. Did the Kentucky court prepare itself for its decision by a study of Ihering, Savigny, Saleilles, Huber, Pollock? Perhaps. But I venture with a little diffidence to suggest that a court in such cases does something very different. A court feels that drinking ought or ought not to be punished in the interests of prohibition enforcement. If it feels it ought to be, it cannot say so directly, because the law does not make drinking punishable, but the court will in that case get as near to punishing drinking as it can. If the court does not wish to extend the inhibitions of the Volstead act, it will not approach drinking more closely than it must.

I wish to state that the Kentucky court found that defendant had

Reprinted from the *American Bar Association Journal*, vol. 11 (1925), pp. 357, 358–59, 362, by permission.

not been in possession of the brown jug or its contents. Of course they might have learned that from Savigny and von Ihering and from the fragments of Julius Paulus contained in the Digest of Justinian.

[This case] illustrate[s] . . . a common way in which judges arrive at their conclusion. The category into which to place the situation presented to them for judgment, does not leap into their minds at once. On the contrary, several categories struggle in their minds for the privilege of framing the situation before them. And since there is that struggle, how can they do otherwise than select the one that seems to them to lead to a desirable result. . . .

Is the question which forms the title of this paper merely a study of psychology, normal or otherwise? Far from it. It is the most practical of all questions for us. What judges thought, *was* the law and, what they will think, *is* the law. It is quite impossible—if there are judges at all—that it can be otherwise. It is as true of such places as 18th century Prussia in which the judges were humble and timid ministerial officials as in the Paradise of judicial indiscretion, Great Britain of the 18th and 19th centuries, where the maxim certainly prevailed, *boni iudicis est ampliare iurisdictionem*.[1]

If that is true, we must at our peril think the way judges do, we must reach the result they do, or rather we must reach the result they will reach just one jump ahead of them. And if they act more frequently than otherwise by discovering the desirable result first and summing their category to justify it, afterwards, we really ought to know what test they employ in determining that a result is desirable.

What makes [a] certain result seem desirable to a judge? Judges, we know, are people. I know a great many. Some were my school-mates— some I met elsewhere than in school. They eat the same foods, seem moved by the same emotions, and laugh at the same jokes. Apparently they are a good deal like ourselves. If, therefore, in a controversy in which we are engaged, we could rid ourselves of the personal interest in it, we might shrewdly guess that a great many judges would like to see the same person win who appeals to us. But we must be quite sure we have performed that difficult feat of ridding our minds completely of our personal interest in the case. You remember the Missouri mountaineer woman who watched a fight between her husband and a bear and remarked as she inhaled smoke through her clay pipe that this was the first fight she ever saw in which she did not care who won. If a case comes into our office and we can view it for a few fleeting moments with this Missouri detachment, we shall have opened up vistas of what the decision is likely to be—unless we can prevent it.

What gives judges this opportunity of working their judgment backward, from a desirable conclusion to one or another of a stock of logical premises, is the notable fact of human nature that conduct tends to run in types. We are none of us really individuals. Most of the things we do are pattern things, groups of acts rather than wholly separate acts, and many of these groups have at some time or other been considered by courts. The shifting character of human experience rearranges groups, rather than creates wholly new ones, and it will go hard with any situation that a court has to deal with if one or another of its elements does not point to a category in which a desirable conclusion is snugly bundled up, ready to be discovered by strictly logical reasoning according to the rules of the Aristotelian syllogism. . . .

. . . Judges are people and the economizing of mental effort is a characteristic of people, even if censorious persons call it by a less fine name. If in investigating a transaction which comes before him, element after element appears and a great many of them seem to fit quite neatly into a type situation that has somehow been early called up in his mind, a judge economic of mental effort, may decline to disturb it by searching for new elements which might compel the substitution of a wholly different situation. That may happen just as well in the case of the most industrious and energetic judge, who without a disinclination to work, must have the natural tendency to regard with favor suggestions that have arisen in his own mind.

The situations that will so arise will generally be a pleasing or a satisfactory situation. And it is highly likely that a situation which seems pleasing to a judge would seem so to us, if we could omit reflection on our pecuniary interest in a particular result. What difference then need it make to us whether the movement of the judicial mind is from the type situation forward to the particular one, or from the particular one backward to a type situation that is selected—often quite consciously—because it leads to a desirable result? And yet it does make a difference. In order to perform this feat, judges have recourse to a great many devices. They relate back. They presume. They impute. They take judicial notice. They refuse to take judicial notice. They construe. They charge with knowledge. They impress trusts. And they don't always do this in the same way. What one judge reaches by presumption, another will, by relation.

When we are searching for type situations which we can suggest to the bench to base a judgment in our favor, we find them with all these products of judicial activity and we frequently have to take them as a whole with all these products around them and disentangle them afterwards. That is hard work and lawyers are as reasonably economic of mental effort as any other branch of the community. They wish to confine their efforts to doing what I am told some lawyers can do very well. They paint the situation they would like to have the judge find desirable so charmingly that they sometimes succeed in pushing the judicial preference aside altogether and inducing under the hypnotic spell of their skill, the judge to sign their painting as his own work. Naturally they don't want to be put to the additional trouble of finding a frame for the painting.

Does all this make for anarchy and destroy all sense of security? I think not. Real security, absolute security, one hundred per cent certainty, we cannot have. We can approximate it, but no more. Our business is prophecy, and if prophecy were certain, there would not be much credit in prophesying. But, as I have said, we can come fairly near certainty.....

But in that great mass of transactions which will not fit readily or quickly into established types, or will fit into one just as easily as another, the judge ought to be a free agent. We need not fear arbitrariness. Our Cokes and Mansfields and Eldons derive their physical and spiritual nourishment from the same sources that we do. They will find good what we find good, if we will let them. And if they had not prescribed to themselves the curious necessity of putting the transaction to be regulated into one type-form rather than another—assuming that it could go into either and will not without pushing go into any—they would have no need of their relations and imputations, their presumptions and suppositions, their gyrations and concatenations, and could cut straight to the desirable result which they in common with ourselves as members of the community prefer.

We are all of us not only lawyers but teachers of law. We must teach law, if to nobody else, at least to our clients. We must therefore teach them what judges will think about their business. If we say to them "The transaction in which you were engaged resembles any one of half a dozen standard situations. It resembles No. 1 a little more closely than No. 2 or 3 or 4. But to put it under No. 1 would lead to an undesirable result. What the judge ought to do is to state these facts and admit that he has created a new type, which I can keep in mind or know where to find, because of its similarity to No. 1. But he will probably not do that. He will try to squeeze it into No. 2 which it only slightly resembles but which will lead to a desirable result, and in consequence when something very like our transaction occurs again, we shall have a great deal of trouble in finding it. In fact we had better examine all cases of type No. 2, to see whether a transaction like ours has not already been put in that place. For if we know how they have thought once, we are helped to guess how they will think again."

It is an undoubted fact that the chief purpose courts fulfill in giving us not merely a judgment but a classification of the judgment by types and standards, is to make it easy for us to find out how they think. The technique which has become traditional in Europe and America seems to me to make it hard.

Are judges under any obligations to make things easy for lawyers? After all, why should they? We don't always make things easy for them.

HERMAN OLIPHANT

"A Return to Stare Decisis"[1]

(1928)

*[In 1927, Oliphant was President of the Association of American Law
Schools. He delivered this essay as his Presidential Address at the annual meeting of the association (held in Chicago in December,
1927).—Ed]*

Not the judges' opinions, but which way they decide cases will be
the dominant subject matter of any truly scientific study of law. This is
the field for scholarly work worthy of best talents because the work to
be done is not the study of vague and shifting rationalizations but the
study of such tough things as the accumulated wisdom of men taught
by immediate experience in contemporary life,—the battered experiences
of judges among brutal facts. The response of their intuition of experience to the stimulus of human situations is the subject-matter having
that constancy and objectivity necessary for truly scientific study. When
we pin our attention to this, we may more freely criticize what courts
have said but we shall more cautiously criticize what they have done, realizing, as we shall, that they were exposed to the impact of more of the
facts than we.

This surer thing for scholarly purpose is also the inner secret of
what is soundest in the enfeebled *stare decisis* in judicial government of
today. With eyes cleared of the old and broad abstractions which curtain
our vision, we come to recognize more and more the eminent good
sense in what courts are wont to do about disputes before them. Judges
are men and men respond to human situations. When the facts stimulat-
ing them to the action taken are studied from a particular and current
point of view, which our present classification prevents, we acquire a
new faith in *stare decisis*. From this viewpoint we see that courts are
dominantly coerced, not by the essays of their predecessors but by a
surer thing,—by an intuition of fitness of solution to problem,—and a
renewed confidence in judicial government is engendered. . . .

One sampling of this proposed subject-matter of a real science of

Reprinted from the *American Bar Association Journal*, vol. 14 (1928), pp. 159–61, by
permission.

law must suffice. There are two lines of old cases involving the validity
of promises not to compete. They are considered in square conflict. But
when the opinions are ignored and the facts re-examined all the cases
holding the promises invalid are found to be cases of employees' promises not to compete with their employers after a term of employment.
Contemporary guild regulations not noticed in the opinions made their
holding eminently sound. All the cases holding the promises valid were
cases of promises by those selling a business and promising not to compete with the purchasers. Contemporary economic reality made these
holdings also eminently sound. This distinction between these two lines
of cases is not even hinted at in any of the opinions but the courts' intuition of experience led them to follow it with amazing sureness and
the law resulting fitted life. That is a sample of the stuff capable of scientific study....

   ... In recent times the world of scientific thought has been turning
dark places into light. We now can see that the choice between the legal
principles competing to control the new human situations involved in
the cases we pass upon is not dictated by logic. Neither deduction nor
induction can do more than suggest the competing analogies and to indicate promising directions for trial and error testing. Neither the as-
tuteness of legal scholarship not the authority of judicial position can
transcend these limitations inherent in logic. The final choice of analogy
can be made only in reliance upon practical considerations or upon pure
chance. Rejecting sheer guess as a basis of sound judicial action and of
worthwhile scholarship, then discovering and marshalling decisive practical considerations inevitably constitute the essence of both an improved judicial process and of a more useful scholarly effort. A return to
the sounder empiricism of *stare decisis* of former times should reckon
with the recent advances in scientific thought referred to. That ancient
empiricism was intuitive. It worked well because judges sat close to
problems and viewed them as current problems. It would have worked
better still had it been conscious and methodical. Remembering always
that the final choice for both judge and scholar in deciding a case or
criticizing a decision is always a practical one, whether consciously or
unconsciously so, the problem, how a more conscious and methodical
process can be substituted for an intuitive empiricism in making that
choice, transcends in importance all other problems of legal education.
Until its solution is attempted, a socialized jurisprudence will continue a
. mere aspiration and social engineering will be the profession of many
but the occupation of none....

   An examination of some of the presuppositions of intuitive empiricism as a method of deciding cases and evaluating decisions may shed
some light on the solution of that problem. Good as it has been, it assumes that we know social reality and shape our actions to it merely because we live in it. It presupposes that the affairs of life cannot be more
wisely controlled than by men of affairs. But none of us knows social

reality merely because we live in it. The experience of any man, however broad, is limited largely to one period of time. The future he cannot know and the past is reported to him by men of equally limited experience. The social experience of most of us is limited largely to one people, yet social reality encircles the globe. Our social experience is limited to one class of people though we must govern all classes. Indeed, it is limited to but one occupation and the part often most decisive in determining our attitudes is the experience of but a single family group. Complete reliance upon an intuition of fitness of solution to problems was better placed when used in the solution of the legal problems emerging from the simpler life of early England. Some parts of current social life are no more complex now than then, but great areas of it— and the areas of most frequent dispute—are most complex, being knit together by a social and mechanical technology which only experts can hope to understand. Complete reliance upon an intuition of such a limited experience is a policy of doubtful wisdom.

But more can be said. If our individual experience were as broad as the life whose problems we work on, still our intuition of experience would be no certain guide. Not all of our experience goes to make up that intuition. Individual temperament and our self-interest cause us, in the most subjective fashion, to select from the totality of our experience that which satisfies our temperament, and fortifies our interest. Thus but a small fraction of total social reality forms our attitudes and grounds our intuition of experience. To distill a guide from so little of the immense and complex social reality about us is a procedure for which the modern scientific thought must offer some better substitute. Such an unconscious empiricism, such a common-sense pragmatism can be improved upon by borrowings from the accumulated wisdom of the sciences. . . .

JOSEPH C. HUTCHESON, JR.

"The Judgment Intuitive: The Function of the 'Hunch' in Judicial Decision"

(1929)

[At the time he wrote this article, the author was a federal district judge in the Southern District of Texas.—Ed]

Many years ago, at the conclusion of a particularly difficult case both in point of law and of fact, tried to a court without a jury, the judge, a man of great learning and ability, announced from the Bench that since the narrow and prejudiced modern view of the obligations of a judge in the decision of causes prevented his resort to the judgment aleatory by the use of his "little, small dice" he would take the case under advisement, and, brooding over it, wait for his hunch.

To me, a young, indeed a very young lawyer, picked, while yet the dew was on me and I had just begun to sprout, from the classic gardens of a University, where I had been trained to regard the law as a system of rules and precedents, of categories and concepts, and the judge had been spoken of as an administrator, austere, remote, "his intellect a cold logic engine," who, in that rarified atmosphere in which he lived coldly and logically determined the relation of the facts of a particular case to some of these established precedents, it appeared that the judge was making a jest, and a very poor one, at that.

I had been trained to expect inexactitude from juries, but from the judge quite the reverse. I exalted in the law its tendency to formulize. I had a slot machine mind. I searched out categories and concepts and, having found them, worshiped them.

I paid homage to the law's supposed logical rigidity and exactitude. A logomachist, I believed in and practiced logomancy. I felt a sense of real pain when some legal concept in which I had put my faith as permanent, constructive and all-embracing opened like a broken net, allowing my fish to fall back into the legal sea. Paraphrasing Huxley, I believed that the great tragedy of the law was the slaying of a beautiful concept by an ugly fact. Always I looked for perfect formulas, fact proof, concepts so general, so flexible, that in their terms the jural relations of mankind could be stated, and I rejected most vigorously the suggestion that there was, or should be, anything fortuitous or by chance in the law. Like Jurgen I had been to the Master Philologist and with words he had conquered me.

I had studied the law in fragments and segments, in sections and compartments, and in my mind each compartment was nicely and logically arranged so that every case presented to me only the problem of arranging and re-arranging its facts until I could slip it into the compartment to which it belonged. The relation of landlord and tenant, of principal and agent, of bailor and bailee, of master and servant, these and a hundred others controlled my thinking and directed its processes.

Perceiving the law as a thing fullgrown, I believe that all of its processes were embraced in established categories, and I rejected most vigorously the suggestion that it still had life and growth, and if anyone had suggested that the judge had a right to feel, or hunch out a new category into which to place relations under his investigation, I should have repudiated the suggestion as unscientific and unsound, while as to the judge who dared to do it, I should have cried "Away with him! Away with him!" . . .

I knew, of course, that some judges did follow "hunches,"—"guesses" I indignantly called them. I knew my Rabelais, and had laughed over without catching the true philosophy of old Judge Bridlegoose's trial, and roughly, in my youthful, scornful way, I recognized four kinds of judgments; first the cogitative, of and by reflection and logomancy; second, aleatory, of and by the dice; third, intuitive, of and by feeling or "hunching;" and fourth, asinine, of and by an ass; and in that same youthful, scornful way I regarded the last three as only variants of each other, the results of processes all alien to good judges. . . .

[Now, however,] after eleven years on the Bench following eighteen at the Bar, I, being well advised by observation and experience of what I am about to set down, have thought it both wise and decorous to now boldly affirm that "having well and exactly seen, surveyed, overlooked, reviewed, recognized, read and read over again, turned and tossed about, seriously perused and examined the preparitories, productions, evidences, proofs, allegations, depositions, cross speeches, contradictions . . . and other such like confects and spiceries, both at the one and the other side, as a good judge ought to do, I posit on the end of the table in my closet all the pokes and bags of the defendants—that being done I thereafter lay down upon the other end of the same table the bags and satchels of the plaintiff."

Thereafter I proceed "to understand and resolve the obscurities of these various and seeming contrary passages in the law, which are laid claim to by the suitors and pleading parties," even just as Judge Bridlegoose did, with one difference only. "That when the matter is more plain, clear and liquid, that is to say, when there are fewer bags," and he would have used his "other large, great dice, fair and goodly ones," I decide the case more or less offhand and by rule of thumb. While when the case is difficult or involved, and turns upon a hairsbreadth of law or of fact, that is to say, "when there are many bags on the one side and on the other and Judge Bridlegoose would have used his "little small dice," I, after canvassing all the available material at my command, and duly cogitating upon it, give my imagination play, and brooding over the cause, wait for the feeling, the hunch—that intuitive flash of understanding which makes the jump-spark connection between question and decision, and at the point where the path is darkest for the judicial feet, sheds its light along the way.

And more, "lest I be stoned in the street" for this admission, let me hasten to say to my brothers of the Bench and of the Bar, "my practice is therein the same with that of your other worships."

For let me premise here, that in feeling or "hunching" out his decisions, the judge acts not differently from, but precisely as the lawyers do in working on their cases, with only this exception; that the lawyer, having a predetermined destination in view,—to win his law suit for his client— looks for and regards only those hunches which keep him in the path that he has chosen, while the judge, being merely on his way with a roving commission to find the just solution, will follow his hunch wherever it leads him, and when, following it, he meets the right solution face to face, he can cease his labors and blithely say to his troubled mind—"Trip no farther, pretty sweeting, journeys end in lovers meeting, as every wise man's son doth know."

Further, at the outset, I must premise that I speak now of the judgment or decision, the solution itself, as opposed to the apologia for that decision; the decree, as opposed to the logomachy, the effusion of the judge by which that decree is explained or excused. I speak of the judgment pronounced, as opposed to the rationalization by the judge on that pronouncement. . . .

If these views are even partly sound, and if to great advocacy and great judging the imaginative, the intuitional faculty is essential, should there not be some change in the methods of the study and of the teaching of the law in our great law schools? Should there not go along with the plain and severely logical study of jural relations study and reflection upon, and an endeavor to discover and develop, those processes of the mind by which such decisions are reached, those processes and faculties which, lifting the mind above the mass of constricting matter whether of confused fact or precedent that stands in the way of just decision, enable it by a kind of apocalyptic vision to "trace the hidden equities of divine reward, and to catch sight through the darkness, of the fateful threads of woven fire which connect error with its retribution?"

JEROME FRANK

Law and the Modern Mind

(1930)

Is it not absurd to keep alive the artificial, orthodox tradition of the "ideal judge?" The rational alternative is to recognize that judges are fallible human beings. We need to see that biases and prejudices and conditions of attention affect the judge's reasoning as they do the reasoning of ordinary men. Our law schools must become, in part, schools of psychology applied to law in all its phases. In law schools, in law offices and law courts there must be explicit recognition of the meaning of the phrase "human nature in law."[1] The study of human nature in law (to paraphrase Graham Wallas, who has done so much to emphasize the evil of divorcing the study of human nature from the study of politics) may not only deepen our knowledge of legal institutions but open an unworked mine of judicial wisdom.

It has been argued that judges will go far towards abandoning "medievalism" when they begin to procure, and to rely on, carefully prepared factual data as to the social setting of the cases which come before them for decision. Something of the sort has occasionally been done, as for instance in cases dealing with statutes regulating the hours of labor for women or with the inapplicability to wage contracts of the rules growing out of mercantile contracts. This technique has, indeed, wide possibilities. Our judges can well afford to get expert advice as to the customs and usages (and the consequences of such customs and usages) of business men in dealing with commercial paper, banking credit, reorganizations of financially embarrassed corporations and other like and unlike situations. More than that, there deserves to be studied the possible employment, throughout the field of law, of that method of patient investigation, by disinterested experts, of the facts and background of individual cases now used by our more enlightened juvenile courts and courts of domestic relations. Today the judge's knowledge of the individual aspects of cases comes to him off the record, sometimes improperly, sometimes accidentally, sometimes through his reading between the lines of the evidence formally presented. We need to develop a more explicit technique for individualizing cases.[2]

But the systematic, deliberate and openly disclosed use of the unique facts of a case will not be of much service until the judges develop the notion of law as a portion of the science of human nature. And that development cannot come to fruition until the judges come to grips with the human nature operative in themselves.[3]...

Getting Rid of the Need for Father-Authority

No intelligent person can question the wisdom of the revised attitude toward the law which our Pounds, Wurzels, Demogues and Cardozos would have the lawyers and the laity adopt. They want our "courts to perceive what it is they are doing" and thus be "enabled to address themselves consciously to doing it in the best way." They want an effective, intelligent fusion of the two competing tendencies towards stability and change; a working principle of growth; a constant revision of the law's heritage of knowledge and thought; the frequent adaptation of the legal rules so as to relate them to the realities of contemporary social, industrial and political conditions. They desire that traditional premises should be so shaped as to give effect to social interests, with reference not to the abstract claims of abstract individuals, but to the concrete situation; they picture law as continuously more efficacious social engineering, satisfying, through social control, as much as is possible of the whole body of human wants.

They urge that lawyers and judges should deal realistically with their materials and their technique, and that there should be an adult recognition, by the public generally, of the possibilities and limitations of the law with consequent improvement of its legitimate functioning.

All this is no easy task. Men in any of life's relations will never be completely free of delusion. But delusions can be diminished. And those who desire the healthy growth of the law will with courage seek to diminish legal delusions and, to that end, to comprehend the nature and sources of their own weaknesses,[4] and of the powerful yearning in themselves as well as others for unrealities in law.

Just in so far as we ourselves are childish, do we want to keep our children from growing up. So say the modern educators. It is weak, it is unworthy, to over-protect the children. This is the "snare of patronage," the great sin of parenthood: to obstruct the psychological freedom of the child. The prolongation of infancy is essential to the development of the human infant, but to prolong infancy unduly at the expense of the child's development is to violate the eleventh commandment.

A coming-of-age has its perils for the children and its pains for the parents. Yet, if our legal critics are to play the rôle of wise fathers, they must have the courage to let their "children" grow up. Myth-making and fatherly lies must be abandoned—the Santa Claus story of complete legal certainly; the fairy tale of a pot of golden law which is already in existence and which the good lawyer can find, if only he is sufficiently diligent; the phantasy of an aesthetically satisfactory system and harmony, consistent and uniform, which will spring up when we find the magic wand of a rationalizing principle. We must stop telling stork-fibs about how law is born and cease even hinting that perhaps there is still some truth in Peter Pan legends of a juristic happy hunting ground in a land of legal absolutes.

To the extent that lawyers, whether more or less consciously, join the conspiracy of silence about, or denial of, the ineradicable mutability of law, they do an injury to their fellows. For to that extent—and in one of the most important life activities—they are keeping men in subjection to a falsehood and, worse, to the debilitating irresponsibility arising from reliance on supposed safety-conferring external authority. Not only is there involved an injury to the maturation of law, but as well to the spirit of men generally. For, if what we have suggested is true, if something of a paralyzing father-worship is one of the hidden causes of men's belief in a body of infallible law, then the perpetuation of that belief means that everywhere the noxious thralldom to mere authority and tradition is strengthened.

Growing up means throwing off dependence upon external authority.[5] It means self-reliance, the acceptance of responsibility. It means questioning—not hastily, angrily, rebelliously, but calmly and dispassionately—our bequests from the past, our social heritage.

A great religious thinker, George Berman Foster, writing of religion, has put the matter in words which, slightly modified, might well be heeded by the leaders of the legal profession:

"The true and wise lover and leader of his brothers will not shield them against doubt but make them equal to doubt, inspire them with strength to doubt. They will say to their brothers that religious doubt is not a disease of the soul; but is necessary to the health of the soul; that it does not signify decay or degeneration but re-birth—the mounting upward of never-resting, never-rusting life. . . . Whoever fears doubt, fears truth; for it is truth that casts the first shadow of doubt into the human spirit. . . . It is in religious doubt that we begin to acquire the power of a true self-confidence."

Increasing constructive doubt is the sign of advancing civilization. We must put question marks alongside many of our inherited legal dogmas, since they are dangerously out of line with social facts.

Indeed, we may throw some light on our problem by asking what, in general parlance, we mean by a "fact." Holmes has answered that it is something one can't help believing. "What gives it objectivity is that I find my fellow man to a greater or less extent (never wholly) subject to the same Can't Helps." Barry more recently has defined a fact as a "coercive" or "compulsory" experience "established by common agreement which is indicated by similar behavior with reference to it." And Eddington speaks of it as a "symposium" of presentations to individuals in all sorts of circumstances.

Now these common agreements as to "coercive experiences," these symposia with respect to the nature of Can't Helps, keep changing, even where the subject-matter has reference to what we call the laws of nature. In other words, stubborn facts are, in a sense, not so stubborn as we are wont to suppose. In the natural sciences the rate of change in the accepted symposia is rapid because there the habit of constant questioning, of unremitting doubt, has come to be accepted, at least by the scientists, as a virtue. Even in those sciences, it took thousands of years to justify doubt. And outside of the sciences, most of our facts have remained unchanged for at least several hundred generations. A large part of our accepted or unquestioned "truths" are the "unverified world-pictures of vanished barbaric (prehistoric) peoples." The toughness of these facts is due—to what? To the vast power of the authority behind them. They have become sacred; they are protected from close scrutiny by terrifying taboos.

Primitive man could not endure the terrors that surrounded him. He made masks to conceal the menace they involved, so that now, says Shaw, "every mask requires a hero to tear it off." In each man's infancy, generation after generation, his father has taught him the eternal verity of these masking "truths." Wherefore he is coerced by them and treats them as if they were nature's irreducibles. And if the tendency to tear off the masks, to question man-made Can't Helps, has progressed far less rapidly in the law than in the natural sciences—if, that is, our "law facts" need to be brought in line with our "science facts"—this is no doubt because in the law father-authority has found a firmer lodgment.

This point is so important that we venture to state it once more in slightly variant terms. As we have often remarked in the foregoing pages, our legal abstractions can only be approximations. They are, by definition, drawn off—abstracted—from the facts. Hence, the results can never be precise, perfect. They must be inexact. If the "environment" were stable, the degree of inexactness could become more negligible and remain relatively fixed.[6] But the economic, political and social problems are ever-shifting. So that, in the very nature of the situation, the approximations must be revised frequently and can never be accepted as final in terms of satisfactory consequences. We must be content with modest probabilities, as Dewey puts it, and not foolishly pretend that our legal abstractions are mathematically accurate, for that pretense obstructs the will to modify and adjust these abstractions in the light of careful observation of their working results.

These abstractions, that is to say, are tools whose whole value is instrumental. They have been contrived to meet particular problems. As new problems arise, the old tools must be adapted to cope with them. But when the old tools have been authoritatively pronounced to be once-and-for-all perfect, when, that is, they have the father-sanction, then to question their everlasting sufficiency is difficult. Then the tools seem not human contrivances but a very part of the nature of things. The questioning, when it begins, has to be oblique, the adaptations surreptitious. Even the questioner, the adapter, must not let himself know that he is daring to depart from the accepted ways. Science made large strides when man began to treat the traditional formulations as no longer completely correct and definite knowledge of objective nature but as hypotheses or fictions; in other words, when men were ready to treat as tentative the guesses about the external world which had been handed down to them. Then only could they fearlessly observe the events, dispassionately consider new guesses about the character of these events.

All the guesses are human and, therefore, subject to question. But the old guesses come to us as the father's truths and are, therefore, sacrosanct. Humanity increases its chances of survival and of progress to the extent that it becomes able to question—neither blindly to accept nor violently to defy—the father's guesses, and to discontinue calling them self-evident truths. In the sciences this attitude has won out. Although the law is a more patently human construction than, say, physics, yet, in the calm reconsideration of the value of inherited truths, law is decades behind physics. Why? Because in law, the father is more deeply entrenched. The law is a near substitute for that father, a belief in whose infallibility is essential to the very life of the child. And in the life of the adult that authority now no longer usefully, but still potently, often holds sway.

The fear of change is an ancient one. We may, with Elsie Clews Parsons, define civilization as man's steps in his escape from that fear. Whitehead puts the same thought somewhat differently: Development in life means wandering. Modern science has imposed on humanity the necessity for increased wandering, for migrations into uncharted seas. The future will disclose dangers. "It is the business of the future to be dangerous; and it is among the merits of science that it equips the future for its duties." We must not confuse civilization and security, for security and stability will, with advancing civilization, grow less. Too much insecurity is perhaps inconsistent with civilization. "But, on the whole, the great ages have been unstable ages."

Whence it follows that, if we are to grow more civilized, we must arrive at a more adult attitude towards chance and change. And here a nice distinction must be made between the adult position with respect to danger and a less developed sentiment which falsely resembles it.

Early in this essay we spoke of the bewilderment of the infant, of his seeking for sureness and security in the confused environment into which he has suddenly been ejected; of his finding, in a reliance upon his idealized father, some measure of relief from his confusion. And we traced the effects of the persistence in adult life of this reliance upon the father. But the child is motivated not only by the desire to escape the terrors of the unknown; he has also within him a store of vital energy, he is a growing dynamic organism. His dynamic capacities constantly assert themselves; the child is never completely a mere creature of parental authority. In a

certain sense, danger and risk, as well as safety and security, make their
appeal to him. As sometimes he runs away from chance and change, so
at other times he seeks them.

Now the curious fact is that such childish courting of danger may be,
in part, a product of father-authority. All children have a dual attitude
towards the father. The child needs a belief in an all-powerful, all-wise
parent. Yet that parent ever and again takes on the aspect of a harsh tyrant
who cruelly and unfairly interferes with the child's aims and purposes.
Even the most loving and obedient child feels occasional animosity towards
the father and, at times, revolts against the father. His conduct, in such
circumstances, may be in the direction of healthy growth, but, in so far
as it is merely expressive of revolt, it is purely negative in meaning. The
child, that is, may not be forging ahead, but only running away from a
new terror—the terror of too strict fatherly authority.

Recent writings in criminology have a decided bearing here. Many
criminals, we learn, are driven to lawlessness by an inner, subconscious
revolt against the authority of the father. In opposing the law they are
reacting to it as a father-substitute. They, too, so to speak, demand (but
"contrary-wise") an authoritarian law in order that they may rebel against
it. Fatherly authority in their childhood was too oppressive and as a consequence the anti-authority bias developed as a determining conduct-factor
throughout life. The violent rebel against authority is no more "free" than
the slave of authority; he is in bondage to a compulsion to revolt; his is
a constrained attitude, which Cooley has happily called the "subservience
of contradiction."[7]

And so we must distinguish between that growth towards maturity
which produces an acceptance of danger and that childish reaction against
fatherly authority which takes on the appearance of adult courage. The
constrained rebellion against paternalism is not a symptom of development
but of prolonged infantilism. It is another form of slavish obedience. The
person engaged in such rebellion is not free of paternal authority, but is
still subjectively dependent upon it.[8]

True growth involves healthy encouragement of the inherent spon-
taneity of the child, an encouragement of wakeful vitality and the dis-
couragement of half-blind adherence to, or half-blind breaking away from,
the traditional.

And so in law. If the search for the father-judge is ended,[9] if the
authority-ridden mode of regarding law is eliminated, if men see law as a
human adjustment and not as a gift or mandate from some external source,
no violent transformation need or will occur. The relief from fear of chance
need not result in the adoption of a policy of incessant, hectic change, but
should lead to a policy of healthy and vital growth.

Today, excessive regard for certified stability yields to an excessive
desire for modification, so that there is a constant unconscious struggle
between these two impulses, a struggle unnecessarily violent. There is
vacillation in the mind even of the average man between worship and

denunciation of legal certainty. The demand for too much change is as little based on practicality as the demand for too much rigidity. Holmes has warned us that continuity with the past is not a duty. It is no less true that there is no obligation to effect discontinuity with the past. A recognition of those two truths, resulting from a thoroughly adult attitude towards fatherly authority, will produce a balanced, not an anarchic, attitude towards law.[10] When men are free of childish compulsions away from or towards the traditional, it will be possible for them to have an open mind on the question of the advisability of radical alterations of law.

In other words, such a revised attitude will not entail constant inquiry into the sufficiency of all legal formulations. *It is unnecessary and undesirable to attack on all fronts at once.* Certain formulations must have been and will be at any given moment treated as, for the time being, fixed and settled while others are being investigated. But those "rules" that are thus, for the time being, taken for granted, will be only temporarily dealt with as permanent. They will be considered as *temporary absolutes.* Some of them will be accepted because repeated checkings show them still to be working well; others because the attention, at the moment, will be too occupied.[11]

Modern civilization demands a mind free of father-governance. To remain father-governed in adult years is peculiarly *the* modern sin. *The modern mind is a mind free of childish emotional drags, a mature mind.* And law, if it is to meet the needs of modern civilization must adapt itself to the modern mind. It must cease to embody a philosophy opposed to change. It must become avowedly pragmatic. To this end there must be developed a recognition and elimination of the carry-over of the childish dread of, and respect for, paternal omnipotence; that dread and respect are powerful strongholds of resistance to change. Until we become thoroughly cognizant of, and cease to be controlled by, the image of the father hidden away in the authority of the law, we shall not reach that first step in the civilized administration of justice, the recognition that man is not made for the law, but that the law is made by and for men.

FELIX S. COHEN

"Transcendental Nonsense and the Functional Approach"

(1935)

I. The Heaven of Legal Concepts

Some fifty years ago a great German jurist had a curious dream. He dreamed that he died and was taken to a special heaven reserved for the theoreticians of the law. In this heaven one met, face to face, the many concepts of jurisprudence in their absolute purity, freed from all entangling alliances with human life. Here were the disembodied spirits of good faith and bad faith, property, possession, *laches,* and rights *in rem.* Here were all the logical instruments needed to manipulate and transform these legal concepts and thus to create and to solve the most beautiful of legal problems. Here one found a dialectic-hydraulic-interpretation press, which could press an indefinite number of meanings out of any text or statute, an apparatus for constructing fictions, and a hair-splitting machine that could divide a single hair into 999,999 equal parts and, when operated by the most expert jurists, could split each of these parts again into 999,999 equal parts. The boundless opportunities of this heaven of legal concepts were open to all properly qualified jurists, provided only they drank the Lethean draught which induced forgetfulness of terrestrial human affairs. But for the most accomplished jurists the Lethean draught was entirely superfluous. They had nothing to forget.

Von Jhering's dream has been retold, in recent years, in the chapels of sociological, functional, institutional, scientific, experimental, realistic, and neo-realistic jurisprudence. The question is raised, "How much of contemporary legal thought moves in the pure ether of Von Jhering's heaven of legal concepts?" One turns to our leading legal textbooks and to the opinions of our courts for answer. May the Shade of Von Jhering be our guide....

II. The Functional Method

That something is radically wrong with our traditional legal thought-ways has long been recognized. Holmes, Gray, Pound, Brooks, Adams, M. R. Cohen, T. R. Powell, Cook, Oliphant, Moore, Radin, Llewellyn, Yntema, Frank, and other leaders of modern legal thought in America, are in fundamental agreement in their disrespect for "mechanical jurisprudence," for legal magic and word-jugglery. But mutual agreement is less apparent when we come to the question of what to do: How are we going to get out of this tangle? How are we going to substitute a realistic, rational, scientific account of legal happenings for the classical theological jurisprudence of concepts?

Attempts to answer this question have made persistent use of the phrase "functional approach." Unfortunately, this phrase has often been used with as little meaning as any of the magical legal concepts against which it is directed. Many who use the term "functional" intend no more than the vague connotation which the word "practical" conveys to the "practical" man. Again, the term "functional approach" is sometimes used to designate a modern form of animism, according to which every social institution or biological organ has a "purpose" in life, and is to be judged good or bad as it achieves or fails to achieve this "purpose." I shall not attempt to be faithful to these vague usages in using the term "functional." I shall use the term rather to designate certain principles or tendencies which appear most clearly in modern physical and mathematical science and in modern philosophy. For it is well to note that the problem of eliminating supernatural terms and meaningless questions and redefining concepts and problems in terms of verifiable realities is not a problem peculiar to law. It is a problem which has been faced in the last two or three centuries, and more especially in the last four or five decades, by philosophy, mathematics, and physics, as well as by psychology, economics, anthropology, and doubtless other sciences as well. Functionalism, operationalism, pragmatism, logical positivism, all these and many other terms have been used in diverse fields, with differing overtones of meaning and emphasis, to designate a certain common approach to this general task of redefining traditional concepts and traditional problems.

It may perhaps clarify the significance of the functional approach in law to trace some of the basic contributions which the functional method has made in modern science and philosophy. ·

1. The Eradication of Meaningless Concepts

On its negative side (naturally of special prominence in a protestant movement), functionalism represents an assault upon all dogmas and devices that cannot be translated into terms of actual experience.

In physics, the functional or operational method is an assault upon such supernatural concepts as absolute space and absolute time; in mathematics, upon supernatural concepts of real and imaginary, rational and irrational, positive and negative numbers. In psychology, William James inaugurates the functional method (of which behaviorism is an extreme form) by asking the naive question: "Does consciousness exist?" Modern "functional grammar" is an assault upon grammatical theories and distinctions which, as applied to the English language, simply have no verifiable significance—such empty concepts, for instance, as that of noun syntax, with its unverifiable distinction between a nominative, an objective, and a possessive case. And passing to the field of art, we find that functional architecture is likewise a repudiation of outworn symbols and functionless forms that have no meaning,—hollow marble pillars that do not support, fake buttresses, and false fronts.

So, too, in law. Our legal system is filled with supernatural concepts, that is to say, concepts which cannot be defined in terms of experience, and from which all sorts of empirical decisions are supposed to flow. Against these unverifiable concepts modern jurisprudence presents an ultimatum. Any word that cannot pay up in the currency of fact, upon demand, is to be declared bankrupt, and we are to have no further dealings with it. Llewellyn has filed an involuntary petition in bankruptcy against the concept Title, Oliphant against the concept Contract, Haines, Brown, T. R. Powell, Finkelstein, and Cushman against Due Process, Police Power, and similar word-charms of constitutional law, Hale, Richberg, Bonbright, and others against the concept of Fair Value in rate regulation, Cook and Yntema against the concept of Vested Rights in the conflict of laws. Each of these men has tried to expose the confusions of current legal thinking engendered by these concepts and to reformulate the problems in his field in terms which show the concrete relevance of legal decisions to social facts.

2. The Abatement of Meaningless Questions

It is a consequence of the functional attack upon unverifiable concepts that many of the traditional problems of science, law, and philosophy are revealed as pseudo-problems devoid of meaning. As the protagonist of logical positivism, Wittgenstein, says of the traditional problems of philosophy:

> "Most propositions and questions, that have been written about philosophical matters, are not false, but senseless. We cannot, therefore, answer questions of this kind at all, but only state their senselessness. Most questions and propositions of the philosophers result from the fact that we do not understand the logic of our language. (They are of the same kind as the question whether the Good is more or less identical than the Beautiful.) And so it is not to be wondered at that the deepest problems are really no problems."

The same thing may be said of the problems of traditional juris-prudence. As commonly formulated, such "problems" as, "What is the holding or *ratio decidendi* of a case?" or "Which came first,—the law or the state?" or "What is the essential distinction between a crime and a tort?" or "Where is a corporation?" are in fact meaningless, and can serve only as invitations to equally meaningless displays of conceptual acrobatics.

Fundamentally there are only two significant questions in the field of law. One is, "How do courts actually decide cases of a given kind?" The other is, "How ought they to decide cases of a given kind?" Unless a legal "problem" can be subsumed under one of these forms, it is not a meaningful question and any answer to it must be nonsense.

3. The Redefinition of Concepts

Although the negative aspect of the functional method is apt to assume peculiar prominence in polemic controversy, the value of the method depends, in the last analysis, upon its positive contributions to the ad-vancement of knowledge. Judged from this standpoint, I think it is fair to say that the functional method has justified itself in every scientific field to which it has been actually applied, and that functional redefini-tion of scientific concepts has been the keynote of most significant the-oretical advances in the sciences during the last half century. . . .

The parallel between the functional method of modern physics and the program of realistic jurisprudence is so well sketched by a distin-guished Chinese jurist that I can only offer a quotation without comment:[1]

> "Professor Eddington, in a recent book on "The Nature of the Physi-cal World," observes: "A thing must be defined according to the way in which it is in practice recognized and not according to some ulterior signif-icance that we suppose it to possess." So Professor Bridgman, in "The Logic of Modern Physics":
> "Hitherto many of the concepts of physics have been defined in terms of their properties." But now, "in general, we mean by any concept nothing more than a set of operations; *the concept is synonymous with the corresponding set of operations.* If the concept is physical, as of length, the operations are actual physical operations, namely, those by which length is measured; or if the concept is mental, as of mathematical con-tinuity, the operations are mental operations, namely those by which we determine whether a given aggregate of magnitudes is continuous."
> Now, this way of dealing with concepts was precisely what Holmes intro-duced into the science of law early in the '80's. Before discussing the signif-icance and possibilities of the new method, let me list here some of his definitions of things juridic:
> Law: "The prophecies of what the courts will do in fact, and nothing more pretentious, are what I mean by the law."

• • •

"But for legal purposes a right is only the hypostasis of a prophecy—the imagination of a substance *supporting* the fact that the public force will be brought to bear upon those who do things said to contravene it—just as we talk of the force of gravitation accounting for the conduct of bodies in space."

Duty: "A legal duty so called is nothing but a prediction that if a man does or omits certain things he will be made to suffer in this or that way by judgment of the court; and so of a legal right."

• • •

Contract: "The duty to keep a contract at common law means a prediction that you must pay damages if you do not keep it and nothing else. If you commit a tort, you are liable to pay a compensatory sum. If you commit a contract, you are liable to pay a compensatory sum, unless the promised event comes to pass, and that is all the difference."

"It may be conceded at the outset that all these definitions are capable of being further developed or improved upon: The important point to note is the complete departure from the way the old Classical Jurisprudence defined things. Hostile as he was to the traditional logic, Holmes touched the springs of the neo-realistic logic in his analysis of legal concepts. He departed entirely from the subject-predicate form of logic, and employed a logic of relations. He did not try to show how a legal entity possesses certain inherent properties. What he was trying everywhere to bring out is: If a certain group of facts is true of a person, then the person will receive a certain group of consequences attached by the law to that group of facts. Instead of treating a legal concept as a substance which in its nature necessarily contains certain inherent properties, we have here a logic which regards it as a mere signpost of a real relation subsisting between an antecedent and a consequent, and, as one of the New Realists so aptly puts it, all signposts must be kept up to date, with their inscriptions legible and their pointing true. In short, by turning the juristic logic from a subject-predicate form to an antecedent-consequent form, Holmes virtually created an inductive science of law. For both the antecedent and the consequent are to be proved and ascertained, empirically."

In brief, Holmes and, one should add, Hohfeld have offered a logcial basis for the redefinition of every legal concept in empirical terms, *i.e.* in terms of judicial decisions. The ghost-world of supernatural legal entities to whom courts delegate the moral responsibility of deciding cases vanishes; in its place we see legal concepts as patterns of judicial behavior, behavior which affects human lives for better or worse and is therefore subject to moral criticism. Of the functional method in legal science, one may say, as Russell has said of the method in contemporary philosophy, "Our procedure here is precisely analogous to that which has swept away from the philosophy of mathematics the useless menagerie of metaphysical monsters with which it used to be infested."

4. The Redirection of Research

It is often easier to distinguish a school of thought by asking not, "What basic theory does it defend?" but rather, "What basic question does it propound?"

A failure to recognize that the law is a vast field, in which different students are interested in diverse problems, has the unfortunate effect of making every school of legal thought an *ex officio* antagonist of every other school. Dean Pound's classification of jurists into mutually exclusive "analytical," "historical," "philosophical," and "sociological" schools, with sub-species too numerous to mention, has given a good deal of prestige to the idea that a new school of jurisprudence must offer a revolutionary threat to all existing schools. It would be unfortunate to regard "functionalism" in law as a substitute for all other "isms." Rather, we must regard functionalism, in law as in anthropology, economics, and other fields, as a call for the study of problems which have been neglected by other scientific methods of investigation.

In general, when one comes upon a strange fact and seeks to understand it, there are four inquiries he can pursue.

In the first place, our investigator can *classify* the fact—either by putting an arbitrary label upon it or by discerning in the fact to be explained the significant similarities and differences which relate it to other facts.

Again, one may seek to discover the *genesis* of the fact in question, to trace its historical antecedents.

In the third place, one may inquire into the *nature* of the fact presented, endeavoring by logical analysis to resolve it into simpler elements.

A fourth possible approach seeks to discover the *significance* of the fact through a determination of its implications or consequences in a given mathematical, physical or social context.

It is this last approach to which the term "functional" has been applied. Obviously, it is not the *only* way of gathering useful information, and obviously, it is largely dependent upon the results of classificatory or taxonomic investigation, genetic or historical research, and analytical inquiries. . . .

The age of the classical jurists is over, I think. The "Restatement of the Law" by the American Law Institute is the last long-drawn-out gasp of a dying tradition. The more intelligent of our younger law teachers and students are not interested in "restating" the dogmas of legal theology. There will, of course, be imitators and followers of the classical jurists, in the years ahead. But I think that the really creative legal thinkers of the future will not devote themselves, in the manner of Williston, Wigmore, and their fellow masters, to the taxonomy of legal concepts and to the systematic explication of principles of "justice" and "reason," buttressed by "correct" cases. Creative legal thought will more and more look behind the pretty array of "correct" cases to the actual facts of judicial behavior, will make increasing use of statistical methods in the scientific description and prediction of judicial behavior, will more and more seek to map the hidden springs of judicial decision and to weigh the social forces which are represented on the bench. And on the critical side, I think that creative legal thought will more and more look behind the traditionally accepted principles of "justice" and "reason" to appraise in ethical terms the social values at stake in any choice between two precedents.

"Social policy" will be comprehended not as an emergency factor in legal argument but rather as the gravitational field that gives weight to any rule or precedent, whether it be in constitutional law, in the law of trade-marks, or in the most technical details of legal procedure.

There is implied in this shifting of the paths of legal research a change in the equipment needs of the student of law. Familiarity with the words of past judicial opinions and skill in the manipulation of legal concepts are not enough for the student who seeks to understand the social forces that control judicial behavior, nor for the lawyer who seeks to use these forces.

The vested interests of our law schools in an "independent" science of law are undermined by every advance in our knowledge of the social antecedents and consequences of judicial decision. It becomes the part of discretion, in law schools aware of such advances, to admit that legal science necessarily involves us in psychology, economics, and political theory. Courses in our more progressive law schools are beginning to treat, most gingerly, of the psychological doctrines embedded in our rules of evidence, the sociological theories assumed in our criminal law, the economic assumptions embalmed in our doctrines of constitutional law, and the psychological, sociological, and economic *facts* which give force and signficance to rules and decisions in these and other fields of law. The first steps taken are clumsy and evoke smiles of sympathy or roars of laughter from critics of diverse temperaments. The will to walk persists.

For the lawyer, no less than for the legal scholar, handling of materials hitherto considered "non-legal" assumes increasing importance....

III. The Uses of the Functional Method in Law

The significance of the functional method in the field of law is clarified if we consider the bearings of this method upon four traditional legal problems: (1) The definition of law; (2) The nature of legal rules and concepts; (3) The theory of legal decisions; and (4) The role of legal criticism.

1. The Definition of Law

The starting point of functional analysis in American jurisprudence is found in Justice Holmes' definition of law as "prophecies of what the courts will do in fact." It is in "The Path of the Law," that this realistic conception of law is first clearly formulated:

> "If you want to know the law and nothing else, you must look at it as a bad man, who cares only for the material consequences which such knowledge enables him to predict, not as a good one, who finds his reasons for conduct, whether inside the law or outside of it, in the vaguer sanctions of conscience.... Take the fundamental question, What constitutes the law? You will find some text writers telling you that it is something different from what is decided by the courts of Massachusetts or England, that it is a system of reason, that it is a deduction from principles of ethics or admitted axioms or what not, which may or may not coincide with the decisions. But if we take the view of our friend the bad man we shall find that he does not care two straws for the axioms or deductions, but that he does want to know what the Massachusetts or English courts are likely to do in fact. I am much of his mind. The prophecies of what the courts will do in fact, and nothing more pretentious, are what I mean by the law."

A good deal of fruitless controversy has arisen out of attempts to show that this definition of law as the way courts actually decide cases is either true or false. A definition of law is *useful* or *useless*. It is not *true* or *false*, any more than a New Year's resolution or an insurance policy. A definition is in fact a type of insurance against certain risks of confusion. It cannot, any more than can a commercial insurance policy eliminate all risks. Absolute certainty is as foreign to language as to life. There is no final insurance against an insurer's insolvency. And the words of a definition always carry their own aura of ambiguity. But a definition is useful if it insures against risks of confusion more serious than any that the definition itself contains. . . .

2. The Nature of Legal Rules and Concepts

If the functionalists are correct, the meaning of a definition is found in its consequences. The definition of a general term like "law" is significant only because it affects all our definitions of specific legal concepts.

The consequence of defining law as a function of concrete judicial decisions is that we may proceed to define such concepts as "contract," "property," "title," "corporate personality," "right," and "duty," similarly as functions of concrete judicial decisions.

The consequence of defining law as a hodge-podge of political force and ethical value ambiguously amalgamated is that every legal concept, rule or question will present a similar ambiguity.

Consider the elementary legal question: "Is there a contract?"

When the realist asks this question, he is concerned with the actual behavior of courts. For the realist, the contractual relationship, like law in general, is a function of legal decisions. The question of what courts *ought* to do is irrelevant here. Where there is a promise that will be legally enforced there is a contract. So conceived, any answer to the question "Is there a contract" must be in the nature of a prophecy, based, like other prophecies, upon past and present facts. So conceived, the question "Is there a contract?" or for that matter any other legal question, may be broken up into a number of subordinate questions, each of which refers to the actual behavior of courts: (1) What courts are likely to pass upon a given transaction and its consequences? (2) What elements in this transaction will be viewed as relevant and important by these courts? (3) How have these courts dealt with transactions in the past which are *similar* to the given transaction, that is, *identical in those respects which the court will regard as important*? (4) What forces will tend to compel judicial conformity to the precedents that appear to be in point (*e.g.* inertia, conservatism, knowledge of the past, or intelligence sufficient to acquire such knowledge, respect for predecessors, superiors or brothers on the bench, a habit of deference to the established expectations of the bar or the public) and how strong are these forces? (5) What factors will tend to evoke new judicial treatment for the transaction in question (*e.g.* changing public opinion, judicial idiosyncrasies and prejudices, newly accepted theories of law, society or economics, or the changing social context of the case) and how powerful are these factors?

These are the questions which a successful practical lawyer faces and answers in any case. The law, as the realistic lawyer uses the term, is the body of answers to such questions. The task of prediction involves, in itself, no judgement of ethical value. Of course, even the most cynical practitioner will recognize that the positively existing ethical beliefs of judges are material facts in any case because they determine what facts the judge will view as important and what past rules he will regard as reasonable or unreasonable and worthy of being extended or restricted. But judicial beliefs about the values of life and the ideals of society are *facts,* just as the religious beliefs of the Andaman Islanders are facts, and the truth or falsity of such moral beliefs is a matter of complete unconcern to the practical lawyer, as to the scientific observer.

Washed in cynical acid, every legal problem can thus be interpreted as a question concerning the positive behavior of judges.

There is a second and radically different meaning which can be given to our type question "Is there a contract?" When a judge puts this question, in the course of writing his opinion, he is not attempting to predict his own behavior. He is in effect raising the question, in an obscure way, of whether or not liability *should* be attached to certain acts. This is inescapably an ethical question. What a judge ought to do in a given case is quite as much a moral issue as any of the traditional problems of Sunday School morality.

It is difficult for those who still conceive of morality in other worldly terms to recognize that every case presents a moral question to the court. But this notion has no terrors for those who think of morality in earthly terms. Morality, so conceived, is vitally concerned with such facts as human expectations based upon past decisions, the stability of economic transactions, and even the maintenance of order and simplicity in our legal system. If ethical values are inherent in all realms of human conduct, the ethical appraisal of a legal situation is not to be found in the spontaneous outpourings of a sensitive conscience unfamiliar with the social context, the background of precedent, and the practices and expectations, legal and extra-legal, which have grown up around a given type of transaction.

It is the great disservice of the classical conception of law that it hides from judicial eyes the ethical character of every judicial question, and thus serves to perpetuate class prejudices and uncritical moral assumptions which could not survive the sunlight of free ethical controversy.

The Blackstonian conception of law as half-mortal and half-divine gives us a mythical conception of contract. When a master of classical jurisprudence like Williston asks the question "Is there a contract?", he has in mind neither the question of scientific prediction which the practical lawyer faces, nor the question of values which the conscientious judge faces. If he had in mind the former question, his studies would no doubt reveal the extent to which courts actually enforce various types of contractual obligation. His conclusions would be in terms of probability and statistics. On the other hand, if Professor Williston were interested in the ethical aspects of contractual liability, he would undoubtedly offer a significant account of the human values and social costs involved in different types of agreements and in the means of their enforcement. In fact, however, the discussions of a Williston will oscillate between a theory of what courts actually do and a theory of what courts ought to do, without coming to rest either on the plane of social actualities or on the plane of values long enough to come to grips with significant problems. This confused wandering between the world of fact and the world of justice vitiates every argument and every analysis.

Intellectual clarity requires that we carefully distinguish between the two problems of (1) objective description, and (2) critical judgement, which classical jurisprudence lumps under the same phrase. Such a distinction realistic jurisprudence offers with the double-barreled thesis: (1) that every legal rule or concept is simply a function of judicial decisions to which all questions of value are irrelevant, and (2) that the problem of the judge is not whether a legal rule or concept actually exists but whether it *ought* to exist. Clarity on two fronts is the result. Description of legal facts becomes more objective, and legal criticism becomes more critical.

The realistic lawyer, when he attempts to discover how courts are actually dealing with certain situations, will seek to rise above his own moral bias and to discount the moral bias of the legal author whose treatise he consults.

The realistic author of textbooks will not muddy his descriptions of judicial behavior with wishful thinking; if he dislikes a decision or line of decisions, he will refrain from saying, "This cannot be the law because it is contrary to sound principle," and say instead, "This is the law, but I don't like it," or more usefully, "This rule leads to the following results, which are socially undesirable for the following reasons . . . "

The realistic advocate, if he continues to use ritual language in addressing an unrealistic court, will at least not be fooled by his own words: he will use his "patter" to induce favorable judicial attitudes and at the same time to distract judicial attention from precedents and facts that look the wrong way (as the professional magician uses his "patter" to distract the attention of his audience from certain facts). Recognizing the circularity of conceptual argument, the realistic advocate will contrive to bring before the court the human values that favor his cause, and since the rules of evidence often stand in the way, he will perforce bring his materials to judical attention by sleight-of-hand—through the appeal of a "sociological brief" to "judicial notice," through discussion of the background and consequences of past cases cited as precedents, through elaboration and exegesis upon admissible evidence, or even through a political speech or a lecture on economics in the summation of his case or argument.

The realistic judge, finally, will not fool himself or anyone else by basing decisions upon circular reasoning from the presence or absence of corporations, conspiracies, property rights, titles, contracts, proximate causes, or other legal derivatives of the judicial decision itself. Rather, he will frankly assess the conflicting human values that are opposed in every controversy, appraise the social importance of the precedents to which each claim appeals, open the courtroom to all evidence that will bring light to this delicate practical task of social adjustment, and consign to Von Jhering's heaven of legal concepts all attorneys whose only skill is that of the conceptual acrobat.

3. The Theory of Legal Decisions

The uses of the functional approach are not exhausted by "realistic jurisprudence." "Realistic jurisprudence," as that term is currently used, is a theory of the nature of law, and therefore a theory of the nature of legal rules, legal concepts, and legal questions. Its essence is the definition of law as a function of judicial decisions. This definition is of tremendous value in the development of legal science, since it enables us to dispel the supernatural mists that envelop the legal order and to deal with the elements of the legal order in objective, scientific terms. But this process of definition and clarification is only a preliminary stage in the life of legal science. When we have analyzed legal rules and concepts as patterns of decisions, it becomes relevant to ask, "What are judicial decisions made of?"

If we conceive of legal rules and concepts as functions of judicial decisions, it is convenient, for purposes of this analysis, to think of these decisions as hard and simple facts. Just as every physical object may be analyzed as a complex of positive and negative electrons, so every legal institution, every legal rule or concept may be analyzed as a complex of plaintiff decisions and defendant decisions. But simplicity is relative to the level of analysis. For the chemist, the atom is the lowest term of analysis. But the physicist cannot stop the process of analysis with the atom or even the electron. It would be heresy to the faith of science to endow either with final simplicity and perpetual immunity from further analysis. Unfortunately, certain advocates of realistic jurisprudence, after using the functional method to break down rules and concepts into atomic decisions, refuse to go any further with the analytic process. They are willing to look upon decisions as simple unanalyzable products of judicial hunches or indigestion.

The "hunch" theory of law, by magnifying the personal and accidental factors in judicial behavior, implicitly denies the relevance of significant, predictable, social determinants that govern the course of judicial decision. Those who have advanced this viewpoint have performed a real service in indicating the large realm of uncertainty in the actual law. But actual experience does reveal a significant body of predictable uniformity in the behavior of courts. Law is not a mass of unrelated decisions nor a product of judicial bellyaches. Judges are human, but they are a peculiar breed of humans, selected to a type and held to service under a potent system of governmental controls. Their acts are "judicial" only within a system which provides for appeals, rehearings, impeachments, and legislation. The decision that is "peculiar" suffers erosion—unless it represents the first salient manifestation of a new social force, in which case it soon ceases to be peculiar. It is more useful to analyze a judicial "hunch" in terms of the continued impact of a judge's study of precedents, his conversations with associates, his reading of newspapers, and his recollections of college courses, than in strictly physiological terms.

A truly realistic theory of judicial decisions must conceive every decision as something more than an expression of individual personality, as concomitantly and even more importantly a function of social forces, that is to say, as a product of social determinants and an index of social consequences. A judicial decision is a social event. Like the enactment of a Federal statute, or the equipping of police cars with radios, a judicial decision is an intersection of social forces: Behind the decision are social forces that play upon it to give it a resultant momentum and direction; beyond the decision are human activities affected by it. The decision is without significant social dimensions when it is viewed simply at the moment in which is it rendered. Only by probing behind the decision to the forces which it reflects, or projecting beyond the decision the lines of its force upon the future, do we come to an understanding of the meaning of the decision itself. The distinction between "holding" and "dictum" in any decision is not to be discovered by logical inspection of the opinion or by historical inquiry into the actual facts of the case. That distinction involves us in a prediction, a prophecy of the weight that courts will give to future citiations of the decision rendered. This is a question not of pure logic but of human psychology, economics and politics.

What is the meaning of a judicial decision, summed up in the words, "Judgement for the plaintiff"? Obviously, the significance of the decision, even for the parties directly involved in the case, depends upon certain predictable uniformities of official behavior, *e.g.* that a sheriff or marshall will enforce the decision, in one way or another, over a period of time, that the given decision will be respected or followed in the same court or other courts if the question at issue is relitigated, and that certain procedures will be followed in the event of an appeal, etc. When we go beyond the merely private significance of an actual decision, we are involved in a new set of predictions concerning the extent to which other cases, similar in certain respects, are likely to receive the same treatment in the same courts or in other courts within a given jurisdiction. Except in the context of such predictions the announcement of a judicial decision is only a noise. If reasonably certain predictions of this sort could never be made, as Jerome Frank at times seems to say, then all legal decisions would be simply noises, and no better grist for science than the magical phrases of transcendental jurisprudence.

If the understanding of any decision involves us necessarily in prophecy (and thus in history), then the notion of law as something that exists completely and systematically at any given moment in time is false. Law is a social process, a complex of human activities, and an adequate legal science must deal with human activity, with cause and effect, with the past and the future. Legal science, as traditionally conceived, attempts to give an instantaneous snapshot of an existing and completed system of rights and duties. Within that system there are no temporal processes, no cause and no effect, no past and no future. A legal decision is thus conceived as a logical deduction from fixed principles. Its meaning is expressed only in terms of its logical consequences. A legal system, thus viewed, is as far removed from temporal activity as a system of pure geometry. In fact, jurisprudence is as much a part of pure mathematics as is algebra, unless it be conceived as a study of human behavior,—human behavior as it molds and is molded by judicial decisions. Legal systems, principles, rules, institutions, concepts, and decisions can be understood only as functions of human behavior.

Such a view of legal science reveals gaps in our legal knowledge to which, I think, legal research will give increasing attention.

We are still in the stage of guesswork and accidentally collected information, when it comes to formulating the social forces which mold the course of judicial decision. We know, in a general way, that dominant economic forces play a part in judicial decision, that judges usually reflect the attitudes of their own income class on social questions, that their views on law are molded to a certain extent by their past legal experience as counsel for special interests, and that the impact of counsel's skill and eloquence is a cumulative force which slowly hammers the law into forms desired by those who can best afford to hire legal skill and eloquence; but nobody has ever charted, in scientific fashion, the extent of such economic influences. We know, too, that judges are craftsmen, with aesthetic ideals, concerned with the aesthetic judgements that the bar and the law schools will pass upon their awkward or skillful, harmonious or unharmonious, anomalous or satisfying, actions and theories; but again we have no specific information on the extent of this aesthetic bias in the various branches of the law. We know that courts are, at least in this country, a generally conservative social force, and more like a brake than a motor in the social mechanism, but we have no scientific factual comparison of judicial, legislative, and executive organs of government, from the standpoint of social engineering. Concretely and specifically, we know that Judge So-and-so, a former attorney for a non-union shop, has very definite ideas about labor injunctions, that another judge, who has had an unfortunate sex life, is parsimonious in the fixing of alimony; that another judge can be "fixed" by a certain political "boss"; that a series of notorious kidnappings will bring about a wave of maximum sentences in kidnapping cases. All this knowledge is useful to the practicing lawyer, to the public official, to the social reformer, and to the disinterested student of society. But it is most meager, and what little of it we have, individually, is not collectively available. There is at present no publication showing the political, economic, and professional background and activities of our various judges. Such a reference work would be exceedingly valuable, not only to the practical lawyer who wants to bring a motion or try a case before a sympathetic court, but also to the disinterested student of the law. Such a Judicial Index is not published, however, because it would be disrespectable. According to the classical theory, these things have nothing to do with the way courts decide cases. A witty critic of the functional approach regards it as a *reductio ad absurdum* of this approach that law schools of the future may investigate judicial psychology, teach the art of bribery, and produce graduate detectives. This is far from a *reductio ad absurdum*. Our understanding of the law will be greatly enriched when we learn more about how judges think, about the exact extent of judicial corruption, and about the techniques for investigating legally relevant facts. Of course, this knowledge may be used for improper purposes, but cannot the same be said of the knowledge which traditional legal education distributes?

If we know little today of the motivating forces which mold legal decisions, we know even less of the human consequences of these decisions. We do not even know how far the appellate cases, with which legal treatises are almost exclusively concerned, are actually followed in the trial courts. Here, again, the experienced practitioner is likely to have accumulated a good deal of empirical information, but the young law clerk, just out of a first-rate law school, is not even aware that such a problem exists. Likewise, the problem of the actual enforcement of judgements has received almost no critical study. Discussion of the extent to which various statutes are actually enforced regularly moves in the thin air of polemic theory. It is usually practically impossible to find out whether a given statute has ever been enforced unless its enforcement has raised a legal tangle for appellate courts.

When we advance beyond the realm of official conduct and seek to discover the social consequences of particular statutes or decisions, we find a few promising programs of research but almost no factual studies. Today the inclusion of factual annotations in a code, showing the extent and effects of law enforcement, would strike most lawyers as almost obscene. But notions of obscenity change, and every significant intellectual revolution raises to prominence facts once obscure and disrespectable. It is reasonable to expect that some day even the impudencies of Holmes and Llewellyn will appear sage and respectable.

4. Legal Criticism

It is perhaps the chief service of the functional approach that in cleansing legal rules, concepts, and institutions of the compulsive flavors of legal logic or metaphysics, room is made for conscious ethical criticism of law. In traditional jurisprudence, criticism, where it exists, is found masked in the protective camouflage of transcendental nonsense: "The law *must* (or *cannot*) be thus and so, because the *nature* of contracts, corporations or contingent remainders so requires." The functional approach permits ethics to come out of hiding. When we recognize that legal rules are simply formulae describing uniformities of judicial decision, that legal concepts likewise are patterns or functions of judicial decisions, that decisions themselves are not products of logical parthenogenesis born of pre-existing legal principles but are social events with social causes and consequences, then we are ready for the serious business of appraising law and legal institutions in terms of some standard of human values.

The importance for legal criticism of clear, objective description of judicial behavior, its causes and its consequences, is coming to be generally recognized. What is not so easily recognized is the importance for objective legal science of legal criticism.

Since the brilliant achievements of Bentham, descriptive legal science has made almost no progress in determining the consequences of legal rules. This failure of scholarship, in the light of encouraging progress of modern research into the antecedents and social context of judicial decision, calls for explanation.

Possibly this gap is to be explained in terms of an inherited assumption that statutes and decisions are self-executing, that the consequences of a law or a judgement are, therefore, clearly indicated by the language of the statute or decision itself, and that factual research is therefore a work of supererogation. Possibly this failure of research is to be explained in terms of the dominance of the private lawyer in our legal education. The private attorney is interested in the *causes* of judicial decisions, but his interests in consequences is likely to stop with the payment of a fee. I am inclined to think, however, that the failure of our legal scholarship in this direction may be attributed to a more fundamental difficulty. The prospect of determining the consequences of a given rule of law appears to be an infinite task, and is indeed an infinite task unless we approach it with some discriminating criterion of what consequences are *important*. Now a criterion of *importance* presupposes a criterion of values, which is precisely what modern thinkers of the "sociological" and "realistic" schools of jurisprudence have never had. Dean Pound has talked for many years of the "balancing" of interests, but without ever indicating which interests are more important than others or how a standard of weight or fineness can be constructed for the appraisal of "interests." Contemporary "realists" have, in general, either denied absolutely that absolute standards of importance can exist, or else insisted that we must thoroughly understand the facts as they are before we begin to evaluate them. Such a postponement of the problem of values is equivalent to its repudiation. We never shall thoroughly understand the facts as they are, and we are not likely to make much progress towards such understanding unless we at the same time bring into play a critical theory of values. In terms of such a theory, particular human desires and habits are important, and the task of research into legal consequences passes from the realm of vague curiosity to the problem form: How do these rules of law strengthen or change these important habits and satisfy or impede these important desires?

The positive task of descriptive legal science cannot, therefore, be entirely separated from the task of legal criticism. The collection of social facts without a selective criterion of human values produces a horrid wilderness of useless statistics. The relation between positive legal science and legal criticism is not a relation of temporal priority, but of mutual dependence. Legal criticism is empty without objective description of the causes and consequences of legal decisions. Legal description is blind without the guiding light of a theory of values. It is through the union of objective legal science and a critical theory of social values that our understanding of the human significance of law will be enriched. It is loyalty to this union of distinct disciplines that will mark whatever is of lasting importance in contemporary legal science and legal philosophy.

KARL N. LLEWELLYN

"Remarks on the Theory of Appellate Decision and the Rules or Canons About How Statutes Are to Be Construed"

(1950)

Canons of Construction

Statutory interpretation still speaks a diplomatic tongue. Here is some of the technical framework for maneuver.

Thrust	but	Parry
1. A statute cannot go beyond its text.		1. To effect its purpose a statute may be implemented beyond its text.
2. Statutes in derogation of the common law will not be extended by construction.		2. Such acts will be liberally construed if their nature is remedial.
3. Statutes are to be read in the light of the common law and a statute affirming a common law rule is to be construed in accordance with the common law.		3. The common law gives way to a statute which is inconsistent with it and when a statute is designed as a revision of a whole body of law applicable to a given subject it supersedes the common law.
4. Where a foreign statute which has received construction has been adopted, previous construction is adopted too.		4. It may be rejected where there is conflict with the obvious meaning of the statute or where the foreign decisions are unsatisfactory in reasoning or where the foreign interpretation is not in harmony with the spirit or policy of the laws of the adopting state.

© Copyright 1950 by Vanderbilt Law Review. Reprinted from the *Vanderbilt Law Review*, vol. 3 (1950), pp. 395, 401–6, by permission.

5. Where various states have already adopted the statute, the parent state is followed.

6. Statutes *in pari materia* must be construed together.

7. A statute imposing a new penalty or forfeiture, or a new liability or disability, or creating a new right of action will not be construed as having a retroactive effect.

8. Where design has been distinctly stated no place is left for construction.

9. Definitions and rules of construction contained in an interpretation clause are part of the law and binding.

10. A statutory provision requiring liberal construction does not mean disregard of unequivocal requirements of the statute.

11. Titles do not control meaning; preambles do not expand scope; section headings do not change language.

12. If language is plain and unambiguous it must be given effect.

13. Words and phrases which have received judicial construction before enactment are to be understood according to that construction.

5. Where interpretations of other states are inharmonious, there is no such restraint.

6. A statute is not *in pari materia* if its scope and aim are distinct or where a legislative design to depart from the general purpose or policy of previous enactments may be apparent.

7. Remedial statutes are to be liberally construed and if a retroactive interpretation will promote the ends of justice, they should receive such construction.

8. Courts have the power to inquire into real as distinct from ostensible—purpose.

9. Definitions and rules of construction in a statute will not be extended beyond their necessary import nor allowed to defeat intention otherwise manifested.

10. Where a rule of construction is provided within the statute itself the rule should be applied.

11. The title may be consulted as a guide when there is doubt or obscurity in the body; preambles may be consulted to determine rationale, and thus the true construction of terms; section headings may be looked upon as part of the statute itself.

12. Not when literal interpretation would lead to absurd or mischievous consequences or thwart manifest purpose.

13. Not if the statute clearly requires them to have a different meaning.

14. After enactment, judicial decision upon interpretation of particular terms and phrases controls.

15. Words are to be taken in their ordinary meaning unless they are technical terms or words of art.

16. Every word and clause must be given effect.

17. The same language used repeatedly in the same connection is presumed to bear the same meaning throughout the statute.

18. Words are to be interpreted according to the proper grammatical effect of their arrangement within the statute.

19. Exceptions not made cannot be read.

20. Expression of one thing excludes another.

21. General terms are to receive a general construction.

22. It is a general rule of construction that where general words follow an enumeration they are to be held as applying only to persons and things of the same general kind or class specifically mentioned (*ejusdem generis*).

23. Qualifying or limiting words or clauses are to be referred to the next preceding antecedent.

14. Practical construction by executive officers is strong evidence of true meaning.

15. Popular words may bear a technical meaning and technical words may have a popular signification and they should be so construed as to agree with evident intention or to make the statute operative.

16. If inadvertently inserted or if repugnant to the rest of the statute, they may be rejected as surplusage.

17. This presumption will be disregarded where it is necessary to assign different meanings to make the statute consistent.

18. Rules of grammar will be disregarded where strict adherence would defeat purpose.

19. The letter is only the "bark." Whatever is within the reason of the law is within the law itself.

20. The language may fairly comprehend many different cases where some only are expressly mentioned by way of example.

21. They may be limited by specific terms with which they are associated or by the scope and purpose of the statute.

22. General words must operate on something. Further, *ejusdem generis* is only an aid in getting the meaning and does not warrant confining the operations of a statute within narrower limits than were intended.

23. Not when evident sense and meaning require a different construction.

24. Punctuation will govern when a statute is open to two constructions.

25. It must be assumed that language has been chosen with due regard to grammatical propriety and is not interchangeable on mere conjecture.

26. There is a distinction between words of permission and mandatory words.

27. A proviso qualifies the provision immediately preceding.

. 28. When the enacting clause is general, a proviso is construed strictly.

24. Punctuation marks will not control the plain and evident meaning of language.

25. "And" and "or" may be read interchangeably whenever the change is necessary to give the statute sense and effect.

26. Words imparting permission may be read as mandatory and words imparting command may be read as permissive when such construction is made necessary by evident intention or by the rights of the public.

27. It may clearly be intended to have a wider scope.

28. Not when it is necessary to extend the proviso to persons or cases which come within its equity.

7

Law as Social Science

"Science" was powerfully attractive to the social scientists of the 1920s. The leftists among them had concluded that the progressive effort to educate the poor to rework capitalism had failed. Politics had given them Harding and his "return to normalcy," the Teapot Dome scandal, and the collapse of the League of Nations. The people could not be taught to lead themselves. Walter Lippman had argued as much in his sardonic *Public Opinion* (1922). John Dewey came to a complementary conclusion in *The Quest for Certainty* (1929), claiming that people clung hardest to "eternal truths" when the times were most uncertain; their hold must be broken through scientific method. Others put the matter more strongly still—that scientific study of contemporary problems and their solution was the only sure means of social control. The new world order, considered by intellectuals as diverse as Edward Bellamy and Justice Holmes,[1] amounted to this—here, in the words of a leading social scientist of the 1920s, Charles Merriam:

> We are very rapidly approaching a time when it may be possible to decide not merely what types of law we wish to enact, but what types of person we wish to develop, either by the process of education or of eugenics ... to determine what sorts of creature are to be born, within important limits at least.[2]

In their own discipline, the social scientists' grand dream, as Huntington Cairns put it at the time, was "to duplicate in the statement of social laws the tremendous success of the natural sciences in formulating the laws of nature."[3] As their belief in genetic engineering shows, for the reformers, "formulating" meant not merely holding a mirror up to nature, but changing the basis for the social order, even for nature itself.

Among the Legal Realists, the attraction of social science was also in the working out of the proposition (in Walter Wheeler Cook's words) that "human laws are devices, tools which society uses as one of its methods to regulate human conduct and to promote those types of it which are regarded as desirable."[4] By 1919, the view of law as a social phenomenon was commonplace enough that the editors at the Yale Law Journal could announce a new emphasis in legal analysis. No system of justice, they claimed, was fixed or permanent. Law was to be adjusted to mores, an aim that could be furthered through a constant refashioning of legal terminology, and the shaping of a more exact legal science.[5] While most Realists debunked the notion of legal doctrine working independently as a motive force in social life, it was only extremists among them such as Underhill Moore who considered that legal rules were wholly determined by custom or culture, having no gravitational power of their own.[6]

For the Realists, "social science" and "sociology" captured a half-worked-out idea, the means towards fusing in our laws the ideal and the real, the key to undoing the ethical dilemma embedded in such projects as Karl Llewellyn's "*temporary* divorce of Is and Ought for purposes of study."[7] Social science was not a neutral method; instead, it was packed with reformist energy. Cardozo declared in *The Nature of the Judicial Process* (1921) that the greatest force in reconstructing law is "the power of social justice which finds its outlet and expression in the method of sociology. The final cause of law is the welfare of society. The rule that misses its aim cannot permanently justify its existence."[8] If the possibility of "social justice" was treated more skeptically by the Realists a decade later,[9] sociology and "quantitative analysis"[10] nonetheless retained some of their magic resonance.

Thus conceived, social science had an additional, more humble effect—it meant casting aside Langdellian pieties. Langdell had considered that "printed books are the ultimate sources of all legal knowledge"; if law is a science, then the library is its "proper workshop."[11] But after Pound and others (following Weber and Durkheim) had emphasized that law was a social institution, that legal rules could be tested against the way people acted,[12] Realists were quick to show that meant Langdell's educational prescriptions were outmoded and wrong. Unfortunately, the promise of this new scientific method led Realists with a social science bent to claims far more grandiose than Langdell's.[13] Some scholars labored mightily at empirical research, only to find conclusions elusive, their hard-won data so incomplete as to be unpublishable, their work useless for suggesting reform. William O. Douglas, for example, began, at Yale in 1928, a study of business failures, meant, he said, to expose the "functioning of the whole credit system of the country."[14] In 1932, he published two articles, neither fulfilling the promise of his earlier substantial research. Taken together, they presaged his abandonment of the project.[15]

By the late 1920s, the group of law professors deeply engaged in social science included Clark, Cook, Douglas, Marshall, Moore, Oliphant, and Yntema—all of them at Columbia, Yale, or Johns Hopkins.[16] The contributors to the Brookings Institute's *Essays on Research in the Social Sciences* (1931) give a quick sense of the movement: W.F.G. Swann on science; W.W. Cook on social science; Charles Beard on political science; John Clark on economics; Karl Llewellyn on "legal tradition and social science method"; Madison Bentley on psychology; Arthur Schlesinger on history; and William Ogburn and William Thomas, writing separately, on research problems in the social sciences.

As a further sign of the breakdown of Langdell's ideal of the legal scholar, social scientists also joined law faculties. At Yale, for example, Walton Hamilton, an institutional economist, joined the faculty in 1924; Leon Marshall, an economist with no legal training, was there already. Bronislav Malinowski, who had written *Crime and Custom in Savage Society* (1926), taught a course in legal anthropology beginning in the late twenties. From 1927 to 1929, Yale's dean, Robert Hutchins, tirelessly raised funds for the Institute of Human Relations, which was to unite study in psychology, medicine, and law. The Institute of Law of The Johns Hopkins University was founded in 1928 to afford legal scholars the time to conduct research by scientific method rather than by traditional common law technique. During its six years of existence, the Institute published many Realist collaborative efforts in social science.[17]

The social scientist law professor was no longer to work in the manner of Ames, Gray, or Langdell; or of Williston, Corbin, Hohfeld, or Beale. He was instead to set law in the frame of anthropology, economics, political science, psychology, and sociology. There were scattered predecessors, well-known to the Realists. Sir Henry Sumner Maine had deployed anthropology in *Ancient Law* (1864); and, with greater sophistication, so too had Josef Kohler.[18] In their *Evolution of Law* (1915), even traditionalists like Wigmore and Kocourek turned their hands to anthropology. Dean Pound urged and, to some extent, fostered a shift in research from appellate to trial courts, from arid studies in legal concepts to a theory of social interests, from "law in books" to "law in action."[19] And social science arguments had proved valuable to reformers. For example, in *Muller v. Oregon* (1908),[20] Justice Brewster, moved by Brandeis' sociological brief, declared patriarchal society to be a core truth in anthropology, just as Maine had done.

But it was the Realists of the twenties and thirties who were, as Llewellyn styled them, consistent, persistent, insistent about the usefulness of social science. In law and economics, Berle and Means wrote on methods of corporate control,[21] and John R. Commons, in an institutionalist study that inspired Karl Llewellyn, examined the *Legal Foundations of Capitalism* (1924). In the 1920s, there was a spate of articles on debtor and lender practices, stimulated in part by Llewellyn's pioneering essay, "The Effect of Legal Institutions upon Economics"

(1925).[22] Dean Hutchins collaborated briefly with Mortimer Adler, and for several years with another psychologist, Donald Slesinger, and produced a series of penetrating essays on psychology in the law of evidence.[23] Thurman Arnold's *Symbols of Government* (1935) was a free-ranging commentary based in contemporary psychology—and, his critics alleged, on the work of the "patron saint of fascism," Vilfredo Pareto.[24] Edward Corwin, the constitutional law scholar, proposed a complex scheme to the American Political Science Association summer conference in 1923, when he "discussed the need to specify criteria in the light of value judgments about political outcomes and outlined a sophisticated series of questions, taking into account differences in historical period, field of constitutional law, interplay of state and federal courts, and changes over time in the canons of interpretation."[25] Harold Laski, an intellectually flamboyant disciple of Holmes—and the "*doyen* of living pluralists*" according to a contemporary—wrote widely in politics and law.[26]

Also under the rubric of the social science of law went Frederick Beutel's work in "experimental jurisprudence"—a method of "scientific decisionmaking" by experts that, when elaborated, struck commentators as anti-democratic[27]—; Hessel Yntema's attacks on those who contended legal rules must be studied as parts of a self-contained system—"the restriction of a science of dietetics to the norms of a cookbook since they are used by the *chef*"[28]—; and Underhill Moore's early, raw-boned essays in legal behaviorism.[29] Perhaps of all this Realist work, the legal anthropology of Llewellyn and E. Adamson Hoebel among the Cheyenne has worn best.[30]

The chief method of social science, practiced by some, honored by all, was statistics. Statistical science—a nineteenth-century obsession, now turned out in twentieth-century dress—was to reveal society's natural laws. With uncharacteristic harshness, Karl Llewellyn later remarked:

> I doubt whether in all of the quest for social science there has ever been such hastily considered, ill-planned, mal-prepared large-scale so-called research as was perpetrated by Cook and Oliphant at Hopkins. But it was at Yale that the nadir of idiocy was achieved when Underhill Moore "tested out" whether law has mystical operation by an elaborate observation, metering and statisticking of the noneffect on the parking practices of New Haveners of a change in the official traffic regulations which he had arranged to keep carefully from coming to the knowledge of any trafficker.[31]

But Moore's notion, and it was a belief held by all the avowed social scientists, was that only through such a scientific method could progress—no longer felt to be part of the American birthright—be guaranteed. Moore is easy to mock, but his particular method of statistical analysis is no more naive than that undertaken by William Ogburn or Wesley Mitchell, trained social scientists, as Moore was not.[32]

Besides, there were some limited successes in this mode of study. Pound and Frankfurter led the Cleveland Crime Survey of 1922, a novel statistical examination of both criminal law and procedure.[33] Yale's Institute of Procedure aided Charles Clark's massive study of state and federal courts, in which he was helped on and off by William O. Douglas and Arnold.[34] Clark also developed an impressively detailed automotive accident survey for the New York Bar Association.[35]

In 1929, it did not seem absurd when the new social science building at the University of Chicago had, incised above its main door, "When you cannot measure your knowledge is meager and unsatisfactory."[36] But statistical surveys are only part of the story. Social science promised the Realists dramatic new forms of research, a driving reason for legal reform, and a means for yoking together law and ethics. No wonder Cardozo found the "power of social justice" expressed in the "method of sociology."

LOUIS BRANDEIS AND JOSEPHINE GOLDMARK

Muller v. *Oregon*

208 U.S. 412 (1908)
Brief for Defendant in Error

[*Before Brandeis' appointment to the Supreme Court in 1916, he was a successful Boston lawyer, leading diverse reform projects, such as the creation of savings bank life insurance. He was also deeply influential in the American Zionist movement. In* Muller v. Oregon, *208 U.S. 412 (1908), the Supreme Court reviewed maximum-working–hours regulations for laundresses. In a series of decisions, and most famously in* Lochner v. New York, *198 U.S. 45 (1905) (reprinted above), the Court had closely scrutinized various pieces of economic legislation, invalidating them when the means used by legislators were not closely tailored to the ends they sought. In practice, that standard of close scrutiny permitted the Court to hold unconstitutional statutes it believed interfered with the private market. Only those kinds of work traditionally held ultrahazardous at common law, such as coal mining, were properly subject to state regulation. That sort of reasoning was later ridiculed as highly artificial by the Realists, just as it was by Justice Harlan at the time (as in his dissent in* Lochner *itself). Brandeis' challenge in writing his brief for the Court in* Muller *was to obtain a sympathetic hearing for the facts supporting the legislators' statute, for that would show means fitted to ends. The Court was usually quite skeptical about such arguments. See, for example,* Adkins v. Children's Hospital, *261 U.S. 525, 559–560 (1923); and Bikle, "Judicial Determination of Questions of Fact Affecting the Constitutional Validity of Legislative Action," Harvard Law Review, 38 (1924): 6. The "Brandeis brief" method triumphant in* Muller *was also used successfully in* Brown v. Board of Education of Topeka, *347 U.S. 483 (1954), and in many of the criminal law decisions of the Warren Court, including* Miranda v. Arizona, *384 U.S. 436 (1965).—Ed]*

This case presents the single question whether the Statute of Oregon, approved Feb. 19, 1903, which provides that "no female [shall]

be employed in any mechanical establishment or factory or laundry"
"more than ten hours during any one day," is unconstitutional and
void as violating the Fourteenth Amendment of the Federal
Constitution.

The decision in this case will, in effect, determine the constitutionality
of nearly all the statutes in force in the United States, limiting the hours
of labor of adult women. . . .

Argument

The validity of the Oregon statute must . . . be sustained unless the Court
can find that there is no "fair ground, reasonable in and of itself, to say
that there is material danger to the public health (or safety), or to the
health (or safety) of the employees (or to the general welfare), if the hours
of labor are not curtailed." *Lochner* v. *New York*, 198 U.S. 45, 61. The
Oregon statute was obviously enacted for the purpose of protecting the
public health, safety, and welfare. . . .

The facts of common knowledge of which the Court may take judicial notice . . . establish, we submit, conclusively, that there is reasonable ground for holding that to permit women in Oregon to work in
a "mechanical establishment, or factory, or laundry" more than ten
hours in one day is dangerous to the public health, safety, morals, or
welfare.

These facts of common knowledge will be considered under the following heads:

Part I. Legislation (foreign and American) restricting the hours of
labor for women.

Part II. The world's experience upon which the legislation limiting
the hours of labor for women is based. . . .

Part Second

The World's Experience Upon Which The Legislation Limiting The
Hours Of Labor For Women Is Based. . . .

Report of the Maine Bureau of Industrial and Labor Statistics, 1888

Let me quote from Dr. Ely Van der Warker (1875):

Woman is badly constructed for the purposes of standing eight or
ten hours upon her feet. I do not intend to bring into evidence the peculiar position and nature of the organs contained in the pelvis, but to
call attention to the peculiar construction of the knee and the shallow-
ness of the pelvis, and the delicate nature of the foot as part of a sustaining column. The knee joint of woman is a sexual characteristic. Viewed
in front and extended, the joint in but a slight degree interrupts the

gradual taper of the thigh into the leg. Viewed in a semi-flexed position, the joint forms a smooth ovate spheroid. The reason of this lies in the smallness of the patella in front, and the narrowness of the articular surfaces of the tibia and femur, and which in man form the lateral prominences, and thus is much more perfect as a sustaining column than that of a woman. . . .

Massachusetts Bureau of Statistics of Labor. Domestic Labor and Woman's Work, 1872.

In the cotton mills at Fitchburg the women and children are pale, crooked, and sickly-looking. The women appear dispirited, and the children without the bloom of childhood in their cheeks, or the elasticity that belongs to that age. Hours, 60 to 67 3/4 a week. . . .

Report of Select Committee on Shops Early Closing Bill. British House of Commons, 1895.

Testimony of Dr. W. Chapman Grigg (formerly out-patient physician for the diseases of women at Westminster Hospital, and senior physician to the Queen Charlotte Lying-in Hospital and the Victoria Hospital for Children). . . .

I believe [sterility] is one of the greatest evils attached to these prolonged hours. I have seen many cases in families where certain members who have pursued the calling of shop-girl assistants have been sterile, while other members of the family have borne children. I know of one case where four members of a family who were shop-girls were sterile, and two other girls in the family, not shop-girls, have borne children; and I have known other cases in which this has occurred. . . . I have patients come to me from all parts of London. It appears to be a most common condition. . . .

Report of the British Chief Inspector of Factories and Workshops, 1873. Dr. R. H. Leach, Certifying Surgeon for over Thirty Years.

Shorten their hours of labor, for I believe that scores of infants are annually lost under the present system. As things now stand, a mother leaves her infant (say of two months old) at 6 a.m., often asleep in bed, at 8 she nurses it, then until 12:30 the child is bottle fed, or stuffed with indigestible food. On her return at noon, overheated and exhausted, her milk is unfit for the child's nourishment, and this state of things is again repeated until 6 p.m.; the consequence is, that the child suffers from spasmodic diarrhoea, often complicated with convulsions and ending in death....

La Réglémentation Légale du Travail des Femmes et des Enfants dans l'Industrie Italienne. Lionel Baudoin.

At the International Congress at Milan, on accidents among the laboring class, in May, 1894, Mr. Luigi Belloc (Factory Inspector of the Department of Labor) represented Italy. He stated that the continuous motion of the body taxes the nervous system, causing the gravest troubles. The sewing-machine, which requires of the operator 40,000 movements a day, causes in the long run abdominal and renal troubles, disarrangement of the menstrual function, and falling and deviations of the uterus. Functional weaknesses and paralysis are the result of the continual performance of the same movement. The necessity of standing or sitting for the whole day causes malformation of the body or curvature of the spine, as a result of the strained position. The attention required in watching a machine, especially an automatic one, is very fatiguing, on account of the large number of wheels operating at the same time which need attention....

Report of the British Chief Inspector of Factories and Workshops, 1900.

The existence of an exemption in the fish-curing trade has rendered the administration difficult and uncertain in result. It is noteworthy that in this trade, in which overtime is permissible to women on sixty occasions in the year, I have never found overtime notices in use in any workshop. The occupiers do not find them necessary. Starting with an exemption for one process, that of "gutting, salting, and packing," the industry would seem to have shaken itself gradually free from control, until now we find fish that have been in salt for several weeks dealt with as perishable articles. Given plenty of time and unsuitable surroundings, every article of food is to some extent perishable, and when a herring has been kept in salt for some weeks there is no reason for working on it at night except the reason that the day will bring other work, and in this seems to lie the cause of much of the late and irregular hours of the fish-curing trade....

One of the evils to which this want of regulation leads is the practice of employing the same person in the same day in processes controlled by the Acts, and in those outside their control.

...In another case in which a curer had a factory and also a kippering shop in the same town, the workers went from one to the other, always sure of their full day's work in the factory, followed very often by five or six hours' work in the other shop....

Dangerous Trades. Thomas Oliver, *Medical Expert on Dangerous Trades Committees of the Home Office.* 1902. *Chapter XLVII. Laundry Workers.*

The "calender machine" has been adapted to laundry work, and is now commonly found in quite small laundries; it consists of huge steam or gas heated cylinders, varying from four to eight or nine feet long, either revolving singly in a metal bed, as in the case of the "decoudun," or on each other, as in the case of the multiple-roller calenders. The linen is generally drawn in under the hot, revolving rollers, which thus "iron" it smooth and glossy, a cloud of steam arising as each damp article passes under the roller. Constant care is required to so put the work under the machine that the hands are not also drawn under; want of attention may be followed by an accident, and even where care is exercised the fingers may be entangled in a string or hole in the material and the hand thus drawn in. The heat given off by these machines is sometimes very great; a temperature of over 90° F. may be registered even in winter on the feeding-step in front of this machine. . . . at which little girls stand all day long. . . .

The ten minutes or quarter-hour "lunch" of "beer" is common, and the "beer-man" who goes his rounds at 10 a.m. and 6 or 7 p.m. to all the laundries, delivering his cans of beer from the nearest public house, is an institution which is, I believe, unknown in any other trade. Imagine the amazement of the master of a mill or weaving factory if his employees were to stop in a body for a quarter of an hour twice a day between meals to drink beer! Yet in many laundries the beer is kept on the premises for the purpose, and it is certain that as long as time thus wasted (to put it on the lowest grounds) can be made up by each separate woman "working it out" at the end of the day, irregular dawdling and intemperate habits will be encouraged. On the other hand, a woman who is expected on Thursdays or Fridays to be in the laundry from 8 or 8:30 in the morning till 9 or 10 or 11 at night may claim with some show of reason that only by some kind of spur can she keep her over-tired body from flagging.

WALTER W. COOK

"Scientific Method and the Law"

(1927)

It is common to say that beginning with the early years of the seventeenth century scientific workers abandoned the rationalistic approach of
the middle ages and entered upon the study of the empirical facts of antecedents and consequences, appealing to experiment and what is called
the inductive method. Like most broad generalizations, this proves
upon examination to be misleading unless taken with many qualifica-
tions and limitations. It will be found that much of the rationalistic approach remained until the present century. Consider the situation in
physics a generation ago. We were told by leading scientists of that day
that atoms were indestructible units out of which an indestructible universe was built. It was believed that in a certain sense finality had been
reached; that one consistent scheme of interpretation of the physical
universe which would apply to all cognizable occasions had been attained. This idea influenced workers in other fields. Biologists, for example, struggled, perhaps some are still struggling, with the problem,
given configurations of matter with locomotion in space as assigned by
physico-chemical laws, to account for living organisms. The laws of the
conservation of energy, of mass, of matter, were apparently established
on a firm basis. The phrase, "As unchangeable as the law of gravitation," expressed the dominant attitude of mind. As Whitehead has said,
it was the dullest period in science in the last three hundred years.

Had one scanned the horizon, as indeed Pearson, Mach, and Poin-
caré were already doing, he might have detected signs of a coming
change. Indeed, as men look back now they perhaps wonder that those
signs were not seen and understood by more. The reason, I venture to
suggest, lies near at hand. Underlying all variant systems of thought in
a given epoch there are always certain fundamental assumptions which
are unconsciously presupposed. As Whitehead says, "Such assumptions
appear so obvious that people do not know what they are assuming because no other way of putting things has ever occurred to them." It is
believed that there underlay the scientific thought of the period to
which we are referring an assumption of the validity of the logic of Ar-

Reprinted from the *American Bar Association Journal*, vol. 13 (1927), pp. 303–09, by
permission.

istotle, at least in its more essential features. Fundamentally, as I understand it, that logic assumes two things: (1) That in some way or other we can arrive at certain propositions which we know are factually true of the world in which we live; these propositions being either general or universal truths or particular truths—e.g., All men are mortal; Socrates is a man. These constitute the premises of our syllogisms. (2) That by combining these general and particular truths in accordance with the laws of the syllogism we can arrive at new truths about the world by deduction, without new observation.

Based upon this logical system there had come down to the modern world the system of Euclidean geometry, the first great example of what the modern mathematical philosopher calls an autonomous doctrine, that is, a body of propositions all derived by pure deduction from a relatively small and logically compatible set of propositions known as postulates. It is important for our purposes to note two things: (1) That Euclidean geometry was regarded as a set of factually true propositions about the properties of the physical space in which we live. Geometry was thus thought of as the science of physical space. (2) That the postulates were regarded as self-evident truths. This was the view even in Kant's day, and made it possible for him and his predecessors to take the position that we can have an *a priori* knowledge of nature, since by deduction from self-evident truths new truths can be arrived at. By the middle of the last century we find a change. Under the influence of nineteenth century scientific thought we find John Stuart Mill arguing that the postulates are not self-evident truths. He insists that while they are truths they are proved by the logical process of induction. It does not occur to him to deny that they are truths about physical space; he merely insists that the proof of their truth is by means of inductive logic. That is, he still has his general and his particular truths which he knows to be objectively true of the physical world; and from these he can deduce new truths. Deduction is thus still recognized as a legitimate tool to use in gaining new truths about the world without further resort to observation and induction. The only change in point of view is as to the method of arriving at the premises of syllogisms; that they are objective truths from which new truths can be deduced is not questioned. Would it be untrue to say that this view is still held today by many people who commonly regard themselves as educated? Most of us learned in high school to prove that the square of the hypotenuse of a right triangle is equal to the sum of the squares on the other two sides. As Bertrand Russell recently said, the only difficulty is that the proof proved nothing, and the only way to prove it is not by logic but by experiment. To this I would add, we need to find out what we mean by proof of the factual truth of a proposition before we conclude that it can be done even by experiment.

Be this as it may, men's notions of the validity of Euclid's geometry as the science of physical space were challenged when in the first half of

the nineteenth century the Hungarian Bolyai and the Russian Lobach-
evski almost simultaneously but independently created non-Euclidean
geometries, which were soon followed by that of Riemann. This was accomplished merely by substituting a different postulate for the celebrated parallel postulate of Euclid. Mathematicians, physicists, and
philosophers were then compelled as never before to scrutinize the
methods of science and indeed the concept of scientific truth itself. For,
if two or more doctrines about the properties of physical space exist,
each logically autonomous, but differing from the others as to at least
one of its postulates, men are bound sooner or later to ask, which one
is the true geometry of the physical space of our world; and this in turn
leads ultimately to the more fundamental question, by what tests do we
decide whether a proposition or doctrine is factually true?

As many of us know, the development of these new types of geometry, each one of which was developed by deduction from its set of
postulates, has played an important part in bringing about a revolution
in our ideas as to the scope of mathematics and of the function of deductive logic in the search for scientific truth. In seeking the answer to
the question, Which one of these geometries is true, factually true, important discoveries were made. Let us note those of them which are important for our purposes. One is that as a branch of pure mathematics
geometry has nothing to do with space. Apparently Euclid is from his
.postulates deducing the properties of space. These postulates all talk ostensibly of space. Any two points determine a straight line; any three
points not in the same straight line determine a plane; etc., etc. Note
now, as any book on modern mathematical philosophy will show, that
we can replace the words, point, line, plane, etc., with any meaningless
vocables whatever, and yet deduction can go on as before. If, following
Keyser, we say that any two *loigs* determine a *boig*, that any two *loigs* not
in the same *boig* determine a *ploig*, etc., we certainly do not know what
we are talking about; nevertheless we can still deduce all the propositions with exactly the same logical rigor as before, only we shall not be
able to associate with them concepts of space. As Keyser says, "The fact
which thus leaps naked to view is that logical deduction depends entirely upon the form of the premises or postulates and not at all upon
any specific meanings which we assign to their terms."

Suppose we say:

> All gostaks are doshes,
> All doshes are galloons:

again we do not know what we are talking about, but if we assume that
these mysterious terms stand for classes of things, we can by the strictest
of logic draw the inference that

> All gostaks are galloons.

And so it comes about that the mathematicians tell us that mathematics is but the details of the tree of formal logic, and that it is the science in which we never know what we are talking about or whether what we are saying is true (Russell). As a branch of pure mathematics, then, geometry has nothing to do with space. If you examine any rigorous treatise on plane geometry you will find, as Morris Cohen puts it, that "it will make no difference in the form and sequence of the propositions if the indefinable points are replaced by complex numbers or if 'distance between points is replaced by differences of holiness in a multidimensional series of saints.' " . . .

Noteworthy is it that almost contemporaneously with this development in mathematics came the work of Charles Darwin in the field of biology. His great work on the *Origin of Species* added its influence to the undermining of the belief which had ruled men's thoughts for over two thousand years that is was possible to arrive at "universals" in the Aristotelian sense, i.e., at factually true propositions which could be applied by syllogistic reasoning to the demonstration of new truths about the world without further observation and experiment. Underlying that belief is the idea of classes; that the objects in the universe can be classified in a mode which is objectively valid. Darwinism carries with it a denial that genera and species in biology are more than subjective conveniences. If we adopt the Darwinian hypothesis of the evolution of species, then, as Schiller puts it, "if the course of events could be recalled to life, we should watch each species gradually fusing with its congeners, the genera coalescing with their families, individuals exhibiting the qualities of what have since become divergent kinds, and at last learn that all the various forms of life have had a common ancestry, and are never realized except in individuals. . . . Thus a species is merely a temporary grouping of individuals. . . . We happen to snapshot them in that stage of their racial development at which they may conveniently be grouped together." Moreover, today's observations in many fields show one species gradually fading off into another through all the intermediate stages, so that the line between them must be drawn more or less arbitrarily, the only test being that of convenience for the purpose in view. To be sure, in strict logic this work in biology does not apply to inorganic things; nevertheless when added to developments in other fields it has had a tremendous influence in altering men's views of logic and of what we call the "laws of nature."

The significance of these developments in mathematics and biology was not fully apparent until the discovery of a whole series of new phenomena in the field of the inorganic sciences of physics and chemistry. X-rays, radium, radio-activity, the disintegration of atoms, the transmutation of one chemical element into another, electrons and protons, the Michelson-Morley experiment, the abandonment of the doctrines of the conservation of mass, of matter, and of energy as principles of universal applicability, the refusal of electrons to obey the accepted laws of me-

chanics; the quantum theory—all these and others have left modern physical science gasping for breath. Leading scientists admit that at present no
one consistent scheme for the interpretation of physical phenomena is
feasible, and many would perhaps hesitate to assert that it is to be expected.
We have reached the era of relativity. By this is not meant the specific
theories of Einstein and others, commonly associated with that term, but
a point of view which, whatever may happen to specific doctrines, seems
destined to remain as a permanent achievement in human thought. With
much diffidence I venture to suggest what seem to me to be some of the
characteristics of this point of view.

First and foremost, we find a frank and clear recognition of the extent
to which all our thinking is based upon underlying postulates of which
frequently we are entirely unaware but which color all our mental processes
and in particular often give to those generalizations which we are in the
habit of calling "natural laws" the form which they assume. Discard the
postulates, and this form is altered. Frequently when we drag these postulates out into the light of day we find on examination that they are not
in accord with anything in our experience. . . .

A second feature of the newer point of view is the surrender of the
hypothesis that the universe can be fully described or explained in terms
of matter in motion, i.e., in terms of the changing configurations of par-
ticles of matter, the patterns altering in accordance with the classical laws
of mechanics. This does not mean that the laws of mechanics have been
discarded, thrown away, as of no further use; far from it. They still hold,
i.e., are useful, in dealing with phenomena within a given range. Beyond
that range, they do not apply. . . .

As a third element in what I have called the relativity point of view
is the recognition of the limitations of the process of deductive and inductive logic. In the first place, it is coming to be recognized that this
"big blooming buzzing confusion" of a universe with which we are confronted does not present itself to us in classes, or so that it can be handled
merely by a class logic. . . .

By experience we find that we may for a particular purpose group
together into a class a larger or smaller number of situations, each to some
extent unlike the others, conceiving that their differences are irrelevant
for the purpose in view. The essential characteristic chosen as the basis
of our classification will vary with our purpose and must be relevant
to it. . . .

Any grouping . . . appears as at most a working hypothesis, to be
tested by its consequences, and subject to revision in the light of further
experience. Classification thus disappears as the statement of objectively
valid and final truths about the world, and reappears as the adoption of
working hypotheses, mental devices to which we resort in order to deal
more effectively with our experiences. Classification is thus to be tested
by its results and to be altered if those results are not satisfactory.
When confronted by a new situation, i.e., one which is apparently

different from any previously dealt with, so that we are in doubt what to do with it and are led to reflect upon the matter, we find that we can not deal with it merely as a new specimen of a given class. Our real task is to determine whether the differences involved which make us think of it as new, are as a practical matter, i.e., as tested by their consequences, important for the purpose we have in view; and so whether or not we can safely enlarge our class so that when we have finished our thinking it will include the new situation.... "Universals," general rules, "natural laws," thus appear as working hypotheses or postulates; general ways of stating that for a given purpose we have in the past found by experience that it worked satisfactorily to group together a number of situations, no two of which are exactly alike; the validity of the grouping depending on whether it leads to desired results.... [A]s Keyser has so strikingly put it, that "the old cosmic absolutes absolute space, absolute time, absolute matter, absolute natural law, absolute truth—are gone. The reign of relativity thus inaugurated by the basic sciences, is destined to work a corresponding revolution, deep, noiseless it may be, but inevitable, in all the views and institutions of man." ...

Apparently I have wandered far from my field. What, doubtless many of you are asking, has all this to do with law. More than may at first sight appear, I venture to say. For, in spite of these developments which we have been considering, the naive belief that men think in syllogisms and that new truth about the world can be deduced from general laws arrived at by induction, still persists in much of the thinking that goes on in the field of the social sciences. It is a curious paradox that when men are confronted with situations still more complex than those found in the physical and biological sciences, as is the case in economics, sociology, ethics, and law—situations which therefore are more difficult to deal with by scientific technique—the more insistent do they become as to the prior existence of fixed and universal principles or laws which can be discovered and directly applied and followed. Instead of thinking of principles as "methods of inquiry," as "instrumentalities for the investigation" of new situations, by means of which the "net value of past experience is rendered available for the scrutiny of new perplexities," they are prone to assimilate the problems in these fields to those of mathematics. As a result they either fail to discover what their problems are or to deal adequately with them if they do.

It may seem incredible, but it is still possible for eminent members of the bar to assert that all a court does in deciding doubtful cases is to deduce conclusions from fixed premises, the law; or what comes to the same thing, to assert that all the Supreme Court of the United States does in holding a statute of Congress unconstitutional is to apply by logic a preexisting rule found in the constitution. Let me quote the relatively recent utterance of an eminent member of the bar, a well known student of legal history and jurisprudence.

"Every judicial act resulting in a judgment consists of a pure deduction. The figure of its reasoning is the stating of a rule applicable to certain facts, a finding that the facts of the particular case are those certain facts, and the application of the rule is a logical necessity. The old syllogism. 'All men are mortal, Socrates is a man, therefore he is mortal,' states the exact form of a judicial judgment.... It must be perfectly apparent to any one who is willing to admit the rules governing rational mental action that unless the rule of the major premise exists as antecedent to the ascertainment of the fact or facts put into the minor premise, there is no judicial act in stating the judgment. The man who claims that under our system courts make law is asserting that the courts habitually act unconstitutionally."

Is it not obvious that from the point of view of present day ideas of logic and of scientific method [the] "traditional and known technique of the common law," as Dean Pound calls it, is as grotesquely inadequate for legal purposes as the childish mechanical notions of the nineteenth century have shown themselves to be in the field of physics? If we approach the problems which confront the lawyer and the judge in the light of what we may call the newer logic, what do we find? First of all, we discover that the practicing lawyer, as much as, let us say, an engineer or a doctor, is engaged in trying to forecast future events. What he wishes to know is, not how electrons, atoms, or bricks will behave in a given situation, but what a number of more or less elderly men who compose some court of last resort will do when confronted with the facts of his client's case. He knows how they or their predecessors have acted in the past in many more or less similar situations. He knows that if without reflection the given situation appears to them as not differing substantially from those previously dealt with, they will, as lawyers say, follow precedent. This past behavior of the judges can be described in terms of certain generalizations which we call rules and principles of law. If now the given situation appears to the court as new, i.e., as one which calls for reflective thinking, the lawyer ought to know, but usually does not because of his unscientific training, that his case is "new" because these rules and principles of law do not as yet cover the situation. If they did, the case would be disposed of more or less automatically. As it is, the lawyer finds competing analogies and so competing rules or principles which are possibly applicable. A familiarity with modern studies of human thinking would reveal to him that his job is, not to find the preexisting meaning of the terms in the rules and principles which he wishes the court to apply, but rather to induce the court to give to those terms for the first time a meaning which will reach the desired result.

If we shift our point of view from that of the practicing lawyer to that of the judge who has to decide a new case, the same type of logical problem presents itself. The case is by hypothesis new. This means that there is no compelling reason of pure logic which forces the judge to apply any one of the competing rules urged on him by opposing counsel. His task is not to find the preexisting but previously hidden meaning of the terms in these rules; it is to give them a meaning. A few judges are fully aware of this, men of the type of Holmes and Cardozo; others see it dimly; and still others apparently not at all.

The logical situation confronting the judge in a new case being what it is, it is obvious that he must legislate, whether he will or no. By this is meant that since he is free so far as compelling logical reasons are concerned to choose which way to decide the case, his choice will turn out upon analysis to be based upon considerations of social or economic policy. An intelligent choice can be made only by estimating as far as that is possible the consequences of a decision one way or the other. To do this, however, the judge will need to know two things: (1) what social consequences or results are to be aimed at; and (2) how a decision one way or other will affect the attainment of those results. This knowledge he will as a rule not have; to acquire it he will need to call upon the other social sciences, such as economics. Note now that our traditional technique makes no adequate provision whereby counsel can furnish the court with the needed data; neither does it provide the court itself with the machinery to acquire it. Why? I take it, because the assumption is that with nothing but his experience as a man and a judge he can by reasoning, by logic, decide the case—it is purely a question of law, and no evidence is required after the facts of the situation have been ascertained.

Underlying any scientific study of the law, it is submitted, will lie one fundamental postulate, viz., that human laws are devices, tools which society uses as one of its methods to regulate human conduct and to promote those types of it which are regarded as desirable. . . . [L]et us attempt to sketch in rough outline a university school of law or jurisprudence. . . . Such a school I visualize as a community of scholars, devoted to the scientific study of law as a social institution and to the training of other scholars for the same pursuit. . . .

First and foremost, the members of such a group would need to have and to give to their students a clear conception of what the scientific study of anything involves, and of the available tools for pursuing it in the legal field. This would require them to take account of modern investigations into logic and human reasoning, and to survey in general outline at least the development of science and scientific method. . . .

In the second place, a scientific approach to the study of law will demand observation and study of the actual structure and functioning of modern social, economic, and political life, so that in dealing with what are in the last analysis problems of social and economic policy those working in their difficult field will not rely upon hit-or-miss information which has been picked up accidentally.

In the third place, studies will need to be made of the existing rules of law, so as to ascertain just what they are. . . .

In the fourth place, in a school of the kind we are considering there would be carried on studies in the actual operation of our law. This would involve research into the conflicts of interest which arise in the community and into the adjustments of these which we seek to bring about by legal means. In this connection would be made studies in legal history, and comparative law, so that we may take advantage of the experience of other times and other peoples in solving similar problems. Here also would be required the study of present day social, economic, and political relations affected by particular bodies of law. The cooperation of students in the other social sciences would be needed—of students of economics in the field of commercial law; of students of the family in what lawyers call the law of domestic relations; of psychologists, in the field of evidence; of psychologists, psychiatrists, criminologists, and others in the criminal law, etc., etc. Time fails in which to go into details; I content myself with mere suggestions of the possibilities. . . .

KARL N. LLEWELLYN AND
E. ADAMSON HOEBEL

The Cheyenne Way

(1941)

Homicide and the Supernatural

The homicide record of the Cheyennes—sixteen recorded killings within the tribe in two generations (1835–1879), or an annual rate of almost one killing to a theoretical ten thousand of population—is another evidence of the conflict between the aggressive personal ego of the individual male and the patterns of restraint which were also ideationally promulgated by the culture.

The killing of one Cheyenne by another Cheyenne was a sin which bloodied the Sacred Arrows, endangering thereby the well-being of the people. As such it was treated as a crime against the nation.... Much of the crystallization of Cheyenne community consciousness into political reality was due to the action of this social catalytic. Fear of supra-social consequences and the resultant efforts of the Cheyenne community to purify itself from the stain of Cheyenne blood on Cheyenne hands are most probably what brought homicide under the public law. Killing became a crime; its criminal aspect came then to dwarf its aspects as sin, though by no means to displace the latter; and the criminal aspect had in law gone far to actively displace the private wrong concerned: homicide had ceased to be legally a matter for blood-revenge. So far as concerns total discountenancing of blood-revenge, this is a logical consequence of the social calamity of bloodying the Arrows. But there is no reason in logic, and no premise in the culture, which with any necessity stood in the way of purifying the Arrows, say by ritualized and consecrated execution of the offender....

When murder had been done, a pall fell over the Cheyenne tribe. There could be no success in war; there would be no bountifulness in available food. "Game shunned the territory; it made the tribe lonesome." So pronounced Spotted Elk; so assent all Cheyennes.

There is thus a branding synonym for "murder" in Cheyenne,

(*he'jɔxowɜs*), *putrid*. Such was the murderer's stigma. With murder a man began his internal corruption, a disintegration of his bodily self which perhaps contrition could stay, but never cure. About the killer clung the murderer's smell, an evil mantle eternally noisome to fellow men and the sought-after animal denizens of the plains. Though the tribe, after ridding itself of the murderer's presence through banishment, could purify itself by the sacred ritual of renewing the Medicine Arrows, the murderer was tainted beyond salvation. Hence, the immediate consequence of murder was a conference of the tribal chiefs—such as were in the population of the band at the moment. By them a decree of exile was given.

It is too often said that in primitive life banishment from the group is tantamount to a death sentence. That depends on the conditions of physical and social environment. For the banished Cheyenne circumstances were relatively kind. The friendly Dakota or Arapaho would seemingly receive him with open hospitality and no questions asked. . . .

The ceremony of purifying the Arrows is in itself of no direct legal significance; the compulsion to perform the ceremony is. For the murderer's transgression *the tribe* paid penalty, until the ceremony was performed. The control significance of such a penalty must not be overlooked. It must not be overlooked, even though active references to it when a killing seemed toward, are not found. For instance, people intervened when men quarreled violently. What they said was "You must not." "You must not be a murderer." "You will disgrace yourself." "It is not worth it." This is the language of law and morals, reputation and horse sense, not of religion and sin and supernatural visitation upon the people. But we hold the shadow of this latter to have been present and felt, despite the powerful secularization of overt expression. When Sweet Medicine gave the Holy Arrows to the tribe so many generations ago, it is told that he then instructed the Cheyennes in the rituals of purification. They were to keep the Arrows forever sweet and clean. This the Cheyennes have faithfully done. Were there to be a murder among either the Northern or Southern Cheyennes today, an abridged form of the renewal ritual would be performed in Oklahoma, well shielded from the prying eyes of white men. In the old days, the renewal occasioned the presence of every living Cheyenne, except murderers, their families and followers. The military societies saw to the presence of all citizens in good standing and enforced the absence of the others. . . .

. . . [T]he more direct importance of the Medicine Arrow complex for law lies not in the ceremonies, but in the associated notions. These notions brought forth not only measures punitive and measures absolvent; they engendered preventive measures as well. When violent emotions were brewing, "the thought of the Arrows kept lots of people back." . . .

Immediately after murder was done, such tribal chiefs as were in the group at the time met to pronounce the sentence of banishment. The procedure on such occasions should be of crucial interest, but unfortunately we learned nothing about it. Was there a trial? What was done above evidence? These are, thus far, unanswerable questions. The deficiency does not rest on failure to inquire. Though an informant could cite the color of the horse the victim rode, he could not (possibly, would not) state the way in which the High Court took its action. No living Cheyenne has participated in a session of the Council of Forty-Four when it was giving consideration to a sentence of banishment. There seems to have been no public knowledge of what took place. Since in cases of forthright murder the evidence is unequivocally clear, there may have been little need for court procedure in the ordinary case; but questions of fact did arise. The Council had to determine whether one killing was murder or accident. . . .

The native view is that it was the function of the soldiers to enforce the chiefs' decree of exile, an act which, however, was never necessary. The criminal always went.

Banishment of the murderer was not for life. In theory the sentence was to run for five or ten years. Actually, the ban was in the nature of an indeterminate sentence with commutation possible on a number of grounds. First of these was absence of intent. In peculiar instances, as will appear later, this removed homicide from the category of murder, as evidenced by the chiefs' failure to "convict" in such cases. In some such instances, however, the soldiers invaded the chiefs' sphere of jurisdiction. This happened in the case of White Bear, who accidentally killed his mother when drunk. According to Dog and others, White Bear was not at first exiled. But when the time for the great communal hunts was at hand, the soldier societies began to fear bad luck. On word from them White Bear departed with a few of his friends. In the fall when the hunt season was over, it was decided that because White Bear's misadventure was accidental, he could be permitted to rejoin the community. This homicide took place on the North Platte River in 1874. The real legal problem, which was the tribe's source of perplexity in this situation, was the question of the personal culpability of the drunken man. Could a drunkard who has revealed no malice aforethought be excused for an accidental homicide? This was a new problem to the Cheyennes. In this case the chiefs apparently deemed banishment unnecessary. The Arrows, however, were renewed for White Bear's mother almost immediately. Manslaughter, intentional or not, was a sin to be cleansed; at least, any doubt there might be was too grave to be let continue. The military acceded to the killer's presence at first, only to raise misgivings when the time for the great hunt came. Hence the semibanishment. The first season successfully met, the probationer was allowed to return. Even though reinstated, White Bear for many years could not eat from other men's dishes, nor could he put their pipes to his lips. That this held "for many years," and not for life, evidences in our view that the religious point was one of doubt, rather than of conviction, that the Arrow-renewal, like the uncleanliness tabus and the soldiers' halfhearted action, rested on precaution rather than on certainty. The legal and secular side of the case could be dealt with, decisively, according to the purpose of the penalty; but, lacking a vision, the supernatural uncertainty was handled as a lawyer should handle a matter of moment, by charting the safe course against even the unfavorable event. . . .

It would appear certain that absence of premeditation or intent was at least a mitigating factor in homicide, reducing manslaughter of this type to the "second" or "third" degree. . . .

. . . In Cheyenne culture, whatever the disposition of the woman's kin toward the husband, the expectation would be that [wife killing] should be looked upon as murder, and it was. . . . [O]nly one such instance could be found. . . . . This story has in it a peculiar twist of vision compulsion. According to Stump Horn, whose account is offered, there was little choice for Dying Elk.

> He was a holy man [medicine man]. Maiyun kept telling him he would have to kill his wife. Maiyun said not to send her away, but to kill her. If Dying Elk had failed to heed Maiyun, he would have died, or have gone crazy; he did it to save his own body.
>
> He was mean to his wife. It happened one day that she did not hear him call. He kept bawling at her, but she was gossiping with a bunch of women. When she came back to his lodge, he was waiting with his gun. She died there.
>
> The soldiers ordered him out; it would be a terrible thing to have him in camp. He went to the Sioux for two years, and then went south to other tribes. In his absence he was lost track of, until he turned up after five years had passed. The Dog Soldiers had it announced that he should be received in camp. He returned, and as long as he was with his family he could eat from their dishes, but not with the public; he could not smoke from the common pipe in gatherings of the men; nor was he ever allowed in the Sacred Arrow Lodge, though he could go to the Holy Hat Lodge.

This case, alone, might indicate that killing one's wife was a slightly attenuated crime. Distinctly more probable is the view that the supernatural urge to do the killing was held to make Dying Elk slightly less responsible, or to give him somewhat mitigating circumstances. The fact is not determinable.

But one notes in the account a point of grave legal importance. "The soldiers ordered him out." In White Bear's case the soldiers' suggestion was proper interstitial policing precaution, and the case went to the competent authority. Had the soldiers in Dying Elk's case arrogated to themselves the solemn jurisdiction of the Great Council?

Commutation of sentence for a murderer whose case was clear-cut and simple was not a matter for government alone to decide. The action in such instances shows ever so clearly the survival of kin urges to do damage to the murderer and the public's recognition of the kin's feelings in the matter. . . .

If the power of the government was not so supreme as to make unnecessary the consultation of a dead man's kin in the process of commuting a decree of exile, so also was it too weak wholly to prevent the outbreak of blood-revenge. What was once law and now illegal was still present, and human, with a lingering touch of customary right....

In the year 1854, White Horse, then chief of the Fox Soldiers, stole the wife of Walking Coyote, who was very fond of her and brooded much over the trouble. He sent word to White Horse to send back the woman, saying that if he did not do so he would kill him. No attention was paid to the message, and after a time Walking Coyote went to Yellow Wolf, who had adopted him, and said: "Father, as you know, White Horse has stolen my woman and I have sent word to him many times to send her back, but he does not do so. Now I intend to kill him, and I ask you not to interfere with my trouble, not to ask me to refrain from killing this man."

Walking Coyote knew that Yellow Wolf loved him better than he did any of his own sons and daughters, and he suspected that Yellow Wolf might ask him not to take revenge on White Horse, and if Yellow Wolf asked this, Walking Coyote felt he must obey him.

One day in the summer of 1854 Walking Coyote with War Bonnet rode up to St. Vrain's Fort (on the South Fork of Platte River in Colorado) from their camp twenty miles below. White Horse was living in a camp of Cheyennes there. Walking Coyote rode into the fort and saw White Horse and his wife—not the woman who had been stolen—sitting on a bench in the hall of the fort. When the two saw Walking Coyote, they arose and walked toward the men's messroom, and Walking Coyote jumped off his horse and shot White Horse with his gun, the ball passing through the upper part of the chest and killing him at once. Then Walking Coyote and War Bonnet led their horses outside the gate of the fort, and sat down there, and Walking Coyote said, "If anyone has anything to say to me, I am here."

After they had sat there for a short time, Little Wolf, a cousin of Yellow Wolf, came out and said to Walking Coyote, "This is all over with; you should now go back to your camp." The two men mounted and rode to camp.

Shortly after this the woman returned to Walking Coyote's lodge. After this killing, Winnebago (*Nāhk to wun*) renewed the arrows because of the killing. A little later he stole from Walking Coyote the woman that White Horse had stolen and went up north with her.

Walking Coyote sent word to him, saying, "I am not going to kill another man for this woman, but I shall take your wife, Spirit Woman (*A si mon i*)." Before Nahktowun returned from the North, Walking Coyote went to Nahktowun's lodge, and, entering, took Spirit Woman by the arm and said, "Come along now!" She went with him, for she feared him.

When Nahktowun returned from the North and found what had happened, he was angry, so that night he took his gun, went to the lodge of Walking Coyote, looked in at the door, saw him sitting on his bed, where he was resting after returning from the buffalo hunt, and putting the muzzle of his gun through the door he shot Walking Coyote, killing him.

Next morning he went again to Walking Coyote's lodge, took Spirit Woman, and made her go back to his lodge.

After the killing of Walking Coyote the arrows were renewed, perhaps by Red Moon.

One day, eight years later, in the spring of 1863, Nahktowun was sitting behind his lodge filing arrowpoints, which he had fastened into a cottonwood stick to hold them. While he was doing this Kutenim came up and began to discuss with him the question of a horse, the ownership of which had been in dispute between the two. Kutenim was a distant relative of White Horse. As Nahktowun was working away, Kutenim became more angry at him and abused him, and finally Nahktowun jumped to his feet and raising the stick which he had been using to file his arrowpoints, struck Kutenim on the head with it and knocked him down. Kutenim jumped up and ran to his lodge, which was near by, to get his rifle, while Nahktowun strung his bow and took a handful of arrows from his quiver. Presently Kutenim ran out of his lodge and fired at Nahktowun, and the ball passed close to his head. Nahktowun drew his bow and shot Kutenim in the left breast. Kutenim dropped his gun, and drawing his butcher knife, rushed at Nahktowun, who ran away, but Kutenim overtook him and slashed him on the arm, and then fell dead.

The men round about, seeing what had happened, did not go near the two. Only old women and old men ran up to them.

The Bowstring Soldiers, who then had charge of the camp, wanted to punish Nahktowun for killing Kutenim by whipping him. They consulted the chiefs, who advised them not to notice the affair at all, and nothing was done to Nahktowun.

The Arrows were renewed not long afterward.

In the summer of 1864 Nahktowun was living with the Arapahoes. He had an Arapaho woman, and some people began to talk as if Rising Fire, *Ho ist ó ha a* (Smoke Rising), were trying to steal the woman. This made Rising Fire unhappy, and the more he thought of it the worse he felt, and the angrier he became toward Nahktowun. Finally he said to some of his friends, "I shall have to kill Nahktowun; he killed my cousin and now he is talking about me."

His friends replied: "You ought to do so, because if you do not kill him, he will kill you. He has already killed two men and is an outlaw, and if he feels like it he may cut your throat or shoot you."

Not long after this, Nahktowun, who was a Dog Soldier, was invited by one of the Dog Soldiers to come over and eat at his lodge. He therefore moved over from the Arapaho camp near Fort Larned on the Arkansas and camped with the Cheyennes who were on the Saline. On the day of the feast he started, with Little Robe and Good Bear, to walk to the lodge of the host. On their way they passed the lodge of Rising Fire, who was sitting inside looking out the door, and as they passed he shot Nahktowun with a gun and broke his spine. When Nahktowun fell, Little Robe and Good Bear stepped to one side, and Little Robe called out to Rising Fire, "Well, you have begun your work; now come out and finish it."

Rising Fire took an old brass-mounted horse pistol, walked over to where Nahktowun lay, and blew out his brains. *Meh him ik* (Eagle's Head) renewed the arrows on the Solomon.[1]

In interpretation four things stand out. The first is the persistence of the vengeance urge, community and religious notions to the contrary notwithstanding. The second is the possibility that where there was sufficient provocation to murder, banishment did not necessarily follow, even when the Arrow-renewal did. Walking Coyote seems not to have been exiled; nor are the events leading to his own death easy to understand save in terms of his continuance with the tribe.

There are many obscure angles to Winnebago's (Nahktowun's) role in the case and his final demise in the story as Mr. Grinnell has given it. There appears, in the first place, no adequate reason for his killing of Walking Coyote. Nothing is said of Winnebago's reinstatement in the tribe, but it will be noted that eight years elapsed between his first killing and his reappearance in the narrative. This was time enough for the banishment to have run its course. When Winnebago killed a second time, two years elapsed before he appeared again, but this time he was among the Arapahoes—from which we infer he was in exile. Thus, though Grinnell observed that "nothing was done to him," he was apparently out, and the soldiers had put to the chiefs the question of whether they might not whip Winnebago. This it would seem was thought of as a punishment for brawling in the camp, for his consequent murder of Kutenim could conceivably be regarded as self-defense, and it was hardly in the character of the soldier societies of the time to delay a whipping in order to consult the tribal Council, if the cause for whipping was unequivocally clear. It is more probable that the soldiers were making a wholly novel proposal to the chiefs at the time they were holding their meeting to consider the banishment of Winnebago, namely, that whipping be added to the traditional and solemn decree of banishment, where the murderer was guilty of brawling.

And finally, there seems to have been a distinction between Cheyenne attitudes toward murderers and bully-murderers, i.e., between decent men who happened to kill and mean, bullying men, who in their overbearing conduct kill. It is clear that in a quarrel the murder stigma could be called upon to put the murderer out of countenance....

Winnebago with his two murders had gone so far beyond the Cheyenne pale that his position had become precarious and untenable—both for himself and for other Cheyennes....

The actual destruction of Winnebago...shows how far some of the Cheyennes could go in ignoring the religious injunction against killing when there was a Cheyenne around who had twice demonstrated that the religious and legal injunctions meant nothing to him. The circumstances of his death have all the marks of a social conspiracy. Suggestion and public gossip built up a grudge ("he is picking a fight") feeling on the part of Rising Fire toward Winnebago, which was compounded with a blood-grievance and fear of what Winnebago might do. The invitation of the Cheyenne Dog Soldiers for Winnebago to leave the Arapaho camp to visit them is an amazing invitation. It is too amazing for coincidence that Winnebago should be escorted right past the door where Rising Fire sat waiting for him. Even more amazing is the remark of Winnebago's two Dog Soldier companions when he fell, if they were, or were acting as, his friends; or even if they were concerned, as soldiers and citizens regularly were, with heading off killings within the tribe. The only credible interpretation is that Winnebago was lured into an ambuscade for his assassination, that this was deliberately planned by members of his own former military society, and that Rising Fire was more or less deliberately built up psychologically to be the trigger man. . . .

Justifiable homicide did receive recognition by the Cheyennes, though in their strict theory any killing of a fellow tribesman was an evil act. Doubt as to the right course of action is reflected in the situations which revolve about homicide for "justifiable cause" . . . because though the Arrows were renewed in any event, banishment did not inevitably follow by pronouncement of the Council of Forty-Four. When the buffalo failed of procurement, however, then the doubts simmered to the surface, and one notes some soldier society "advising" the slayer to leave camp until the meat supply had been obtained.

The evidence has thus far formed a picture of supernatural factors playing a powerful role in control of Cheyenne non-religious behavior. But only at this one point does such a conception hold true. Conditional curse, or self-curse, for instance, while an existent mechanism in Cheyenne legal techniques, was not extensively used for legal purposes or otherwise; nor does vengeance-sorcery loom at all large in the culture. But disputants sometimes swore upon the Holy Hat, especially if adultery was involved.

Thus, the prevalent conception that "ordeal is not found in the New World" requires qualification. The elements lumped to make up the "ordeal" concept include appeal to the supernatural to determine a disputed question of fact, of legal import, the procedure being known and standard and conclusive. . . . What [does not appear] is the element of priestly administration, with its possibilities of manipulation (toward justice or toward injustice). And the Cheyenne cases show no machinery for inflicting the test on a wholly unwilling person, nor for shaping penalty to outcome.

Owl Head, for example, accused Chief Eagle and Stump Horn's friend, Brady, of intimacy with his wife. The accusation was expressed through action; Owl Head just came up and seized the defendants' horses. Chief Eagle gave up his; Brady refused and denied the implicit charge. He led Owl Head to the Medicine Hat Lodge. Chief Eagle acquiesced in the still implicit joinder of issue: he went along. When they entered the lodge, they were asked no questions, for it was naturally a place for people to gather. Brady spoke to the Hat-Keeper, telling him the story, asserting that he wanted to swear on the Hat. The Keeper said nothing, but led them outside, where the Hat, in its bundle, hung on the pole. Both Chief Eagle and Brady addressed it as though talking to Maiyun, saying, "They have accused us of being with that woman. It is not true." No names were mentioned.

Owl Head did not swear, says Stump Horn, because he knew they were guilty and would get their just deserts. But Chief Eagle got back his horse. Legally, the oath cleared him. Stump Horn knew that Brady was guilty, too, for he was Brady's friend. As they rode away, he asked Brady why he had done it. Brady made no answer. He had challenged one of the fundamental beliefs of the Cheyennes, the power of the Buffalo Hat. Now his friend reproached him with his anxious question. There was nothing to say.

The dogma of the Hat was substantiated when Brady was wounded in the next fight with the Crows. In the second fight Chief Eagle was killed, though he stood a long way from the firing.

Suspected wives were not forced to take an oath or conditional curse, as Comanche women were,[2] though if nagged by a suspicious husband, women sometimes declared their intention to swear by the Medicine Hat. Stump Horn insists that they never did so, however, for the husband was wont to drop it then with the feeling that "this woman is going too far; she must be a true wife." The total absence of such cases in our recordings would seem to substantiate him.

Other symbols were used for oaths, as well. A pipe or four arrows, said to represent the Medicine Arrows, or a specially painted buffalo skull to represent the Holy Hat could be used as the equivalents of the modern Bible in oath. . . .

[R]eligion . . . solidified community sentiment to such a point that matters regarded as a subject for kin-vengeance by most primitive hunting peoples could no longer, for the Cheyennes, be considered such in law . . . [T]he machinery of tribal government supervened with a secularization of sanction which, while wholly harmonious with the religious, gave a tangibility and flexibility of power and beauty. These factors, rooted as both were in the tribal world philosophy, combined with the developing police activities of the soldier societies to advance Cheyenne society far along the road to statehood. . . .

The device of exile combined with an almost certain ultimate commutation was a technique of multiple excellence. By removing the murderer it lessened provocation to revenge; it disciplined the offender; allowance was made for the return of the culprit; but only when dangers of social disruption were over. . . .

Suicide is self-inflicted homicide and very much a cultural fact expressing definite social patterns rather than a mere individual urge. . . . [A]mong the Cheyennes, as with other Plains Indians, suicide played an important social role. Death courted on the field of battle could be sought as an act of great public service, . . . as a means of self-effacement when life appeared empty and pointless, and above all as a face-saving and protest device with legal repercussions; so also, death by self-violence.

All the present cases of direct suicide, and some of the glorious death type, involve a grievance within the closest family and amount either to sacrificial reestablishment of own and family prestige, or to an appeal to the public for redress of a wrong beyond the cognizance of existing tribal law. Suicides could indeed occur over trivial matters without consequent repercussions.

On the Little Horn River, Hankering Wolf used his sister's horse in a buffalo hunt. When the kill was brought in, the sister took two hides for the use of the horse, but Hankering Wolf's wife objected. Reappropriating the hides, she remarked that her sister-in-law could look elsewhere for hers. That night the sister disappeared, not to be seen again until in the leafless fall her body hung exposed on a skeleton tree. Hankering Wolf, it is said, no more than reproved his wife.[3]

The incident illustrates one typical phase of primitive law: when the bargaining (or shall we say the haggling) pattern is absent, then refusal of any person's offer constitutes a rebuke, sometime unbearable, and occasion for fight or flight. In such a situation, a person has a social obligation to diagnose what is right beforehand, and not only that, but what will be acceptable. The Cheyenne patterns were all built to make the first offer reach within the range of decency. In this instance they failed, in tragedy. . . .

In several other recorded cases there was no marshaling of community forces to chastise the one who had so aggravated as to cause a suicide. Indeed when Goes To Get A Drink hanged herself because Morning Star, her husband, took a Pawnee captive to wife, her own grandmother remarked that she was foolish to hang herself over such a little thing.

It here seems to be another conflict between a sane general social organization and an individualism never tamed. The individual's machinery of protest was live and available, but, as will show in the succeeding histories, it produced results only in circumstances which stirred the social body. The cases to follow show that growing and trusted social organization was suddenly perceived not only to have failed to produce the results desired, but somehow to have missed badly. This means, it would seem, that suicide as a pattern of protest, or as the case may be, of release from shame, or both, was existent, but in social consciousness was definitely uncertain in response. . . .

Thus one comes to the suicide which effected the desired result: an aroused social sympathy and shocked reaction.

> When Red Owl's daughter eloped, the infuriated mother went after her. As she drove the girl home, lashing her with whip and tongue, she declared, "I hate that family of his. If you go back, I'll beat you to death." At home, her scolding annoyed her son. As his sister sat silent under their mother's tirade, he declared he was getting out.
>
> Soon Red Owl also shuffled out, grumbling. Then two shots were heard, and people came running. The girl was dead. Seeing what had happened, Seminole, who was standing by, smashed Red Owl to the ground with one blow. The brother ran up, and in horror, he forgot that Red Owl was his mother; he too knocked her down. It was the needed release for the crowd. In mad frenzy they beat her with everything at hand, with fists and tearing fingers. Only the persuasive intervention of her faithful sister saved her from death.

When they were through with her, she was forced out of the camp. She was made to live by herself in the willows. "I used to see her peeping out at us," said Calf Woman. "Whenever she ventured forth, people assailed her with bad names. They would say, 'Oh, there is that loose woman. There is that nice woman.' " After many years, they gradually let her partake again of community life. But whenever she ventured to offer an opinion, she was quashed with a summary: "Oh, you are a nice one to be speaking. You killed your daughter. Sit down!"

Though ostracized, she continued to be abusive. She berated her son for generosity. So nasty was she that he, too, attempted suicide without success (possibly, only intended as a threat). This near-calamity at last brought a change of personality. Red Owl became a decent person and a respected storyteller among the young.[4]

In this instance, causing the daughter to take her life was akin to taking her life. The Arrows were renewed for the girl by Holy Bear. The shedding of Cheyenne blood by another Cheyenne is murder. Though, in fact, the daughter was the killer, in the public emotion (and by its action, in the law) the mother, as the responsible party, was the murderess. This reaction was given expression in law, for Calf Woman states that a soldier band (Elk or Fox), declaring that Red Owl's smell scared the buffalo, placed a ban of exile upon her. In order to support her, her family had to leave the camp to take abode with her in exile. This suicide occurred in the 1860s. . . .

The suicide pattern of self-sought death at enemy hands was not so strongly institutionalized among the Cheyennes as it has been found to be with the Comanches. In marital imbroglios such suicides were much less common, probably as a result of the fact that because Cheyenne settlement techniques normally involved no face-to-face weighing of individual prowess, there was no call for face-saving on the part of the defeated litigant. Only among brothers whose sibling authority had been flaunted by eloping sisters . . . or young men, harshly spoken to by shrew-tongued mothers, were personality wounds because of women found to be so deep as to require release in the "glorious death."

This glorious death, rooted as it was in a military culture, was adequate compensation for the most damaged prestige. . . .

Scalp Cane in his misadventure revealed the drive of worldweariness and sorrow, when upon the death of his brother at Crow hands he publicly announced his intention of joining his beloved sibling.

When the whereabouts of the Crow camp had been reported, Scalp Cane mounted an old man on his horse, and together they rode up and down the Cheyenne village, the old man crying for all to hear, "Here we have Scalp Cane with us today. Look at him now, ye Cheyenne. Tomorrow he will have left us. Behold him! Tomorrow he will be with us no more." From then on Scalp Cane could take meat from anybody or whip up any laggards on the march. People were a little afraid of him, for they considered him already dead because he had given his life to the enemy.

The next day they charged the Crow camp in the morning, fighting until the sun was low. The Cheyennes and their Dakota allies were driven back and back. Scalp Cane was running, too, not dying as he had vowed he would. Some boys caught him a pack horse with two saddles to change for his own winded charger. So he outstripped the pursuing Crows. After that day the standard greeting for Scalp Cane was, "Hello, you are back? You don't look like a ghost. How do you like riding two saddles, eh?"[5]

Death was not thus the inevitable result of the declared intention to die in battle. And the Cheyennes did not demand it when the end to be served by the announcement of the intention had been fulfilled. . . . But what a difference is seen in the social reaction to the circumstances under which death was missed without honor. Scalp Cane was ridiculed and shamed—not released. . . .

Possessed of more fortitude than Scalp Cane was the maiden of whom High Forehead's father-in-law told him long ago. Her lover was killed charging through the enemy. She dressed in her best elk-tooth dress and walked backward off a cliff, singing, with her face to the camp, of the greatness of her love and the barrenness of life without him whom she loved alone.

Touching, too, is the story of the old blind man, Spit, who at the Wagon-Box Fight with the United States Army said he was always looking for just such a chance to die, for he was tired of only half seeing his way; where were the soldiers? Young ones took his hand, lined his face toward the firing enemy. Serene, he walked toward death, until a bullet brought it to him. Whenever we led Walks Last by the hand, he in his blindness muttered, "If only I had been brave as a youth, I would never have come to this." He would have died in glory, in his prime.

These last suicides and glorious deaths or glorious exposures are not legal in flavor; but they are necessary to round out the picture of similar behavior when it rests not on act of fate or the public enemy, but on act of a fellow-Cheyenne, and more intensely, of a family member. One can imagine protest suicide, in substantially similar default of the event of strikingly unjust action of the organs of the law. But Cheyenne suicide as a legal, or better, extra-legal proceeding, involved more than shame or grief or weariness or glory; it was an appeal, direct and extreme, to justice beyond the law—and so, in its groping way, for better law.

Aftermath[6]

The Cheyenne Law of Killing

Following is a somewhat modernized and consciously articulate statement of the norms, as they appear in action, in the recorded cases and opinions. [Note: A question mark accompanying a given phrase means that the point is indicated in the material, but not definitely established.]

ARTICLE 1. Definition and Effect of Homicide.

Killing within the tribe is a crime, and a sin, but it is no longer even a fully recognized tort.

(a) The killing of a Cheyenne by another Cheyenne is a sin which bloodies the Sacred Arrows and endangers the people; it is a crime against the peace and the people, and normally within the exclusive jurisdiction of the tribal authorities.

(b) The rule that the kin of the victim of a killing are privileged to seek self-redress in their own right, or to retaliate, is no longer law. However, the authorities are directed to take due account of the natural feelings of the victim's kin.

(c) It is the expected duty of every citizen, and especially of the military societies, to intervene in disputes before they reach the stage of killing.

(d) Within the meaning of this Article, the person killed is a Cheyenne:

(i) if it be a recognizable fetus, carried by a Cheyenne woman;

(ii) if he be a resident alien [or captive?] substantially identified with the Cheyennes and notably deserving of the people.

(e) Within the meaning of this Article, such outrageous treatment of a daughter [child? family member? person?] as must be viewed as causing a suicide in protest, constitutes killing.

ARTICLE 2. Jurisdiction and Punishment.

(a) The chiefs present in a body of Cheyennes at the time of a homicide shall have exclusive jurisdiction over the offense of killing, if they exercise jurisdiction; but, in the absence [pending?] of a ruling by the chiefs, a military society may take such [minor?] measures as they may deem required, including temporary banishment during a hunt [or even a general banishment?].

(b) Save as provided in Article 3, the chiefs shall decree the banishment of the killer. Unless otherwise expressly provided in the decree, the banishment shall be for a period of ten [five?] years.

(c) Banishment involves permanent disability to attend renewal of the Arrows, or to eat or smoke from a Cheyenne utensil without polluting it. It involves during the period of effective banishment disability to acquire coup honors [or other civil honors, or to officially perform acts of chieftainship ? but not disability to effectively engage in ordinary civil transactions of marriage, gift, and the like?].

(d) The chiefs present in a band or in the assembled tribe or tribal division may at any time in their discretion, but not in general in less than two years' time, on being persuaded of the penitence of the culprit and of the safety of his return, remit any banishment. Provided, however, in the interest of public order, that no such remission shall be ordered without prior consent of the several military associations and the representatives of the kin of the victim.

      (i) Remission of banishment involves readmission to performance of tribal function, except for such permanent disabilities as are provided under section (c) above.
- (e) Non-murderers who band up with a murderer in banishment incur the murderer's disqualifications with regard to coup by voluntary choice. Even signal service allows no relaxation of this rule.
- (f) Visitation of corporal penalties by the authorities upon a killer is improper; but spontaneous expression of general indignation at a particular offense, not resulting in death of the offender, is itself no offense.
- (g) No person, not even a military society, shall impose other and further punishment specifically for killing, save with the consent of the chiefs in the camp.
- (h) When any further dispute arises with an obnoxious killer, the other party to the dispute may properly raise the tone of his demands and conduct.

ARTICLE 3. Exceptions and Mitigations.
- (a) A killing is justified:
  - (i) Where necessary in self-defense against incestuous rape; or
  - [(ii) Where necessary to remove a homicidal recidivist generally felt to be dangerous to the people;?] or
  - [(iii) Where utterly and absolutely necessary to military police in the execution of an important duty?]
- (b) A killing is excused if [within the family, and?] demonstrably accidental.
- (c) Provocation, drunkenness, seeming necessity for self-defense, or other mitigating circumstances, are for consideration of the authorities in admeasuring, or later, in remitting banishment.
- (d) the authorities may adjudge the killing secularly excused or justified and yet take such measures as may seem to them desirable in pursuance of communal safety, in regard to possible supernatural effects of a killing. Only in extraordinary cases are the Arrows not to be renewed.
- [(e) Voluntary withdrawal by a notable head chief who has killed under extenuating circumstances may serve in lieu of banishment?].

UNDERHILL MOORE AND CHARLES C. CALLAHAN

"Law and Learning Theory: A Study in Legal Control"

(1943)

This study lies within the province of jurisprudence. It also lies within the field of behavioristic psychology. It places the province within the field and, in doing so, fragments the province into disconnected pieces. The problems of jurisprudence become psychological problems to be attacked by the use of the propositions of a psychological theory of behavior and by quantitative and experimental methods.

Although analytical, natural-law, historical, sociological, and "realistic" jurists, legislators, administrators, cultural anthropologists, sociologists, and others have dealt with positive law and with whatever each classifies as law, they have not undertaken investigations, empirical, experimental, and quantitative of the quantity and degree of conformity to a rule of positive law to the end that the propositions describing that quantity and degree of conformity may be subsumed under a general theory of human behavior....

[We hypothesize] that a proposition of law is an artifact and its administration behavior, the effect of which may be described by the same laws as describe the effect of any artifact or behavior, for example, the effect of the ringing of a telephone bell on the behavior of the listener, and secondly, by a combination of logical and empirical processes attempting to verify hypotheses deduced from propositions of a general theory accounting for human behavior....

The data of the investigation were obtained by observing the effect of certain ordinances regulating the parking and driving of automobiles upon certain aspects of the behavior of parkers and drivers. The investigators, however, had no particular interest in parking and driving or in generalizations applicable to traffic alone. It happened that at the time and place of work experiments with traffic ordinances could be made. It was possible to make relatively accurate observations of behavior yielding quantitative data.

Reprinted by permission of The Yale Law Journal Company and Fred B. Rothman & Company from *The Yale Law Journal*, vol. 53 (1943), pp. 1–3, 76–78, 82–84.

The quantity and degree of conformity to the ordinances which the investigation discloses are in accord with the theorems of a psychological behavioristic theory of learning, in particular, the propositions of that theory referring (1) to stimulus situations in which mutually conflicting responses have been learned to the cues which are present and (2) to the gradient of reward. The investigation suggests that the quantity and degree of conformity to any proposition of law will be in accord with the propositions of such a learning theory. And, since by the propositions of such a theory a proposition of law is nothing more than a sensible object which may arouse a drive and cue a response, the investigation further suggests that there is reason not to isolate the study of law from the study of other behavior phenomena.

During the years 1933 thorugh 1937 certain aspects of the behavior of persons who drove or parked automobiles in fifteen different areas located on six streets in the City of New Haven, Connecticut, were observed....

[The Unregulated Period.]

[A]n individual who parks on the observed site during the unregulated period is thought of as being motivated by a drive of unknown quality and strength; the cue is the combination of the drive, the car, the street, and something which identifies the situation as one in which parking will lead to reward; the response is the moving of the car to a position in which the right wheels are near the curb and parallel to it; the goal reward is of unknown quality and strength and is obtained at the end of the period during which the car remains standing at the curb; the instrumental response of parking is reinforced by a reward the strength of which is a function of (1) the strength of the goal reward—which factor is eliminated by the assumption that rewards of varying strengths are distributed proportionately among all studies and all duration categories of all studies—and (2) the person's impression as to the delay which will ensue between the giving of the instrumental response and the obtaining of the reward. This impression is determined by the person's impression as to his relative position in a distribution of parking durations on that site and this latter impression is, in turn, indexed by an actual measurement of the relative position of the duration of each parking with respect to the others. By this process, the strength of the reinforcement for any response of parking, which parking will be categorized according to the elapsed time between parking and leaving, is related to the percentage of the total parkings which are in categories denoting durations less or greater than the particular parking. In other words, the per cent of the total unregulated distribution to the left of a particular category, on a time axis, is a measurement of the strength of the reinforcement for parkings which fall in that category.

The Regulated Period.

The second series of observations in each parking study was made under conditions as nearly like those of the first series as the means of control would permit, with the exception that there was introduced into the situation, before the beginning of the second series, a notice of the regular police pattern stating that parking on the site was prohibited or limited to some specified duration.

The Drive. The drive which motivates action in this new cue-response relationship is an acquired drive of anxiety. The anxiety is an anxiety which arises upon the site of the posted notice in conjunction with the other parts of the cue.

The Cue. Like other cues, the cue in the new cue-response relation includes the drive. It also includes the car, the street, and the posted notice stating the regulation. These items alone are sufficient to identify the situation as one in which the giving of the response will be followed by reward.

The Response. The response is the driving of the car past the area, as opposed to parking it in the area, the latter being the response conflicting with the new cue-response relation.

The Reward. The reward which suppports the response in this new cue-response relation is, of course, the relief of the anxiety, the reduction of the drive which motivated the response.

The Degree of Reinforcement of the Response. The degree of support (reinforcement) of the response in this new cue-response relation, which is the significant factor in the determination of whether the response will be given in a conflict situation, varies with the strength of the anxiety which is to be relieved, the extent to which the anxiety (of whatever stength) will be relieved by the giving of the response, and the lapse of time between the giving of the response and the obtaining of the reward. . . .

From the above, the following propositions with respect to the differences in absolute frequencies between the unregulated and regulated periods in the parking studies may be deduced:

(1) If, in a given parking study situation, there are more potential parkings (parkings which would occur were sufficient parking space available) than there are parking spaces available, the number of observed parkings will increase when the number of available parking spaces is increased.

The number of occurrences of a response is limited by the number of concurrences of a drive and a cue. If there are more drives than cues, the number of responses will increase upon the creation of more cues. The creation of additional parking space is the creation of more cues.

(2) The amount of the increase in the number of observed parkings referred to in (1) above will vary with the number of potential parkings

previously unrealized and the number of additional parking spaces made available.

If the situations in the parking studies reported here be taken, as they are, as situations in which, prior to the introduction of the ordinances and the posted notices, there was an unsatisfied demand for parking space, then each of the two deductions above is verified by by the fit of the formula $u = 12 + 1.4x - 1.01v$, in which formula u may be said to represent the increase attributed to this unsatisfied demand, x is a measurement of the number of additional parking spaces created, and v is a measurement (index) of the number of potential parkings unrealized prior to the introduction of the ordinances and posted notices.

The Theory Applied to the Administrative Studies

. . . [T]he hypothesis on the basis of which the analysis of the administrative studies proceeded was that the effect of the tagging which was done in those studies was to prevent all further parking for durations longer than the tagging time, by the persons whose cars were tagged or alternatively, if a slight improvement in results be accepted as significant, by persons who, prior to the tagging period, had been parking repeatedly in the area for durations greater than the tagging time.

During both the no-tagging and the tagging periods of each study the persons who parked were giving a response in a learning situation [to] the drives, cues, responses, and rewards. . . . During the tagging period of each study some of the individuals in the situation faced a conflict. A new cue-response relationship appeared in the situation. This new cue-response relation was similar to that introduced into the parking study situations in that the response was driving past the area (as distinguished from parking in the area), the drive was an anxiety drive aroused by the cue, and the reward was relief of the anxiety. With respect to the cue, however, the cue-response relation differed from the new relation which appeared in the parking studies. In the administrative studies no notice was posted stating that all cars staying over eighty or forty-five minutes were being tagged. The tags, relatively inconspicuous to persons approaching in cars, were placed on the cars which remained longer than the designated period and, of course, remained there for varying periods of time until the the car was removed. But during most of the time during the tagging period the physical appearance of the area was no different than during the no-tagging period. It is, therefore, not unreasonable to correlate the tag itself with the concept of cue in the new cue-response relation, and to assert that the only persons who got the cue, which cue aroused anxiety, and which anxiety in conjunction with the tag formed a cue for the delayed response of driving past the area on future occasions, were the persons whose cars were actually tagged.

On the basis of this correlation the following deductions from learning theory may be made with respect to the differences between the no-tagging and tagging distributions:

(1) There will be no change in the frequency of parkings by persons who did not receive tags.

Since there is no new cue for these persons there will be no response. As to such persons there is no new cue-response relation, no conflict, and hence no change.

(2) There will be a decrease in the frequency of parkings of duration longer than the tagging time by persons who do receive tags and this decrease will account for the entire difference between the no-tagging and tagging distributions of each study (temporarily eliminating, again, the difference attributed to unsatisfied demand).

As stated above these persons are faced with a conflict and it is likely that for some, at least, the reinforcement of the parking response will be so slight that it will be overcome by the reinforcement of the response of driving past the area on occasions in the near future.

Except for the elimination of *all* parkings by repeaters, rather than of repetitions only, these two deductions are verified by the regularities obtained in the distribution analysis of the administrative studies....

8

Legal Education and Legal Scholarship

While the Realist debates over educational policy concerned curriculum primarily, they fall into a broader set of arguments conducted among lawyers in the 1920s and 1930s, arguments that had themselves been ebbing and flowing over the course of a century.

Justice Story had warned a local bar association in 1835 of the "fearful calamity which threatens us, of being buried alive . . . in the labyrinths of the law." Story believed that the only way out of these catacombs was through the "habits of generalization," to be furnished by a separate university education in law.[1] By 1870, Dean Christopher Columbus Langdell had begun to achieve such a school at Harvard. Langdell's pioneering case method, while not original—instruction in the principles of law through carefully selected appellate opinions had been tried in the 1860s, notably at New York University—did permit the law, in Holmes' words, to be "generalized and reduced to a system."[2] And it was economical: no student needed regularly to recite a lesson, thus taking up the faculty's time; instead, all the students in a class, numbering up to two hundred, had to prepare to be asked questions each day. As practiced by Langdell himself, however, the result was no more compelling than the old-fashioned law lectures mocked by Flaubert and Swift. Roscoe Pound admitted that as a student he found Langdell boring. But although Langdell did all the talking, nonetheless, he "was always worried about 'Why?' and 'How?' He didn't care particularly whether you knew a rule or could state the rule or not, but how did the court do this and why did it do it?"[3]

Until 1920, one part of the story of American legal education concerns the tentacular grip of the case method on the leading law schools, where it had spread from Harvard, and the rise of scholar teachers like James

Barr Ames, who had little or no lawyering experience. Those professors helped form the Association of American Law Schools in 1900, separate from the American Bar Association. By 1920, the AALS, having been prodded by its president of 1916, Walter Wheeler Cook, advocated law school attendance as prerequisite to admission to the bar. Law schools that qualified for the organization's imprimatur included only those institutions with three full-time instructors and 5,000 volume libraries.[4] Such standards were meant to press hard on the lesser night schools.[5] The AALS standards, which grew increasingly stringent through the 1920s, also worked against the Black law schools, almost all of which closed by the late 1920s, the exceptions being Howard (which was accredited by the ABA in 1931), Terrell, in the District of Columbia, and Lincoln University of Missouri (both of which struggled into the 1950s).[6] The Jesuit schools, challenged by both the Depression and the AALS, and heavily reliant on funds from their Order, managed to remain open. Along with the night schools, they were among the few institutions open to Italian and Irish immigrants.[7]

Between 1910 and 1940, the members of the ABA and the AALS debated at their yearly meetings what the proper contours of the legal profession were to be—the role of law school admissions standards, the prerequisites for acceptance to the Bar, the purpose of ethical canons. This debate stemmed in part from the members' fear of the supposedly swelling ranks of the legal profession and law's falling prestige, at least compared to medicine.[8] But there was a dark side to the lawyers' desires to maintain income and standing, for some among them were rankly antisemitic and racist: immigrants, the poor, Jews, Blacks, and women should be kept from joining the profession.[9] Most often, though, the debates were conspicuously high-minded, and modes of legal instruction generally furnished their main subject.

In 1914, Josef Redlich wrote a report for the Carnegie Foundation attacking the case method as elitist.[10] Alfred Reed, in a more influential pair of reports building on Redlich's efforts, also criticized Langdellian instruction, opposed universal legal standards, and proposed a differentiated bar on the English model, with lawyers segregated not only by specialty, but by degrees of talent and training.[11] Responding for the ABA, Elihu Root of Harvard asserted the old verities and argued for a fully unified national bar, but one with exacting standards. Root's report drew sharp criticism—it was "reactionary," "narrow," "unfair."[12]

Thus, by the 1920s, lawyers and law professors tangled over the function of the law schools and the shape courses were to take. The Realists were stimulated by this spirit of reassessment, but although they were by temperament and training well-equipped to examine the anticompetitive, monopolistic aspects of the legal guild[13] and to determine how much of the debate over standards and night schools was shaped by racial prejudice or bigotry, these larger social questions the Realists mostly failed to address.[14] Instead, they focused more narrowly on curriculum reform within elite law schools. Nonetheless, while they may have failed to create any broad-ranging changes, their hard look at the arrangement of law courses was the last such examination in this century.

Between 1927 and 1929, Yale Law School had as its fiery dean Robert Hutchins, appointed when he was just shy of his twenty-eighth birthday. William O. Douglas and Underhill Moore aided him in his effort to rework law courses, and to make the law school a part of Yale's Institute of Human Relations, thus firmly establishing law as one of the empirical sciences. More than three decades later, Thurman Arnold recalled this flourishing period. "Needless to say, Yale was an exciting place in the days of the Depression. Harvard represented, to us at least, the conventional attitude toward the law, the traditional forces dividing the law into separate fields and the lack of emphasis on procedure. We at Yale were busy tearing up the old courses and devising new ones that we thought were far better adapted to the realities of judicial institutions.... The conservatives charged that we were not operating a law school, but instead were denizens of a cave of the winds."[15]

At Columbia, ten committees worked for two years on the curriculum, producing more than one hundred separate reports. Their work was provoked in part by Wesley Hohfeld's 1914 address to the AALS, "A Vital School of Jurisprudence and Law," which Walter Wheeler Cook considered a "summons to the law schools of the country."[16] Reed had emphasized in his 1921 report that "no single school has devised its curriculum upon any reasoned plan."[17] Pound's promotion of sociological jurisprudence formed a further powerful impetus to educational reform; as the law was an engine of social control, Pound argued, it had to shift and change to conform to our developing sense of proper ends—unvarying rules could never compose a proper basis for instruction.[18] As a measure of its faith in the new credo, Columbia promptly appointed business experts, philosophers, and political scientists to its faculty.

But in 1928 a new dean was to be appointed at Columbia; and the appointment turned into a battle between the old guard and the Realists. Some of the Chief Realists, after losing the contest, left the faculty. Douglas and Moore went to Yale. Oliphant and Yntema, joined by Cook, went to form The Johns Hopkins Institute for the Study of Law.[19]

Meanwhile, Harvard, under the direction of Roscoe Pound, had become thoroughly involved in the Restatements of the American Law Institute. The Restatement project, which began in 1923, aspired to state the correct principles of law, shorn of case citations, in five fields: agency, conflict of laws, contracts, torts, and trusts.[20] In a remark typical of his scorn for the Restatement, Thurman Arnold called Harvard the "high church of abstract legal theology."[21] Although Harvard professors undertook a few empirical projects, including Pound's own study of the Volstead Act for the President's Wickersham Commission (1929), the school emphasized the common law and the case method, and, despite the presence of sardonic constitutional law scholar Thomas Reed Powell (who had come from Columbia in 1925), it remained a target for the Realists.[22]

In general, the Realists shared Jerome Frank's conclusion that American law schools had become too academic, too remote from legal life—in short, that the program established by Langdell and improved by Ames had succeeded too well. Legal aid work—performed at the University of Pennsylvania, Harvard, and Northwestern, among other schools—was one answer.[23] Such changes began to return legal instruction to Blackstone's ideal of liberal education, and to reintroduce political and economic issues, just what Langdell sought to avoid. Broadened teaching materials, including textbooks of "cases and materials" (materials being digests, statutes, annotations, and social science statistics), instead of merely cases, was another response. Columbia's proposed functional division of the law—into family, business, and political relations, as well as administrative law—was the most comprehensive and far-reaching reform proposal. And students there felt the difference, in popular courses like Noel Dowling's Industrial Relations, or Herman Oliphant's Illegal Combinations (which brought together concepts from contracts, corporations, criminal law, torts, and equity).[24] Such were Columbia's efforts to counter "major defects in the legal education."[25] At Johns Hopkins, Realists attempted to put the scholarly study of law on its own footing, with no pretension of teaching practicing lawyers at all. Unfortunately, that experiment, begun in 1928 with five years funding, was crushed by the Depression.[26]

In 1936, looking back over this period of debate and reform, a special committee at Harvard announced with satisfaction that its own curriculum, untouched by the struggles without, should remain just as it was: "no major additions . . . are now required." Institutes of this or that were expensive frauds, or worse. Scholarship is a solitary calling; organization means "regimentation."[27] These thin and uninspiring remarks were nonetheless prophetic for the elite law schools of the next generation.

HERMAN OLIPHANT, ED.

Summary of Studies in Legal Education

(1929)

Chapter VIII
General Plan of Organization of the Law School
Curriculum

The Faculty began its study of this question by asking what principles or standards of curriculum organization underlie the general structure of existing law school curricula and then went on to consider a possible general plan based on some conscious standards to be applied in such curriculum planning.

The General Framework of Existing Law School Curricula

Almost all, if not all, the work in the first of the three years of practically every American law school is prescribed. . . .

. . . [T]he law curricula of this country are, as to the second and third years, substantially planless. Courses comprising these years are independent, self-contained and interchangeable units, free from the sequential and horizontal inter-tyings which result from consistent curricular construction, based on articulated educational policies and practices. . . .

. . . [T]he most significant fact about the existing standard first year is the joint presence therein of Contracts, Torts, Property and Agency. In these courses, as now given, are to be found the great mass of the substantive law concepts which, in various combinations and with various modifications, go to make up the content of the greater part of the present second and third year courses as those courses are now constituted.

Pre-legal training is unsupervised. The law student today begins his study of law without any discipline in the social structure to which it relates, and without such a scientific attitude and approach as could be obtained from an adequate study of the history of scientific thought and the nature of the thought/processes and methods involved in evaluating and extending the boundaries of truth. By beginning with Contracts,

Torts, Property and Agency, he begins, not with the preliminary background and method just outlined, but with the broad and abstract concepts which constitute these general subjects. Of course, he must, in any event, begin with abstractions, but he could begin with abstractions less broad than those of Contracts, Torts, Property and Agency and with abstractions of greater current significance because more recently drawn from the current of social reality about us.

The Outlines of a Plan for a Law School Curriculum Consciously Drawn in Accordance with Articulated Educational Standards

Distinguishable phases of the total educational process in legal training are:

1. The acquisition of a background for the study of law, consisting of an understanding of the structure and functioning of modern society, an appreciation of the devices and processes of all forms of social control in contemporary society, and an orienting knowledge of the agencies and processes of law, viewed as but one form of social control in modern society.
2. An appreciation of what a truly scientific attitude of mind toward any work in any of the social sciences, including law, involves.
3. The acquisition of the tool skills widely involved in legal study, that is, the acquisition of those methods of collecting, observing, and evaluating social data, and of erecting autonomous systems of thought embracing and "accounting for" them.
4. Working through the main corpus of substantive and adjective law in which training is indicated, the student starting with the scientific attitude of mind and equipped with background and methods needed for the study of law.
5. Getting a synthesizing view of all the fields of law thus covered in order to see elements common to all the fields and to see significant differences among them; this being done in order that the student's knowledge of the law may be an organized whole instead of a confusing mass of loose ends.
6. Making a general survey of the law and its administration for the purpose of evaluating the effectiveness of the latter and the long-time social implications of the former.

It may be argued that no separate courses, dealing with background, scientific attitude of mind and methods of legal study (1, 2 and 3 above), should be given, but rather that all of these things should be developed in connection with the work on the main body of the subject-matter of legal education (4 above). However that may be, it seems clear that, if separate work is to be done by the student in these first three of the five phases of legal education just enumerated, the point at which such work should be stressed is at the beginning of the law school curriculum because of their obvious introductory character.

Likewise, it may be argued that no separate work should be organized for law students, the main objectives of which are synthesis and evaluation. However this also may be, it seems clear that, if such work is to be given, it should be at the end of the law school curriculum so that the student, before attempting comparison and evaluation, may have an abundance of legal and other social data to serve as the subject-matter and basis of attempts at synthesis, comparison, and evaluation.

These two propositions being established, the third and main phase of legal education drops naturally into the middle reaches of the curriculum, and this gives us a set of standards for the construction of a curriculum. . . .

The accompanying diagram represents in general outline form a law school curriculum constructed along the lines just set out. The areas sharply separated by straight lines are not thought of as mutually exclusive. There would be unavoidable and desirable over-lapping in any actual curriculum. Neither are they here thought of in terms of courses, only in terms of subject-matter. No attempt is here made to represent what courses should be given, or how much time should be consumed by any one of these subject-matters or by all of them combined, nor do the names appearing in the diagram indicate anything as to the method of instruction which should be used. Each of the labels appearing in this diagram is the subject of a later short paragraph indicating in a general way the subject-matter which it is intended to cover.

Evaluation and Criticism			
Synthesis and Comparison			
Law Administration	Political Relations	Business Relations	Familial Relations
Methods of Legal Study			
Societal Background			
Scientific Attitude			

1. *Scientific Attitude.* The history of the scientific habit of thought should be studied and seen in terms of the history of thought in the social sciences. The subject-matter should disclose what effects on current practices in legal thinking flow from the coming of the scientific habit of thought into the field of the social sciences.

2. *Societal Background.* A knowledge of modern society organized in terms of social agencies, social processes and social ends is the content of this subject-matter. Part of it is specialized to include a rather detailed knowledge of those aspects of the total social phenomenon which may be called social control and to include a yet more detailed knowledge of the agencies for, and processes of, legal intervention in social life.

3. *Methods of Legal Study.* These include the ability to use a case and a statute as tools for getting new knowledge; to use objective sampling methods besides the case method; to use the objective methods, accounting and statistics; to use the historical method; and to understand the limitations and uses of the various logical forms of thought.

4. *Familial Relations.* This subject-matter includes all those bodies of law wherein the practical considerations judged most important by contemporary thought affect dominantly the social relations in, and clustering about, the family.

5. *Business Relations.* This area is devoted to those portions of the law wherein the practical considerations judged more important by contemporary thought relate, in the main, to industry and commercial activities.

6. *Political Relations.* By this rectangle is designated those areas of law in which the practical considerations judged most important by contemporary thought relate to communal standards and practices and to the structure and functioning of that gradation of larger and larger social groupings running up to a state.

7. *Law Administration.* This body of knowledge is thought of as covering the set-up and operation of all the social devices, both implicit and explicit, which operate to cause adherence to the lines of social conduct disclosed by a study of substantive law.

8. *Synthesis and Comparison.* The subject-matter represented by this portion of the diagram includes all the substantive and adjective law which has gone before in the curriculum, as well as the law of other times and of other peoples. Calling it "Analytical Jurisprudence" might help to convey the idea. Gathering loose ends together and constructing a self-consisting body of autonomous doctrine, embracing the whole law, or selected areas of it, is to state the thing in terms of its objective.

9. *Evaluations and Criticism.* Describing this area in terms of its objectives, the purpose at this stage should be to go over the whole or selected areas of the law to note the immediate and long-time social

consequences of particular rules of law and to sense the difficulty of forming judgments as to desirable social ends. How other peoples and our own people at other times have solved legal problems should be drawn into the picture. . . .

Chapter IX
Classification of the Subject-Matter of Legal Education

. . . [I]t is assumed that the student is equipped with the proper scientific attitude, background and methods for legal study. The question here is: In what way or ways should the whole of the thing called "law" be classified in order to fix the student's and also the profession's approach or approaches to it. . . .

If one studies the classifications of law, represented by the divisions and subdivisions of it which go to make up the law courses listed in the catalogues of any of our good law schools, no conscious or consistent plan of classification is to be found. Four factors have operated, all more or less fortuitously, to give us our present classification of law for legal study.

1. Some titles are, in essence, of procedural origin, they representing categories of a procedural system either no longer in existence or no longer potent to suggest significant substantive law categories.
2. Many of the headings correspond to the titles adopted by text book writers on law during the latter part of the eighteenth and the early part of the nineteenth centuries. Story, for instance, decided to write a book on Agency. His book gave us this division of law and its scope is largely fixed by the exigencies of his interests, industry, and leisure.
3. Publishers of digests, encyclopediae, and similar all-embracing works of law have made efforts at comprehensive classification. Their efforts, largely uninfluenced by any notions scholars may have had, have given us some titles such, for example, as "vendor and purchaser" in connection with real estate.
4. The last fifty years has seen a rapid development in law along certain specialized lines such, for example, as that of public utilities. These have pressed for attention in the law school. The existing so-called basic courses not having a grasp upon those things which are really basic in the evolution and functioning of law, such hidden matter naturally keeps cropping out. It appears to be largely *sui generis* and apparently pretty much unrelated to any thing in existing courses. To meet the need for treatment of these newly developed and specialized areas of the law, law schools did not go back and attempt a reorganization of their basic courses so as to integrate these new areas, but instead attempted to meet it by adding new courses covering these bodies of evolving law. This process has been a source of some of

the divisions into which law is partitioned in present law school curricula.

Whatever the sources of the present divisions of the law, it is clear from an inspection of them that they are largely the result of haphazard growth. No major contribution to this problem of a comprehensive and more useful classification of law has been made or attempted during the last century. So far as is known, the subject has not been studied in any comprehensive way. It may be that the situation cannot be improved, but the prolonged absence of effort in this direction is itself enough to indicate that, by taking thought, significant improvements can be made. If any one thing is to be picked out of the many things undertaken by the Faculty in its study of legal education as of capital importance, it would be this matter of getting a more significant classification of law for purposes of its study and its administration.

Something on a Technique of Classification

If we are to exploit the full advantages of attempting a wholly conscious and reasoned classification to replace one largely unplanned and accidental, we should begin with a preliminary consideration of some of the principles and techniques of classification in general, considering such questions as: Why do we classify at all? How many kinds of classifications are possible? What dictates the choice of one rather than the other?

The subject-matter of law is large. It has to be divided in order that the whole may be separated into manageable portions.

Here is a pile of apples. These apples can be sorted (classified) into an indefinite number of groups of barrels, according to their color, size, shape, soundness, acidity, place or season of growth, etc., etc. Is some one of these the "true" basis of sorting (classification) to the exclusion of all others and, if not, in terms of what attribute or attributes shall we sort (classify) these apples and why? In like manner, visualize the whole mass of what we know, or are on the point of knowing, about law. Imagine all of the interstitial tissue, which now ties the whole of this together into various thought systems, wholly dissolved so that it lies as an unorganized mass of unsorted units. What shall be the bases of our master classification of these units? They can, as a matter of outside possibility, be thrown into an indefinite number of groups of categories, depending on as many different things as the number of attributes of the procedural devices used, of the persons affected, of the things involved, of the places in question, of the history of our thinking about them, etc., etc. Is there some one of these which is the "true" basis of classification to the exclusion of all others and, if not, what basis or bases of classification shall be chosen and why?

The Faculty's study of the reclassification of law proceeded upon the assumption, which need not be here argued, that there is no one basis of classification true to the exclusion of all others, and that the choice of a basis of classification must of necessity turn either upon chance or accident on the one hand, or upon practical considerations on the other. This being granted, a methodology of classification would involve: making a list of all those practical advantages which can be obtained by adopting the several different bases of classification which are possible; next deciding which ones of these advantages should be sought; and finally choosing that basis or those bases of classification calculated to procure the advantages sought.

The technique actually pursued by the Faculty involved the same process except that it was turned around. The Faculty tried to make up its mind as to what the proper objectives of legal education were, that is, as to what ends, values or advantages it wanted to attain. It then undertook to find that basis or those bases of classification of law which would tend most effectively to secure the objectives chosen.

The choice of a basis of classification of any subject-matter tends pretty effectively to determine one's whole approach to it. The Faculty recognized that, while the classification of law is only one means to use in attaining the ends or advantages sought, it is a very important one. A catalogue of objectives or advantages to be sought, sufficient in number and detailed to the degree useful at this point, is as follows:

1. In actual practice, the administration of law, both criminal and civil, is ineffective and wasteful. Much of the study and teaching of law in law schools is unreal, not merely because too much time is given to the consideration of problems which do not arise in actual life, but also, and probably more importantly, because the problems considered are detached from the procedural or other governmental agencies and processes which constitute their vital setting.

2. Any classification of law requires abstraction, but our present classification embodies unnecessarily broad abstractions. Many of them are antiquated partly because they were made in terms of a procedural set-up long since obsolete and partly because made prior to the industrial and financial revolutions and prior to the beginning of the present marketing revolution. Our present classification is pretty much out of touch with life. Among the things which we need to do is to come to study law from points of view more intimate than the abstractions of our present classifications permit and more significant than their age makes possible.

3. New angles of approach, as just suggested, and the incorporation of non-legal material from the other social sciences involves adding to our vocabulary some terms unfamiliar to many of the conventionally trained lawyers and judges. This creates the problem of developing in the student the skill to pour some new wine into old bottles so that those accustomed to drink only out of old bottles will continue to do

so. Existing word pictures in the minds of the conventionally trained lawyers and judges to some extent condition their way of looking at things. In considering the solutions of particular problems indicated by the social science data incorporated into legal training of the new sort, allowance for this factor will have to be made somewhat as gunners allow for the wind.

4. Lawyers occupy key-positions in the matter of social change. Students have been taught law pretty much as if it were a mechanized art, barren of teleological implications. Students should be made aware of the direction and significance of social change and of the possibilities, difficulties, and dangers involved in manipulating it. Even though legal education should not seek to manufacture social "uplifters" yet it should at least equip men to make articulate such social-mindedness as they may possess.

5. Indispensably conditioning all of the foregoing are high ideals of scholarship. These involve the matter of cultivating a zeal for creative and exact scholarship and a sense of pride in a fine craftsmanship exercised on worth-while tasks. . . .

To put the matter figuratively, the discussion and study of any subject-matter, including law, based on any classification is like a weaving process. The categories arising from the basis chosen for the master classification constitute the warp into which is woven day by day a woof, whose strands are the categories arising from another basis or other bases of classification. Equipped as law teachers, lawyers and judges are, and will be for some time to come, it is perfectly clear that an abundance of such day to day discussion will be in terms of existing legal concepts, however radically different from them may be the categories into which the master classification of the subject-matter divides it.

To say that, if one thing is the warp, some other thing must be the woof, is not to say that it is a matter of indifference as to which is the warp and which is the woof. The whole point to the pragmatic implications of classification is that, by the choice of the warp, we designate the aspects of the matter under treatment which is to receive special emphasis. Thus, for example, if the need of our day and time is that more attention shall be given by law students and, in turn, by lawyers and judges, to the practical operation of rules of law, one way to bring that about is to make the human relations affected by the rules of law in question the basis of our master classification of the subject-matter being studied. This is made abundantly clear by considering how a legal scholar approaches his subject and in what a different fashion an accountant who sought to use the accounting data contained in the law reports would classify those same data for his purposes. Finally, it may be said that, if the same subject matter is not to be examined more than once and if the potency of classification in attaining objectives is to be exploited, there is no escape from the necessity of choosing that objec-

tive or advantage which seems most urgent here and now and making
that the test in the choice of the basis of the master classification of that
subject-matter.

Law Administration

For attaining the first of the five objectives enumerated above, we find a
good part of the law already classified in terms of the procedural and administrative devices and processes operative to secure adherence to
norms of human conduct. This is true, for example, of the law of pleading, practice, evidence, and administrative law. But all such subjects
taken together do not comprise a comprehensive treatment of the whole
field. Numerous devices functioning indirectly as devices of law administration are hidden under the crust of substantive law rules. New forms
of administrative bodies, such, for example, as the quasi-judicial—quasi-
administrative boards and commissions have recently grown up. Their
structure and processes are not being adequately treated. Numerous
non-governmental law administrative agencies are operative. Unofficial
governing groups of all sorts are in constant action and are affecting the
administration of law in substantial ways. Their study is at present no
part of a law student's training.

All of these things need to be pulled together so that a comprehensive view of the structure and functioning of law administrative devices
can be had, their detailed consideration in some areas, however, being
de-centralized and taking place in connection with a study of the particular rules of conduct which they are administering in one way or
another. . . .

THURMAN W. ARNOLD

"Institute Priests and Yale Observers— A Reply to Dean Goodrich"

(1936)

Most of the literature of jurisprudence, to paraphrase William James, is tedious, not as hard subjects like physics and mathematics are tedious, but as throwing feathers, endlessly, hour after hour, is tedious. Therefore it had been the habit of the more red blooded students at Yale to ignore the subject. With the advent of the February issue of the *University of Pennsylvania Law Review*, this attitude suddenly changed. It was discovered that fighting words might lie concealed in the dreary terminology of legal theory. Whereupon sales of Professor Robinson's recent book, *Law and the Lawyers*, increased at the local bookstore, the *University of Pennsylvania Law Review* had to be put on reserve to meet the student demand, and interest in Jurisprudence at Yale achieved a new high.

The proximate cause of this intellectual renaissance was a paragraph by Dean Goodrich in his article, *Institute Bards and Yale Reviewers*, reading as follows:

"In all the pages of writing concerned the project as a whole, a particular subject of the law, or an individual point or doctrine, the examination of issues has been on a high plane of impersonal discussion. The one exception seems to me to be that by Professor Edward Stevens Robinson, professor of psychology at Yale University, in his recent book on *Law and the Lawyers*. His interest in the Institute, it should be said, is incidental to a broader consideration of the shortcomings of those who follow the law. But speaking of the Institute and its Restatement he says: 'Our main interest, however, is in the general philosophy of the undertaking, which is plainly founded upon the belief that too much truth about the law is disastrously confusing and that the remedy may be found in an authoritative suppression of the facts rather than in better education of the public and the bar as to the actual psychological and sociological nature of the law.' These are fighting words, clearly passing the limit of fair comment. If the expression 'authoritative suppression of the facts' does not charge intellectual dishonesty against those responsible for the Institute's Restatement, I can think of no words which will do so. Such vituperations are still bandied

Reprinted from the *University of Pennsylvania Law Review,* vol. 84 (1936), pp. 811–15, 817–19, 821–24, by permission.

about in the political arena, but it is a novel thing to see them appear in the field of scholarship. Whether Professor Robinson likes the American Law Institute and its works or not is a matter with which he is alone concerned. But all of us who have put in a share of the sweat and tears which have gone into the effort thus far, bitterly resent such an attribution of malignancy to our motives as the one quoted above."

The interest created by this paragraph offers a rare pedagogical opportunity to restate the point of view which Professor Robinson takes in his recent book, and which the writer reflects in his companion volume, *The Symbols of Government*. Dean Goodrich completely misunderstands what Professor Robinson is trying to say, and interprets the paragraph, quoted out of context, as a personal attack on himself and his collaborators. It is not important to discuss whose fault this is. On Dean Goodrich's behalf it should be said that an objective examination of any institution always appears irritating to its devout supporters, and hence his reaction is entirely natural. It is the same type of reaction experienced by moral and ethical philosophers when they first examined the psychoanalytical approach to love and morals. They felt that the whole foundation of human character was being attacked by these objective observations. It should be expected that this same sort of approach to institutional habits and behavior would provoke the same sort of hostility. An objective or naturalistic approach taken by Professor Robinson emphasizes the effects of ideals on human or institutional conduct. It has as yet no recognized place among the conventional "fields" of the law. It has no accepted terminology. Hence it is bound to be confusing to devout and sincere scholars like Dean Goodrich, concerned not with the effects of ideals, but with their dialectic expression and their proper veneration.

There is, however, no reason why a legal scholar should be alarmed by an objective description of what he is doing, in spite of the fact that it seems to contradict all the assumptions on the basis of which legal dialectic is written. His difficulty is that he instinctively feels that everything which concerns the law should be capable of presentation in court. A point of view which must be concealed behind the scenes, and which would look out of place in any formal statement of the law seems to the conventional scholar either to be wrong or to prove the law is wrong. Confronted by such a dilemma the scholar naturally rallies to the defense of the law against what seems to him an unjustified attack.

This spiritual trouble would be avoided if the scholar realized that there is need for both a science of law and a science about law—the one for ceremonial use inside the institution and the other for observation from above. An objective or naturalistic attitude toward human institutions is one that can be taken only by one writing about them from the outside. It is not pragmatically successful as a public attitude for one working as a minister of the institution. An objective history of a church can scarcely be written by its bishop, if he wishes to maintain the church as it is. He may use the understanding which he derives from such an attitude in order to make the operation of the church more effective, but while he is on the public stage he must play his part in accordance with the assumptions underlying the lines which he speaks. The reason is obvious. It applies to the law, the church, the speech of a college football coach to inspire his team before a game, indeed to any activity which represents the symbols and ceremonies which are the cement binding human institutions together.

The symbols of the law, both primitive and modern, arise out of a series of contests which dramatize the various conflicting ideals hidden under the term "justice." Out of those contests parables are spun, and maxims derived which reflect the contradictory moral and economic notions of the man on the street. These maxims can never get far from those notions, or the man on the street will complain of the law as unjust or uneconomic. The man on the street is not one character, but a whole cast of characters. His firmly held beliefs contradict each other, and he reconciles them in mysticism, or loses them in elaborate dialectic. The most important institution wherein such conflicts are reconciled, either by ceremony or logic, is the judicial system. It cannot, therefore, be a place where hard, cold truth is sought, yet it must be a place where everyone thinks that truth is searched for. For this paradoxical function the technique of trial by battle seems admirably fitted. Both sides state their positions with the utmost exaggeration possible, and the ordinary decision permits all the conflicting ideals to stand which may be reconciled with its decision. When the Supreme Court upheld the T.V.A. on the theory that the distribution of electricity at the Wilson Dam was really a continuation of the World War, it left all the conflicting economic ideals represented by the parties still arguable. Where the Court itself decides to uphold some general ideal and oppose another the doctrine making a distinction between decision and dicta still permits opposing ideals to be argued. The Restatement is seeking formulae through which those functions can be performed. It is not seeking the "truth" about the institutional habits of our complex judicial system. The very necessities of its task in seeking a formula to reconcile contradictory ideals, prevents it from stating, as part of that formula, the reasons why such a formula is necessary.

Dean Goodrich is a disciple of a science *of* law. Mr. Robinson is talking in terms of a science *about* law....

The traditions of America give a mystical significance to a "rule of law" rather than to a "personality" as a symbol of the unity of our institutions. We feel safer thinking in this way. We dramatize that rule of law in our judicial system and in our constitution.... Our ceremonies are built on the pattern of a feast of pure reason. The spectacle of a hundred or so prominent lawyers and scholars sitting in a great hotel listening to the Restatement discussed section by section is congenial to our protestant way of looking at the symbols of our government. It was this love of dialectic and fear of ceremony which made the Restatement take the form it did. Yet that same distrust of ceremony forced the members of the American Law Institute to deny that their function was ceremonial at all. . . .

. . . Law . . . shades all the way from the dramatization of conflicting ideals to practical and detailed directions. One can always tell where a Jubilee ceremony begins and ends. One can never tell just where rules of law are primarily pure symbols and where they are detailed instructions. Most of them are used in both ways. However, the necessities of the Institute's task forced them to leave out the more practical element as much as possible. The Restatements have been criticized for the fantasy of some of their parables—for instance, the parable of the man leading a lion with a small rope[1] is thought to be helpful in the Restatement of Agency. Yet, those who find such parables humorous forget that wherever the Institute was confronted with a choice between discussion of a modern practical situation and the dramatization of conflicting moral, economic, or procedural ideals, the nature of their task compelled it to emphasize the latter. It was this reason that compelled them to abandon consideration of statutes and to leave out the citation of authorities. A parable which becomes too complicated ceases to be a parable.

It is impossible to make such observations within the confines of a science *of* law, because the emotional necessity which creates that science binds it to certain narrow dramatic canons. That is the reason why the so-called realists were usually voted down in all their major suggestions. The reaction was due to an unconscious realization that nothing but black letter type, supported by parables, would work. Yet, within the science of the law the matter could not be stated quite so frankly. . . .

The abstract picture in the background of the Restatement is something like a mining operation, by which gold is extracted from that vast body of ore, the judicial opinion. There is gold in those hills but experts are needed to extract it. The refuse is then relegated to an ore dump where it will be out of the way, and instead of huge unwieldy lumps of ore only pure gold will pass back and forth in the exchange of ideas between court and counsel. The idea is slightly different from the formulation of a code, which resembles a manufacturing process, producing a new and fabricated product, rather than a mine. It was not the function of the Restatement to fabricate but only to assay and extract the nuggets which, being pure gold, did not even need gilding. The notion of nuggets being dug up from unassayed literary material was familiar to those who had listened to the sermons of the last half of the nineteenth century. The idea behind the religious dialectic was to dig truths out of the Bible by the light of pure reason, and it was sustained by the faith that the more truths that were dug out, classified and stored away, the less doubt there would be in the world, and the clearer religion would become. The theologians would not more have dreamed of legislating their religious principles than the restaters would have advocated a code of substantive law. A stream can rise no higher than its source. The source of religion was the Bible, which needed only exposition. The source of the law was the cases, which needed only to be boiled down. The completed product of the Restatement which is now before us represents the results of that great intellectual smelter. Perhaps it has not extracted all the gold, but the up-to-date machinery and the care with which it was assembled should lead any reasonable man to assume that they got most of it. To deny this is to express doubt on the efficiency of organized cooperative logical analysis.

From the point of view of a science *about* law, the picture is entirely different. To understand the problem as an observer of human affairs rather than as a priest, it is necessary to describe the great post-war legal inflation of cases and concepts which has not yet reached its peak. It is a characteristic of all inflations that those who are in power while they are going on never realize that they are inflations. In 1928 substantial men were proving that we were on a permanently high level in the stock market. Today legal scholars act constantly on the assumption that a system which pours out 25,000 cases a year can be kept in control by West Publishing Company digests and the smelting and assaying operations, conducted on a grand scale every so often by an American Law Institute and on a continuous smaller scale by a hundred law reviews. The complaining consumer of all this literature, the practicing lawyer, like all consumers, was at first inarticulate. He cut down on his amusements to pay the growing cost of his library and accepted the explanation that the reason law was getting so much more complicated was that life is so much more complicated. Certainly legal scholars were doing all they could for him by clearing up the various fields of the law one by one in law reviews. They were also getting out new law reviews as fast as they could be supported. A few binding precedents could run a simple country like Sweden; eight hundred volumes could supply the intellectual gasoline for a small island like England, but a great complex social machine like America needed about twenty-five thousand cases a year to keep it within the principles of the common law.

As time went on this explanation wore a trifle thin. The lawyers demanded relief from the huge burden of unorganized cases, articles and texts. Naturally they sought help from the scholars, and so the Restatement was launched as a great philanthropic undertaking. A practical man facing the practical problem would have seen several possibilities. If there are too many cases for the lawyers to read, one obvious remedy would be to limit Supreme Courts to ten opinions a year on their favorite topics. Or the system in France might be adopted by publishing only a few of the cases. The association of law schools might have been asked to refuse admission to a school which published articles without a certificate of public convenience. This certainly would have cut down the flood of literature. Yet if the legal profession had been in a frame of mind to consider such suggestions, that very fact would have ended the legal inflation, and the suggestions would not have been needed. Since it was not in such a frame of mind, the inflation has to take the accustomed course of all uncontrolled inflations. A code would have been a way of control, but we were not yet ready for such an amount of governmental interference with private law. The rugged individualism of separate cases, each standing sturdily on its own four legs in a little empire of its own, whose boundaries were fixed by stare decisis and maintained by constant fighting, could not be destroyed without loss of national character....

... The idea that the old system was perfect and needed only clearness and accuracy on the part of lawyers and judges was so fixed that had anything else been tried it would not have obtained even a scattering support. For it is important to note that the realists were as unaware that they were seeing a repetition of the pleading inflation of the 19th century as were the so-called fundamentalists. Neither they nor their opponents regarded the substantive law as a series of parables by means of which conflicting moral and economic ideals were dramatized. It was disrespectful to speak of the law as an argumentative technique. Realists wanted only a classification according to their own terms.... And like all members of the opposition, they could not get together. Some wanted to force the courts to talk in figures and statistics, unmindful of the fact that this is a language congenial only to expert accountants. Others, whose myopia the writer shared, wanted a reclassification along the lines of practical problems, unaware that when legal objectives become sufficiently clear to talk practically about them they are automatically turned over to administrative tribunals, where the whole formal atmosphere of a law court disappears and the need of restatement with it. It is difficult to see how the Restatement could have taken any other form in the climate of opinion in which it was created.

... [T]he Restatement [has not] stopped the great post-war substantive law inflation. It has become another book which must be consulted, while the cases and texts pour out as before....

The writer, however, suspects that the end may be somewhere in sight....

It would indeed be curious, if the climate of opinion which produced the Florida Boom and the 1928 stock market should not achieve something similar in the field of scholarship. And perhaps the mysterious psychological forces which cause all these booms to rise and fall have something in common.

The present legal inflation has been worse than any in the past, yet that seems true of all inflations....

The fact that the Restatement has not stopped the flood of legal literature is certainly not the fault of the reporters, if one believes as the writer does that no other type of restatement was possible in the intellectual atmosphere of the time. It has to be tried.... Therefore nothing but praise should be accorded those who worked so conscientiously within the narrow confines of the peculiar artificial reasoning of the law.... [A]s attitudes toward precedents in pleading changed, so may the attitude toward piles of books in substantive law change, and the day may come when more practical measures may be taken.

The writer suggests no formula because at present it is only too evident that no new formula will be accepted. It is sufficient to illustrate the possibilities of a science *about* law by an analogy. The so-called Copernican revolution had a significance in human culture far beyond the specific astronomical discovery. For the first time, in ceasing to think of the earth as the center of the universe, men began to look at it from the outside. Amazing advances in man's control over his physical environment followed that change of attitude. Discoveries were made which would have been impossible for men bound by fetters of earlier pre-conceptions. Today there is beginning to dawn a similar change in attitude towards creeds, faiths, philosophies and law. Looked at from within, law is the center of an independent universe with economics the center of a co-ordinate universe. Looked at from outside, we can begin to see what makes the wheels go round and catch a vision of how we can exercise control not only of physical environment but of mental and spiritual environment. When men begin to examine philosophies and principles as they examine atoms and electrons, the road to discovery of the means of social control is open. . . .

FRED RODELL

"Goodbye to Law Reviews"

(1936)

There are two things wrong with almost all legal writing. One is its style. The other is its content. That, I think, about covers the ground. And though it is in the law reviews that the most highly regarded legal literature—and I by no means except those fancy rationalizations of legal action called judicial opinions—is regularly embalmed, it is in the law reviews that a pennyworth of content is most frequently concealed beneath a pound of so-called style. The average law review writer is peculiarly able to say nothing with an air of great importance. When I used to read law reviews, I used constantly to be reminded of an elephant trying to swat a fly.

Now the antediluvian or mock-heroic style in which most law review material is written has, as I am well aware, been panned before. That panning has had no effect, just as this panning will have no effect. Remember that it is by request that I am bleating my private bleat about legal literature.

To go into the question of style then, it seems to be a cardinal principle of law review writing and editing that nothing may be said forcefully and nothing may be said amusingly. This, I take it, is in the interest of something called dignity. It does not matter that most people—and even lawyers come into this category—read either to be convinced or to be entertained. It does not matter that even in the comparatively rare instances when people read to be informed, they like a dash of pepper or a dash of salt along with their information. They won't get any seasoning if the law reviews can help it. The law reviews would rather be dignified and ignored.

Suppose a law review writer wants to criticize a court decision. Does he say "Justice Fussbudget, in a long-winded and vacuous opinion, managed to twist his logic and mangle his history so as to reach a result which is not only reactionary but ridiculous"? He may think exactly that but he does not say it. He does not even say "It was a thoroughly stupid decision." What he says is—"It would seem that a contrary conclusion might perhaps have been better justified." "It

Reprinted from the *Virginia Law Review*, vol. 23 (1936), pp. 34–45, by permission.

would seem—," the matriarch of mollycoddle phrases, still revered by the law reviews in the dull name of dignity.

One of the style quirks that inevitably detracts from the forcefulness and clarity of law review writing is the taboo on pronouns of the first person. An "I" or a "me" is regarded as a rather shocking form of disrobing in print. To avoid nudity, the back-handed passive is almost obligatory:—"It is suggested—," "It is proposed—," "It would seem—." Whether the writers really suppose that such constructions clothe them in anonymity so that people can not guess who is suggesting and who is proposing, I do not know....

Long sentences, awkward constructions, and fuzzy-wuzzy words that seem to apologize for daring to venture an opinion are part of the price the law reviews pay for their precious dignity....

... [T]he explosive touch of humor is considered just as bad taste as the hard sock of condemnation. I know no field of learning so vulnerable to burlesque, satire, or occasional pokes in the ribs as the bombastic pomposity of legal dialectic. Perhaps that is the very reason why there are no jesters or gag men in legal literature and why law review editors knit their brows overtime to purge their publications of every crack that might produce a real laugh. The law is a fat man walking down the street in a high hat. And far be it from the law reviews to be any party to the chucking of a snowball or the judicious placing of a banana-peel.

Occasionally, very occasionally, a bit of heavy humor does get into print. But it must be the sort of humor that tends to produce, at best, a cracked smile rather than a guffaw. And most law review writers, trying to produce a cracked smile, come out with one of those pedantic wheezes that get an uncomfortably forced response when professors use them in a classroom. The best way to get a laugh out of a law review is to take a couple of drinks and then read an article, any article, aloud. That can be really funny.

Then there is the business of footnotes, the flaunted Phi Beta Kappa keys of legal writing, and the pet peeve of everyone who has ever read a law review piece for any other reason than that he was too lazy to look up his own cases. So far as I can make out, there are two distinct types of footnote. There is the explanatory or if-you-didn't-understand-what-I-said-in-the-text-this-may-help-you type. And there is the probative or if-you're-from-Missouri-just-take-a-look-at-all-this type.

The explanatory footnote is an excuse to let the law review writer be obscure and befuddled in the body of his article and then say the same thing at the bottom of the page the way he should have said it in the first place. But talking around the bush is not an easy habit to get rid of and so occasionally a reader has to use reverse English and hop back to the text to try to find out what the footnote means. It is true, however, that a wee bit more of informality is permitted in small type. Thus "It is suggested" in the body of an article might carry an explanatory footnote to the effect that "This is the author's own suggestion."

It is the probative footnote that is so often made up of nothing but a long list of names of cases that the writer has had some stooge look up and throw together for him. These huge chunks of small type, so welcome to the student who turns the page and finds only two or three lines of text above them, are what make a legal article very, very learned. They also show the suspicious twist of the legal mind. The idea seems to be that a man can not be trusted to make a straight statement unless he takes his readers by the paw and leads them to chapter and verse. Every legal writer is presumed to be a liar until he proves himself otherwise with a flock of footnotes.

In any case, the footnote foible breeds nothing but sloppy thinking, clumsy writing, and bad eyes. Any article that has to be explained or proved by being cluttered up with little numbers until it looks like the Acrosses and Downs of a cross-word puzzle has no business being written. . . .

Exceptions to the traditions of dumpy dignity and fake learnedness in law review writing are as rare as they are beautiful. Once in a while a Thomas Reed Powell gets away with an imaginary judicial opinion that gives a real twist to the lion's tail. Once in a while a Thurman Arnold forgets his footnotes as though to say that if people do not believe or understand him that is their worry and not his. But even such mild breaches of etiquette as these are tolerated gingerly and seldom, and are likely to be looked at a little askance by the writers' more pious brethren.

In the main, the strait-jacket of law review style has killed what might have been a lively literature. It has maimed even those few pieces of legal writing that actually have something to say. I am the last one to suppose that a piece about the law could be made to read like a juicy sex novel or a detective story, but I can not see why it has to resemble a cross between a nineteenth century sermon and a treatise on higher mathematics. A man who writes a law review article should be able to attract for it a slightly larger audience than a few of his colleagues who skim through it out of courtesy and a few of his students who sweat through it because he has assigned it. . . .

Harold Laski is fond of saying that in every revolution the lawyers are liquidated first. That may sound as if I had jumped the track but it seems to me to be terribly relevant. The reason the lawyers lead the line to the guillotine or the firing squad is that, while law is supposed to be a device to serve society, a civilized way of helping the wheels go round without too much friction, it is pretty hard to find a group less concerned with serving society and more concerned with serving themselves than the lawyers. The reason all this is relevant is that if any among the lawyers might reasonably be expected to carry a torch or shoot a flashlight in the right direction, it is the lawyers who write about the law.

I confess that "serving society" is a slightly mealy phrase with a Sunday school smack to it. There are doubtless better and longer ways of expressing the same idea but it should still convey some vague notion of what I mean.

I mean that law, as an institution or a science or a high-class mumbo-jumbo, has a job to do in the world. And that job is neither the writing of successful briefs for successful clients nor the wide-eyed leafing over and sorting out of what appellate court judges put into print when, for all sorts of reasons, some obvious and some hidden in the underbrush, they affirm or reverse lower court decisions.

Yet it would be hard to guess, from most of the stuff that is published in the law reviews, that law and the lawyers had any other job on their hands than the slinging together of neat (but certainly not gaudy) legalistic arguments and the building up, rebuilding and sporadic knocking down of pretty houses of theory foundationed in sand and false assumptions. It would be hard to guess from the mass of articles dedicated to such worthy inquiries as "The Rule Against Perpetuities in Saskatchewan," "Some New Uses of the Trust Device to Avoid Taxation," or "An Answer to a Reply to a Comment on a Criticism of the Restatement of the Law of Conflicts of Laws."

Law review writers seem to rank among our most adept navelgazers. When they are not busy adding to and patching up their lists of cases and their farflung lines of logic, so that some smart practicing lawyer can come along and grab the cases and the logic without so much as a by-your-leave, they are sure to be found squabbling earnestly among themselves over the meaning or content of some obscure principle that nine judges out of ten would not even recognize if it hopped up and slugged them in the face.

This centripetal absorption in the home-made mysteries and sleight-of-hand of the law would be a perfectly harmless occupation if it did not consume so much time and energy that might better be spent otherwise. And if it did not, incidentally, consume so much space in the law libraries. It seems never to have occurred to most of the studious gents who diddle around in the law reviews with the intricacies of contributory negligence, consideration, or covenants running with the land that neither life nor law can be confined within the forty-four corners of some cozy concept. It seems never to have occurred to them that they might be diddling while Rome burned.

I do not wish to labor the point but perhaps it had best be stated once in dead earnest. With law as the only alternative to force as a means of solving the myriad of problems of the world, it seems to me that the articulate among the clan of lawyers might, in their writings, be more pointedly aware of those problems, might recognize that the use of law to help toward their solution is the only excuse for the law's existence, instead of blithely continuing to make mountain after mountain out of tiresome technical molehills. . . .

When it comes right down to laying the cards on the table, it is not surprising that the law reviews are as bad as they are. The leading articles, and the book reviews too, are for the most part written by professors and would-be professors of law whose chief interest is in getting something published so they can wave it in the faces of their deans when they ask for a raise, because the accepted way of getting ahead in law teaching is to break constantly into print in a dignified way. The students who write for the law reviews are egged on by the comforting thought that they will be pretty sure to get jobs when they graduate in return for their slavery, and the super-students who do the editorial or dirty work are egged on even harder by the knowledge that they will get even better jobs.

Moreover, the only consumers of law reviews outside the academic circle are the law offices, which never actually read them but stick them away on a shelf for future reference. The law offices consider the law reviews much as a plumber might consider a piece of lead pipe. They are not very worried about the literary or social service possibilities of the law, but they are tickled pink to have somebody else look up cases and think up new arguments for them to use in their business, because it means that they are getting something for practically nothing.

Thus everybody connected with the law review has some sort of bread to butter, in a nice way of course, and all of them—professors, students, and practicing lawyers—are quite content to go on buttering their own and each other's bread. It is a pretty little family picture and anyone who comes along with the wild idea that the folks might step outside for a spell and take a breath of fresh air is likely to have his head bitten off. It is much too warm and comfortable and safe indoors.

And so I suspect that the law reviews will keep right on turning out stuff that is not fit to read, on subjects that are not worth the bother of writing about them. Yet I like to hope that I am wrong.

Maybe one of these days the law reviews, or some of them, will have the nerve to shoot for higher stakes. Maybe they will get tired of pitching pennies, and of dolling themselves up in tailcoats to do it so that they feel a sense of importance and pride as they toss copper after copper against the same old wall. Maybe they will come to realize that the English language is most useful when it is used normally and naturally, and that the law is nothing more than a means to a social end and should never, for all the law schools and law firms in the world, be treated as an end in itself. In short, maybe one of these days the law reviews will catch on. Meanwhile I say they're spinach. . . .

Notes

Introduction

1. Among the other common descriptions are "formalism" and "mechanical jurisprudence."

2. See, for example, *Walker* v. *Cronin*, 107 Mass. 555 (1871); *In re Debs*, 158 U.S. 564 (1895); *Vegalahn* v. *Guntner*, 167 Mass. 92 (1896); Arnold M. Paul, *Conservative Crisis and the Rule of Law: Attitudes of Bar and Bench, 1887–1895* (1960; reprint, Gloucester, Mass.: Peter Smith, 1976), 104–58.

3. See, for example, *United States* v. *E.C. Knight Co.*, 156 U.S. 1 (1895).

4. See, for example, *Chicago, Milwaukee & St. Paul Ry. Co.* v. *Minnesota*, 134 U.S. 418 (1890); *Reagan* v. *Farmers' Loan and Trust Co.*, 154 U.S. 362 (1894); *Lochner* v. *New York*, 198 U.S. 45 (1905).

5. See Morton J. Horwitz, *The Transformation of American Law, 1780–1860* (Cambridge: Harvard Univ. Press, 1977), chap. 1; William Nelson, "The Impact of the Anti-Slavery Movement upon Styles of Judicial Reasoning in Nineteenth-Century America," *Harvard Law Review* 87 (1974): 513; William Fisher, "Ideology, Religion, and the Constitutional Protection of Private Property: 1760–1860," *Emory Law Journal* 39 (1990): 65, 112–21.

6. See, for example, *Coppage* v. *Kansas*, 236 U.S. 1, 14 (1915); Samuel D. Warren and Louis D. Brandeis, "The Right to Privacy," *Harvard Law Review* 4 (1890): 193.

7. See Duncan Kennedy, "Toward an Historical Understanding of Legal Consciousness: The Case of Classical Legal Thought in America, 1850–1940," *Research in Law and Sociology* 3 (1980): 3; Robert Gordon, "Legal Thought and Legal Practice in the Age of American Enterprise, 1870–1920," in G. Geison, ed., *Professions and Professional Ideologies in America* 70, 82 (Chapel Hill: Univ. of North Carolina Press); Morton Horwitz, *The Transformation of American Law, 1870–1960: The Crisis of Legal Orthodoxy* (New York: Oxford Univ. Press, 1992), chap. 1.

8. See Thomas C. Grey, "Langdell's Orthodoxy," *University of Pittsburgh Law Review* 45 (1983): 1, 6–28; Committee on the Establishment of a Perma-

nent Organization for the Improvement of the Law, "The Law's Uncertainty and Complexity," American Law Institute, *Proceeding*, 1 (Part 1, 1923), 66–76 (initiating the Institute's "restatement" project—discussed in Chapter 8).

9. See, for example, Roscoe Pound, "Mechanical Jurisprudence," *Columbia Law Review* 8 (1908): 605; Horwitz, *Transformation of American Law, 1780–1860*, chap. 8; Peter Gabel and Jay Feinman, "Contract Law as Ideology," in David Kairys, ed., *The Politics of Law: A Progressive Critique* (New York: Pantheon, 1982), 172–84.

10. See Grey, "Langdell's Orthodoxy," 32–39.

11. See Herbert Hovencamp, *Enterprise and American Law, 1836–1937* (Cambridge: Harvard Univ. Press, 1991).

12. See David Trubek, "Max Weber on Law and the Rise of Capitalism," *Wisconsin Law Review* (1972): 739–48.

13. See Harry Scheiber, "Instrumentalism and Property Rights: A Reconsideration of American 'Styles of Judicial Reasoning' in the Nineteenth Century," *Wisconsin Law Review* (1975): 1.

14. See Michael Les Benedict, "Laissez-Faire and Liberty," *Law and History Review* 3 (1985): 293; David P. Currie, "The Constitution in the Supreme Court: The Protection of Economic Interests, 1889–1910," *University of Chicago Law Review* 52 (1985): 325, 381.

15. See, for example, *Coppage* v. *Kansas*, 236 U.S. 1, 4–5 (1915) (argument of John S. Dawson, Attorney General of Kansas).

16. See G. Edward White, *Patterns of American Legal Thought* (Charlottesville, Va.: Bobbs-Merrill, 1978), 99–135. The work of this group is discussed at greater length in Chapter 1.

17. See Edward A. Purcell, Jr., *The Crisis of Democratic Theory: Scientific Naturalism and the Problem of Value* (Lexington: Univ. Press of Kentucky, 1973), 74–94.

18. The debate among the Realists themselves concerning the membership of their movement is considered in Chapter 2.

19. See generally Arthur Schlesinger, *The Age of Roosevelt: The Coming of the New Deal* (Boston: Houghton-Mifflin, 1957).

20. See, for example, Richard Danzig, "A Comment on the Jurisprudence of the Uniform Commercial Code," *Stanford Law Review* 27 (1975): 621; Zipporah Batshaw Wiseman, "The Limits of Vision: Karl Llewellyn and the Merchant Rules," *Harvard Law Review* 100 (1987): 465.

21. See Karl Klare, "Contracts Jurisprudence and the First-Year Casebook," *New York University Law Review* 54 (1979): 876.

22. See William Fisher, "The Development of Twentieth-Century American Legal Theory and the Judicial Interpretation of the Bill of Rights," in Michael Lacey and Knud Haakonssen, ed., *A Culture of Rights* (Cambridge: Cambridge Univ. Press, 1991).

23. See Mark Tushnet, "Following the Rules Laid Down: A Critique of Interpretivism and Neutral Principles," *Harvard Law Review* 96 (1983): 781–82 (citing the confirmation hearings of Judge Wald and Justice O'Connor).

24. See, for example, Thurgood Marshall, "The Continuing Challenge of the Fourteenth Amendment," *Georgia Law Review* 3 (1968): 9; Jon O. Newman, "Between Legal Realism and Neutral Principles: The Legitimacy of Institutional Values," *California Law Review* 72 (1984): 200; Harry T. Edwards, "The Role of a Judge in Modern Society: Some Reflections on Current Practice

in Federal Appellate Adjudication," *Cleveland State Law Review* 32 (1983): 388–403; William H. Rehnquist, "Remarks on the Process of Judging," *Washington & Lee Law Review* 49 (1992): 263–64, 269–70.

Chapter 1

Introduction

1. See, for example, Felix Cohen, *Ethical Systems and Legal Ideals: an Essay on the Foundations of Legal Criticism* (1933; reprint, Greenwood Press, 1976), 104–5.

2. *Law and the Modern Mind* (1930; reprint, Gloucester, Mass.: Peter Smith, 1970), 270. Many testimonials to Holmes by Legal Realists are collected in Felix Frankfurter, ed., *Mr. Justice Holmes* (New York: Coward-McCann, 1931).

3. *The Common Law,* ed. Mark DeWolfe Howe (Boston: Little, Brown, 1963), 5.

4. Benjamin Cardozo, "Mr. Justice Holmes," in *Mr. Justice Holmes,* 3.

5. This interpretation gains credibility from Holmes' sarcastic description of Langdell as "the greatest living legal theologian." Book Review, *American Law Review* 14 (1880): 233, 234.

6. See, for example, Morris Cohen, "Justice Holmes and the Nature of Law," *Columbia Law Review* 31 (1931): 353, 356.

7. See Chapter 7, below.

8. See Thomas C. Grey, "Holmes and Legal Pragmatism," *Stanford Law Review* 41 (1989): 792.

9. First delivered as a speech at Boston University, "The Path of the Law" was published simultaneously in the *Harvard Law Review* 10 (1897): 457 and *Juridicial Review* 9 (1897): 105. It is now most easily available in Richard A Posner, ed., *The Essential Holmes* (Chicago: Univ. of Chicago Press, 1992), 160–77. While he was writing it, Holmes was carrying on an unusually impassioned correspondence with Lady Clare Castletown in Ireland. For speculations concerning the connection between the emotions evinced by his letters and the content of the essay, see Morton J. Horwitz, *The Transformation of American Law, 1870–1960: The Crisis of Legal Orthodoxy* (Cambridge: Harvard Univ. Press, 1992), 142–43.

10. The passage is reprinted in context on p. 17.

11. See Thomas A. Reed, "Holmes and the Paths of the Law," *American Journal of Legal History* (1993) (forthcoming).

12. Cohen, "Justice Holmes," 357.

13. The efforts of Llewellyn and others to establish an intermediate position are examined in Chapter 6.

14. See Morton J. Horwitz, *The Transformation of American Law, 1780–1860* (Cambridge: Harvard Univ. Press, 1977), chaps 1, 8.

15. See, for example, Yosal Rogat, "The Judge as Spectator," *University of Chicago Law Review* 31 (1964): 213; G. Edward White, "The Rise and Fall of Justice Holmes," *University of Chicago Law Review* 39 (1971): 51; Thomas C. Grey, "Holmes, Pragmatism, and Democracy" (unpublished paper, originally presented as the Colin Ruagh Thomas O'Fallon Memorial Lecture on Law and American Culture, University of Oregon Law School, April 6, 1992).

16. See David Wigdor, *Roscoe Pound: Philosopher of Law* (Westport, Conn.: Greenwood, Press, 1974), 249–51.

17. See Chapter 2.

18. See Horwitz, *Crisis of Legal Orthodoxy*, 118–21.

19. Excerpts from the first of his two papers are reprinted below. The other is "Fundamental Legal Conceptions as Applied in Judicial Reasoning," *Yale Law Journal* 26 (1917): 710. For secondary studies of Hohfeld, see Duncan Kennedy and Frank Michelman, "Are Property and Contract Efficient?," *Hofstra Law Review* 8 (1980): 748–58; Joseph Singer, "The Legal Rights Debate in Analytical Jurisprudence from Bentham to Hohfeld," *Wisconsin Law Review* (1982): 986–89.

20. See Chapter 4.

21. See Chapter 6.

ROSCOE POUND

"Liberty of Contract"

1. *Adair* v. *United States*, 208 U.S. 11, 175.

2. Ward, *Applied Sociology*, 28.

ROSCOE POUND

"Law in Books and Law in Action"

1. [The cases to which Pound is referring are: *People* v. *Coler*, 166 N.Y. 1 (1901); *People* v. *Lochner*, 177 N.Y. 145 (1904); *United States* v. *Martin*, 94 U.S. 400 (1876); and *Lochner* v. *New York*, 198 U.S. 45 (1905).—Ed]

Chapter 2

Introduction

1. *Columbia Law Review* 30 (1930): 431.

2. *American Economic Review* 15 (1925): 665.

3. The first casebooks, like Langdell's *A Selection of Cases on the Law of Contracts* (1871, 1880), offered court decisions—mostly English, not United States or colonial—without much commentary by the editor.

4. See Charles Beard, "Germany Up to Her Old Tricks," *The New Republic* 80 (October 24, 1934): 299; and David Wigdor, *Roscoe Pound: Philosopher of Law* (Westport, Conn.: Greenwood Press, 1974) 250–51.

5. Llewellyn also drafted a book on Sacco and Vanzetti, *Who are these Accused?*, Karl Llewellyn Papers, Section G, University of Chicago Law School. And see William Twining, *Karl Llewellyn and the Realist Movement* (Norman: University of Oklahoma Press, 1973), 341–49; N.E.H. Hull, "Reconstructing the Origins of Realistic Jurisprudence: A Prequel to the Llewellyn—Pound Exchange Over Legal Realism," *Duke Law Journal* (1989): 1302; Morton Horwitz, *The Transformation of American Law 1870–1960: The Crisis of Legal Orthodoxy* (New York: Oxford University Press, 1992), 170–80.

6. Pound himself was styled by Frank a rule-fetishist. Jerome Frank, *Law and the Modern Mind* (New York: Brentano's, 1930), 37, 228n.

7. "A Realistic Jurisprudence," 434.

8. Ibid., 435.

9. N.E.H. Hull, "Some Realism About the Llewellyn-Pound Exchange Over Realism: The Newly Uncovered Private Correspondence, 1927–1931," *Wisconsin Law Review* (1987): 921, 935.

10. Karl N. Llewellyn, "The Bar Specializes—With What Results?," *Annals of the American Academy of Political and Social Science* (May, 1933): 167.

11. *Harvard Law Review* 44 (1931): 697.

12. *Harvard Law Review* 44 (1931): 1222.

13. For a different view, and a summary of the commentary on the debate, see Hull, "Some Realism About the Llewellyn-Pound Exchange."

14. *Hynes* v. *New York Central R. Co.*, 231 N.Y. 229, 236 (1921).

15. "Some Realism About Realism," 1236. Llewellyn repeated his appeal for the temporary separation of law and ethics in "Legal Tradition and Social Science Method—A Realist's Critique," in *Essays in Research in the Social Sciences* (New York: Brookings Institute, 1931), 101. Later, he reconsidered. See, for example, "On the Good, the True, the Beautiful, in Law," *University of Chicago Law Review 9* (1942): 260.

16. See Chapter 1, p. 17.

17. Benjamin Kaplan, "Encounter with Oliver Wendell Holmes, Jr.," *Harvard Law Review* 96 (1983): 1828, 1836. And see Llewellyn, "Holmes," *Columbia Law Review* 30 (1935): 488.

18. See Twining, *Karl Llewellyn and the Realist Movement*, 124–26 (arguing that, despite vicissitudes, Llewellyn was essentially a "liberal").

19. "Some Realism About Realism," 1238.

KARL LLEWELLYN

"A Realistic Jurisprudence—The Next Step"

1. *Law and Morals* (1924), 25 *et seq*.

2. Pound's work in this aspect is as striking in its values as in its limitations. It is full to bursting of magnificent insight. It is to Pound we owe the suggestion of "the limits of effective legal action" (worked out in terms of *court* decisions). It is to Pound we owe the contrast of law-in-books and law-in-action....

Critical reading of Pound's work, it may be noted in passing, and especially the phrasing of any concrete criticism, are embarassed by the constant indeterminacy of the level of his discourse. At times the work purports clearly to travel on the level of considered and butressed scholarly discussion; at times on the level of bed-time stories for the tired bar; at times on an intermediate level, that of the thoughtful but unproved essay. Most often, it is impossible to tell the intended level of any chapter or passage, and the writing seems to pass without notice from one to another. Now it is obvious that three successive, mutually inconsistent generalizations, though no one of them sustainable as the deliberate propositions of a scholar, may all be illuminating and indeed all true at once— on the level of the after-dinner speech, or even of the thought-provoking essay. All of which gags the critic at the same time that it perhaps stimulates his critical faculties....

KARL N. LLEWELLYN

"Some Realism About Realism— Responding to Dean Pound"

1. Jerome Frank refused me permission to sign his name as joint author to this paper, on the ground that it was my fist which pushed the pen. But his generosity does not alter the fact that the paper could not have been written without his help.

2. *The sampling of men.* We set up the following criteria: (a) those chosen must fit the general and the more specific items set forth above; (b) they must include the leading figures in the new ferment; (c) in order that we may turn up most passages supporting the items we challenge, the men chosen must include all who may be reputed to have taken extreme positions; (d) a wide range of views and positions must be included..

(1) Bingham and Lorenzen are included as of course. (2) We add those whom we believe recognized as figures of central stimulus in the new ferment: C. E. Clark, Cook, Corbin, Moore, T.R. Powell, Oliphant. (3) We add further men peculiarly vocal in advocating new or rebellious points of view: Frank, Green, Radin. (4) We stir in all others whom we have heard criticized as extremists on one or another point mentioned by the dean: Hutcheson, Klaus, Sturges. (5) We fill out with as many more as time permits: Douglas, Francis, Patterson, Tulin, Yntema—chosen partly because their writing has explicitly touched points of theory, partly because their writing was either familiar to us or not too bulky. (6) We throw in Llewellyn, as both vociferous and extreme, but peculiarly because he and he alone has issued a "Call for a Realist Jurisprudence" under that peculiar label. . . . This gives us twenty names. There are doubtless twenty more. But half is a fair sample. We check back and find that our men range from right to the four or five prevailing lefts. They are either characteristic or extreme. They are in print more fully than most on these matters. If they do not bear out Dean Pound's challenged points of description, we feel safe in saying that those points can not stand. . . .

3. [Llewellyn's citations of particular authors in support of each point are omitted.—Ed]

4. As to each of the following points I have attempted to check over not only the general tone of work but several specific writings of the twenty men named and a number of others—*e.g.,* Kidd, Maggs, Breckenridge, Morse, Durfee, Bohlen, Bryant Smith and Goble—and to make sure that each point was applicable to each. Errors may have crept in. Note how closely the description fits Holmes' work as early as 1871–72: "It commands the future, a valid but imperfectly realized ideal."

Chapter 3

Introduction

1. William Blackstone, *Commentaries on the Laws of England,* 4 vols. (1765–1769; facsimile ed., Chicago, University of Chicago Press, 1979), 2:440–70. Until well into the nineteenth century, most American lawyers derived much of their working knowledge from annotated versions of the *Commentaries.*

2. See, for example, Jay Feinman, "The Development of the Employment at Will Rule," *American Journal of Legal History* 20 (1976): 118; Minda, "The Common Law of Employment at Will in New York," *Syracuse Law Review* 36 (1985): 939.

3. See Lawrence M. Friedman, *A History of American Law,* 2d ed. (New York: Simon & Schuster, 1985), 427.

4. See Morton J. Horwitz, *The Transformation of American Law, 1870–1960: The Crisis of Legal Orthodoxy* (New York: Oxford University Press, 1992), 39–45.

5. See Morton J. Horwitz, *The Transformation of American Law, 1760–1860* (Cambridge: Harvard University Press, 1977), 204–7.

6. See ibid., 207–10; Lawrence M. Friedman and Jack Ladinsky, "Social Change and the Law of Industrial Accidents," *Columbia Law Review* 67 (1967): 60.

7. See Horwitz, *Transformation of American Law, 1760–1860,* 180–88.

8. See ibid., 262; Robert Hale, "Bargaining, Duress, and Economic Liberty," *Columbia Law Review* 43 (1943): 616.

9. See Horwitz, *Crisis of Legal Orthodoxy,* 36–37.

10. See Friedman, *History of American Law,* 442–62.

11. See Horwitz, *Crisis of Legal Orthodoxy,* 46–51.

12. William Keener, *A Treatise on the Law of Quasi-Contracts* (Baker, Voorhis, 1893), 3–25.

13. See "The Path of the Law," reprinted in Chapter 1, above.

14. The emergence of this doctrine is discussed in the Introduction on page xi.

15. See *Adair* v. *United States,* 208 U.S. 161 (1908); *Coppage* v. *Kansas,* 236 U.S. 1 (1915). A "yellow-dog contract" is a promise by an employee not to join a union or, if already a member of a union, to resign from it.

16. See Herbert Hovencamp, *Enterprise and American Law* (Cambridge: Harvard University Press, 1991), 171–204.

17. Other essays in this vein include: Clarence Ashley, "Mutual Assent in Contract," *Columbia Law Review* 3 (1903): 71; idem, "Should There Be Freedom of Contract?," *Columbia Law Review* 5 (1905): 36; Arthur Corbin, "Quasi-Contractual Obligations," *Yale Law Journal* 21 (1912): 553; idem, "Discharge of Contracts," *Yale Law Journal* 22 (1913): 513; idem, "Does a Pre-Existing Duty Defeat Consideration?—Recent Noteworthy Decisions," *Yale Law Journal* 27 (1918): 362; idem, "Contracts for the Benefit of Third Persons," *Yale Law Journal* 27 (1918): 1008; William Draper Lewis, "The Liability of the Undisclosed Principal in Contract," *Columbia Law Review* 9 (1909): 116.

18. The quotation is from Corbin, "Offer and Acceptance, And Some of the Resulting Legal Relations," reprinted on pp. 80–81, below.

NATHAN ISAACS

"The Standardizing of Contracts"

1. I am gratefully adopting Professor Wesley N. Hohfeld's eight fundamental legal conceptions. See *Fundamental Legal Conceptions as Applied in Judicial Reasoning* (1913) 23 Yale Law Journal 16, and (1917) 26 Yale Law Journal 710. I have made but one verbal change: "limitation" instead of "no right."

Chapter 4

Introduction

1. See Oscar Handlin and Mary Flug Handlin, *Commonwealth: A Study of the Role of Government in the American Economy, Massachusetts, 1774–1861* (Cambridge: Harvard University Press, 1969), 51–133; Hendrik Hartog, *Public Property and Private Power* (Chapel Hill: Univ. of North Carolina Press, 1983), chaps. 1–5; Joan Williams, "The Development of the Public/Private Distinction in American Law," *Texas Law Review* 64 (1985): 225.

2. For varying views of the origins of this shift in attitude, see Gerald Frug, "The City as a Legal Concept," *Harvard Law Review* 93 (1980): 1059, 1099–1109; Carol Rose, "Public Property, Old and New," *Northwestern University Law Review* 79 (1984): 216.

3. See E. Merrick Dodd, *American Business Corporations Until 1860, With Special Reference to Massachusetts* (Cambridge: Harvard University Press, 1954); Louis Hartz, *Economic Policy and Democratic Thought: Pennsylvania, 1776–1860* (Cambridge: Harvard University Press, 1948); Oscar & Mary Handlin, "The Origins of the American Business Corporation," *Journal of Economic History* 5 (1945): 1, 8–9; Note, "Incorporating the Republic: The Corporation in Antebellum Political Culture," *Harvard Law Review* 102 (1989): 1883.

4. See, for example, *Dartmouth College* v. *Woodward*, 4 Wheat. (17 U.S.) 518 (1819); *Santa Clara County* v. *Southern Pacific Railroad*, 118 U.S. 394 (1886); R. Kent Newmyer, "Justice Story's Doctrine of Public and Private Corporations and the Rise of the American Business Corporation," *DePaul Law Review* 25 (1976): 825.

5. See Frug, "The City as a Legal Concept," 1105; Hartog, *Public Property*, chaps. 8–9.

6. See Morton Horwitz, "The History of the Public/Private Distinction," *University of Pennsylvania Law Review* 130 (1982): 1423, 1424.

7. See ibid., 1425; William W. Fisher III, "The Law of the Land: An Intellectual History of American Property Doctrine, 1776–1880" (Ph.D. diss., Harvard University, 1991), 233–38.

8. See Joseph William Singer, "Legal Realism Now," *California Law Review* 76 (1988): 465, 477–82; Duncan Kennedy, "Toward an Historical Understanding of Legal Consciousness: The Case of Classical Legal Thought in America, 1850–1940," *Research in Law and Sociology* 3 (1980): 3.

9. For essays in addition to those reprinted below that make similar claims, see Robert Hale, "Law Making by Unofficial Minorities," *Columbia Law Review* 20 (1920): 451; Morris Cohen, "The Basis of Contract," *Harvard Law Review* 46 (1933): 553; Robert Hale, "Bargaining, Duress, and Economic Liberty," *Columbia Law Review* 43 (1943): 603; and John Dawson, "Economic Duress—An Essay in Perspective," *Michigan Law Review* 45 (1947): 253.

10. 334 U.S. 1 (1948). It is no accident that Robert Hale, the most trenchant and persistent of the Realist critics of the public/private distinction, helped draft the brief in *Shelley*. See Barbara Fried, *Robert L. Hale and Progressive Legal Economics* (forthcoming 1994), chap. 4; cf. Robert Hale, *Freedom Through Law: Public Control of Private Governing Power* (New York: Columbia Univ. Press, 1952), 366–79 (discussing *Shelley*). For a recent extension of the doctrine in *Shelley*, see *Edmonson* v. *Leesville Concrete Company*, 111 S.Ct. 2077

(1991) (holding that the Fourteenth Amendment is violated when a judge allows a civil trial to proceed after the lawyer for a private party uses his peremptory challenges to exclude members of a particular race from the jury).

11. See, for example, Robert Ellickson, "Cities and Homeowners Associations," *University of Pennsylvania Law Review* 130 (1982): 1519; Duncan Kennedy, "The Stages of the Decline of the Public/Private Distinction," *University of Pennsylvania Law Review* 130 (1982): 1349.

12. See *First National Bank* v. *Bellotti*, 935 U.S. 765 (1978).

13. See *Anderson* v. *City of Boston*, 380 N.E.2d 628 (Mass. 1978), appeal dismissed, 439 U.S. 1060 (1979); Steven Shiffrin, "Government Speech," *UCLA Law Review* 27 (1980): 565.

14. See Christopher D. Stone, "Corporate Vices and Corporate Virtues: Do Public/Private Distinctions Matter?," *University of Pennsylvania Law Review* 130 (1982): 1441.

MORRIS R. COHEN

"Property and Sovereignty"

1. [Cohen is referrring here to *Adkins* v. *Children's Hospital*, 261 U.S. 525 (1923), in which the Supreme Court declared unconstitutional a federal statute authorizing an administrative board to set minimum wages for adult women in the District of Columbia.—Ed]

M. Witmark & Sons v. *Fred Fisher Music Co.*

1. The present value of the renewal right to the song in suit is not estimated in the moving papers. However, it was used 6,335 times on the radio in 1939, and there are a number of prospective profitable uses that have come into being since the date of the assignment, such as electrical transcriptions for radio, motion-picture sound tracks, coin-operated public phonographs and radio broadcasting. In its moving paper, appellee's president urges that the song "is one of the most celebrated ballads of our times," and that an injunction is necessary to prevent "substantial monetary damage."

There were similar renewal rights to several other songs sold by Graff to the plaintiff in the same contract—including the well-known 'Till The Sands of the Deserts Grow Cold,—which have admittedly "become world famous."

2. The defendants seem not to be financially responsible. That alone, however, is no ground for a preliminary injunction, and surely not when there are other means of protecting plaintiff, should it ultimately win, without doing unnecessary harm to defendants should they ultimately succeed. At most (assuming that any agreement made prior to the renewal date to sell a renewal right can be valid) the interim order should not have gone beyond an impounding, pendente lite, of the receipts of defendants from sales of the song.

3. See Coercion and Distribution in a Supposedly Non-Coercive State, 38 *Pol. Sci. Q.* (1923) 475; Force and The State, 35 *Col. L. Rev.* (1935) 149; Our Equivocal Constitutional Guaranties, 39 *Col. L. Rev.* (1939) 563.

4. Hale's ideas were subsequently restated (although independently) by M. R. Cohen, who says that our "law of contract . . . puts the sovereign power

of the State at the disposal of one party to a contract.... From this point of view, the law of contract may be viewed as a subsidiary branch of public law, as a body of rules according to which the sovereign power of the State will be exercised as between the parties to a more or less voluntary bargain.... If then the law of contract confers sovereignty on one party over another (by putting the State's force at the disposal of the former) the question naturally arises: For what purposes and under what circumstances shall that power be conferred?" M. R. Cohen, The Basis of Contract," in Cohen, Law and The Social Order (1933) 69, 103–104; cf. Cohen, Property and Sovereignty, 13 *Corn. L. Q.* (1927) 8; cf. J. M. Clark, Social Control of Business (1926), 132.

5. Dean Pound, for instance.

6. Of course, the labels "medieval," "mercantilism" and "laissez-faire" are each vague catchwords. Each of them symbolizes a complex or congeries of acts and attitudes having many sources. As to some of the many facets and components of laissez-faire, see, e.g., Wingfield-Stratford, The Victorian Cycle (1935); Clarke, 3 *Pol. Sci. Q.* (1888) 549, reprinted in Beard, Introduction to The British Historians (1906) 609, 612ff; Hamilton and Braden, The Special Competence of the Supreme Court, 50 *Yale L. J.* (1941) 1319, 1320, note 11; Sabine, A History of Political Theory (1937) 656–665, 672.

7. Informed by the past, we should, with proper scepticism, regard the view now prevailing as a new fashion, not certain to last forever, even if we admire it. Certainly there are other opposing views not far below the surface. That is no cause for regret: They may prevent a drift of opinion from becoming a flood which will erode too much....

8. M. R. Cohen, Property and Sovereignty, 13 *Corn. L. Q.* (1927) 8, reprinted in Cohen, Law and The Social Order (1933) 41, 57.

9. M. R. Cohen, The Basis of Contract, 46 *Harv. L. R.* (1933) 553, reprinted in Cohen, Law and The Social Order (1933) 69, 75, 76.

10. "To put the matter more generally, ought every person of full age, acting with his eyes open and not the victim of fraud but who nevertheless is placed in a position in which from the pressure of his needs he can hardly make a fair bargain, to be capable of binding himself by a contract? If these and the like questions be answered in the affirmative, an individual's full contractual capacity is preserved, but he is in danger of parting, by the very contract which he is allowed to make, with all real freedom.... The difficulty is in all these cases ... the same; there is a perpetual danger that unlimited contractual capacity which is looked upon as an extension of individual freedom, may yet be so used by some individual as to deprive himself of the very freedom which it is assumed to be the exercise." Dicey, Law and Opinion in England (2d ed. 1914), 152, 153; cf. 260 ff.

See also Dawson, Economic Duress and Fair Exchange in French and German Law, 11 Tulane L. Rev. (1937) 346; 12 ibid. (1937) 43; Cohen, The Basis of Contract, supra.

11. See e.g., Holmes, Science and The Common Law (1879) reprinted in Holmes, Book Notices, etc., (Shriver, 1936) 10, 11; Vegelahn v. Guntner, 167 Mass. 92, 44 N.E. 1077 (1896); "The Path of the Law" (1897), [reprinted in] *Collected Legal Papers* (1920) 181, 184.

12. For candid avowals that there is and (within proper limits) must be judicial legislation, see Holmes, J., Southern Pacific Company v. Jensen, 244 U.S. 205, 221 (1917); Cardozo, *The Nature of the Judicial Process* (1921) 10, 103, 113, 146–149; Dicey, *Law and Opinion in England* (2d ed. 1914) 361–398, 483–494;

Thayer, *A Preliminary Treatise on Evidence* (1898) 318, 319, 327, 331; Dickinson, *Administrative Justice and the Supremacy of Law* (1927) 122, note 22; 209, note 23.

"What was the law in the time of Richard Coeur de Lion on the liability of a telegraph company to the persons to whom a message was sent?" Gray, *The Nature and Sources of Law* (1900) Sec. 222.

13. Our system recognizes divers restraints on complete liberty of contract. Among them are the enforcement of spendthrift trusts; refusal to enforce the contract of a man to stay out of business forever or to allow his arm to be cut off; punishment of those who make suicide pacts, etc. As to the use of standardized contracts of insurance and the like, required by statute, see Isaacs, "Standardizing the Contracts," 27 *Yale Law Journal* 34 (1917); Llewellyn, "What Price Contract?," 40 *Yale Law Journal* 704, 731ff (1931); Goebel, "Trends in The Theory of Contracts in the United States," 11 *Tulane Law Review* 413, 421 (1937); M.R. Cohen, "The Basis of Contract," *supra*.

The concept of "Coercion by economic pressure" has received overt judicial recognition in United States v. Butler, 297 U.S. 1, 71. It has been applied to "contract law" in many ways. For a recent case decided by this court, see United States Navigation Co. v. Black Diamond Lines, 2 Cir., 124 F.2d 508. Cf. Havighurst, "Consideration, Ethics and Administration," 42 *Columbia Law Review* (1942) 1, 27–30.

Chapter 5

Introduction

1. See W. Elliot Brownlee, *Dynamics of Ascent: A History of the American Economy*, 2d ed. (New York: Knopf, 1979), 269–300; Robert Higgs, *The Transformation of the American Economy, 1865–1914: An Essay in Interpretation* (New York: Wiley, 1971); Herman E. Krooss and Martin R. Blyn, *A History of Financial Intermediaries* (New York: Random House, 1971).

2. See Brownlee, *Dynamics of Ascent*, 302–7; Alfred D. Chandler, Jr., *The Visible Hand: The Managerial Revolution in American Business* (Cambridge: Harvard Univ. Press, 1977), 484–90.

3. See Alfred D. Chandler, Jr., *Strategy and Structure: Chapters in the History of the Industrial Enterprise* (Cambridge: MIT Press, 1966), chap. 4; Tony Freyer, *Regulating Big Business: Antitrust in Great Britain and America, 1880–1990* (Cambridge: Cambridge Univ. Press, 1992), 11–42; Morton Keller, *Affairs of State: Public Life in Late Nineteenth Century America* (Cambridge: Harvard Univ. Press, 1977), 434–38; Ralph L. Nelson, *Merger Movements in American Industry* (Princeton: Princeton Univ. Press, 1959).

4. See Chandler, *The Visible Hand*, especially 1–12, 207–500.

5. See Robert Wiebe, *The Search for Order, 1877–1920* (New York: Hill & Wang, 1967).

6. See pp. 20–21. This argument is also discussed in the Introduction to Chapter 1 on p. 5.

7. 248 U.S. 215 (1918).

8. Brandeis' argument here shows the influence on him of the new trends in legal theory. Contrast his early essay, with its inventive use of analogical reasoning, "The Rights to Privacy," *Harvard Law Review* 4 (1890): 193.

9. See Morton J. Horwitz, *The Transformation of American Law, 1870–1960: The Crisis of Legal Orthodoxy* (New York: Oxford Univ. Press, 1992), 65–108.

10. See ibid., 105–7.

Chapter 6

Introduction

1. Oliver Wendell Holmes, Jr., "The Path of the Law," *Harvard Law Review* 10 (March 1897): 457. The crucial portions of the essay are reprinted on p. 17.

2. "A Realistic Jurisprudence—The Next Step," *Columbia Law Review* 30 (April 1930): 448.

3. See, for example, Jerome Frank, "What Courts Do In Fact," *Illinois Law Review* 26 (1932): 645, 654–56; Leon Greene, "The Negligence Issue," *Yale Law Journal* 37 (1928): 1029 ("The definitions of scholars are sieves, the opinions of judges are little more than a succession of mirages").

4. See, for example, Felix Cohen, *Ethical Systems and Legal Ideals: An Essay on the Foundations of Legal Criticism* (New York: Harcourt, Brace, 1933), 240–49; Llewellyn, "Realistic Jurisprudence," 444.

5. On the indeterminacy of deductive logic, see, for example, Walter Wheeler Cook, "Scientific Method and the Law," *American Bar Association Journal* 13 (June 1927): 305–6 and the essay by John Dewey reprinted below. On the indeterminacy of analogical reasoning, see for example, Karl Llewellyn, *The Bramble Bush: On Our Law and Its Study* (New York: Columbia School of Law, 1930), 67–71.

6. See, for example, Karl Llewellyn, "Remarks on the Rules or Canons About How Statutes are to be Construed," *Vanderbilt Law Review* 3 (1949): 395 (reprinted below).

7. See, for example, Walter Wheeler Cook, Review of *The Paradoxes of Legal Science* by Benjamin Cardozo, *Yale Law Journal* 38 (1929): 406; Laura Kalman, *Legal Realism at Yale, 1927–1960* (Chapel Hill: University of North Carolina Press, 1986), 22.

8. See Joseph Hutchinson, "The Judgment Intuitive: The Function of the 'Hunch' in Judicial Decision, *Cornell Law Quarterly* 14 (1929): 274 (reprinted below).

9. See, for example, Frank, "What Courts Do in Fact," 655; idem, *Law and the Modern Mind* (1930; reprint, Gloucester, Mass.: Peter Smith, 1970), 114 (reprinted below).

10. See, for example, Felix Cohen, "Transcendental Nonsense and the Functional Approach," *Columbia Law Review* 35 (1935): 843–45 (reprinted below); Charles G. Haines, "General Observations on the Effects of Personal, Political and Economic Influences in the Decisions of Judges," *Illinois Law Review* 17 (1922): 96; Harold D. Lasswell, "Self-Analysis and Judicial Thinking," *International Journal of Ethics* 40 (1930): 354; Hessel Yntema. "The Handbook Method and the Conflict of Laws," *Yale Law Journal* 37 (1928): 480–81.

11. See, for example, Max Lerner, "Constitution and Court as Symbols," *Yale Law Journal* 46 (1937): 1317; Leon A. Tulin, "The Role of Penalties in Criminal Law," *Yale Law Journal* 37 (1928): 1052.

12. See, for example, Lon Fuller, "American Legal Realism," *University of Pennsylvania Law Review* 82 (1934): 443–47.

13. See, for example, Herman Oliphant, "Facts, Opinions, and Value-Judgments," *Texas Law Review* 10 (1932): 134.

14. For discussion of the respects in which these convictions were derived from contemporaneous movements in philosophy and the natural and social sciences, see Edward Purcell, *The Crisis of Democratic Theory: Scientific Naturalism and the Problem of Value* (Lexington, Ky.: University Press of Kentucky, 1973), 21–23.

15. See Cohen, "Transcendental Nonsense," 839–40; Wesley Sturges and Samuel O. Clark, "Legal Theory and Real Property Mortgages," *Yale Law Journal* 37 (1928): 713–14.

16. See Chapter 1, p. 45.

17. Walter Wheeler Cook, "Privileges of Labor Unions in the Struggle for Life," *Yale Law Journal* 27 (1918): 785–96.

18. See, for example, Charles E. Clark, "Relations, Legal and Otherwise," *Illinois Law Quarterly* 5 (1922): 26; Arthur L. Corbin, "Jural Relations and their Classification," *Yale Law Journal* 30 (1921): 226.

19. See, for example, Thurman W. Arnold, Review of *The Law of Trusts and Trustees* by George Gleason Bogert, *Columbia Law Review* 36 (1936), 687; Ernest G. Lorenzen and Raymond J. Heilman, "The Restatement of the Conflict of Laws," *University of Pennsylvania Law Review* 83 (1935): 561.

20. Frank, *Modern Mind,* 157–58, nn.26–27. In some of his early writings Roscoe Pound seemed to take this extreme position, arguing that judges should strive for "reasonable and just solutions of individual cases." "The Scope and Purpose of Sociological Jurisprudence," *Harvard Law Review* 25 (1912): 515. He gradually retreated from this stance (see White, *Patterns of Legal Thought,* 114–15) until by the 1930s he was denouncing the Realists for their fascination with "the unique single case" (see "Call for Realist Jurisprudence," 707).

21. The principal exponents of this view were Felix Cohen and Karl Llewellyn. See Cohen, *Ethical Systems,* 238 (criticizing his fellow Realists for "an unrealistic view of single cases as divorced from the uniformities which lend them significance"); Karl Llewellyn, *The Common Law Tradition in Deciding Appeals* (Boston: Little, Brown, 1960), 121–26.

22. See, for example, Karl Llewellyn, *Jurisprudence: Realism in Theory and Practice* (Chicago: University of Chicago Press, 1962), 217. The principal exception to the generalizations ventured in this paragraph was Benjamin Cardozo. In his many years as a judge, Cardozo helped reshape several important fields of private and public law. But he often concealed—or only partially revealed—the purposes that underlay his innovations. For some speculations concerning the roots of Cardozo's circumspection, see the forthcoming biography by Andrew Kaufman.

23. Karl Llewellyn, "On the Good, the True, the Beautiful, in Law," *University of Chicago Law Review* 9 (1942): 260 (emphasis in original).

24. Ibid., 250 (emphasis in original).

25. Llewellyn's largely unsuccessful effort to adhere to this proposition when drafting the Uniform Commercial Code is described in Zipporah Batshaw Wiseman, "The Limits of Vision: Karl Llewellyn and the Merchant Rules," *Harvard Law Review* 100 (1987): 465.

26. "The Good, the True, the Beautiful," 250.

27. Ibid., 264; Llewellyn, *Common Law Tradition*, 426. Llewellyn's vision of the appropriate role of judges in reconceiving the "purposes" of *statutes* was more ambiguous than this picture of common law adjudication. See Wiseman, "Limits of Vision," 499–501 (describing his awkward position concerning the "mandatory" character of his proposed statements of the purposes of the Uniform Commercial Code); Llewellyn, "The Good, the True, the Beautiful," 251 (referring to a judge's obligation to remain within the "limits" of his office).

28. See, for example, Oliver Wendell Holmes, Jr., "Privilege, Malice, and Intent" (1894), reprinted in *Collected Legal Papers* (New York: Peter Smith, 1952), 120 ("Whether, and how far, a privilege shall be allowed is a question of policy. . . . When the question of policy is faced it will be seen to be one which cannot be answered by generalities, but must be determined by the particular character of the case").

29. The most famous expression of this belief is Holmes' argument that, after the question whether a particular sort of behavior constituted "negligence" had been submitted to several different juries, the courts should extract from the juries' answers a rule of law, which thereafter would govern all such cases. The net result would be that "the featureless generality, that the defendant was bound to use such care as a prudent man would do under the circumstances" would gradually give way to a matrix of more specific, "fixed" rules prescribing what a person might and might not do in certain situations. *The Common Law*, 110–24.

30. On rare occasions Realists spoke wistfully of the possibility of "raising the [legal] walls within which men must live and work by just laying one [decisional] brick upon another, letting a keener awareness of the needs of life and labor which they are to house guide our hands." Oliphant, "Stare Decisis—Continued," 160 (reprinted below). But most often their sense of the instability of each such brick led them to despair of completing the building.

31. This is part of what Lon Fuller meant when he accused the Realists of carrying a "reactionary principle" in their loins. *The Law in Quest of Itself* (Chicago: Foundation Press, 1940), 51–65.

32. "The Good, the True, the Beautiful," 250–63.

33. "Modern Ethics," 50.

34. Moore, "Rational Basis of Legal Institutions," 612. For similar views, see Joseph W. Bingham, "The Nature of Legal Rights and Duties," *Michigan Law Review* 12 (1912): 2–3; Walter Nelles, Review of *Ethical Systems and Legal Ideals* by Felix Cohen, *Columbia Law Review* 33 (1933): 767.

35. Cohen, *Ethical Systems*, 227–29. For a similar relance on "faith," see Llewellyn, "The Good, the True, the Beautiful," 255–57.

36. See White, *Patterns of Legal Thought*, 109.

37. Cohen, *Ethical Systems*, 145, 187–8, 220, 229.

38. See Llewellyn, "Some Realism about Realism," 1236 (discussed in Chapter 2, pp. 49–52).

39. Oliphant, "Facts, Opinions, and Value-Judgments," 137. See also Cook, "Scientific Method and the Law," 308–9; Yntema, "The Rational Basis of Legal Science," 943.

40. The notion that positive law derives from custom has very deep roots in Anglo-American law. For a few of its tendrils, see E. Donald Elliot, "The Evolutionary Tradition in Jurisprudence," *Columbia Law Review* 85 (1985): 38. The Realists' ideas on this score were probably most influenced by Holmes' early writings on the importance of custom. See Morton Horwitz, *The Transformation*

of American Law, 1870–1960: The Crisis of Legal Orthodoxy (New York: Oxford University Press, 1992), 109–44.

41. Moore, "Rational Basis of Legal Institutions," 614.

42. See, for example, Llewellyn, "Realism About Realism," 1236; William Douglas, "A Functional Approach to the Law of Business Associations," *Illinois Law Review* 23 (1929): 675.

43. Llewellyn, *Common Law Tradition*, 122. See also Note, "Legal Theory and Legal Education," *Yale Law Journal* 79 (1970): 1170. As Richard Danzig has argued, the clearest manifestation of this view of the proper origins of law is Article II of the Uniform Commercial Code, which was drafted in substantial part by Llewellyn. Danzig, "A Comment on the Jurisprudence of the Uniform Commercial Code," *Stanford Law Review* 27 (1975): 621. Many of the crucial provisions of the article do not purport to establish a rule of decision, but instead direct judges to decide controversies among merchants on the basis of commercial practice and customary standards of fair dealing. The code does not mandate slavish deference to business practice; not all provisions are based upon custom and those that are frequently advert not to average levels of conduct but to the behavior of "commercially *decent* dealers." But "commercial standards" provide the principal criteria of decisionmaking.

BENJAMIN N. CARDOZO
The Nature of the Judicial Process

1. [*Law and the Modern Mind* (New York: Brentano's, 1930), 252.—Ed]

2. [After praising the scholars he described as "neo-realists" for their seriousness and insight, Cardozo chastised them for exaggerating the importance of emotion and raw hunch in judicial decisionmaking, neglecting the role of reason and precedent, and generally for failing to appreciate the values of coherence and order in law. In the end, however, he suggested that the difference between the "neo-realists" and himself might not be all that great. Posing the question whether he himself should be considered a member of the group, he answered coyly: "The high priests of the new movement will have to decide." Frank responded to the speech with an angry and disappointed letter, to which Cardozo made no substantive reply. For discussion of these exchanges and, more generally, the relationship between Cardozo and the (other) Realists, see chapter 17 ("Beyond the Nature of the Judicial Process") of the forthcoming biography of Cardozo by Andrew Kaufman.—Ed]

Pennsylvania Coal Company v. *Mahon*

1. [Justice Holmes is referring here to a series of cases decided during the nineteenth century by state appellate courts holding that it was constitutionally permissible for city officials to order the destruction of privately owned buildings, thereby creating an open space that would stop the spread of a fire. Several states adopted statutes providing for indemnification of the owners of such buildings. But, in the absence of such a statute, most courts ruled that the owners could not recover damages either from the city governments or from the officials who issued the orders. See, for example, *Russell* v. *Mayor of New York City*,

2 *Denio's Reports* 461 (N.Y. 1845); *American Print Works* v. *Lawrence*, 23 *New Jersey Law Reports* 590 (1851).—Ed]

    2. [Justice Holmes is referring to three cases decided in the early 1920s, in which the Court upheld rent-control ordinances instituted to alleviate wartime housing shortages. See *Block* v. *Hirsh*, 256 U.S. 135 (1921); *Marcus Brown Holding Co.* v. *Feldman*, 256 U.S. 170 (1921); *Levy Leasing Co.* v. *Siegal*, 258 U.S. 242 (1922).—Ed]

    3. [Justice Brandeis is referring to *Mugler* v. *Kansas*, 123 U.S. 623 (1887), in which the Supreme Court upheld a Kansas statute that prohibited the manufacture or sale of "intoxicating liquors" for use as beverages, and *Powell* v. *Pennsylvania*, 127 U.S. 678 (1888), in which the Court upheld a Pennsylvania statute that prohibited the manufacture of oleomargarine or imitation butter.—Ed]

    4. [From the depths to the heavens.—Ed]

MAX RADIN

"The Theory of Judicial Decision: Or How Judges Think"

    1. [It is the duty of a good judge to enlarge or extend justice.—Ed]

HERMAN OLIPHANT

"Stare Decisis"

    1. [The phrase *stare decisis* refers roughly to the practice of courts to adhere to precedent—in other words, to abide by the rules announced or implicit in prior judicial decisions.—Ed]

JEROME FRANK

Law and the Modern Mind

    1. *Indeed the dishonesty of judges and other government officials is a proper subject-matter for study by lawyers.* That a certain judge is corrupt is highly important to the honest lawyer and his client. It may be imperative to avoid trying a case before a judge suspected of being dominated by a political boss interested in the case.

    2. The dishonest judge learns much that does not appear in the record. The honest judge, in certain kinds of cases, permits himself the privilege of procuring backdoor information, as, for instance, in receivership cases, where the receiver consults with the judge in chambers, often in the absence of the parties to the proceedings. Also, judges fitfully and sporadically avail themselves of the doctrine of judicial notice to obtain knowledge privately from experts whose names and opinions are usually not revealed to the litigants.

    Why cannot all cases be given the same careful study (openly disclosed), with respect to the facts, which is given to cases, say, of juvenile delinquents in our best juvenile courts? Lawyers need to learn more of the ideals of Hippocratic medicine in which the cure of the patient is considered of more importance than the ("aesthetically" satisfying) cataloguing of diseases.

    3. What this implies is that the judge should be not a mere thinking-

machine but well trained, not only in rules of law, but also in the best available methods of psychology. And among the most important objects which would be subject to his scrutiny as a psychologist would be his own personality so that he might become keenly aware of his own prejudices, biases, antipathies, and the like, not only in connection with attitudes political, economic and moral but with respect to more minute and less easily discoverable preferences and disinclinations.

4. One recalls Gilbert's fairies who, chided for falling in love with mortals, exclaimed, "We know it's weakness, but the weakness is so strong."

5. It is worth noting once more that prolonged dependence on fatherly authority may exist in adult years even when the childish fears which brought about such dependence are absent. The child-father relation, no longer a necessary means of adaptation, has acquired subjective end value.

6. No complete rigidity would be attained, even so, unless and until the personalities of all judges became approximately uniform.

7. Compare Gilbert's observation:

> "I often think it's comical
> How nature always does contrive
> That every boy and every gal
> That's born into the world alive
> Is either a little Liberal
> Or else a little Conservative."

8. There is a measure of deep insight in the facetious remarks of Mr. Justice Darling: "I cannot avoid noticing an error into which they fall who complain of the uncertainty of law as though it were a weakness. Rather should it be considered the chiefest of all sanctions. . . . Many would dare to do wrong, did they know for certain what would follow."

9. If the child indeed becomes father of the man, *i.e.,* each individual becomes his own father and thus eliminates the need for fatherly authority.

10. From the genetic point of view, development towards maturity might be roughly schematized as follows:

(1) At first the child's thinking is egocentric, "autistic," unsocialized. He accepts his own thoughts as self-evident; he is totally unaware of any subjectivity in his thinking. (2) Later, doubts arise as to the self-evident character of his own thoughts. Their subjective character becomes somewhat apparent. He now substitutes the father's dogmas for his own. Father's thoughts are objectively real. (3) Still later, other authorities are substituted for the father. But, in this substitutive manner, fatherly authority still continues. Truths which emanate from authority are objectively real. (4) Then all authority may come into question, all human thought being conceived as subjective and therefore invalid and unreal. (5) The stage of complete maturity is reached when the relativity of all truths is accepted but seem to be compatible with the provisional validity and utility of such truths.

Once more, note that we are using a "*partial* explanation."

11. Whitehead has expressed this idea in generalized terms: "There are two principles inherent in the very nature of things, recurring in some particular embodiments, whatever field we explore—the spirit of change, and the spirit of conservation. There can be nothing real without both. Mere change without conservation is a passage from nothing to nothing. Its final integration yields mere transient nonentity. Mere conservation without change cannot conserve. For after

all, there is a flux of circumstance, and the freshness of being evaporates under mere repetition."

FELIX S. COHEN

"Transcendental Nonsense and the Functional Approach"

1. John C. H. Wu, "Realistic Analysis of Legal Concepts: A Study in the Legal Method of Mr. Justice Holmes" (1932) 5 *China L. Rev.* 1, 2.

Chapter 7

Introduction

1. See Holmes' opinion in *Buck* v. *Bell*, 274 U.S. 200 (1927); Edward Bellamy, *Looking Backward* (Boston: Houghton, Mifflin & Co., 1888), chap. 25.

2. Charles Merriam, *New Aspects of Politics* (Chicago: University of Chicago Press, 1925), 21–22. Cited in Dorothy Ross, *The Origins of American Social Science* (Cambridge: Cambridge University Press, 1991), 455. And see generally Ross, chap. 10, "Scientism," 390–470.

3. Huntington Cairns, *Law and the Social Sciences* (New York: Harcourt, Brace, 1935), 3.

4. "Scientific Method and the Law," *American Bar Association Journal* 13 (1927): 305, 308.

5. *Yale Law Journal* 29 (1919): 83–85. The editors' call for more precise legal terminology was inspired by the recent death of Wesley Hohfeld. See p. 8. Theirs was a wholly different project than the classificatory method of Langdell, of organizing law around natural, logical concepts. See Pound, "Classification of the Law," *Harvard Law Review* 37 (1924): 933.

6. William Underhill Moore began as a conventional academic expert on bills and notes. He first proclaimed his new beliefs (a "legal institution is human behavior") in "Rational Basis of Legal Institutions," *Columbia Law Review* 23 (1923): 609.

7. "Some Realism About Realism—Responding to Dean Pound," *Harvard Law Review* 44 (1931): 1222, 1236. Cf. Chapter 2, pp. 49–52, and Chapter 6, pp. 168–70.

8. Benjamin N. Cardozo, *The Nature of the Judicial Process* (New Haven: Yale University Press, 1921): 65–66.

9. See, for example, Thurman Arnold, "Law Enforcement—An Attempt at Social Dissection," *Yale Law Journal* 42 (1932): 1.

10. *The Nature of the Judicial Process*, 13.

11. C. C. Langdell, *Record of The Commemoration . . . on the Two Hundred and Fiftieth Anniversary of the Founding of Harvard College* (1887).

12. Pound was the chief progenitor of "sociological jurisprudence." See "The Scope and Purpose of Sociological Jurisprudence," *Harvard Law Review* 24 (1911): 591, and 25 (1912): 140, 489.

13. Langdell's best known remarks on law as a science come from the preface to his *Selection of Cases on the Law of Contracts* (1871). Langdell was there trying to find a means for dealing with the rapidly increasing number of reported cases, of tracing a path through centuries of decisions to display, for students, the limited

number of crucial "principles and doctrines." His labors were taxonomic and pedagogical. "If these doctrines could be so classified and arranged that each should be found in its proper place, and nowhere else, they would cease to be formidable in their number."

14. Cited in John Schlegel, "American Legal Realism and Empirical Social Science: From the Yale Experience," *Buffalo Law Review* 28 (1979): 459, 522, and see 519–532.

15. "Some Functional Aspects of Bankruptcy," *Yale Law Journal* 41 (1932): 329; Douglas and Marshall, "A Factual Study of Bankruptcy Administration and Some Suggestions," *Columbia Law Review* 32 (1932): 25.

16. For a chastened view of the reach of science and social science, see Herman Oliphant, "Facts, Opinions, and Value-Judgments," *Texas Law Review* 10 (1932): 127.

17. See, for example, *Monographs of Survey of Litigation in New York* (1931–1932); Marshall, *Unlocking the Treasures of the Trial Courts* (1933); Yntema, *Analysis of the Ohio Municipal Court Acts* (1933). For a full listing of the Institute of Law's publications, see *Current Research in Law*, Oliphant, ed., published periodically after 1928 by the Institute. See also the introduction to Chapter 8, below.

18. Kohler's work appears in the pages of the *Zeitschrift für vergleichende Rechtswissenschafte* in the late nineteenth century. For a contemporary treatment of social science theory, including what amounts to a descriptive bibliography, see Huntington Cairns, *Law and the Social Sciences* (New York: Harcourt, Brace, 1935).

19. See, for example, Roscoe Pound, "The Scope and Purpose of Sociological Jurisprudence;" "Law in Books and Law in Action," *American Law Review* 44 (1910): 12; "A Theory of Social Interests," *Proceedings of the American Society of Sociology* 15 (1921): 16. For a discussion of the "Poundian paradigm," see James E. Herget, *American Jurisprudence, 1870–1970* (Houston: Rice University Press, 1990), 147–227.

20. See p. 237.

21. See Chapter 5. See also Edward A. Ross, *Social Control: A Survey of the Foundations of Order* (New York: Macmillan, 1901), arguing that law is the chief means for controlling society.

22. *American Economic Review* 15 (1925): 665.

23. Hutchins and Slesinger began their collaborative publications with "Some Observations on the Law of Evidence," *Columbia Law Review* 28 (1928): 432. For a complete list of their articles, see John Schlegel, "American Legal Realism and Empirical Social Science: From the Yale Experience," *Buffalo Law Review* 28 (1979): 459, 480–82.

24. Review of *Symbols of Government, Cornell Law Quarterly* 21 (1936): 686.

25. Ross, *The Origins of American Social Science*, 450.

26. See, for example, Harold Laski, *Authority in the Modern State* (New Haven: Yale Univ. Press, 1919), *A Grammar of Politics* (Yale Univ. Press, 1925), *Studies in Law and Politics* (Yale Univ. Press, 1932); and Huntington Cairns, *Law and the Social Sciences* (New York: Harcourt, Brace, 1935): 230.

27. See, for example, Frederick Beutel, "Some Implications of Experimental Jurisprudence," *Harvard Law Review* 48 (1943): 169; *Some Potentialities of Experimental Jurisprudence as a New Branch of Social Science* (Lincoln: Univ. of Nebraska Press, 1957). And see David Cavers, "Science, Research, and the Law: Beutel's 'Experimental Jurisprudence,' " *Journal of Legal Education* 10 (1957): 162.

28. Hessel Yntema, "The Rational Basis of Legal Science," *Columbia Law Review* 31 (1931): 925, 952. And see Herget, *American Jurisprudence, 1870–1970,* 208–13, and generally chap. 8, "The Social Science of Law."

29. See, for example, Underhill Moore, "The Rational Basis of Legal Institutions, *Columbia Law Review* 23 (1923): 609; Moore and Hope, "An Institutional Approach to the Law of Commercial Banking," *Yale Law Journal* 38 (1929): 703.

30. *The Cheyenne Way* (Norman: University of Oklahoma Press, 1941). Their book remains in print. Leon Lipson and Stanton Wheeler, eds., *Law and the Social Sciences* (New York: Russell Sage Foundation, 1986), 3, single it out as the principal "monument" of legal realism. *The Cheyenne Way* was widely praised when it appeared, by Boas and Levi-Strauss among others.

31. "On What Makes Legal Research Worthwhile," *Journal of Legal Education* 8 (1956): 400–401.

32. On Moore, see John Schlegel, "American Legal Realism and Empirical Social Science: The Singular Case of Underhill Moore," *Buffalo Law Review* 29 (1980): 195.

33. *Criminal Justice in Cleveland,* Roscoe Pound and Felix Frankfurter, eds. (1922, reprint, Montclair, N.J.: Patterson Smith, 1968). And see Arthur Sutherland, *The Law at Harvard: A History of Ideas and Men, 1817–1967* (Cambridge: Harvard University Press, 1967): 271–272.

34. Clark's first study appeared as "An Experiment in Studying the Business of Courts of a State," *American Bar Association Journal* 18 (1928): 318; it was reformulated as "Fact Research in Law Administration," *Connecticut Bar Journal* 2 (1928): 211.

35. See John Schlegel, "American Legal Realism and Empirical Social Science: From the Yale Experience," *Buffalo Law Review* 28 (1970): 459, 532–538; and on Clark's studies in procedure, 495–519.

36. Cited in Edward Purcell, *The Crisis of Democratic Theory: Scientific Naturalism and the Problem of Value* (Lexington: University Press of Kentucky), 1973: 31.

KARL LLEWELLYN AND E. ADAMSON HOEBEL

The Cheyenne Way

1. Grinnell, *The Cheyenne Indians,* I, 350–53. The case is presented verbatim as given by Grinnell.

2. Hoebel, *Political Organization . . . of the Comanche Indians,* 96 ff.

3. Informant: Spotted Elk.

4. Calf Woman's version.

5. Informant: Walks Last.

6. This method of formulation is inspired by Professor A. L. Kroeber's concise handling of the Yurok data in his *Handbook of the Indians of California* (Bureau of American Ethnology, *Bulletin 78,* 1925): 20ff.

Chapter 8

Introduction

1. Joseph Story, *Miscellaneous Writings* (1835), 405, 436, cited in Brainerd Currie, "The Materials of Law Study," *Journal of Legal Education* 3

(1951): 331, 365. For Story's reform of Harvard Law School, see R. Kent Newmyer, *Supreme Court Justice Joseph Story: Statesman of the Old Republic* (Chapel Hill: University of North Carolina Press, 1985), 237–270.

2. Oliver Wendell Holmes, Jr., "The Path of the Law," *Harvard Law Review* 10 (1897): 457; reprinted in *Collected Legal Papers* (New York: Harcourt, Brace & Howe, 1920), 167, 169.

3. Cited in Arthur E. Sutherland, Jr., "One Man in His Time," *Harvard Law Review* 78 (1964): 7, 10.

4. *Handbook of the Association of American Law Schools, 1921.*

5. John Wigmore, the evidence scholar, put the matter abruptly: "The Bar is over-crowded with incompetent, shiftless, ill-fitted lawyers, who degrade the methods of the law and cheapen the quality of services by unlimited competition. The number of lawyers should be reduced by one-half." *Report of The American Bar Association, 1915:* 737. But the AALS was traditionally more hostile to the night schools than the ABA. See, for example, *Handbook of the AALS, 1912:* 45, resolving that to offer night classes "tends inevitably to lower educational standards." For a summary of the debate, see Henry Ballantine, "The Place in Legal Education of Evening and Correspondence Law Schools," *Report of The ABA, 1918:* 418. However, by the 1920s, the two organizations reached an accommodation, which meant leaving alone more established night and part-time schools (in Boston, for example, the YMCA and Suffolk), while together trying to close smaller schools.

6. Harold R. Washington, "History and the Role of Black Law Schools," *Howard Law Journal* 18 (1974): 385.

7. Robert Stevens, *Law School: Legal Education in America from the 1850s to the 1980s* (Chapel Hill: University of North Carolina Press, 1983), 80, 198.

8. See, for example, *Reports of The ABA, 1915* and *1916.*

9. For example, one representative argued that college preparation should be required for "Russian Jew boys," who were otherwise prone to professional abuses. *Reports of The ABA, 1929:* 623. Yale's Dean Swan proposed that foreign-born students should be required to do more preparatory work before law school. Simply raising grades to make admissions selective would never do. That would mean too many foreigners, and, Swan maintained, an "inferior student body ethically and socially." Cited in John Schlegel, "American Legal Realism and Empirical Social Science: From the Yale Experience," *Buffalo Law Review* 28 (1980): 459, 479. Often, leaders of the bench and bar offered reassurance. Arthur Corbin, President of the AALS, maintained, "Our collegiate law schools are not now filled with rich men. We find there the poor and hard-working . . . we find black as well as white; jew and gentile; male and female; Russian, Irishman, Italian, and American; farmer, merchant, and laborer." *Handbook of The AALS, 1921:* 52. However, Corbin's placid view is belied by the AALS and ABA reports. For the ABA, see, for example, the yearly debates on legal ethics and its relation to immigrants, including the reports of the committee on immigration and crime, particularly *Reports of The ABA, 1916:* 825; Kate Cleghorn, "Crime and Immigration: A Clinical Study of Two Hundred and Thirteen Immigrants Admitted to Sing Sing Prison," *1917:* 735; and the beleaguered sensibility shown by the slogan of the ABA's Committee on Promotion of American Ideals, "to reestablish the Constitution of the United States and the principles and ideals of our government in the minds and hearts of the people," *1923:* 442; and such remarks as this one, by a member of the legal education section: "[w]e have no desire to

subject ourselves to the accusation that we have become a conspiracy rather than a profession," *1931:* 603.

10. Josef Redlich, *The Common Law and the Case Method in American University Law Schools* (New York: Carnegie Foundation, 1914).

11. Alfred Z. Reed, *Training for the Public Profession of Law: Historical Development and Principal Contemporary Problems of Legal Education in the United States, with Some Account of Conditions in England and Canada* (New York: Carnegie Foundation, 1921); *Present-Day Law Schools in the United States and Canada* (New York: Carnegie Foundation, 1928).

12. *American Law School Review* 4 (1921): 682. For an account of the debate over these reports, see Stevens, *Law School,* 112–30.

13. Llewellyn for one considered the bar associations grossly anticompetitive, virtually a trust looking for market domination. "The Bar Specializes—With What Results?," *Annals of the American Academy of Political and Social Science* (May 1933): 167. For other commentary by Llewellyn, see N.E.H. Hull, "Reconstructing the Origins of Realistic Jurisprudence: A Prequel to the Llewellyn-Pound Exchange Over Realism," *Duke Law Journal* (1989): 1302.

14. For the argument that all admissions "standards" are purposely racist, anti-semitic, anti-poor, see Jerold L. Auerbach, *Unequal Justice: Lawyers and Social Change in Modern America* (New York: Oxford Univ. Press, 1976). See also Alan M. Dershowitz and Laura Hanft, "Affirmative Action and the Harvard College Diversity-Discretion Model: Paradigm or Pretext?," *Cardozo Law Review* 1 (1979): 379; Donna Fossum, "Law School Accreditation Standards and the Structure of American Legal Education," *American Bar Foundation Research Journal* (1978): 515.

15. Thurman Arnold, *Fair Nights and Foul* (New York: Harcourt, Brace & World, 1965), 67–68. And see William Twining, *Karl Llewellyn and the Realist Movement* (Norman: University of Oklahoma Press, 1973), 26–40, 67–69, 94–103; Laura Kalman, *Legal Realism at Yale, 1927–1960* (Chapel Hill: University of North Carolina Press, 1986), 67–144.

16. Reprinted in *Fundamental Legal Conceptions as Applied in Legal Reasoning,* ed. W.W. Cook (New Haven: Yale University Press, 1919), 21.

17. *Training for the Public Profession of Law,* 346.

18. Roscoe Pound, "The Scope and Purpose of Sociological Jurisprudence," *Harvard Law Review* 24 (1911): 591; 25 (1912): 140, 489.

19. See Twining, *Karl Llewellyn and the Realist Movement,* 41–59; Kalman, *Legal Realism at Yale,* 67–97.

20. The Restatement project cut wholly against the Realist grain. Charles E. Clark considered the Restatements a "straightjacket," a "dry pulp" of "pontifical and vague black letter generalities." "The Restatement of the Law of Contracts," *Yale Law Journal* 42 (1933): 643, 647 (providing a brief history of the project). See also, for example, Hessel Yntema, "The Hornbook Method and the Conflict of Laws," *Yale Law Journal* 37 (1927): 468; Thurman Arnold, "Restatement of the Law of Trusts," *Columbia Law Review* 31 (1931): 800; Ernest Lorenzen and Raymond Heilman, "The Restatement of the Conflict of Laws," *University of Pennsylvania Law Review* 83 (1935): 555; Edwin Patterson, "The Restatement of the Law of Contracts," *Columbia Law Review* 33 (1933): 397. And for equally sharp criticism by a non-realist, see William Reynolds Vance, "The Restatement of the Law of Property," *University of Pennsylvania Law Review* 86 (1937): 173. The volumes, complains Vance, are "inaccurate," "obscure," "ponderous," "dull,"

"disappointing," "unintelligible." Put simply, the Realists claimed that, fairly examined, any given area of case law yielded a multitude of rules, conflicting in matters small and large. Thus, however it was that the Restatements came to declare a single rule on a contested issue, that choice of rule could not be a mere "restatement."

21. *Fair Nights and Foul*, 58.

22. See, for example, Jerome Frank, "Why Not a Clinical Lawyer School," *University of Pennsylvania Law Review* 81 (1933): 907. Karl Llewellyn delivered an explosive address to a packed hall at Harvard Law School in 1935. The following quotations give a fair sample of the lecture (which was not directed at Harvard alone): "Law school education, even in the best schools, is...so inadequate, wasteful, blind and foul that it will take twenty years of unremitting effort to make it halfway equal to its job." Schools are carefully producing "the legal factory-hand, dedicated to the upper reaches of the corporation-factory." "Freak persons and freak policies are needed." "On What is Wrong with So-Called Legal Education," *Columbia Law Review* 35 (1935): 651, 677, 654, 651. On Harvard Law School in the Realist period, see also Arthur Sutherland, *The Law at Harvard: A History of Ideas and Men, 1817–1967* (Cambridge: Harvard University Press, 1967) 226–299; Twining, *Karl Llewellyn and the Realist Movement*, 10–25; Kalman, *Legal Realism at Yale*, 45–66.

23. See generally, "Report of the Committee on Legal Aid Work," *Reports of the ABA, 1923:* 374, and the reports made in subsequent years. See also John Maguire, "Poverty and Civil Litigation," *Harvard Law Review* 36 (1923): 361.

24. Twining, *Karl Llewellyn and the Realist Movement*, 45–46.

25. Herman Oliphant, ed., *Summary of Studies in Legal Education, Faculty of Law* (New York: Columbia University Press, 1929), 1.

26. Hessel Yntema, "Walter Wheeler Cook," *Illinois Law Review* 38 (1944): 347, 352–353.

27. *Confidential Report of the Committee on Curriculum, Harvard Law School, June 15, 1936* (Cambridge: 1936), 5, 109. In solitary dissent, the contracts scholar Samuel Williston drew attention to the report's only controversial aspect: a library smoker. "To have a pleasant place to lounge and smoke, directly connected with the reading room, where vacations from work could be taken at any time, would in my opinion inevitably operate to form or confirm bad habits of work and play." Ibid., 142.

THURMAN W. ARNOLD

"Institute Priests and Yale Observers—A Reply to Dean Goodrich"

1. Restatement, Agency (1934) § 355, Comment *b:* "So, a person appointed to guard the patrons of a circus from a lion is not liable because the pike with which he is supplied as a preventive means is obviously insufficient. If, however, such agent is a participant in causing the thing over which he has such partial control to cause harm, he is subject to liability for such harm (see Comment *c* on § 343). Thus, if the agent were to lead a lion down the street holding him by a small rope, this being the means supplied by his employer, he would

be guilty of affirmative negligence and therefore would be liable to a person harmed by the lion after escaping."

The picture of two men walking down the street, one leading a lion with a small rope, and the other guarding him with an obviously insufficient pike has all the appeal of a new testament parable, and the answer is so ingenious and so unexpected that it sticks indelibly in one's mind.

Bibliography

The body of writing by Realists and about Realism is enormous, and this bibliography is not designed to present it all. Its purpose, instead, is to provide a student or scholar whose interest in Realism has been piqued by this volume a roadmap for further exploration of the field. To that end, we have set forth a representative sample of Realist books and essays and a list of what we consider the best of the secondary works on the movement. More complete bibliographies may be found in several of the secondary studies.

Primary Sources

Adler, Mortimer. "Legal Certainty." *Columbia Law Review* 31 (1931): 91.

Arnold, Thurman. "Criminal Attempts—The Rise and Fall of an Abstraction." *Yale Law Journal* 40 (1930): 53.

———. "Restatement of the Law of Trusts." *Columbia Law Review* 31 (1931): 800.

———. "The Role of Substantive Law and Procedure." *Harvard Law Review* 45 (1932): 617.

———. "Law Enforcement—An Attempt at Social Dissection." *Yale Law Journal* 42 (1932): 1.

———. *Symbols of Government.* New Haven: Yale Univ. Press, 1935.

———. "Institute Priests and Yale Observers—A Reply to Dean Goodrich." *University of Pennsylvania Law Review* 84 (1936): 811.

———. Review of *The Law of Trusts and Trustees* by George Gleason Bogert, *Columbia Law Review* 36 (1936): 687.

———. *Fair Fights and Foul.* New York: Harcourt, Brace & World, 1965.

Berle, A.A. & Means, Gardner C. *The Modern Corporation and Private Property.* New York: Macmillan, 1932.

Beutel, Frederick. "Some Implications of Experimental Jurisprudence." *Harvard Law Review* 48 (1934): 178.

——. *Some Potentialities of Experimental Jurisprudence as a New Branch of Social Science.* Lincoln: Univ. of Nebraska Press, 1957.

Bingham, Joseph. "What is the Law?" *Michigan Law Review* 11 (1912): 1.

——. "The Nature of Legal Rights and Duties." *Michigan Law Review* 12 (1913): 1.

Cairns, Huntington. "Law and Anthropology." *Columbia Law Review* 31 (1931): 32.

——. *Law and the Social Sciences.* New York: Harcourt, Brace, 1935.

Cardozo, Benjamin. The Nature of the Judicial Process. New Haven: Yale University Press, 1921.

Clark, Charles E. "Relations, Legal and Otherwise." *Illinois Law Quarterly* 5 (1922): 26.

——. "An Experiment in Studying the Business of Courts of a State." *American Bar Association Journal* 18 (1928): 318.

——. "Fact Research in Law Administration." *Connecticut Bar Journal* 2 (1928): 211.

——. "The Restatement of the Law of Contracts." *Yale Law Journal* 42 (1933): 643.

Cohen, Felix. *Ethical Systems and Legal Ideals: An Essay on the Foundations of Legal Criticism.* Westport, Conn.: Greenwood Press, 1933.

——. "Modern Ethics and the Law." *Brooklyn Law Review* 4 (1934): 33.

——. "Transcendental Nonsense and the Functional Approach." *Columbia Law Review* 35 (1935): 809.

——. "The Ethical Basis of Legal Criticism." *Yale Law Journal* 41 (1938): 201.

——. "Dialogue on Private Property." *Rutgers Law Review* 9 (1954): 357.

——. *The Legal Conscience: Selected Papers of Felix S. Cohen.* Edited by Lucy Kramer Cohen. New Haven, 1960.

Cohen, Morris. "The Process of Judicial Legislation." *American Law Review* 48 (1914): 161.

——. "Property and Sovereignty." *Cornell Law Quarterly* 13 (1927): 8.

——. "Justice Holmes and the Nature of Law." *Columbia Law Review* 31 (1931): 361.

——. "The Basis of Contract." *Harvard Law Review* 46 (1933): 553.

Cook, Walter Wheeler. "Privileges of Labor Unions in the Struggle for Life." *Yale Law Journal* 27 (1918): 785.

——. "The Logical and Legal Bases of the Conflict of Laws." *Yale Law Journal* 33 (1924): 457.

——. "Scientific Method and the Law," *American Bar Association Journal* 13 (1927): 305.

——. Review of *The Paradoxes of Legal Science* by Benjamin Cardozo. *Yale Law Journal* 38 (1929): 406.

Corbin, Arthur L. "Law and the Judges." *Yale Review* (1913).

——. "Offer and Acceptance, and Some of the Resulting Legal Relations. *Yale Law Journal* 26 (1917): 167.

——. "Jural Relations and their Classification." *Yale Law Journal* 30 (1921): 226.

———. "The Restatement of the Common Law by the American Law Institute." *Iowa Law Review* 15 (1929): 19.

Corwin, Edward S. *The Twilight of the Supreme Court: A History of Our Constitutional Theory.* New Haven: Yale Univ. Press, 1934.

Dewey, John. "Logical Method and the Law." *Cornell Law Quarterly* 10 (1924): 17.

———. "The Historic Background of Corporate Legal Personality." *Yale Law Journal* 35 (1926): 655.

Dickinson, John. "Legal Rules: Their Function in the Process of Decision." *University of Pennsylvania Law Review* 79 (1931): 833.

———. "Legal Rules: Their Application and Elaboration." *University of Pennsylvania Law Review* 79 (1931): 1052.

Douglas, William O. "A Functional Approach to the Law of Business Associations." *Illinois Law Review* 23 (1929): 675.

———. "Vicarious Liability and Administration of Risk." Parts 1,2. *Yale Law Journal* 38 (1929): 584, 720.

———. "Some Functional Aspects of Bankruptcy." *Yale Law Journal* 41 (1932): 329.

Douglas, William O., and Jerome Frank. "Landlord Claims in Reorganizations." *Yale Law Journal* 42 (1933): 1003.

Douglas, William O., and J. Howard Marshall. "A Factual Study of Bankruptcy Administration and Some Suggestions." *Columbia Law Review* 32 (1932): 25.

Frank, Jerome. *Law and the Modern Mind.* New York: Brentano's, 1930.

———. "Are Judges Human?" *University of Pennsylvania Law Review* 80 (1931): 17.

———. Review of *The Bramble Bush* by Karl Llewellyn, *Yale Law Journal* 40 (1931): 1123.

———. "Mr. Justice Holmes and Non-Euclidean Thinking." *Cornell Law Quarterly* 17 (1932): 586.

———. "What Courts Do In Fact." *Illinois Law Review* 26 (1932): 645.

———. "Why Not a Clinical Lawyer School?" *University of Pennsylvania Law Review* 81 (1933): 911.

Fuller, Lon L. "American Legal Realism." *University of Pennsylvania Law Review* 82 (1934): 429.

Fuller, Lon L., and William R. Purdue, Jr. "The Reliance Interest in Contract Damages." Parts 1,2. *Yale Law Journal* 46 (1936): 52 and 46 (1937): 373.

———. *The Law in Quest of Itself.* Chicago: Foundation Press, 1940.

Gray, John Chipman. *The Nature and Sources of the Law.* New York: Columbia Univ. Press, 1909.

Green, Frederick. "The Relativity of Legal Relations" *Illinois Law Quarterly* 5 (1923): 187.

Green, Leon. *Judge and Jury.* Kansas City, Missouri: Vernon, 1930.

———. "The Negligence Issue." *Yale Law Journal* 37 (1928): 1029.

Haines, Charles Grove. "General Observations on the Effects of Personal, Political, and Economic Influences in the Decision of Judges." *Illinois Law Review* 17 (1922): 96.

Hale, Robert Lee. *Valuation and Rate-Making: The Conflicting Theories of the Wis-*

consin Railroad Commission, 1905–1917. New York: Columbia Univ. Press, 1918.

———. "Coercion and Distribution in a Supposedly Non-Coercive State." *Political Science Quarterly* 38 (1923): 470.

———. "Economic Theory and the Statesman." In *The Trend of Economics,* ed. Rexford G. Tugwell. New York: Knopf, 1924.

———. "Value and Vested Rights." *Columbia Law Review* 27 (1927): 523.

———. "Value to the Taker in Condemnation Proceedings." *Columbia Law Review* 31 (1931): 1.

———. "Force and the State: A Comparison of 'Political' and 'Economic' Compulsion." *Columbia Law Review* 35 (1935): 149.

———. "Our Equivocal Constitutional Guarantees." *Columbia Law Review* 39 (1939): 563.

———. "Bargaining, Duress and Economic Liberty," *Columbia Law Review* 43 (1943): 605.

———. *Freedom Through Law: Public Control of Private Governing Power.* New York: Columbia Univ. Press, 1952.

Hamilton, Walton H. "The Ancient Maxim Caveat Emptor." *Yale Law Journal* 40 (1931): 1133.

———. "Property—According to Locke." *Yale Law Journal* 41 (1932): 864.

Hohfeld, Wesley Newcomb. "Some Fundamental Legal Conceptions as Applied in Judicial Reasoning" *Yale Law Journal* 23 (1913): 16.

———. "Fundamental Legal Conceptions as Applied in Judicial Reasoning" *Yale Law Journal* 26 (1917): 710.

———. *Fundamental Legal Conceptions,* ed. Walter Wheeler Cook. New Haven: Yale Univ. Press, 1923.

Holmes, Oliver Wendell, Jr., *The Common Law.* Boston: Little, Brown, 1881.

———. *Collected Legal Papers.* New York: Harcourt, Brace, & Howe, 1920.

———. *The Essential Holmes: Selections from the Letters, Speeches, Judicial Opinions, and Other Writings of Oliver Wendell Holmes, Jr.,* ed. Richard A. Posner. Chicago: University of Chicago Press, 1992.

Hutcheson, Joseph C., Jr., "The Judgment Intuitive: The Function of the 'Hunch' in Judicial Decision." *Cornell Law Quarterly* 14 (1929): 274.

Hutchins, Robert M., and Donald Slesinger. "Some Observations on the Law of Evidence." *Columbia Law Review* 28 (1928): 432.

Isaacs, Nathan. "The Standardizing of Contracts." *Yale Law Journal* 34 (1917): 27.

———. "How Lawyers Think." *Columbia Law Review* 23 (1923): 555.

Jaffe, Louis L. "Law Making by Private Groups." *Harvard Law Review* 51 (1937): 201.

Kallen, Horace M. "Functionalism." *Encyclopedia of the Social Sciences* ed. Seligman, Johnson, vol. 6 (1930–1935): 523.

Keyserling, Leon H. "Social Objectives in Legal Education." *Columbia Law Review* 33 (1933): 437.

Landis, James M. *The Administrative Process.* New Haven: Yale Univ. Press, 1938.

Laski, Harold. "The Basis of Vicarious Liability." *Yale Law Journal* 26 (1917): 105.

———. *A Grammar of Politics.* New Haven: Yale University Press, 1925.

———. *Studies in Law and Politics.* New Haven: Yale University Press, 1932.

Lasswell, Harold. "Self-Analysis and Judicial Thinking." *International Journal of Ethics* 40 (1930): 354.

Lerner, Max. "The Supreme Court and American Capitalism." *Yale Law Journal* 42 (1933): 668.

———. "Constitution and Court as Symbols," *Yale Law Journal* 46 (1937): 1317.

Llewellyn, Karl N. "A Realistic Jurisprudence—the Next Step." *Columbia Law Review* 30 (1930): 431.

———. *Cases and Materials on the Law of Sales.* Chicago: Callahan and Company, 1930.

———. "Some Realism About Realism—Responding to Dean Pound." *Harvard Law Review* 44 (1931): 1222.

———. "What Price Contract?—An Essay in Perspective." *Yale Law Journal* 40 (1931): 704.

———. "The Bar Specializes—With What Results?" *Annals of the American Academy of Political and Social Science* (May, 1933): 167.

———. "On Philosophy in American Law." *University of Pennsylvania Law Review* 82 (1934): 211.

———. "On What Is Wrong With So-Called Legal Education." *Columbia Law Review* 35 (1935): 653.

———. "On Warranty of Quality and Society," *Columbia Law Review* 37 (1937): 369.

———. "The Rule of Law in Our Case-Law of Contract." *Yale Law Journal* 47 (1938): 1243.

———. "On Reading and Using the Newer Jurisprudence." *Columbia Law Review* 40 (1940): 581.

———. "On the Good, the True, the Beautiful, in Law," *University of Chicago Law Review* 9 (1942): 249.

———. "Remarks on the Theory of Appellate Decision and the Rules or Canons About How Statutes Are to Be Construed." *Vanderbilt Law Review* 3 (1950): 395.

———. *The Common Law Tradition in Deciding Appeals.* Boston: Little, Brown, 1960.

———. *Jurisprudence: Realism in Theory and Practice.* Chicago: University of Chicago Press, 1962.

Llewellyn, Karl, and E. Adamson Hoebel. *The Cheyenne Way.* Norman: University of Oklahoma Press, 1941.

Lorenzen, Ernest G., and Raymond J. Heilman. "The Restatement of the Conflict of Laws." *University of Pennsylvania Law Review* 83 (1935): 561.

Maguire, John. "Poverty and Civil Litigation." *Harvard Law Review* 36 (1923): 361.

Marshall, Leon C. *Unlocking the Treasures of the Trial Courts.* 1933.

Moore, Underhill. "Rational Basis of Legal Institutions." *Columbia Law Review* 23 (1923): 609.

Moore, Underhill, and Charles C. Callahan. "Law and Learning Theory: A Study in Legal Control." *Yale Law Journal* 53 (1943): 1.

Moore, Underhill, and Theodore S. Hope, Jr. "An Institutional Approach to the Law of Commercial Banking." *Yale Law Journal* 38 (1929): 703.

Nelles, Walter. Review of *Ethical Systems and Legal Ideals* by Felix Cohen. *Columbia Law Review* 33 (1933): 767.

Oliphant, Herman. "A Return to Stare Decisis." *American Bar Association Journal* 14 (1928): 71, 159.

———. Summary of Studies in Legal Education, Faculty of Law. New York: Columbia University Press, 1929.

———. "Facts, Opinions, and Value-Judgments." *Texas Law Review* 10 (1932): 127.

Patterson, Edwin W. "The Restatement of the Law of Contracts." *Columbia Law Review* 33 (1933): 397.

Pound, Roscoe. "Do We Need a Philosophy of Law?" *Columbia Law Review* 5 (1905): 339.

———. "The Need of a Sociological Jurisprudence." *The Green Bag* 19 (1907): 607.

———. "Mechanical Jurisprudence." *Columbia Law Review* 8 (1908): 605.

———. "Liberty of Contract." *Yale Law Journal* 18 (1909): 454.

———. "Law in Books and Law in Action." *American Law Review* 44 (1910): 12.

———. "The Scope and Purpose of Sociological Jurisprudence." *Harvard Law Review* 24 (1911): 591 and 25 (1912): 140, 489.

———. "The Theory of Judicial Decision." *Harvard Law Review* 36 (1923): 641, 802, 940.

———. "The Call for a Realist Jurisprudence." *Harvard Law Review* 44 (1931): 697.

Pound, Roscoe, and Felix Frankfurter. *Criminal Justice in Cleveland.* Cleveland, Ohio: The Cleveland Foundation, 1922.

Powell, Thomas Reed. "The Judiciality of Mimimum Wage Legislation." *Harvard Law Review* 37 (1924): 545.

———. "An Imaginary Judicial Opinion." *Harvard Law Review* 44 (1931): 889.

Radin, Max. "The Theory of Judicial Decision: Or How Judges Think." *American Bar Association Journal* 11 (1925): 357.

———. "Legal Realism." *Columbia Law Review* 31 (1931): 824.

———. "Case Law and Stare Decisis: Concerning Prajudizienrecht in Amerika." *Columbia Law Review* 33 (1933): 199.

———. "A Restatement of Hohfeld." *Harvard Law Review* 51 (May 1938): 1141.

Rodell, Fred. "Goodbye to Law Reviews." *Virginia Law Review* 23 (1936): 38.

Sturges, Wesley, and Samuel O. Clark, "Legal Theory and Real Property Mortgages." *Yale Law Journal* 37 (1928): 713.

Thayer, James B. "The Origin and Scope of the American Doctrine of Constitutional Law." *Harvard Law Review* 7 (1893): 129.

Tulin, Leon A. "The Role of Penalties in Criminal Law," *Yale Law Journal* 37 (1928): 1052.

———. "The Rational Basis of Legal Science." *Columbia Law Review* 31 (1931): 943.

Yntema, Hessel. "The Hornbook Method and the Conflict of Laws." *Yale Law Journal* 37 (1928): 468.

———. "The Rational Basis of Legal Institutions." *Columbia Law Review* 31 (1931): 925, 952.

———. *Analysis of the Ohio Municipal Court Acts.* 1933.

Secondary Sources

Ackerman, Bruce. "Law and the Modern Mind by Jerome Frank." *Daedalus* 103 (1974): 119.

Aichele, Gary Jan. *Legal Realism and Twentieth Century American Jurisprudence: The Changing Consensus.* New York: Garland, 1990.

Bechtler, Thomas. "American Legal Realism Reevaluated," in *Law in a Social Context: Liber Amicorum Honouring Professor Lon L. Fuller.* Deventer: Kluwer, 1978.

Cavers, David. "Science, Research, and the Law: 'Experimental Jurisprudence.' " *Journal of Legislative History* 10 (1957): 162.

Danzig, Richard. "A Comment on the Jurisprudence of the Uniform Commercial Code." *Stanford Law Review* 27 (1975): 621.

Diamond, Stephen. "Legal Realism and Historical Method: J. Williard Hurst and American Legal History." *Michigan Law Review* 77 (1979): 784.

———. "In the Twilight of Legal Realism: Fred Rodell and the Limits of Legal Critique." *Oxford Journal of Legal Studies* 11 (1991): 354.

———. "Jerome Frank and the Legacy of Legal Realism." *Journal of Law and Society* 18 (1991): 175.

Duxbury, Neil. "The Birth of Legal Realism and the Myth of Justice Holmes." *Anglo-American Law Review* 20 (1992): 81.

Fried, Barbara. *Robert L. Hale and Progressive Legal Economics.* Forthcoming, Harvard Univ. Press, 1994.

Gilmore, Grant. "Legal Realism: Its Cause and Cure," *Yale Law Journal* 70 (1961): 1037.

Glennon, Robert Jerome. *The Iconoclast as Reformer: Jerome Frank's Impact on American Law.* Ithaca: Cornell University Press, 1985.

Herget, James. *American Jurisprudence, 1870–1970: A History.* Houston: Rice University Press, 1990.

Herget, James E., and Stephen Wallace. "The German Free Law Movement as the Source of American Legal Realism." *Virginia Law Reivew* 73 (1987): 399.

Hopkins, James D. "The Development of Realism in Law and Literature during the Period 1883–1933: The Cultural Resemblance." *Pace Law Review* 4 (1983): 29.

Horwitz, Morton. *The Transformation of American Law, 1870–1960: The Crisis of Legal Orthodoxy.* New York: Oxford University Press, 1992.

Hull, N.E.H. "Some Realism about the Llewellyn-Pound Exchange over Realism: The Newly Uncovered Private Correspondence, 1927–1931." *Wisconsin Law Review* (1987): 921.

———. "Reconstructing the Origins of Realistic Jurisprudence: A Prequel to the Llewellyn—Pound Exchange Over Legal Realism." *Duke Law Journal* (1989): 1302.

Hunt, Alan. *The Sociological Movement in Law.* Philadelphia: Temple Univ. Press, 1978.

Kalman, Laura. *Legal Realism at Yale, 1927–1960*. Chapel Hill: University of North Carolina Press, 1986.

Kennedy, Duncan. "Toward an Historical Understanding of Legal Consciousness: The Case of Classical Legal Thought in America, 1850–1940." *Research in Law and Sociology* 3 (1980): 3.

Kennedy, Duncan, and Frank Michelman, "Are Property and Contract Efficient?" *Hofstra Law Review* 8 (1980): 748.

Klare, Karl. "Contracts Jurisprudence and the First-Year Casebook." *New York University Law Review* 54 (1979): 876.

"Legal Theory and Legal Education." *Yale Law Journal* 79 (1970): 1170.

Purcell, Edward A. *The Crisis of Democratic Theory: Scientific Naturalism and the Problem of Value*. Lexington: University Press of Kentucky, 1973.

"Round and Round the Bramble Bush: From Legal Realism to Critical Legal Scholarship." *Harvard Law Review* 95 (1982): 1669.

Rumble, Wilfred. *American Legal Realism: Skepticism, Reform, and the Judicial Process*. Ithaca, N.Y.: Cornell University Press, 1968.

Schlegel, John. "American Legal Realism and Empirical Social Science: From the Yale Experience." *Buffalo Law Review* 28 (1980): 459.

———. "American Legal Realism and Empirical Social Science: The Singular Case of Underhill Moore." *Buffalo Law Review* 29 (1981): 195.

Singer, Joseph. "The Legal Rights Debate in Analytical Jurisprudence from Bentham to Hohfeld," *Wisconsin Law Review* (1982): 986.

———. "Legal Realism Now." *California Law Review* (1988): 465.

Summers, Robert S. *Instrumentalism and American Legal Theory*. Ithaca: Cornell Univ. Press, 1982.

Tushnet, Mark. "Post-Realist Legal Scholarship," *Journal of the Society of Public Law Teachers* 15 (1960): 20.

Twining, William. *Karl Llewellyn and the Realist Movement*. London: Weidenfeld and Nicholson, 1973.

White, G. Edward. *Patterns of American Legal Thought*. Charlottesville, Va.: Michie, 1978.

White, Morton Gabriel. *Social Thought in America: The Revolt Against Formalism*. New York: Viking, 1949.

Wiseman, Zipporah Batshaw. "The Limits of Vision: Karl Llewellyn and the Merchant Rules." *Harvard Law Review* 100 (1987): 465.

Printed in the USA
CPSIA information can be obtained
at www.ICGtesting.com
BVHW041653140823
668558BV00001B/6